Chinese Culture,

Western Culture

Chinese Culture,

Western Culture

How Cross-Cultural Views of History, Philosophy and Human
Relationships Will Change Modern Global Society

Tai P. Ng, Ph.D
and
Wah-Won Ng, M.Eng, B.ASc

iUniverse, Inc.
New York Lincoln Shanghai

Chinese Culture, Western Culture
How Cross-Cultural Views of History, Philosophy and Human Relationships Will
Change Modern Global Society

iUniverse books may be ordered through booksellers or by contacting:

iUniverse
2021 Pine Lake Road, Suite 100
Lincoln, NE 68512
www.iuniverse.com
1-800-Authors (1-800-288-4677)

Because of the dynamic nature of the Internet, any Web addresses
or links contained in this book may have changed
since publication and may no longer be valid.

The views expressed in this work are solely those of the author and
do not necessarily reflect the views of the publisher, and
the publisher hereby disclaims any responsibility for them.

ISBN: 978-0-595-41846-6 (pbk)
ISBN: 978-0-595-67944-7 (cloth)
ISBN: 978-0-595-86190-3 (ebk)

Printed in the United States of America

Contents

Part Three Mega History, China and the West

Part Four Past, Present, and Future

Acknowledgments

We would like to thank Annette Ng. You are such a wonderful wife and mother, and we could not have finished this book without your continuous stream of love and encouragement. Thank you also to Brian Eng for all your support and understanding throughout this endeavor.

We would also like to thank the editorial board and staff of iUniverse for all their editorial advice and guidance on both the first book and this one. Your insights and help have made a difference to the readability of this version.

Preface

We live at the dawn of the twenty-first century in a new era of globalization and rapid technological advancement. In order to meet many of the unprecedented challenges facing this world, including international terrorism, communal violence, sectarian conflict, or just doing business and traveling overseas, citizens of this global village, especially decision-makers and educators, must be receptive, innovative, and creative. It is inadequate in this global world just to know one's own culture and tradition. Rather, the more we know and understand about those around us, the better we can deal with the events that face us. Cross-cultural knowledge and understanding is increasingly a mandatory prerequisite to successful international ventures and communications.

I (Tai Ng 吳 大 品) was born in Hong Kong, and have studied, worked, and lived throughout Australia, the United States, and Canada for more than fifty years. During all those years living in the Western world, the depth and breadth of my Chinese cultural heritage, especially the history, philosophy, and art, has constantly fascinated me. One of my favorite hobbies was reading Chinese, especially the ancient classics. Another hobby was to venture with curiosity into the subjects of humanities, social sciences, and history.

Professionally, I had a long and interesting career as a geophysicist in petroleum exploration and management. I also enjoyed traveling for the opportunity to interact with different people and cultures. Fortunately, professional and personal travels have brought me to every major region of the world, including the Arctic. I have also traveled widely in North America, Europe, and Asia.

Over the years, I gradually became convinced that Chinese and Western cultures are actually complementary in nature. Many people in both cultures may disagree with me, and I will grant some apparent disparities exist. However, like the representation of the Chinese yin and yang symbol, I strongly believe the two cultures need to learn from each other in order to attain a new dynamic balance. As an example, Western culture has consistently favored yang, or masculine, values and attitudes. It has neglected the complementary yin, or feminine, counterparts. It has favored competition over cooperation, expansion and progress over conservation, analysis and logic over intuitive wisdom, science over religion, self-assertion over integration, and so on. The whole world would benefit if an appropriate dosage of the complementary feminine yin culture of the East could balance out the strong masculine yang culture of the West. This book will present evidence supporting this contention from cultural, philosophical, social, economic, political, and historical viewpoints. My background and familiarity in Chinese and Western cultures, together with a keen interest in both physical and social sciences, should provide readers with a distinctive and, hopefully, interesting perspective.

My daughter, Won Ng 吳 華 耘, has played a significant role in bringing this book to its present form. As a Canadian-born Chinese woman, brought up in the multicultural community of Canadian and American cities, she traveled widely with me around the world. Currently residing in Vancouver, British Columbia, she is an engineer by training and software manager by profession. She represents one of the groups that I am targeting this book toward, that is, people brought up and living/working in our Western society, but keenly interested in learning more about Chinese heritage and history and how to achieve a better harmony and balance in life.

We sincerely hope this book will cater to a much wider audience of readers who can learn a little more about Chinese and Western history, thought, and philosophy. We hope you can take to heart some of the key lessons and conclusions for understanding our world and helping to change our future.

Indeed, the West, encompassing both Europe and America, has led the world in every aspect of technological, economic, political, and social advancement over the past two hundred years. And it will continue to do so in the foreseeable future. What could it possibly learn from the Chinese? Western advancements in science and technology and the free market economy are responsible for incalculable improvements in the standard and quality of life for much of humanity. Important new ideas in social and political philosophy have cultivated profound ideals of freedom and equality for all. The United States is—and will remain for a long time—the only superpower on earth. Humankind would be immeasurably diminished if the United States did not have a resolution to fight tyranny and defend freedom and democracy, especially during the last world war. The Chinese people will always remember fighting alongside Americans against the invading Japanese forces during World War II. Contemporary China has learned—and will continue to learn—from Europe and America.

However, for many centuries before the arrival of the modern era, China was the world leader in technology, commerce, philosophy, and social and political ideas. Even today, many of these ideas, specifically those concerning human relationships with nature, society, and one another, still have relevance.

Thus, Won and I believe it will benefit the world if Chinese and Westerners can learn from each other. China should learn from the successes achieved in the West over the previous two centuries; the Western world should learn from the notions evolved in China prior to the Modern Era.

With this opportunity in mind, I retired early from geophysics and dedicated the past several years to researching some of the questions that have preoccupied me for so long. I eagerly sought to understand the current relevance of ancient Chinese culture. In this endeavor, I am preceded by many Chinese thinkers, who date back to the Opium War and the nineteenth-century incursion of Western ideologies into China. Even today, Chinese thinkers and scholars explore these ideas, especially with increasing relevance since the advent of reforms in China during the past fifteen to twenty years.

Many people are unaware that China actually did quite a bit of experimentation with political and social reform. At one point, some Chinese thinkers advocated complete westernization despite the fact they had adopted Marxist communism as a guiding doctrine. (Ironically, Marxist communism is a Western ideology). Surprisingly, contemporary Chinese intellectuals, industrial entrepreneurs, and even some of the current political leaders have now generally accepted Western liberal ideals, such as freedom, democracy, the market economy, and law-abiding citizenship. But political reality allows only partial implementation.

Chinese leaders have also become aware of the irony that carrying liberalism to an extreme can lead to increased social problems, including crime, violence, illicit drugs, decline in family values, broken homes, and general moral decay. One can argue that this has occurred in some wealthy Western countries. Their challenge now is to build a modern China that incorporates the West's better virtues and traditional Chinese values. As the Chinese become increasingly open to the world, they should also look inward. They may find some of the solutions to their current problems in the well-documented wisdom of their ancestors.

It is not the objective of this book to describe how the contemporary Chinese are reconciling their past. Although this process remains a topic of keen interest to the authors, many excellent books already focus on that subject. A main goal of our writing is to respond to the lack of Western knowledge about China and Chinese civilization. Many excellent studies have been completed in academic institutions across Europe and the United States since the Korean War. However, historical and linguistic factors have left Chinese culture one of the least understood, and sometimes completely misunderstood, cultures, both within and outside China.

In North America, one can observe stereotyping and misrepresentation of Chinese culture almost daily in the media. These representations may or may not have racial overtones. Chinese emigrants living overseas and the mainstream media alike are all guilty of the same offense. Simply, a growing cultural apathy in North America is seen in both the Chinese and non-Chinese population. The general situation, however, is slowly improving as China opens to the world and Western familiarity with Chinese culture broadens. Home to one-fifth of the world's population, China is becoming a major trading nation. Tourism is already an important sector of the Chinese economy. Dialogue between the cultures of the West and the East is therefore bound to improve. Some indications of this are already evident in China's joining of the World Trade Organization (WTO) and World Health Organization (WHO). Beijing will host the 2008 Summer Olympics, and Shanghai will host Expo 2010. Quite possibly, within a few years, a feverish curiosity about China will infect the globe. The general public will then want to know what China is all about. When this happens, market economies suggest that people who care little about Chinese culture or the dialogue between cultures will generate an excessive supply of misinformation from both within and outside China.

Ultimately, our aim is to make unbiased information available in order to respond to the lack of Western knowledge about China and Chinese civilization. We provide some answers to what we believe are pressing questions for the general populace in North America, who mostly do not have the benefit of familiarity with Chinese culture and language. We hope to act as cultural brokers, proposing only our most objective interpretations for our readers. Where possible, we will provide both sides of an argument to maintain objectivity and ideological neutrality. Our selected sources are those we respect as reliable academic authorities in China as well as leading authors and scholars at prominent institutions in Europe and North America. Some information may be controversial or even contradictory to what readers have previously held true. We only ask that you keep an open mind, follow our argument, and come to your own conclusions.

CHAPTER ONE

Introduction

Section One:
Key Questions

For historical reasons, many people in Western societies are not familiar with Chinese culture and language. We believe sincere dialogue and increased understanding, tolerance, and mutual appreciation between people of different cultures can change that viewpoint and improve the situation. If we fail to better understand each other, the consequences could be dire. Many wars have arisen from cultural ignorance. If we can learn to coexist peacefully, we may all benefit from the resulting enhancements in commerce and trade. Both are basic requirements for human survival in our increasingly shrinking global village. By helping each other to meet the new challenges we will each face in the new millennium, we should be able to do better.

With this in mind, the following key questions will be addressed in this book.

- What are the key differences between Chinese and Western culture?

- Why are there such differences?

- Do Chinese people think differently from Westerners? If so, how and why?

- Are Confucianism and Daoism religions or philosophies? How do they compare with their Western counterparts?

- How do the Chinese relate to nature, themselves, and others?

- What are the real aspirations and dreams of the Chinese people?

- China was one of four ancient civilizations on earth. How did Chinese civilization endure to the present while all others failed to continue?

- Until the seventeenth century, China was the most technologically advanced and sociologically sophisticated culture in the world. Why did it gain these advantages? How did it sustain them for so long? Why did it ultimately decline?

- What was the nature of the Chinese monarchy?

- With the exception of brief episodes of invasion by nomads from the northern and western steppes, the Chinese Empire remained cohesive following its unification in the year 221 BC. Why did the Roman Empire fall apart after the invasion of barbarians?

- Is democracy a political ideal in China? What is the future of democracy?

- In this postmodern time and era of globalization, which aspects of Chinese culture have current relevance? What can we learn from Chinese experiences?

- As China rapidly industrializes, what can it learn from the West without repeating some of the mistakes that Europeans and North Americans made in their periods of industrialization?

Section Two:
How to Use This Book

After this introduction, the book is divided into four main parts:
- The first part talks about the development of thought and philosophy in Chinese and Western cultures, specifically how environmental and evolutionary factors impacted how people think and view the world.

- The second part explores the development of human relationships in the two cultures and how their differing thought patterns influence those relationships. It looks at how individuals view themselves and their relationships with family, society, and state.

- The third part presents an overview of historical developments in these two cultures, highlighting developments and events that support the divergence in Chinese and Western thought and relationships.

- The fourth part presents some trends and lessons we can learn from the history and development of these two cultures. It suggests some ways in which we should all learn from each other to better interpret and handle upcoming challenges.

Part One: The Thinking Processes

Chapter two examines the thinking process, that is, "thinking about thinking." This is currently a topic of interest because of its applications in computer and information technologies and artificial intelligence. We will present some current cognitive theories on the development of thinking in pre-humans and humans from psychological, archaeological, neurological, and philosophical perspectives. Of these, we have found the theory of evolutionary development in thinking, knowledge, and intelligence to be the most appealing.

We have found that some of the key characteristics or preferences of Chinese thinking, which contrast with traditional Western thought, can be traced back to the beginning of Western and Chinese cultures sometime during the Ice Age. We will see that natural milieu, climatic conditions, and geographic location played an important role in the formation of these thinking preferences. Essentially, because most of China is situated in low latitude, tropic/subtropic zones, ice sheets did not cover it throughout the Ice Age. This was unlike the situation in Europe. But this is apparently the most important factor in an abundance of fauna and flora observed in China. In contrast, there was a scarcity of this plant life in Europe, which suffered heavily from the severity of the Ice Age. We believe this major difference had profound consequences on the development of our brain and thinking processes during the Paleolithic Era in both China and Europe.

At the end of chapter two, a section describes how human perception of nature has changed throughout history and how these perceptions turn out to be very much culturally specific. Chinese thinkers apparently perceive humanity more as an integral part of nature while Western thinkers seek to overcome or conquer nature. Either way, it is not until the dawn of modern science that people, both Chinese and Western, have really begun to understand how nature operates. Human conceptualizations of nature underpin our views of the world and, consequently, influence our thinking. While our distant ancestors' unique experiences of the Ice Age in the West and China may have stimulated divergent adaptive responses and thinking patterns, so too have our differing views of nature continued to influence the way we think.

Chapter three further explores how the unique and divergent thinking preferences found in China and the West impact the philosophy and worldview of each culture, leading to different interpretations of the natural environments, constructed institutions, and each other. Of particular significance, science and religion are distinctively different in Chinese and Western civilizations. We also explore other conceptual disparities, for example, space-time relationships and how we view the universe, cosmogony, and cosmology.

Thinking preferences or inclinations adopted by cultures directly impact their outlook on life, ideology, and philosophy. Differing perceptions, theories, and practices regarding the human senses, observation, interpretation, experience, knowledge, and attitude distinguished classical Greek from classical Chinese thinking.

The ancient Greeks asked many questions and thought deeply about thinking itself. They pondered the "what" questions. What is truth? What is real? What is the world made of? Simply, what is this? Consequently, Western truth is based upon the knowledge of what is real and what represents that reality. It seeks permanence and substance in things. Humankind is indebted to these Greeks for their logic, mathematics, science, philosophy, arts, and politics. Yet the early Greeks' rejection of empirical and sensory experience and noncausal, less than rational, analytical, logical, and explicit ways of thinking has resulted in enduring dire consequences in the Western world. Only after the Renaissance and Enlightenment were more inclusive perspectives on thought recovered. Even then, dualistic thinking continued to impact us all.

The Chinese asked "where" questions. Where is the Way? The Chinese have long accepted the fact that the only constant in the world is change, and they have sought "the Way" to accommodate this phenomenon or apparent reality. For the Chinese, knowledge is not abstract. It is concrete. It is not representational. It is multifaceted, performative, and participatory. It is not discursive. It is a kind of know-how. Chinese thinkers are not preoccupied with the goal of providing rational accounts of motion and change. Instead, they seek to experience the world rather than understand it. For Chinese people, thinking is actualizing or realizing the meaningfulness of the world, a process that engages the whole person. There is only an ever-changing processional regularity that can be discerned within the world itself. This makes the world, to some degree, coherent and determinate while simultaneously recognizing its inherent indeterminacy, resulting novelty, and unpredictability. Reality is thus a tacit concept, which nevertheless remains grounded in concrete observation and experience. As a result, Chinese attitudes and thought preferences tend to be practical, holistic, tacit, correlative, aesthetic, and dynamic. Western attitude and thought preferences are more abstract, theoretical, atomic, rational, analytical, dualistic, static, and substantial. Of course, one should not overly generalize these points and remember these differences are incidental. They are simply the outcome of environmental and cultural evolution, useful in models for analysis.

One of the most significant outcomes of Western thinking is the development of modern science. A brief description of the development of classical physics demonstrates the use of science in a quest to discover the laws of nature. This scientific revolution occurred mainly in the West. The concept of the laws of nature was actually alien to traditional Chinese philosophical thinking. This is not a surprising fact because Chinese thought is neither analytically nor theoretically inclined. Rather, it is very pragmatic.

Chinese people prefer ethics to religion, applied science over pure science, and practical understanding of human relationships over metaphysics. In contrast, religion and science dominate Western thought. This is not surprising because the search for truth and transcendence has underpinned Western history. The surprising outcome, however, is that the philosophy behind modern Western conceptions of physics, for example, quantum theory and relativity, is better understood in the context of Chinese and Eastern traditions than Western philosophies. The West is increasingly accepting secularization. Postmodern Western philosophies no longer subscribe to traditional religious beliefs. On the other hand, the Chinese worldview is neither supernatural nor preordained by principles. Rather, it is organic, harmonious, and aesthetic, representing a contextual perspective of human experience. This worldview holds that humankind is simply an integral part of nature. Thus, it significantly impacts Chinese conceptualizations of order, truth, reality, value, tradition, and history. These conceptualizations determine Chinese attitudes toward many aspects of life, for example, education, self-cultivation, religion, science, social and political institutions, governance, dreams, and life pursuits.

Part Two: Human Relationships

Chapter four investigates traditional Chinese views of themselves, particularly with reference to psychological and ethical issues. We include discussions regarding the notion of selfhood in modern psychology and traditional Chinese and Western medicine. Central to this discussion is the role of Chinese ethics in demanding foremost that humans self-cultivate and make one's own life significant.

In chapters five and six, we will discuss Chinese relations with other people and institutions in the society and state. These topics concern the psychological, social, economic, and political development of cultures. A moral focus-field model describes Chinese interrelationships between self and family and society and country. Each mimics the order of the universe described in chapter three's exploration of the application of worldviews. This model is overlaid on the foundation of Chinese ethics, that is, the moral integrity of each individual, including rulers. These innate virtues provide the key to our understanding of Confucianism and Chinese culture. The basic unit in ancient Chinese society was the family rather than the individual. The most basic Confucian virtue is filial piety, which demands voluntary and spontaneous love and respect for the elders, particularly parents, in return for their love, care, and protection. Chinese society and the state are a modeled extension of the family. It is not an exaggeration to say that all relationships are familial in the Chinese world.

An exploration of Chinese people's thinking about themselves and their relationships to the world around them necessitates delving into Confucianism. The first social objective of Confucianism is to achieve harmony in family relationships. From the family, social harmony and cohesion is extended until it embraces all human relationships with the ideal of "bringing peace to all under heaven." The Chinese notion of interrelationship comprises those things that induce peace, including the spirit of self-cultivation, the ethic of responsibility, the value of family and social cohesiveness, reciprocity, human solidarity, harmony within diversity, benevolent governance, harmony with nature, and universal peace. Governance of the state follows the model of a family. The leader functions as the father and head of the family. All citizens are his children. The emperor then rules by his Confucian virtues. His moral integrity demonstrates a Mandate from Heaven that demands accountability for the benefit of his people. A bureaucracy of governmental officials, whose legitimacy was also based on their Confucian virtues as well as a system of meritocracy, performed administrative duties.

While on the topic of family relations, we will examine the feminine role in traditional China. We will find that the images of women in China have been changing through history while maintaining a focus on the primacy of the family.

In each of these three chapters concerning human relationships, we will make comparisons between Western and Chinese cultures wherever possible. In some cases, we present relevant modern theories in parallel to provide a reference point for the modern reader. Through these comparisons and presentations, we will discover the ideals, dreams, and aspirations that both Western and Chinese people hold dear. We will examine their similarities and differences in life, beliefs, values, traditions, and institutions. Two important themes emerge. First, Chinese society generally stresses individual obligations; Western society emphasizes rights. Second, contrary to Western thought that seeks differentiation between body and soul, being and nonbeing, individual and family, individual and society, society and state, and human and nature, Chinese thought strives toward coexistence, integration, unity, harmony, and mutual respect and understanding of all things in nature. Such ideals can even transcend time, and they are believed to link together past, present, and the future.

Part Three: Mega History

The historical record provides substantiation for the observations and arguments in the previous chapters. Hence, we dedicate the next six chapters to presenting some macroevents in history. By comparing, we concentrate on different forces behind the occurrence of these events, including technological, cultural, economic, sociological, and political forces. These forces are the results of the human thinking, aspirations, and relationships previously discussed. Their exposition links together different parts of this volume.

The scope and depth of such an historical investigation is potentially limitless. We can only sketch some historical high points for our readers. With a written history that can be traced back more than three thousand years, together with rich legends and myths that date to much earlier, Chinese culture and its writings constitute the best-preserved and longest continuous literary record of humanity. Combining these records with various prehistorical archaeological finds dating back to the Pleistocene epoch, one can study the arrival and development of early humans and the formative process of Chinese civilization in much detail. Only a few archaeologists and anthropologists of other cultures have been afforded this opportunity. An enormous amount of work on this project has been undertaken in China over the last forty years. In these chapters, we will focus on the elements of the historical record that illuminate the evolution of thinking processes in the West and China.

In chapters seven to twelve, we will divide history into three key periods and approach them chronologically. The first period, the subject of chapters seven and eight, entails a review of early history. It focuses on Western civilization from the Neolithic era until the formation of the Roman Empire. In the case of Chinese civilization, we will focus from the Neolithic era to China's first unification into the Qin/Han empires in 221 BC.

The Neolithic era was the age wherein many tenets of civilization, such as basic thinking, language, art, ideology, customs, traditions, and worldview, were developed. Civilizations appeared when Neolithic villages merged to create cities, which then became larger as better technology, organization, and management became available. Urban communities that shared a common cultural heritage grouped themselves by assimilation or conquest into nations. Nations fused through further assimilation or conquest into empires. By tracing the progress and formation of the Roman and Qin/Han empires, one gains a better understanding of the nature and cultural characteristics of Western and Chinese civilizations. The Neolithic civilizations of Europe and the Near East were marked by fission, diffusion, expansion, conquest, counterconquest, barbarian invasion, and colonization, culminating in the formation of the powerful Roman Empire in the first century BC.

The Chinese Neolithic civilizations were distinct in their economic, cultural, and political fission and fusion, assimilation, kinship linkage, intermarriage, social stratification, and integration, which eventually formed the equally powerful Qin/Han empires. We believe these disparate paths to empire are the results of the difference in the two worldviews, cultural philosophies and ideologies, and thinking preferences, which is the prevailing theme of this volume. Chinese civilization was a product of evolution, not the revolution that the West often experienced. We have quoted L. S. Stavrianos extensively in these chapters because we appreciate his global approach to history, especially related to European history. However, his perspectives on Chinese history are no longer tenable in the face of new archaeological evidence.

Chapter eight ends with a comparison of the Roman and Qin/Han Empires, which were broadly comparable in size, population, and historical time period. While they enjoyed the fruits of some similar technological advancement and resulted from the military conquest of a powerful state, the two empires nevertheless developed very distinctive political, sociological, economic, and cultural characteristics.

Chapters nine and ten explore a second period of history, specifically from the peak of the Roman Empire to the late medieval era in approximately the twelfth and thirteenth centuries of Europe. In China, the same period spanned from the Qin/Han dynasties in the second century BC, to the end of the Song dynasty in the thirteenth century.

Historian Joseph R. Strayer of Princeton University described the Roman Empire as a union of people who shared a common Mediterranean civilization under a single, powerful ruler. Nevertheless, this empire never actually achieved the status of a national state.

In contrast, China's governing central and local bureaucracies, intensive agriculture, and market network and economy that the Chinese had been building for many centuries all matured during the Han dynasty and flourished during the Tang and Song dynasties. In addition, most ancient Chinese shared the common ideology of Confucianism and the concept of a legitimate ruler working for the benefit of the people under the Mandate of Heaven. These various elements bound the empire together during this period of great cultural expansion, which was marked by technological advancement, institutional maturity, and economic prosperity, despite the interruption of intervals of political disorder similar to those suffered in Europe. This era was also a golden age for Chinese arts, literature, philosophy, and religion, which neared an apex during the Song dynasty. During these years, China laid legitimate claim to the world's most advanced technology, commerce, and social and political sophistication, in part because it was constantly interacting with and absorbing from foreign cultures and influences. In addition, despite military setbacks experienced in battling nomads in the north, the Song dynasty was a major maritime power with ships ranging freely throughout Southeast Asia and the Indian Ocean that benefited from the use of the mariner's compass.

The fall of the Roman Empire plunged Europe into the Dark Ages when the dominance of the Christian faith provided the sole intellectual activity. Barbarian invasions, political disorder, economic and technological stagnation, black death, and a decline in population all threatened Europe. Because of its unique character and great generative capacity during this period, the Chinese system, in contrast, endured even when the empire was under pressure and experiencing diminishment.

Chapters eleven and twelve deal with the road to modernization that begins in the twelfth century in both Europe and China. This period dates from 1271 when the Mongols conquered China and established the first non-Han Chinese dynasty, the Yuan. East-West communication peaked during the Yuan dynasty when the Mongolian Empire straddled both continental Europe and Asia, dispatching horror and suffering to the Chinese and many Europeans. Yet, the Mongols brought artisans and craftsmen, new technology, and many great inventions of the East to Europe, which was then far more advanced than the West. The Mongolian occupation of China was far more damaging to the Chinese culture than is generally recognized. China would subsequently revert to isolationism with the advent of the Ming dynasty in 1368.

As the Chinese empire began a dramatic decline, European culture simultaneously flourished in the twelfth century, marking a period of peace and stability in the West. Institutions such as economic and social structures were reestablished, education was refocused, and trade burgeoned. The Christian Church became more rationalistic, cautious, and earthbound. Then came the Renaissance. Its French name means "rebirth," which perfectly describes the intellectual and economic changes that occurred in Europe from the fourteenth through the sixteenth centuries. During the Renaissance, Europe emerged from the economic stagnation of the Middle Ages and experienced significant financial growth. Perhaps even more importantly, the Renaissance was an age in which artistic, social, scientific, and political thought turned in new directions. The Reformation and the Age of Discovery that followed provided more impetus for the Europeans to organize their affairs, including religious, political, social, and economic reforms. In China, however, an era of major upheaval was about to begin.

The brief Mongolian occupation of China signaled the beginning of a long period of major cultural, political, and economic decline. Most of the Ming emperors, successors to the Mongols, were incompetent. The authority of the court weakened under the influence of powerful eunuchs, officers of the inner court, and, worst of all, the abolition of the important position of counselor-in-chief, the Chinese equivalent of a prime minister, from the central bureaucracy. All local governments then reported directly to the emperor, whose decisions in state matters were irresponsibly made or based simply on the advice of a handful of close retainers with their own agenda. The previously valuable examination system for the selection of officials was jeopardized due to its new emphasis on form rather than substance. Dogmatic Neo-Confucianism indoctrinated many Chinese people. The government became despotic and oppressive. The creativity and vitality of the people and the society was diminished. After the historic journey of Chenghe to the eastern coast of Africa in 1403, about eighty years before the Portuguese explorer Vasco da Gama's discovery of the same region via the Cape of Good Hope, the Ming administration restricted all ocean travels and closed the country to foreign trade. Despite all these negatives, when the Portuguese first arrived in China in the sixteenth century, they still conveyed a positive new image of China to the European public. Galiote Pereira's *Tratado da China*, written around 1552, openly praised many aspects of Chinese life, including its perfect highways and bridges, the impeccable layout of the cities, the rational organization of economic production, the efficiency of local administration, and the impartiality of the judicial machinery (Loureiro 2000).

As China's march to modernization continued in isolation, the Ming dynasty became so weak that it was totally impotent when another group of nomads, the Manchu, arrived in 1644 and established the Qing dynasty. The Qing emperors were powerful and capable. Most were authorities in Chinese culture. These emperors expanded the empire to its present form. Unfortunately, they inherited and preserved despotic Ming institutions. They distrusted the Han people, fostering racial tensions and rebellions that further weakened the state. As a result, a short period of resurgence in the new empire was followed by a continuing decline that culminated in the end of the imperial era with the establishment of the first Chinese Republic in 1911. Even then, China was unable to recover its past glory and dynamism.

While China endured the dissolution of the Qing era, the West set out upon the adventure of the Age of Enlightenment in the eighteenth century, representing both a culmination and beginning. New ideas and approaches to old institutions were preparing the stage for great revolutions to come. The major themes of this era were rationalism, secularism, scientific method, individualism, utilitarianism, constitutionalism, and cosmopolitanism. People valued liberty and happiness and began challenging the Church's authority and dogmatic doctrines. In the form of this challenge, Europe's Age of Enlightenment shared many of the ideologies and practices of the ancient Chinese who preceded the decline of the Yuan/Ming/Qing dynasties, including, to name a few relevant tenets, humanism, the pursuit of happiness, and education as the foundation of self-fulfillment. The Enlightenment mentality underlies the rise of the modern West as the most dynamic and transformative ideology in human history. Virtually all major spheres of interest characteristic of the modern age are indebted to or intertwined with this mentality, including science and technology, capitalism, market economy, democracy, mass communication, universities, civil and military bureaucracies, and professional organizations. Furthermore, the values we cherish as definitions of modern consciousness, including liberty; equality; human rights; the dignity of the individual; respect for privacy; government for, by, and of the people; and due process of law, are generally, if not structurally, inseparable from Enlightenment mentality.

Then came the age where industrialization, democracy, capitalism, socialism, imperialism, colonialism, and nationalism established societies and institutions that we recognize as modern. Not only did the eighteenth to twentieth centuries usher in major revolutions such as those of the French, Americans, Russians, and Chinese, they also brought two world wars and the Cold War. We will not elaborate on events in modern history except in the use of cases that have significance.

The dramatic shift in the respective global status of China and the Western world is highlighted in the research of Paul Bairoch, which compared historical national output in different areas of the world (Nolan 2004). Bairoch estimated that, in 1750, China's share of global manufacturing output stood at 33 percent, compared with 25 percent for India/Pakistan and just 18 percent in the West. He estimated, at 1960 prices, that China's per capita GNP was $228 (US$) in 1800, compared with $150–200 (US$) for Great Britain and France combined. This contrast would have been even more dramatic if statistics were available for the period prior to the Chinese decline. Nolan pointed out that, until the nineteenth century, the dominant view of European intellectuals was that China was materially superior to Europe. As Europe entered the Industrial Revolution and China around the same time encountered further severe political and economic difficulties, China's role in the global economy changed drastically. By 1913, its share of world manufacturing output had fallen to under 4 percent while the West had risen to 82 percent (Bairoch 1982). When China met face to face with the industrialized European powers in the nineteenth century, it became so entirely ineffectual due to this dramatic change of fortune that the predominant image of China shifted to one of a stagnant, impoverished despotism. Unfortunately, this image of ancient China has persisted to this day, even among some Chinese intellectuals.

Part Four: Past, Present, and Future

In chapter thirteen, we review historical trends and lessons, which are significant in meeting our present and future challenges. We briefly review past efforts to discern such trends, including the works of Oswald Spengler, Arnold Toynbee, Patrick Gardiner, Will and Ariel Durant, L. S. Stavrianos, and Alvin Toffler, in this light. We will concentrate our examination upon the predominant contemporary trends of globalization and technological advancement. We make the case for a post-postmodern reconstruction. Unfortunately, we find that history offers no lesson or general law with any type of predictive power. History never occurs twice under exactly the same conditions. History can provide highly plausible identifications and generalizations of patterns, trends, and structures in our past. This is partially true because the forces behind historical events—economic, social, ethical, or political—are the topics of our better-understood disciplines of social science. The same human psychology, the same human passions we all have, guide all actors in history. Therefore, they are also comprehensible in human terms. With this understanding, we will propose four significant lessons from our own historical observations and perspectives. We hope these lessons, our own historical perspectives, will help our readers to better interpret some of the current and future events.

In chapter fourteen, we will look at the current state of the world, referring to the theme of combining globalization and information revolution. A call to transcend Enlightenment mentality follows. It is our contention that modern ideologies and institutions, for example, capitalism, individualism, democracy, the rule of law, liberalism, and so forth, all need redefinition and reinvigoration in light of globalization and technological changes.

Of particular note technologically is the fact that modern industries rely heavily on fossil fuel, reserves that are exhaustible in the foreseeable future—although not before use of these fuels drastically impacts our environment and threatens the balance of our delicate ecosystem. To avoid disasters that could endanger our civilization and the very existence of our human species, now is the time to call for innovative solutions, both spiritual and material. To begin, we must learn from our spiritual resources, including our traditions, histories, and global and local neighbors. The citizens and governments of our world must unite to face global challenges, such as appropriate governance, the sustainability of industrial development, the realities of limited resources, ecological imbalance, wealth disparities, social and moral degradation, terrorism, and other critical issues.

The West and China must learn from each other. These seemingly divergent traditions are actually more complementary than antagonistic to each other. This connection forms the major theme of this book. The Western world and China face different challenges in the third millennium, challenges that are products or by-products of their distinct cultures, histories, and traditions as well as their differing paces on the paths of cultural, economic, social, and political development.

The United States and Europe are highly industrialized, militarily robust, and culturally and politically influential. They support a large collection of powerful, globally competitive firms, and they can assert control over international capital movements when they deem it necessary to do so. Some of the major challenges facing the West are international terrorism, communal violence, sectarian conflicts, religious and economic fundamentalism, social and moral decadency, and the renewal of dated traditional, spiritual, cultural, social, economic, and political institutions. Some may not be assailable without a critical breakthrough in our thinking, beliefs, attitudes, philosophy, and established traditions. Other cultures and spiritual resources, such as those of the non-Western world, including the Chinese, cannot provide exact answers. But they can help by offering what they have learned from their own traditions, ideas, philosophies, and experiences in meeting similar problems in their own history.

Contemporary China is already learning much from the West. Despite its great economic achievement over the last two decades, China is comparatively weak technologically, economically, politically and militarily. It faces many social and ethical problems typically encountered in developing countries. In addition, there are problems of an historical nature, for example, the threat of segregation across the Taiwanese Strait. China needs a cultural and spiritual renewal, especially after the total deconstruction of the past several decades.

From a more positive point of view, such total deconstruction has left Chinese people free of the notion that tradition and ideology are immutable once established. Thus, China is bestowed with a golden opportunity to construct new traditions, ideals, and institutions from the best components of its own heritage and, indeed, the best from anywhere in the world. Education is one key arena for this renewal in China. China has learned much and is continuing to learn from the West. How Westerners face their challenges in the third millennium will be a source of valuable information, inspiration, and guidance for the Chinese thinkers and planners of the present and future.

The transformation of China and Chinese aspirations will have profound and lasting consequences, individually, locally, nationally, regionally, and globally. With a population of 1.3 billion and limited resources, China cannot afford to employ the same model that the United States and Europe adopted in their era of industrialization, specifically reliance on fossil fuel, overdependence on privately owned automobiles, and disregard for damage to the environment and ecological systems. Sustainability is the key word, and China must be creative and innovative in its development. The rest of the world should offer help wherever they can because we all live in this single global village.

Section Three:
Challenges in a Cultural Study of China

Our quest for cross-cultural, multilinguistic communication will encounter many difficulties of varying degrees. Contrary to the misconception that Chinese culture has been dormant for millennia, it has actually been slowly evolving in a continuously changing process of self-realization and self-actualization. Along the way, Chinese culture has synthesized and absorbed nutrients from its own and many other cultures. For instance, around the time of the Spring and Autumn period, the original Confucianism was distinct from the Confucianism of the Han dynasty a couple of centuries later when aspects of other philosophies, including Daoism, Mohism, Legalism, and others, were reconciled into its doctrine. Then Confucianism was again drastically modified to become the Neo-Confucianism of the Song and Ming dynasties in which teachings from Indian Buddhism were incorporated. Generations of scholars have written many theses on this subject alone. Nevertheless, some issues still remain controversial. This is only a single example, illustrating the difficulty of fairly presenting a dynamically changing concept such as Confucianism, as well as many others, without a lengthy dissertation. The reader must understand the phase "Chinese culture" in conceptual terms. It is a living organism that has changed continuously through time. It is a tradition and a history that spans several millennia. In spatial dimensions, it is a culture that covered an area of East Asia much larger than present-day Europe.

The perception of space is also important because of the vastness and diversity of the landform that China occupies. Upon this immense stage, there coexists one majority Han race and fifty-five official minority races that constitute the people of contemporary China. Most still maintain their own cultures and traditions.

The Han race, in turn, is also a conglomeration of many different cultures and races. Thus, the history and traditions of one race are not necessarily representative of other races in China. The complexities of this vast country cannot be overemphasized nor should one overgeneralize trends based on superficial, local, or casual observations and experiences.

The dynamism and scale of China are not the only challenges we face in this exploration. Another major difficulty of our work lies in the use of concepts or terms with contemporary meanings different from their classical origins, which different connotation in varying cultures compounds. For example, *fengjian* was used in classical Chinese history and literature to describe the way the first emperor of the Zhou dynasty, after winning the eleventh-century BC war against the Shang dynasty, distributed land to his relatives and generals, forming earldoms. Modern application of the same word is much more general and denotes any institution, person, or concept that is old and corrupt. The same term can also be translated as "feudal," which has a different connotation when contrasted with the use of that term in feudal Europe. Despite proper explanations of their usage, these differences in terminology may be confusing and even misleading to readers. In fact, many postmodern philosophers, such as Richard Rorty, suggest that dialogue and even communication between different traditions and cultures is ultimately problematic because there is no single final vocabulary to which all can appeal for common standards of meaning, truth, and value. Different people or groups of people at different times, according to various political or social convictions, understand or interpret divergently important lexicons in classical Chinese history and philosophy. Some interpretations are products of the value judgments unique to a particular time.

The problem of articulating a term or concept that has no equivalence in another culture can represent a major hurdle for cross-cultural communication. All workers in cross-cultural and cross-language arenas face the same challenge. When translating from one culture to another, one often encounters words, concepts, or novel ideas prevalent in one culture, but totally foreign to another culture or tradition. In such cases, we must try to realize the limits of our own culture so we can expand our perspective and gain cross-cultural understanding. Achieving this crucial expansion is not easy, but we believe strongly that it is possible once we are aware of the importance of doing so. Despite our differences, our common human feelings and experiences transcend language and culture and provide the basis of a common understanding. It is true that linguistic, cultural, religious, and other traditions are present throughout our conscious lives, contextualizing the present and serving as a source of ideas and possible solutions to problems that we face. However, it does not follow that our respective traditions do not entirely fix or determine our conscious mental processes. Also, these traditions are not so disparate that those in one tradition cannot understand and make appropriate normative judgments about the activities of those in other traditions. As long as we are aware of the differences, we believe there are always ways in which we can both recognize the value and integrity of each other's traditions and bridge and extend those traditions.

In an effort to deal with the challenges of this cross-cultural comparison, we will take advantage of an expanded view of Chinese tradition presented by David Hall and Roger Ames, whose work we respect and reference throughout this book. Like them, we hope that, by presenting some of the philosophical roots and basic elements of Chinese thought, we can help readers better understand and appreciate the Chinese philosophical traditions that underpin the Chinese mind. For example, Hall and Ames (1998) have identified notions such as self, truth, and transcendence as key concepts that are perceived differently in Chinese and Western traditions. Hall and Ames stressed that, when confronted with such Chinese philosophical concepts, Western readers must not think in terms of transcendence, ontology, or dualism, that is, notions engrained in Western tradition but absent in traditional Chinese culture. Another philosopher, Chenyang Li (1999), considered other common, but important, ideas, such as being, truth, language, ethics, religion, and value, to be confusing in the two cultures. It is required that one be alert in their usage.

Before selecting Chinese philosophical terms or concepts for discussion, we strived to minimize any potential misunderstandings by first surveying as many English writings as possible, focusing on authors who read and write competently in both Chinese and English and have a deep understanding and appreciation of the Chinese people and their philosophy. This objective has been sometimes difficult to achieve because such authors are relatively rare. Hence, we have also selected materials from Chinese sources, authors who have a deep understanding of Western culture and are capable of cross-cultural evaluations.

Part One

The Thinking Processes

Do Chinese people think differently from Westerners? Our experience favors the answer as yes. Various studies published both inside and outside China have continuously modified and reinforced this simple, decisive answer. In our exploration of the differences between East and West, this is the perfect place to start. The differences in thought are the foundation of most of the differences between these two cultures.

The next two chapters investigate the development of thinking in China and the West. We will first study environmental and evolutionary influences before studying how thinking has evolved differently in the two cultures because of those influences.

CHAPTER TWO

Environmental and Evolutionary Influences

Our present study deals with evolution of thinking, specifically how environmental and evolutionary factors have influenced it over time. This study does not cover specific genetic factors in the theory of evolution. Instead, it looks more at how the environment that an individual must adapt to for survival, influences their human behavior, experience, and development.

Section One: Environmental Influences

The southeastern quadrant of the Eurasian landmass, separated from other early civilizations by deserts, mountains, and seas, formed the incubator of Chinese civilization. This region lies more than 4,500 miles from either Asia Minor or southeastern Europe, the two cradles of Western civilization. There is evidence of intermittent communication between these ancient civilizations. However, because of the vast distances and difficult terrains that separated the cultures, early Chinese culture essentially developed in isolation. This isolation persisted until about two thousand years ago with the opening of the Silk Road across the Pamir Mountain passes in Central Asia and the advent of sea trade. Even then, travel was hazardous and time-consuming. Hence, geographic confinement is one of the most important and unifying factors in early Chinese life and history. This is in sharp contrast with the development of ancient civilizations around the Mediterranean, where open communication and cross-cultural exchange were common occurrences.

As we know it today, China is about the same size as the United States with more than three million square miles of territory. Its land abounds with diverse landforms, including many great river valleys and large river basins. The vastness and the scale of China cannot be overemphasized in contrast with other cradles of civilization, particularly Greece and Mesopotamia. All of the Greek city-states would have fit into the smallest of the Chinese kingdoms in the fifth century BC. Both the Yangtze and Yellow Rivers are among the world's ten largest. The larger plains, plateaus, and provinces in China exceed the size of an average-sized country in Europe.

An understanding of this vast and varied geography is clearly necessary to any understanding of the origins of Chinese thought.

Diverse Beginnings

According to leading archaeologist Su Bingyee (1999), there were six major regions of simultaneous cultural development in China, specifically the north, east, central, southeast, southwest, and south. Each progressed at its own speed and with its own character, but they still managed to influence one another, even in prehistory.

The eastern and central regions follow the drainage of the Yellow River, while the southwest and southeast regions follow the Yangtze. Early Chinese culture was comprised of many diverse groups of people scattered in valleys around the feeder channels of the Yellow and Yangtze Rivers. The most prominent divisive element in their landscape was a mountainous region with the east-west trending Qinling Range at its core, tapering down across central China from Tibet toward the Pacific coast and separating the Yellow River drainage zone of the north from the Yangtze River drainage zone of the south and the coastal valleys beyond. Both north and south are also subdivided into smaller areas, separated from each other by stretches of low, but rugged, hills. In addition, both northern and southern China contain a great lowland plain in the east and a highland plateau in the west. The features of this often-forbidding terrain separated people into small regions, where diverse outlooks and maintenance of different customs and dialects endured through time. Even today, one can still witness this. The same holds true for the Pearl River drainage system further south, the ancestral home for many of the Chinese people who emigrated to North America.

Northern China

The Yellow River Highland Plateau is the central region that was previously considered to be the cradle of Chinese civilization. From more recent archaeological finds in other provinces, we now know that this region was only one of six cradles. It was, however, the most important incubator and perhaps one of the first to cross the threshold of civilization.

The Yellow River Highland Plateau was formed by the accumulation of thick loess deposits from the deserts of central Asia's northwest region over a period dating from six to twenty-two million years ago. Even today, cities in the eastern sections of this region, for example, the capital city of Beijing, still suffer from desertification. This pattern can be traced to the mid-Tertiary Miocene period when the Indian subcontinental plate collided with the Eurasian plate, resulting in the creation of the Himalayas. Since that time, desertification has taken place rapidly in central Asia. Winds that previously carried moisture from the Indian Ocean in the south could no longer penetrate the towering mountains. As a result, westerly winds carry the desert particles eastward and differentially deposit them in the Yellow River Highland Plateau according to their grain size. Larger particles settle first. Sand and silt then follow as the wind flows farther eastward. Resulting loess deposits of soft and loose sediment have built up to tens and sometimes hundreds of meters in thickness. These deposits are known to hold water and rich, organic nutrients capable of sustaining intensive farming, particularly for crops not requiring a high moisture environment for growth, for example, soybeans and millets.

This unique pattern of soil deposition occurs in concert with predictable rainfall patterns. Continental Asia encompasses a vast, arid heartland fringed by moist areas facing the oceans. Differential heating of the dry hinterland and surrounding oceans causes air pressure differentials, creating a seasonal reversal of surface airflow known as the Asiatic monsoon system. Monsoons are a dominant factor in the rain distribution patterns of China with heavy rains along the coast. Precipitation only occurs in central China when monsoons meet with the cold, dry cyclones originating in the deserts of the northwest. According to Huang (1997), the Great Wall of China was built to demarcate the herdsmen and nomads of the north and northwest from the farmers of the south and southeast. In fact, it has now been found that the Great Wall was built to coincide with the "twenty-five centimeter isohyet line," the contour of average yearly rainfall. Because of aridity, farming cannot be sustained outside the Great Wall.

Northern China's harsh climate results from proximity to the arid central Asian hinterlands. Annual precipitation, falling mostly in the summer, is only twenty-five to fifty centimeters (ten to twenty inches) in the western highlands and forty to seventy-five centimeters (fifteen to thirty inches) in the eastern plains, depending mainly on the coincidental timing of the monsoons and the storms from the west. Winter is severe. The little precipitation is mostly in the form of snow. The average winter temperatures are approximately minus six degrees Centigrade (twenty one degrees Fahrenheit). In northern China's agricultural areas, 80 percent of the rainfall generally comes in the three summer months. Despite its harsh climate, however, the North China Plain has become the largest, modern agricultural center of China.

Prehistorical evidence suggests the southern part of this loess highland was one of the key centers of ancient Chinese civilization. Archaeologist Zhang Guangzhi contended that, during the postglacial era, which ended several thousand years ago, the North China Plain was warmer and more moist than at present (1983). Combined with the thick, loose layers of fertile loess soil, this warm, moist climate was one of the reasons for the early development of farming in China. Stone ploughs were used very early because of the soft ground conditions. In the Near East, organized farming did not arise until the arrival of the iron plough at a much later time. The Chinese actually domesticated millet in northern China and rice in southern China in the early Neolithic period more than ten thousand years ago.

The Yellow River can be damaging as well as beneficial because of its capacity to carry large amounts of loess sediments, up to 46 percent by volume, in contrast to a great river like the Amazon, which carries only 10 to 12 percent sediment by volume [Huang, 1988]. As a result, the Yellow River has changed course forty-one times throughout history. Over thousands of years, it has created its own beds and channels on the accumulated loess, the layers of which are often higher than the surrounding countryside. Thus, the safety of the countryside depends heavily on the security of the dikes constructed along the river. Yet these dikes are usually built of mud or sand bags and often break under pressure. The resulting floodwaters inundate millions of acres of farmland, threaten many lives, and precipitate significant homelessness in a pattern repeated since the beginning of Chinese civilization. An unofficial estimate suggests there were 1,590 breaches of dikes between 602 and 1938 [Huang, 1988]. During that time, the river changed course seven times. Large-scale famine and pestilence, faithfully documented and vividly described by historians and intellectual observers alike, usually followed such natural catastrophes.

Under such circumstances, mere human survival requires strong leadership, effective technology, and genuine cooperation from all people. In fact, Chinese people often judge the competency of their government via its effectiveness in fighting natural calamities like floods or droughts. Engineers successful in building waterworks to alleviate flooding were worshipped as folk heroes. Traveling around China today, one can still see some of these water projects and folk temples built for the engineers. The most impressive is the controlled water diversion project constructed around the third century BC by the father and son team of Li Bing in Sichuan Province. People today still benefit from this project.

Southern China

Southern China is topographically quite distinct from northern China with an even more diverse landscape. The Yangtze River has its origins in the Tibetan mountain ranges. Unlike the Yellow River, it does not pick up a large amount of loess or other sediments as it flows westward through the Sichuan Basin and ultimately into the Pacific Ocean. The vast Yangtze provinces include the extensive lake country of the middle and lower Yangtze with its hills and alluvial plains, the hilly region of southeastern China, and the plateaus in the west, including the upper Yangtze valley. Although southern China is subject to the effects of the monsoon, its climate is more stable than that of the north. Total precipitation is heavier with a pronounced summer maximum and a heavier winter precipitation, allowing the growth of more luxuriant and varied vegetation. Some areas of southern China are so temperate and receive so much rainfall that two or even three crops a year are common. Even so, crops grown in southern China cannot rely on rainfall alone. This is especially true for rice, which grows exclusively in warm climates and under constant water submersion. For this reason, rice is grown in paddies in southern China.

Archaeologically, the upper Yangtze valley may well be the location of the origins of the Chinese races. Fossil hominids dated at more than two million years have been found in both Sichuan and Yunnan. For a more detailed account of the origin of the Chinese race, consult *The Story of Peking Man* by Jia Lanpo and Huang Weiwen. Archaeological sites of the Paleolithic and Neolithic eras abound, well documented along the river all the way to the Pacific, and include evidence of early rice cultivation during Paleolithic times more than ten thousand years ago.

As a result of these many unique combinations of topography, both northern and southern China have very diverse environments with fertile soil, an abundant supply of water, and a climate conducive to the flourishing of plants and animals. These regions thus became centers for an early transition from hunting and gathering to the development of agriculture in the late Paleolithic and early Neolithic periods. This is in sharp contrast with Mesopotamia, where the environment was too dry for farming without the use of irrigation.

Near East and Europe

The location of the earliest agriculture in the Western world was the Fertile Crescent of the Near East, stretching from the highland of the Levant along the eastern shore of the Mediterranean Sea to the Zagros Mountains of western Iran and the Taurus Mountains of southern Turkey, south of the Caspian Sea. Here, wheat and barley grew wild. The region's fringes were home to the ancestors of domestic sheep and goats. The earliest known domesticates, for example, wheat, barley, peas, lentils, pigs, goats, sheep, and cattle, appeared in this area in the late Paleolithic and early Neolithic periods at approximately the same time as their Chinese counterparts around 10,000 BC. The complete system of Neolithic innovations such as domesticates, village architecture, and pottery was subsequently in place around 7000 BC, and soon spread to the Aegean area and Greece in southeastern Europe and then to the north and west. Because of geographical limitations, the scale of Greek agriculture was in no way a match for that of the Chinese. Greek culture, like other European cultures of the time, was more open to trade and focused on mastery of the seas.

Section Two:
The Effects of the Ice Age

Human Evolution and Geographical Changes

The Pleistocene, commonly referred to as the Ice Age, was a geological epoch that began approximately two million years ago. Active volcanoes, cooling temperatures marked by alternating periods of colder and warmer conditions, and the appearance of *Homo erectus* alongside several modern species of animals characterized the time. The cooling trend, which began in the Pliocene epoch about 3.5 million years ago, coincided with the period of human evolution known as the Basal Paleolithic. During this period, our evolution from Australopithecines began. The following table provides an overview of the geological timescale and the corresponding periods of human development.

	Years B.P.	Period	Stone Industry	Archaelogical Sites	Hominid Species	Major Events
Post-glacial	10,000	Neolithic				Framing Art
Upper Pleistocene		Upper Paleolithic	Blade tools	Lascaus, Pincevent Dolni Vestonice	Homo sapiens sapiens	
Upper Pleistocene	100,000	Middle Paleolithic	Mousterian flake tools	Shanidar Klasies River	Homo sapiens neanderthalensis	Burial of dead Oldest dwellings
Middle Pleistocene	200,000			Kalambo Falls		
Middle Pleistocene	500,000	Lower Paleolithic		Terra Amata Olorgesailie		Use of fire
Middle Pleistocene				Zhoukoudian		
Lower Pleistocene	1,000,000		Clactonian chopping tools	Trinil		Spread out of Africa
Lower Pleistocene			Acheulean handaxes	Ubeidiya Koobi Fora	Homo erectus	Handaxes
Lower Pleistocene	2,000,000	Basal Paleolithic	Oldowan pebble tools	Olduvai		
Lower Pleistocene				Swartkrans	Homo habilis	Large brains First stone tools
Pliocene	3,000,000			Hadar Laetoli		
Pliocene	4,000,000				Australopithecines	
Pliocene	5,000,000			Middle Awash	Ardipithecus	Oldest hominid fossils

Table 1 Archaeological divisions of time (Price and Feinman 2001)

Australopithecine hominids had a skeletal structure similar to our own, but they had a much smaller brain with a cranial capacity of 600 to 650 milliliters (twenty to twenty-two ounces), enabling only the use of simple pebble tools. In contrast, *Homo sapiens*, modern humans of the present day, have a cranial capacity of 1,300 to 1,400 milliliters (forty-four to forty-seven ounces). Around the time that humans began to stand erect, the brain capacity of *Homo erectus* had increased to 800 to 900 milliliters (twenty-seven to thirty ounces), and the stone hand ax first appeared. This phase of human development around 1.8 million years ago marked the beginning of the Lower Paleolithic period. The disappearance at this time of Australopithecines coincided with a large number of non-primate extinctions, leading to the hypothesis of a widespread ecological change.

Current fossil evidence demonstrates that, by the Middle Pleistocene approximately one million years ago, *Homo erectus* began to appear outside Africa. It first appeared in the tropics and then later in higher latitudes. The "out of Africa" theory, however, has become somewhat controversial because fossils of some higher primates and prehuman Australopithecines have been found in many sites in southern Asia, including Yunnan in China, and Indonesia, suggesting indigenous evolutional development. The Upper Pleistocene geological epoch coincides roughly with the onset of the Middle Paleolithic, which marks the appearance of *Homo sapiens neanderthalensis* in Europe and the use of flake core and flake tools.

The Upper Paleolithic is the most important period in human development because it trumpets the arrival of *Homo sapiens sapiens*, the first modern human. This period is also significant for the first archaic evidence of blade tools, that is, the technique of using tools to make other tools, and the use of materials such as bone, antler, ivory, jade, and wood.

The Upper Paleolithic is also the time of the advent of cave arts. It was when, toward the end of the Upper Paleolithic approximately ten thousand years ago, the first farmers appeared. Before then, humans were primarily hunter-gatherers.

The Upper Pleistocene also saw the last major episode of Ice Age climate, namely the Wurm glaciations in Europe, peaking around eighteen thousand years ago and preceding a major warming trend that continues to the present day. During the Ice Age, ice sheets spread across the continents at a rate of 100 to 150 meters (328 to 492 feet) per year. In a thousand years, the sheets expanded 100 kilometers (62 miles). In twenty thousand years, they spread 2,000 kilometers (1,243 miles) from their original center. In fact, during the peak of the last Ice Age, known in North America as the Wisconsin glaciations, ice sheets up to one kilometer (0.6 miles) thick covered America from modern-day Portland, Oregon to New York City. In Europe, the land from Dublin to Berlin would have been a part of the ice cap. When the ice was at its full height, the total volume of ice is estimated to have been 70 million cubic kilometers (17 million cubic miles), three times the Earth's present ice volume of 25 million cubic kilometers (6 million cubic miles).

The large amount of water frozen in the ice created a drastic reduction in the world's sea level, which is estimated to have been 120 to 130 meters (394 to 427 feet) lower than at present, creating a radical change in the landscapes of the continental coastlines. For instance, New York, Baltimore, and Boston would have been 120 to 240 kilometers (75 to 150 miles) inland at that time. Alaska would have joined with Siberia, creating a land bridge that accounted for the migration of early Americans from Asia. In Europe, the English Channel, the North Sea, and the Baltic Ocean would not have existed. The straits of Gibraltar were an open plain. Sicily and Corsica would have joined the Italian Peninsula. There were fewer, but larger, of what we now know as the Greek Islands. In Asia,

Japan would have been linked to the Asian mainland between Russia in the north and Korea in the south. Sumatra, Java, and Borneo were joined to modern-day Malaysia and Thailand in a landmass called the Sunda Shelf. The Sahul Shelf joined New Guinea to Australia and Tasmania. This land bridge may again be responsible for the southerly migration of humans. In China, exposure of the continental shelf of the Yellow Sea, resulting from the drop in the world's sea level, created new landscapes on the Chinese coast with the Yangtze River emptying into the sea about one thousand kilometers (six hundred miles) east of where Shanghai is now located.

The end of the Pleistocene geological epoch is dated at 11,000 years ago (9000 BC) when the last ice sheet retreated. A post-glacial period followed. During that time, the global sea level rose as the huge volume of ice melted. The current consensus is that, between 14000 and 5000 BC, the world sea level rose by no less than 120 to 130 meters. The melting of the thick glacier across the continents had many drastic implications. Many cultures recount the legendary tale of a big flood, the importance of which is well documented and immeasurable. The melting of tremendous amounts of ice also released a large quantity of fresh water, decreasing the salinity of the seawaters and impacting life and microorganisms in the oceans. In 1971, Professor Cesare Emiliani of the University of Miami drilled eleven cores into the seabed of Florida's west coast and dated the organic content. These core findings revealed that marine microorganisms living in approximately 9600 BC inhabited seawater that was significantly less saline than had previously been the case.

As described in ancient Chinese documents, the rise in world's sea levels occurred in small episodes. For instance, at the time of the legendary Chinese sage Fuxi, as described in Chinese legend, the mouth of the Yellow River was located at the foothills of the Tai-Hung Mountains with the North China Plain almost totally submerged and the Tai-San Mountains of eastern China existing as an island in the ocean. The present coastline of the world did not stabilize until around 5000 BC.

In addition to the effect of rising sea levels in the post-glacial period, the sudden relief of pressure caused by the melting of billions of tons of ice resulted in rebounding of the earth's crust, setting off many earthquakes across the continents. Volcanic activity released a large amount of carbon dioxide, resulting in further global warming due to the greenhouse effect. The immense scale of global glaciations and warming produced many catastrophes, leaving a lasting imprint on prehistoric human development during the Pleistocene epoch.

The Pleistocene was also accompanied by what is called the Pleistocene Extinction, the result of violent and unexplained fluctuations of climate with abrupt temperature changes of six to ten degrees Centigrade (forty-three to fifty degrees Fahrenheit) occurring in the Atlantic. According to Charles Darwin, between 15000 and 8000 BC, there were extinctions of seventy kinds of mammals, including seven types of proboscides in North America. Within a period of two thousand years alone, from 11000 to 9000 BC, there were extinctions of forty million species of animals, including mammoth in Siberia and Alaska dying an accidental and sudden death. The sudden nature of these deadly glacial occurrences is demonstrated by the recent discovery in Siberia of a ninety-foot-tall fruit tree that was buried in snow and subsequently preserved in the permafrost with its roots, fruit, and green leaves still intact. Of course, this catastrophic event is not without precedent. There were many known extinctions across boundaries of major geological epochs or even some minor geological episodes. For example, it is commonly known in paleontology that there was an 85 percent species extinction rate at the end of the Ordovician period 439 million years ago. There was a 95 percent extinction rate at the end of the Permian period 230 million years ago. And there was a 75 percent extinction rate at the end of the Cretaceous period sixty-five million years ago. These extinctions were caused by a dramatic breakdown in environmental conditions due to a combination of geological and climatic changes, which resulted in the exhaustion of fauna through overheating, lack of oxygen, and starvation. The Permian Extinction provides an example that was initiated by extreme global warming over a long period of time. Excessive temperatures were eventually responsible for widespread deaths, climaxing when extreme ocean heat killed plankton and severed the food chain.

We believe this brief history is a justifiable tangent to our discussion of the effect of the Ice Age on the development of human thinking. It is clearly evident that our Mother Earth is in a delicate balance. Environmentalists, even Nobel Laureates, have warned of the dangers of our present global warming trend. We must recognize from geological history that extinction could indeed happen to the human race if we are not careful about the way in which we are meddling with our environment.

European Ice Age

Europe lies mainly within the latitudes of forty to sixty degrees north. Madrid and Rome are of similar latitude to New York City and Portland, Oregon. At the peak of the last episode of Pleistocene Glaciations, that is, the Wurm Glaciations approximately eighteen thousand years ago, ice sheets covered Scandinavia, northern England, a part of the Netherlands, northern Germany, Poland, and the northwestern part of the former Soviet Union. These sheets of ice acted like huge bulldozers, grinding down the landscapes beneath their advances. As a result, many species of animals and plants became extinct during the Ice Age. By the end of the last episode, the majority of the small animals and some of the larger ones had moved away or died. Only a few of the larger animals remained to become the quarry of the first modern Europeans.

These early modern Europeans were big game hunters, as evidenced in Paleolithic cave paintings and drawings throughout the continent. These paintings and drawings depict animals familiar to nomadic hunter-gatherer tribes. One of the best examples of this early art is seen in the Lascaux Cavern of France, where hunter-artists engraved and painted pictures of animals, including mammoth, bison, reindeer, and horses, on the walls. It is thought the animals were needed for food, so the paintings were some type of ritual related to the hunt. It is also thought that these animals were sacred and ascribed godlike qualities. It has also been suggested that cave paintings may be primitive calendars or almanacs, records of tribal migrations, or mystic objects central to shamanistic trances. The animal figures are both naturalistic and stylized, often showing fine details that suggest keen familiarity with the animal depicted. Such familiarity would be necessary for the challenge of hunting game much larger than the hunters themselves, a challenge requiring strategy and planning. Thus, it would help to know every detail of the quarry, including the anatomy of the animal, its living habits, and its likes and dislikes.

The first humans in Europe were also skilled in producing clay sculptures. Two unbaked clay bison discovered in Tuc d'Audoubert, France, provide an excellent example. Dating between ten thousand and fifteen thousand years before the present, each measures about sixty centimeters (two feet) in length. These sculptures and paintings, among many others, demonstrate that early European hunters were intimately familiar with the details of the large animals of the time period. This familiarity is very different from the way early Chinese hunter-gatherers looked at their world.

Chinese Ice Age

Most of China lies in the middle to low latitudes, between twenty and forty-five degrees, spanning tropical, subtropical, temperate, and frigid-temperate zones with moisture content increasing toward the coast. Despite this twenty-five-degree span of latitude, there is a crucial difference between Europe and China. With the exception of the peaks in certain high mountain areas, ice sheets did not cover China during the Ice Age. The results of this escape from the ice are profound and evident to this day.

Diverse topography and varied climate makes China a place rich and colorful in fauna and flora. According to a National Wildlife Research and Development Center article on wildlife conservation in China, China has one of the world's most diverse populations of animals and plants with 4,400 species of vertebrates alone constituting more than 10 percent of the total global species. Among these, 210 species are amphibious animals, and 320 species are reptiles. There are 1,186 species of birds, 450 species of beasts, and more than 2,200 species of fish. China is home to 9 of the world's 15 species of crane, 46 out of 148 species of Anserinae-Anatidae, 54 out of 257 species of carnivores, 56 out of 276 species of pheasants, and 11 of the world's 190 species of primates. More than one hundred rare animal species can be found mainly in China. Pandas and South China tigers are among the best known. As yet, no accurate statistics catalog the species of invertebrate animals scattered across China, but they are estimated to number no less than one million.

China's flora is as diverse as its fauna. Altogether, there are 32,800 species of higher plants in China, accounting for more than 12 percent of the world total and ranking third in the world, second only to Malaysia and Brazil. Among China's higher plants are 24,500 species of flowering plants, 236 gymnosperm, 200 bryophyte and 2,600 pteridophyte. Again, due to the fact that most of China was not subject to the influence of the last glaciation episode, many of the ancient and solitary species and specialties now extinct in other regions of the Northern Hemisphere survive in China. For example, there is about 200 genera and more than 10,000 species of rare trees unique to China. China is also one of the three major original centers for the cultivation of domestic plants. The precursors of these plants are kindred species of undomesticated plants, including wild walnut, wild chestnut, wild apple, wild lichee, wild longan, wild red hayberry, wild rice, wild barley, wild soybean, wild tea, and others.

Clearly, the variety and richness in species of animals and plants in China contrast dramatically with the western parts of the continental Old World. This divergence had profound consequences on the development of thinking in hunter-gatherers of the late Pleistocene, both in China and the West. It will form the main topic of our discussion in chapter three.

Section Three: Evolution of the Human Mind

Our examination of human thought begins with psychological development, particularly a recognition of the influence of environmental factors. Prehumans and early humans were closely integrated with their natural environment because of their total dependence on nature for food, water, clothing, and shelter. As they accumulated experience through daily interaction with their natural world, early humans developed knowledge and thoughts that allowed them to slowly change environmental elements to better suit their needs. This evolution was very similar to the way that an infant would learn as he or she progressed through early childhood and into adult life. In this section, we will introduce a few of the theories on how the human mind grows and evolves.

Piaget's Theories

Genetic epistemologist Jean Piaget (1896–1980) studied how children first begin to think and how accumulation of experiences and thoughts becomes knowledge at different stages of life. Piaget hypothesized, and then substantiated with experimentation, that infants are born with operating schemes that he called "reflexes." They use these reflexes to adapt to the environment. Piaget noted that infants used two reflexes in an attempt to adapt to their environment. He called these reflexes "assimilation" and "accommodation." These are both used interchangeably and interactively as a person gradually adapts to the increasing complexity of his or her environment. Assimilation is the process of using or transforming perceptions of the environment so they can be categorized into preexisting cognitive structures. As an example, a very young child may easily identify an airplane as a "bird" because it flies through the air as they have seen other birds do. Accommodation is the process of changing cognitive structures in order to accept stimulus from the environment that does not fit into any preexisting structures. Following our earlier example, over time that same child will update his perceptions to accommodate for the fact that if it is large and metal and doesn't flap its wings, it is in fact an "airplane."

With increasing experience in the environment, the reflexes of assimilation and accommodation are quickly replaced with constructed, rather than innate, schemes. As schemes become increasingly more intricate, they are termed "structures." As a person's structures become more complex, they are organized in hierarchical manner from general to specific. Within this hierarchy, Piaget identified four stages of cognitive development from infancy to adulthood. The first is experience itself, that is, the repetition of observations and motor actions in the context of interacting with the environment. Knowledge is then developed as experiences accumulate. Finally, the ability to think actually results from the accumulation of knowledge. This process of observation, interaction, experience, knowledge, and thinking is a dynamic feedback system. It is a self-reinforcing process.

We believe this process is an evolutionary process that should be equally applicable to an infant and a culture at its infancy. Therefore, before attempting to understand how and why people in different cultures think differently from one another, it would be appropriate to examine the various environments that incubated their corresponding civilizations and investigate how people from different cultures interact with their own environments.

Thought Evolution

Before Darwin, many scholars debated the origins of the human species and beginnings of rational life. Their writings were mainly speculative because there were few agreed-upon facts and many suppositions. Darwin's writings, however, forever changed the nature of human self-reflection about our origins and our minds. His theory continues to be accepted as the most plausible account of the evolutionary origins of life. In a complex and inevitably controversial field such as prehistory, there is unlikely to be adequate archaeological scientific evidence to satisfy all perspectives. Yet, we believe there is already convincing documentation that supports the evolutionary hypothesis.

In recent years, the Canadian neuropsychologist Merlin Donald has undertaken the most impressive effort to understand the human mind within an evolutionary framework. In *Origins of the Modern Mind* (1991), he claimed the human line of descent during the past two million years has passed through three transitions. In the first, which separated hominids from the apes, early humans developed the ability to use their bodies in imitation of older and more sophisticated members of the same group. In the second, humans developed distinctive neuronal and anatomical systems that allowed them to use spoken language and compose and relate stories. In the third transition, which ultimately resulted in the modern human, humans invented symbolic and notational systems that would eventually be used to preserve memories and transmit complex forms of culture, including art and science. Many scholars consider Donald's account to be the most plausible outline of the origin of the thinking human mind.

Mithen's Phases

A more recent book by British archaeologist Steven Mithen, *The Prehistory of the Mind: The Cognitive Origins of Art, Religion, and Science*, represented another effort to support the evolutionary hypothesis, also from key archaeological perspectives. Mithen's work is a genuine attempt to integrate the separate intellectual traditions represented by evolutionary psychology, developmental psychology, brain study, and cognitive archaeology. In this effort, he amalgamated many specific discoveries of cognitive archaeology into a systematic account. Similar to Donald, Mithen maintained the human mind is a product of evolution rather than supernatural creation. In his study, he outlined the elements, timelines, and causative factors in the evolution of the human mind. In addressing the nature and workings of the human mind, Mithen rejected two common metaphors that have wide appeal, that is, the mind as a sponge that soaks up material and the mind as a general purpose computer-learning program. He argued the first image cannot account for how people solve problems or compare and contrast items of information. The second image cannot explain the way the mind thinks, creates, and imagines.

In Mithen's view, ontogeny, the development of an individual organism, recapitulates phylogeny, the development of a species, in three distinct phases. The first phase, occurring in both infants and early hominids, involves the development of a general intelligence that can roughly process information, make connections, and solve problems. The second phase, characterizing young children and hominids of the middle period, involves development of some particular functional structure or module. Each harbors specialized intelligences. Mithen identified at least four modules within the second phase:

- Technology (the development of tools)

- Natural history (sensitivity to plants, animals and the environment)

- Language

- Social understanding

During the historical version of the second phase, the era of our hominid ancestors, the various specialized functions were relatively independent of one another. An individual may have had strong technological and social understanding, for example, but he had no way of integrating those two faculties to work together. Mithen extensively described the emergence and ultimate interaction of the separate faculties during the different phases of human evolution. According to his account, social intelligence emerges first. Natural history intelligence, an ability to assess and take advantage of the natural environment, is second. A tool-using intelligence then follows.

In the third phase, Mithen found the beginning of the capacity to use language, but this is almost exclusively tied to social interchanges. Preverbal hominids spent up to one-third of their time grooming each other as a means of creating and solidifying social bonds. Because language was a much more effective way of sustaining these bonds and took only a fraction of the time to communicate content, it represented a great adaptive advantage. Some important links were made one hundred thousand years ago between the social and natural history capacities and thirty thousand years ago between the technical and naturalistic capacities. It was then that the use of tools began to transform nature, for example, cutting trees and using animal skins. The dramatic climax of this phase features an explosion of the linguistic faculty. Ultimately, it is the capacity to connect the various intelligences, faculties, and modules that characterizes the fully evolved individual—be it *Homo sapiens sapiens* thirty thousand years ago or the mature adult of today. What allows human beings to become truly human is their capacity to bring together the operation of different faculties to solve problems, create products, and make original contributions in art, science, religion, and even cognitive archaeology. The important question addressed by Mithen is, "How do specific modules come to work together to form the creative aspects of human intellect?"

Empirical evidence provided by Mithen shows that the mind, whether human or prehuman, is distinguished precisely by the fact that it does not treat all experiences or problems as equal and does not maintain all-purpose rules or operations. Whether one deals with bees, ants, birds, or human beings, the story is the same. While certain kinds of information are readily apprehended and easily processed and memorized, others are difficult to master. For various reasons, humans from different historical or environmental settings have established different sets of connections of intelligences, faculties, or modules through prehistory and history. This contributed to the formation of different cultural preferences, traditions, or sensibilities.

The implications and consequences of such differences are clearly enormous. They are arguably responsible for the subsequent divergence of Chinese and Western philosophies, political ideals, and interactions with people and nature. First, however, we will examine the origins of these differences in thinking, which can be found in the landscapes that incubated the two cultures.

CHAPTER THREE

Thought and Philosophical Development

The previous chapter presented some of the current theories on the evolution of thinking in both prehumans and humans from three perspectives: psychological, philosophical, and archaeological. We surveyed the key environmental distinctions between the Chinese and Western cultures, including the influence of the Ice Age. As we will assert in this chapter, the abundance and variety of species of plants and animals in China was perhaps one of the most significant factors impacting the development of thinking in our hunter-gatherer ancestors.

In the times of our hunter-gatherer ancestors, survival was predicated on appropriate responses to local environmental conditions. Thus, differing environments led to differing adaptive thought processes. This chapter will demonstrate how thought development diverged early in Western and Chinese culture.

Section One: Development of Western Thought

This section explores Western philosophy and thinking to examine how different emphases and sensibilities ultimately developed in the course of time from prehistory to history.

Causal, Rational, and Analytical Roots

Evidence indicates that early European hunter-gatherers were big game hunters. As such, they needed to be well-informed about the animals they hunted.

Knowledge and intelligence were prerequisites for the survival of such life-threatening ventures. According to Piaget and others, knowledge and intelligence are usually acquired and developed through numerous repetitive observations and the accumulation of experience. In the case of our hunter-gatherer ancestors, the many unanticipated challenges and sporadic catastrophic events of the Ice Age precipitated growth in their brain capacity, resulting in more than a threefold increase in volume during the last three million years.

The early Europeans became preoccupied with hunting animals much larger than themselves. To do this, they needed more than just knowledge and intelligence. As Mithen postulated, humans needed to use social skills to perform effectively as a group and share the fruits of their labor. This was especially true for large game that was hard for one person to handle and required planned tactics and strategies. This led to a focus on tactical and strategic development and, hence, rational and analytical thinking. The vivid details and realistic appearance of large animals depicted in cave paintings and clay sculptures clearly demonstrate such qualities. These depictions are the precursors to Greek fascination with line, shape, form, expression, and attitude, as seen in geometry and early Greek sculpture.

Just as early European cave art and sculpture took forms dictated by the hunter-gathers' responses to their environment, later European art also displays characteristics founded on the thinking patterns that developed during the Ice Age. Greek art is intellectual art, the art of men who were clear and lucid thinkers. It is therefore rather plain and simple. It is axiomatic that Greek art is the dictum of men who would brush aside all obscurity, entanglement, and superfluity and see clearly, plainly, and unadorned that which they wished to express. Classical sculpture focused mostly on the human figure. Depicted in moments of supreme poise or captured in athletic acts, the human body was apotheosized in stone. Artists sought to express the body as a perfect organic unity, an unassailable, archetypal form, with its shape and figure clearly embodying Platonic ideals. Gods and goddesses were imagined in human form, but they were ideal in proportion without imperfection. The unclothed human figure in its most perfect manifestation was admired for its harmonious beauty. The Greek's early commitment to rational, logical, and analytical thinking and perfection as depicted in Greek art is astonishing. Classical Greek scholars' obsession with ontology and the development of causal thinking follows from this tradition.

Dualism, Universality, and Objectivity

All thinking is initiated through human interaction with the environment via sensory stimuli and accumulated experience. Hence, all early humans should have had a similar starting point to their thinking. But the Greeks, with their insistence upon seeking truth through explicit knowledge, ultimately adopted idealistic dualism as a major life philosophy and religion that endured for many years in the Western world. It is widely accepted that the patterns set by the Greeks and Romans permeate Western civilization. In fact, modern English derives well over half of its vocabulary from Latin and Greek. Philosophy, politics, religion, science, art, music, and athletics are all words whose etymology can be traced to the Romans and Greeks. The ideas expressed by these seven words are highly significant because they represent the essence of the Western heritage to which we are indebted.

The Greek notion of thinking began in the sixth century BC. The central question to the early Greeks was how to reconcile the permanence (one, unity, being) required for a unifying explanation of the universe with the appearance of constant change (many, plurality, becoming). Presocratics, which means they came from the era before Socrates, were the first philosophers wrestling with this conundrum and were from either the eastern or western regions of the Greek world. Athens, home for classical Greeks such as Socrates, Plato, and Aristotle, is in the central Greek region and was actually late in joining the philosophy game.

The Presocratics' most distinguishing feature was an emphasis on questions of physics. Aristotle referred to them as "investigators of nature." Their scientific interests included mathematics, astronomy, and biology. They stressed the rational unity of things and rejected any knowledge they considered less than scientific and inexplicit, particularly mythological explanations of the world.

The first group of Presocratic philosophers sought the material principle of things and the mode of their origin and disappearance. The reputed father of Greek philosophy, Thales of Miletus (circa 640 BC), explored the energy of the universe. His perspective on this subject is termed "hylozoism," a view whereby everything in the universe is animate to some degree. He declared water to be the "arche," the life-sustaining property of all things. Next came Anaximander of Miletus (611–547 BC), the first philosophical writer who conceptualized the ultimate principle or original source of life to be an undefined, infinite substance called "apeiron," which was itself without qualities. The primary opposites of hot and cold, moist and dry, differentiated from the apeiron.

With the advent of the Eleatic group of philosophers that followed, Greek philosophy took a dramatic change in outlook and method. The Eleatics explicated problems by a process of pure deductive reasoning that threatened to dismiss the progress made by empirical investigation into nature as illusory. They hypothesized that the world as it appears cannot be real because it is riddled with intrinsic contradictions. The Eleatics drew their conclusions by favoring reasoned logical argument over sensory evidence. By dwelling purely on the concept of existence, reasoned deductions suggest the world as it appears cannot truly exist because such existence is predicated upon factors that contradict deductions arising from examination of the concept of existence. Where reason and experience contradict each other, the Eleatics maintain that reason must oust experience. Notions such as this, characterizing Eleatic philosophy, have persisted through the subsequent history of Western philosophy. The debate continues whether pure reason or the senses reveal most accurately the true nature of reality.

The Eleatics' doctrine of the one, or unity, for example, forwarded by Xenophanes of Colophon (born approximately 570 BC), denied that sensory experience provides access to truth because the world of the senses with its multitudinous nature and constant change cannot be relied on. Reason, however, can furnish knowledge of the nature of the one, or, more accurately, knowledge of what is not the nature of the one. Parmenides, a pupil of Xenophanes influenced by Pythagoras, further argued that "it is" and "it is not" cannot be simultaneously true. He constructed the following syllogism. What cannot be thought cannot exist. What is not cannot enter our thoughts. Therefore, the existence of nonexistence is impossible because it is self-contradictory. By extension, that which exists, despite any contradictory sensory stimulus, must always have existed as a continuous, unchanging, timeless, indivisible unity. Change and becoming as well as diversity and plurality all require the acceptance of "it is not," that is, the existence of nothingness or nonexistence, which is contradictory and, hence, impossible.

One cannot overestimate the influence of Parmenides. Plato's respect for his predecessor ensured that Parmenides' ideas would impact the course of Western philosophy. For example, Greek mathematics has no numeric zero. The denial of a void is still seen centuries later in the ideas of René Descartes (1596–1650). From Parmenides also grew the Platonic metaphysical and epistemological doctrine, which holds that phenomena that can be known must necessarily be real. What is real, eternal, and unchanging cannot be a manifestation of the unstable world perceived through experience. Therefore, there must be objects of knowledge to match the immutable status of knowledge proper. This conclusion fostered skepticism of empirical knowledge, so knowledge was subsequently taken to apply properly only to mathematics, geometry, and deductive reasoning. Parmenides also assumed reality to be a finite sphere because of the necessity for perfection and completeness.

Further support for Parmenides came from Zeno. The famous Zeno's paradoxes applied deductive arguments to a world of apparent plurality (divisibility) and change and motion, resulting in absurd conclusions. He implied the only acceptable alternative must therefore be that reality is actually a changeless Parmenidean unity. The apparent, or experienced, world cannot be real because analysis of the consequences of its features, if taken to be real, leads to paradox, contradiction, and absurdity. An account of Zeno's paradoxes is presented in Shand (2002).

Leucippus (fifth century BC) and his pupil Democritus of Abdera (born circa 460 BC) formed the first explicitly materialistic, rather than phenomenological, system. Theirs was the doctrine of atoms, that is, the nonreducible, indivisible, imperishable small primary element. Infinite in number, moving eternally through an infinite void, atoms collide and unite, thus generating objects that differ in accordance with the number, size, shape, and arrangement of the atoms that compose them.

The school of pluralists, notably Empedocles and Anaxagoras, followed. They accepted the Eleatic argument for the absolute conservation of being in reality. Nevertheless, they acknowledged the possibility of motion and change. The limitless cosmos, as they conceptualized it, was not a unity. Rather, it was a variously mixed plurality of imperishable elements.

The period of Greek philosophy that followed the Presocratics begins around 400 BC. The most important figures are Socrates (477–399 BC), Plato (427–347 BC), and Aristotle (384–322 BC).

More than anyone else in his time, Socrates was responsible for steering philosophical debate away from a material universe, of which humankind was but a part, toward a conception that placed the human race in direct contact with a metaphysical world of divine and eternal values.

Plato, the most famous of Socrates's pupils, had a resounding impact on philosophical trends in the fourth century BC, and he exercised an influence that endures in the modern age. For Plato, the workings of the world, the revolutions of the planets, the succession of night and day, and the endless cycle of the seasons were significant simply because they demonstrated an order and regularity that supported his belief in a moral and rational soul as controller of the universe. Plato turned Socrates's search for definitions of universal, immutable, ethical standards, aimed at understanding the nature of our world, into his theory of forms, in which classifying terms required a reference point anchored to a transcendent object or forms. Not only did knowledge of ethical truths require such forms, all claims to knowledge did so. Plato contended that two main conditions must be met in the highest sort of knowledge: universality (objectivity) and eternality (unchangingness or immutability). In other words, knowledge is not relative to point of view. True knowledge should be true from any perspective. Further, knowledge is unchanging over time. Knowledge, in its highest sense, is infallible and absolutely certain.

Aristotle, another of Plato's pupils, proffered no account of the origin of the world or the creation of the human race. Aristotle believed our world and all species inhabiting it to be eternal and uncreated. Although he rejected Plato's theory of real, separately existing forms, Aristotle retained the notion of forms in his concept of the unchanging reality that provides the basis for knowledge proper of what things are. He posited "substance" as that which has identity and stability through change. Aristotle shared with Plato the notion that if knowledge is possible, knowledge must address only that which is real. What is real is, by nature, eternal and unchanging. Aristotle suggested the world has two aspects: its sensible aspect and its intelligible aspect (the form). Only through the intelligible aspect can we know necessary truths about the sensible world.

The ancient Greeks' quest for truth and knowledge is admirable. In order to obtain true knowledge, they resolved to think causally, rationally, analytically, logically, atomically, and explicitly while simultaneously dismissing knowledge based on sensory experience as illusionary, lacking in permanence, and less than true. Humankind is indebted to these Greeks for their logic, mathematics, science, philosophy, arts, and politics. Yet the early Greeks' rejection of empirical and sensory experience and dismissal of noncausal and less than rational, analytical, logical, and explicit ways of thinking has resulted in enduring dire consequences in the Western world. It was only after the Renaissance and the Enlightenment that more inclusive perspectives on thought were recovered. Even then, dualistic thinking still impacts us all. This contrasts starkly with the perspectives of the Chinese people, whose experiences form the topic of the third section in this chapter.

Section Two:
Nature and Science

It is generally true that Chinese thinkers are more inclined toward perceiving humanity as an integral part of nature while Western thinkers are more inclined to an attitude that seeks to overcome or conquer nature. It is not until the dawn of modern science that people, both Chinese and Western, really begin to understand the operation of nature.

Western conceptions of nature led to science as a mechanism to answer abstract questions about the material world itself. The traditional Chinese relationship with nature centered on applied answers—pragmatic solutions to daily problems—not abstractions or general knowledge. This disparity has strong implications on the subsequent development of these two cultures.

One of the most significant outcomes of the Westerners' persistence on seeking truth and true knowledge and insistence on causal, rational, analytical, logical, and explicit thinking is the subsequent development of science. Science began with our observations of nature. Formalized science developed in the West as a methodology for knowledge acquisition about the physical world and its phenomena. It entailed unbiased observation and/or systematic experimentation. In attempting to make sense of our perceptions of the physical world, we are faced with deciphering and explaining the inner workings of nature so we may predict outcomes. Such prediction is essential because humans rely heavily on nature for sustenance. The accuracy of predictions can mean the difference between life and death.

The obvious question of science is, "What are the natural laws that are independent of our subjective thinking?" The existence of regularities in nature is an objective fact. Thus, we do not impose laws onto nature. Rather, we seek to discover and accept them. What we have termed the "laws of nature" are our attempts to systematically capture the regularities of the world. The essence of science lies in the belief that natural laws exist and the outcome of physical experiments or events is predictable only if we can master understanding of these laws.

Development of Classical Physics

In physics, for instance, the predictability of an astronomical event such as a lunar eclipse is assured if we know the laws that determine the trajectories of the sun, the earth, and the moon. This knowledge depends on knowledge of the mass of all three objects, their relative initial positions, and all of the external forces exerted on each one of them. This is simply one example of the scientific methodology equally applicable to all scientific disciplines. In this book, however, we shall concentrate on physics because of our professional familiarity with the subject.

The explicit laws of nature, as we know them today, emerged slowly in the scientific field. It was not a term in popular use among the Greeks, appearing first in its modern guise in the optical studies of Roger Bacon (1210–1292), wherein the author referred to laws of reflection and refraction and objects and processes "not following the laws of nature." Astronomers, the observers and interpreters of the perpetual laws of celestial motion in the sky, popularized the expression. Tycho Brahe (1546–1601) claimed "the wondrous and perpetual laws of the celestial motions, so diverse and yet so harmonious, prove the existence of God." (Barrow, 1990) Descartes and Johannes Kepler (1571–1630) also associated the regularity of nature with the biblical notion of a lawgiver. Kepler, however, was one of the first scientists to exploit a faith in the underlying simplicity and harmony of nature as a guide in his thinking about the laws of nature. He was also first responsible for expressing laws of nature as mathematical equations. This approach was so successful that the ultimate development of modern science relies heavily on mathematical formulation and representation, allowing science to communicate findings precisely. Kepler's first law of planetary motion, which states that planets move in elliptical orbits, was formulated upon observational data. It transpires that elliptical orbits are true only in the first approximation. Galileo Galilei (1564–1642) was not content to deduce laws of nature from observation. He set about manipulating nature by designing experiments that induced the revelation of the laws of nature. For example, in order to capture nuances of the fall of bodies under gravity, he rolled spheres down inclined planes. Thus, he gradually built up a successful mathematical description of motions. His was the first science that was modern in character.

Sir Isaac Newton (1642–1727) almost single-handedly revolutionized science. He recognized the essential common factors behind superficially different phenomena and was able to isolate a collection of profound laws of nature in mathematical form that survives even today as an excellent approximation of the behavior of bodies moving at speeds much less than that of light. His three laws of motion were so successful that it was widely believed he had found the ultimate laws of the Creator. The most interesting of his three laws is the first, which states, "Every body continues in its state of rest or uniform motion in a straight line unless it is compelled to change that state by forces impressed upon it." This was the first doctrine to discard the ancient idea that motion was some type of process and recognize that the states of rest and steady motion were similar, given the absence of an external force or acceleration. This law is predicated upon a highly idealized condition. It is the result of a mental abstraction, capturing the essential elements of reality because nothing in the universe is actually free from the force of gravitation. As Newtonian physics developed, various idealized situations, or models, appeared. Models include the notion of frictionless surfaces, ideal gases, inelastic collisions, perfect conductors of electricity, perfect laminar flow of fluid, and so forth. None of these entities exist in the real world, yet, from these idealized entities, one can construct models or laws that simulate various degrees of approximation to reality and which one can test through experimentation. This approach maintains the separation of physics and philosophy that Descartes created and simultaneously allows validation of theory against experimental observations. This is the very essence of modern science.

For us, the essential difference between science and religion is simply that science is a methodology utilized to understand and interpret our world. Starting with an observation or experimentation, we construct a hypothesis concerning the interrelationship or internal working relationship of the involved processes. Then we predict an outcome. The formation of a meaningful hypothesis or a new law is not a passive reaction to observed regularities. Rather, it is a creative process of imagination, often involving deep insight into the real properties of nature. The testing of the hypothesis or new law under different contexts invites further observation and experimentation, often leading to the discovery of new, unexpected phenomena. The application of logics, such as deduction, induction, or theory of probability, can retest the rationality and applicability of the hypothesized theory. This retesting demonstrates the existence of actual regularities in nature and ensures we are not imposing on them with our scientific structures. Thus, when the results of new observation or experimentation deviate significantly from the predicted outcome and begin to contradict our hypotheses or laws, we propose new hypotheses or laws to fit the new data and again subject our prediction to testing.

Every hypothesis or law functions within a domain of applicability. We must understand this domain in order to operate within it. For example, Newtonian physics is applicable only within the classical domain. Particles are larger than atomic dimensions, but they are smaller than large celestial bodies when gravitational force begins to dominate and move with a velocity much less than that of light. It was not until we broke through Newtonian physics' domain of applicability by investigating subatomic particles or looking into celestial events such as supernovae that we discovered its limitations. Yet this process led to the discovery of new fields, quantum physics in the former case and the theory of relativity in the latter. Both, in turn, have their own domains of applicability. Quantum physics does not replace Newtonian physics as the truth because both theories work best within their own domain of applicability and remain merely good approximations of reality within their respective domains. As Karl Popper (1902–1994) pointed out, in science, we cannot prove that a theory is true, but we can certainly show that a prediction is false. A scientific test consists of a persevering search for negative, falsifying instances. If a hypothesis survives continuing and serious attempts to falsify it, then it can be provisionally accepted, although it can never be established conclusively. Science progresses through critical testing of theories and adjustment or enlargement of the domain of applicability through falsification.

The belief that the underlying order of the universe can be expressed in mathematical form lies at the heart of modern science. The laws of nature are mathematical primarily because we define a relationship to be fundamental if it can be expressed mathematically. Modern physics, such as particle physics or quantum gravity, relies heavily on mathematical concepts for its formulation and development. Newtonian physics is a mathematical physics wherein the laws of nature are conceived in unambiguous mathematical language. When the necessary mathematics did not exist at the time, Newton developed it himself. This was the case with calculus, by which continuous changes could be mathematically described. With knowledge of initial conditions, differential equations could be formulated to predict the future or reconstruct the past. Since its development, continuous mathematics has been—and always will be—an indispensable tool for scientists in every discipline.

Newton's law of gravitation provides a relatively simple example of the significant achievement in thinking about the laws of nature in mathematical form. It states:

> [G]iven two bodies with masses M and m whose centers are separated in space by a distance r, then the attractive force of gravity between them, F, is proportional to the product of their masses and inversely proportional to the square of the separation, r, of their centers in space, and acts along the line joining those centers.

In the eighteenth century, Laplace expressed this equation in the formula of $F = GMm/r^2$, where G is known as Newton's gravitational constant. By his unification of the effects of gravity, Newton was responsible for identifying G as the first "constant of nature" in the law of nature. Constants of nature are fascinating and significant quantities in modern physics. In the case of G, we have a universal constant stating that all bodies, independent of size, physical properties, or physical conditions, are subject to the same gravitational force once m, M, and r are specified. Because they are universal, the laws of nature are equally applicable to both celestial and subatomic bodies. The application of Newton's law of gravitation was mainly responsible for humankind's success in the exploration of outer space in the late twentieth century through orbiting satellites, journeys to the Moon, and the exploration of other planets.

Along with Newtonian mechanics, including gravitation, electricity, magnetism, and electromagnetic theory formed the backbone of classical physics in the twentieth century. Michael Faraday (1791–1877), along with André-Marie Ampère, Hans Christian Oersted, Jean-Baptiste Biot, and others, revealed that a moving magnetic pole could accelerate an electric charge, creating a current flow. A moving electric charge could create a magnetic field. The field picture of magnetic and electric forces established a revealing delineation of the equivalence between the phenomena of electricity and magnetism. In 1865, James Maxwell further produced a system of four equations that elegantly described all the intertwined phenomena of electricity and magnetism as well as the propagation of the waves of the electromagnetic force field. The electromagnetic wave was found to propagate through space at 300,000 kilometers per second (186,000 miles per second), the speed of light. Different wavelengths in the visible light spectrum represent the different colors that we see, from the shorter wavelength (high frequency) of violet to the longer wavelength (low frequency) of red. Waves outside the light spectrum are not visible, but they are nevertheless very important to modern life. The even-longer wavelengths we cannot visibly perceive are electromagnetic waves. In increasing order of wavelength, they are radio and TV waves, microwaves, and the infrared, or heat, waves. At the other end of the spectrum, the electromagnetic waves with short, invisible wavelengths are known as ultraviolet, X-rays, and gamma rays.

This brief description of the development of classical physics demonstrates the use of science in a quest to discover the laws of nature. This scientific revolution occurred mainly in the West over the last three centuries. Given these Western roots, it is interesting to wonder whether the ancient Chinese shared the concept of laws of nature.

According to Joseph Needham, the concept of laws of nature was actually alien to traditional Chinese philosophical thinking. The majority of science historians appear to agree with Needham on this point. Consequently, there was no scientist like Newton in China, an unsurprising fact because Chinese thought is neither analytically nor theoretically inclined. Rather, it is very pragmatic. Bodde (1991), however, presented a contrasting minority viewpoint by quoting nine passages from ancient Chinese thinkers such as Mozi, Tung Chungshu, and Ko Hung, which illustrate that embryonic laws of nature did actually exist in China. Nevertheless, despite these few exceptions, the ancient Chinese seemed more concerned with technology and practical human issues, occasionally indulging in philosophizing about nature, not theorization or abstraction. Chinese thought preferences are simply not inclined to the theoretical, abstract, rational, or explicit. As a result, China did not produce a modern science despite advancements in technology and conceptualizations of nature.

Human conceptualizations of nature underpin our worldviews and, consequently, order our thinking. Thus, while our distant ancestors' unique experiences of the Ice Age in the West and China stimulated divergent adaptive responses and thinking patterns, so, too, have their views of nature, which grew from those patterns, continued to influence the way we think.

The following three sections will examine selected human understandings of nature that are both significant and significantly different in the West and East.

The Development of Modern Physics

Classical physics further developed into modern physics in the twentieth century by focusing on the subatomic world as well as the macroscopic world of astronomy with galaxies and supernovae, both existing outside the more familiar world of our human experiences. Ironically, modern physics has philosophically developed, without intention, in a direction similar to the metaphysical approach that characterizes the Chinese perceptions of nature detailed later.

The development of the theories of relativity and quantum mechanics in the early twentieth century laid the foundation for a deeper understanding of the microscopic world of subatomic elementary particles as well as the macroscopic world of the universe. These two theories have drastically altered our understanding of nature and nature's laws, which, in turn, have had a profound influence on virtually all aspects of human life. Science and technology have fundamentally changed the conditions of our earth and all life on it, in both beneficial and detrimental ways. In particular, in the information age, the results of atomic and quantum physics have impacted us in such a far-reaching fashion that we can no longer imagine life without the changes that are their legacy. However, the influence of modern physics goes beyond technology, leading us to reexamine many of our traditional conceptions of the universe and our relationship to it. More interesting still, we have found that the new perspectives offered by the philosophy of modern physics actually narrow the gap between the traditional philosophies of China and the West.

The Theory of Relativity

The special theory of relativity, which Albert Einstein published in 1905, has forever changed our views on space-time. By stating that "the laws of physics are the same for all observers moving with uniform relative velocity and the speed of light in vacuum will be found the same by any two observers in uniform relative motion," the twenty-six-year-old Einstein proclaimed that all space and time measurements were relative. His revolutionary claim countered our common experience and intuition and contradicted the notions of absolute space and time assumed by Newtonian physics. For example, because the length of an object depends on its motion relative to the observer and the object changes with the velocity of that motion, it no longer makes common sense to propose the real length of any physical measurement. Similarly, because clocks in motion run slower and time changes from one observer to another, there is no longer an absolute time. How can we fix a time for a meeting in space? Further, in relativistic physics, space and time are treated on an equal footing and are connected inseparably. We can never talk about space without talking about time and vice versa. This new conception of space-time is completely contrary to our common intuition.

Einstein went on to show that space-time and other physical properties as well are unexpectedly interwoven. His most famous equation, $E = mc^2$, provides one of the most important examples. With this equation, Einstein asserted that the energy (E) of an object and its mass (m) are not independent concepts. Instead, they are connected by the velocity of light (c), a universal constant. Because energy manifests itself in many different forms, for example, potential, kinetic, heat, gravitational, chemical, and so forth, the equivalence of mass and energy consequently blurs the distinctions between substance and process. Substance can actually be created from energy and vice versa. This view is strikingly similar to the Chinese notion of space-time, substance, process, and its interrelationship with the universe, as described in the next two sections. Barrow (1990) studied Einstein's theory and its experimental confirmation and distilled a number of revolutionary lessons about the laws of nature:

- Only relative motions are involved in the laws of nature.

- There does not exist either an absolute space or absolute time. They are different concepts for each observer in relative motion.

- There is a maximum speed for the transmission of information.

- Mass and energy are equivalent.

- The presence of mass and energy in space and time determines the geometry of space and rate of passage of time.

- There is no action at a distance involved in gravitation.

These changes in our understanding of nature's laws are not so revolutionary that they completely overthrow Newton's precepts. Rather, they describe what happens over a far wider range of conditions than do Newton's laws. As discussed previously, they represent a new domain of applicability. However, the picture presented here is incomplete because the existence of a cosmic speed limit for the transmission of any signal was incompatible with Newton's law of gravitation.

In 1915, Einstein reconciled this incompatibility with his publication of the general theory of relativity, in which he included the effect of gravity by proposing that the presence of mass or other forms of energy in space is equivalent to an accelerated motion, which could also be considered a distortion in the geometry of space-time. Gravity, according to Einstein, is the warping of space and time. In a curved space-time, the distortions caused by the curvature will impact the spatial relationships described by geometry and the intervals of time. Therefore, time does not flow at the same rate as it would in flat space-time. Because the curvature varies from place to place, according to the distribution of massive bodies, so does the flow of time. The more massive the bodies, the greater the distortion caused in the surrounding space and the greater gravitational influence exerted on other bodies. Conversely, as one moves farther from a massive body, the amount of spatial warping decreases, and the influence of gravity also decreases correspondingly.

Einstein had not merely presented a simple concept to explain gravity. His greatest achievement was uncovering the extraordinarily elegant set of mathematical equations that tells us how to determine the symbiotic relationship between matter and space-time geometry. These field equations harmonize with Riemann geometry and are mathematically sophisticated. Despite the seemingly speculative nature of Einstein's theories, in every instance in which these unusual predictions of curved space-time have so far been tested by observation, they have been verified correct to a high rate of precision. These theories of relativity are behind advancements in cosmology and astronomy over the past decades and have led to our recent identification and understanding of mega-cosmic phenomena, including black holes, neutron stars, quasars, supernovas, galaxies, and so forth. This increased understanding helps humankind to better study our cosmic history, which presently points to a very dynamic, expanding universe.

Quantum Theory

Atomic and nuclear physics has also dramatically influenced our understanding of nature. From the middle of the nineteenth century onward, advancements in chemistry and molecular and atomic physics led to the belief that matter is composed of molecules, which, in turn, consist of atoms. We learned that the molecule was the smallest amount of a chemical compound that could exist and the atoms were the fundamental building blocks of molecules and, thus, of all matter. The question then became, "Is the atom further divisible?"

In 1910, physicist Ernest Rutherford scrutinized an atom by bombarding it with heavier alpha particles and found that the bulk of the atom's mass was concentrated in a tiny nucleus of positive electric charge with electrons of negative charge distributed around it at varying distances. The nucleus was later found to be constituted of subatomic massive particles called protons and neutrons. Each of the protons carries a charge equal and opposite to that of an electron, but with a mass about 1,836 times greater. Neutrons have a mass similar to that of a proton, but they do not possess any electrical charge. The picture of an atom began to emerge. Atoms are composed of massive nuclei no more than 10^{-13} centimeters in diameter that is surrounded by a collection of orbiting electrons extending 10^{-8} centimeters from the central nucleus. The number of protons, neutrons, and electrons and their detailed arrangement within the atom defines the chemical properties of an element. Every element found in the world could be arranged orderly in what is now known as the periodic table. When merged with Bohr's principle of energy quantization, this portrait of the atom produced a model of extraordinary precision with the ability to predict the detailed properties of all types of atoms as well as forecast the discovery of atoms and elements unknown at the time. As a result of these discoveries, the disciplines of chemistry and physics were then simple to delineate. Chemists were interested in the arrangement and energy levels of the electrons in atoms, which determined how atoms could link together into molecules and compounds. Physicists focused their attention upon the structure of the nucleus and the properties of its constituent particles.

Quantum theory was invented to explain why atoms are stable and do not instantly fall apart, as would be predicted by the classical physics of gravitation, electricity, and magnetism. Quantum theory revealed that the deepest laws of the microscopic world govern strange and unobserved aspects of nature. Subsequently, two basic forces of nature were identified within the nucleus: the strong, or nuclear, force, which is responsible for binding together atomic nuclei; and the weak force, which creates some types of radioactivity. Whereas the forces of gravity and electromagnetism are not restricted in the distance over which their influence remains significant, the strong nuclear force has a range roughly equal to the size of the smallest atomic nucleus, about 10^{-13} of a centimeter. The range of the weak force is one hundred times shorter still.

By the middle of the twentieth century, further investigations into the composition of the atomic nucleus had revealed many more of these so-called elementary particles. As a result of decades of active research using quantum field theory, group theory, high-energy physics experiments using accelerators, and observations from cosmic events, such as those seen in cosmic rays, we now know that protons and neutrons in the nucleus are further composed of particles such as the neutrino, muon, tau, and quark. Discussions of these particles very quickly become complex. Our objective here is simply to note their existence. Interested readers should consult the well-written and popular book, *The Elegant Universe*, by Brian Greene, in which the author summarizes these elementary particles and their respective properties as falling into three families tabulated into three tables.

In these three tables, each family contains two quarks, an electron or one of its cousins, and one of the neutrino species. The corresponding particle types across the three families have identical properties except for their mass, which grows larger in each successive family. Greene points out that physicists have now probed the structure of matter to scales of about a billionth of a billionth of a meter, and they have shown that everything encountered to date, whether it occurs naturally or is produced artificially with giant atom smashers, consists of some combination of particles from these three families and their antimatter partners. We must point out, however, that these elementary particles are not in fact particles or building blocks in the ordinary sense of Democritus and Newton. In the words of renowned quantum physicist Niels Bohr, "Isolated material particles are abstractions, their properties being definable and observable only through their interaction with other systems."

In opposition again to our intuition, quantum theory reveals an essential interconnectedness of the universe. Additionally, at the subatomic scale, these so-called particles are the result of mathematical abstractions and are actually processes and not substances, as we previously understood them. For example, an electron neutrino has little mass, no electric charge or other forces, and only a weak charge and a spin of $\frac{1}{2}$, which is a process, as opposed to a substance. This demonstrates that we cannot deconstruct the world into independently existing smallest units, as we once hypothesized we could.

A similar, unusual phenomenon concerns the nature of light. Ever since the discovery of its electromagnetic wave character, physicists have debated this subject for a long time. It was soon learned that, depending upon the observer's perspective, light sometimes appears as particles, called a quantum of photons, and sometimes as waves. It is difficult for our common sense to accept that something can be simultaneously both a particle, an entity confined to a very small volume, and a wave, which is spread out over a large region of space. But it was this very property of the dual nature of light that finally led to the formulation of quantum theory. It almost seems that nothing deduced from quantum theory makes common sense.

The capability to observe a particle is also an issue in practice because one cannot observe a particle, such as an electron, without disturbing the system by means of a measurement because the measurement itself is a form of interference at the subatomic level. As a result, no objective measurement of an event can be made independent of an observer because the observer participates in the measurement process. This principle is based on the quantum field. As mentioned previously, gravitational, electromagnetic, weak, and strong forces are the four basic forces of nature at the microscopic scale. Together, they form the quantum field.

Quantum fields manifest a probabilistic element introduced by our measurement of them, as expressed by the renowned Heisenberg's uncertainty principle that states that two quantities of particles, such as position and momentum or energy and the time of an atomic event, can never be measured simultaneously with precision. Thus, quantum field theories are mathematical descriptions of the average properties of force fields over finite regions of space during finite intervals of time. They predict how those fields will change and how they will interact with one another. Quantum theory has come to recognize probability as a fundamental feature of the atomic and subatomic reality governing all processes and even the existence of matter itself. We can make this argument because subatomic particles do not exist with certainty at definite places. Rather, they have a certain finite chance to exist, and atomic events do not occur with certainty at definite times and in definite ways. Instead, they show tendencies to occur. For example, we can only determine a probability pattern that represents the electron's chance to be in various regions of the atom. We do so through the so-called state function or wave function, a mathematical quantity related to the probabilities of locating the electron in various places and times. Still, these are not probabilities of things. Rather, they are probabilities of interconnections. According to quantum theory, these wave packets are always in a state of motion, the speed of which depends on their temperature and the thermal vibrations of their environment. In vibrating atoms, electrons are bound to the atomic nuclei by electric forces that try to keep them as close as possible. The electrons respond to this confinement by whirling around at speeds approaching the velocity of light. This subatomic reality has again challenged our notions of substance and matter.

In modern physics, the universe is experienced as a dynamic, inseparable whole, which inescapably includes the observer in an essential way. In this experience, the traditional concepts of space-time, isolated objects, and cause and effect lose their meaning. The notion of a space-time continuum becomes more congruous. Thus, the subsequent development of physics actually narrows the philosophical gap between the East and West.

The Dao of Physics: The Convergence

Recognizing the unwitting convergence of Western science and Eastern thinking, Fritjof Capra authored a popular book exploring the parallels between the philosophy of modern physics and Eastern mysticism, *The Tao [or Dao] of Physics*. This book has generated some controversy, but, nevertheless, it makes a very interesting read because of Capra's familiarity with what he calls Eastern mysticism (Buddhism, Hinduism, Daoism, and Zen) and his training as a theoretical physicist working in high-energy physics. He found amazingly strong parallels:

[T]he principal theories and models of modern physics lead to a view
of the world which is internally consistent and in perfect harmony with
the views of Eastern mysticism. For those who have experienced this
harmony, the significance of the parallels between the worldviews of
physicists and mystics is beyond any doubt.

The interesting question is not whether these parallels exist. It is why.
Furthermore, what does their existence imply? Capra argued that physicists derive
their knowledge from experiments and mystics derive their information from
meditative insights. Both are observations. In both fields, these observations are
acknowledged as the only source of knowledge. The object of observation is, of
course, very different in the two cases. The mystic looks within and explores his
or her consciousness at its various levels, which includes the body as the physical
manifestation of the mind. The experience of one's body is actually emphasized
in many Eastern traditions and is often seen as the key to the mystical experience
of the world. When we are healthy, we do not feel any separate parts in our body,
but we are aware of it as an integrated whole. This awareness generates a feeling of
well-being and happiness. In a similar way, the mystic is aware of the wholeness
of the entire cosmos that is experienced as an extension of the body. In contrast
to the mystics, the physicist begins his inquiry into the essential nature of things
by studying the material world. By penetrating into ever-deeper realms of matter,
physicists become aware of the essential unity of all things and events. More than
that, he has also learnt that he himself and his consciousness are an integral part
of this unity. Thus, the mystic and the physicist arrive at the same conclusion, one
starting from the inner realm and the other from the outer world.

Once these parallels between Western science and Eastern mysticism are
accepted, a number of questions arise concerning their implications. With all its
sophisticated machinery, is modern science merely rediscovering ancient wisdom
that the Eastern sages have known for thousands of years? Should physicists abandon the scientific method and begin to meditate? Or can there be a mutual influence between science and mysticism? Perhaps even a synthesis? Capra thought all
these questions have to be answered in the negative. He saw science and mysticism as two complementary manifestations of the human mind of its rational
and intuitive faculties. The modern physicist experiences the world through an
extreme specialization of the rational mind. The mystic experiences it through
an extreme specialization of the intuitive mind. The two approaches are entirely
different and involve far more than a certain view of the physical world. However,
they are complementary, as we have learned to say in physics. Neither is compre-
hended in the other nor can either be reduced to the other. But both are necessary,

supplementing one another for a fuller understanding of the world. Capra paraphrased an old Chinese saying:

> Mystics understand the roots of the *Dao* but not its branches; scientists understand its branches but not its roots. Science does not need mysticism and mysticism does not need science; but men and women need both.

Capra also insightfully prefaced the second edition of his book with these words:

> These discussions have helped me tremendously in understanding the broader cultural context of the strong interest in Eastern mysticism that arose in the West during the last twenty years. I now see this interest as part of a much larger trend that attempts to counteract a profound imbalance in our culture—in our thoughts and feelings, our values and attitudes, and our social and political structures. I have found the Chinese terminology of yin and yang very useful to describe this cultural imbalance. Our culture has consistently favored yang, or masculine, values and attitudes, and has neglected their complementary yin, or feminine, counterparts. We have favored self-assertion over integration, analysis over intuitive wisdom, science over religion, competition over cooperation, expansion over conservation, and so on. This one-sided development has now reached a highly alarming stage; a crisis of social, ecological, moral and spiritual dimensions.

His argument reinforces our strong belief—and one of the major themes of this book—that cultures must learn from each other to attain a new dynamic balance.

Section Three:
Development of Chinese Thought

The factors distinguishing classical Greek and classical Chinese thinking and philosophies lie in different perceptions and perspectives on the human senses, observations, experiences, and knowledge. In addition, there are significant divergences in the theoretical approaches and practices of the two cultures.

Truth-seekers and Way-seekers

Philosophers Hall and Ames observed that the ancient Greeks posed questions about thinking itself. They asked the what questions. What is the truth? What is real? What is the world made of? Simply, what is this? In the West that the Greeks helped to construct, truth is understood to be knowledge of what is real and what represents that reality, a search for permanence and substance in things.

On the other hand, Chinese philosophers asked the where questions. Where is the way? The Chinese have long accepted the fact that the only constant in the world is change, so they have thus sought the way to accommodate this phenomenon or apparent reality. For the Chinese, knowledge is not abstract. Rather, it is concrete. It is not representational. It is multifaceted, performative, and participatory. It is not discursive. It is a knowledge of the way, a kind of know-how.

The contrast between the truth-seekers and the way-seekers is significant. In the words of Hall and Ames (1998):

> Truth-seekers want finally to get to the bottom line, to establish facts, principles, theories that characterize the way things are. Way-seekers search out those forms of action that promote harmonious social existence. For the way-seekers, truth is most importantly a quality of persons, not of propositions. Truth as way refers to the genuineness and integrity of a fully functioning person.

Chinese thinkers were not obsessed with the goal of providing rational accounts of motion and change. They sought to experience the world rather than understand it. Thinking for the Chinese is actualizing or realizing the meaningfulness of the world, a process that engages the whole person.

The ancient Chinese were too pragmatic in their thinking to be concerned with epistemology and ontology. For Confucius (551–479 BC) and the Chinese tradition, thinking is not to be understood as a process of abstract reasoning. Rather, it is fundamentally performative in that it is an activity whose immediate outcome is the achievement of a practical result. Far from being a means for lifting oneself out of the world of experience in an attempt to achieve objectivity, thinking for the Chinese is fundamentally integrative and inclusive. It is a profoundly concrete activity that seeks to maximize the potential of the existing possibilities and the contributing conditions. The absence of ontological assertions in Chinese philosophy means that for the Chinese there is no being behind the myriad beings, no one behind the many, and no reality behind appearance. There is only an ever-changing processional regularity, which can be discerned within the world itself. It makes the world, to some degree, coherent and determinate and, given its inherent indeterminacy, to some degree, novel and unpredictable. Reality is a tacit concept. It is grounded in concrete observation and experience. For the Chinese, reality is immanental. It does not subscribe to absolute and objective principles. Rather than employing norms as a means of evoking appropriate behavioral responses, they use images, models, analogies, and metaphors to communicate and cultivate relationships. The Chinese generally make no distinction between reality and actuality because they believe the validity of principles can be tested only through actual events.

Chinese Thinking Preferences

Imagine you are a hunter-gatherer living in China during the Ice Age. Because most of low-latitude China escaped the spread of the ice sheets, the plants and animals in your environment are abundant and diversified, so much so that you have neither the time nor the need to extensively study any one species of prey or forage. By the late Pleistocene period, your brain size is fully developed at approximately 1,400 cubic centimeters (85.43 cubic inches), so you have the potential intelligence of a modern human.

As your first strategy, you are likely to adopt broad and generalized observation to assess your surrounding environment. After repeated observations over a period of time, you would sort out the similarities and differences of various species of animals and plants, according to their specific characteristics such as overall shape, texture, color, sound, specific posture, personality, and habits. Manifestation of this type of thinking, which focuses on certain characteristics of an object while simultaneously ignoring minor details, can be found in cave paintings in northern China. These depictions contrast markedly with European cave art, which focuses on the real forms and shapes of the objects depicted. Chinese cave art is more abstract and impressionistic. For example, in famous cave paintings discovered in the Yin Mountains north of Beijing, there are vivid expressions of Paleolithic animals such as ostrich, deer, and goats. Each animal is represented through the emphasis of its own distinctive traits. The ostrich is characterized by its long neck. The deer is characterized by its long horns. The goat is characterized by its diminutive mustache and straight horns. Each image emphasizes the spirit and essential character of its object rather than its real form, which would have been the case in the contrasting perspective of the early Greeks. This strong emphasis on the character and spirit of an object, rather than its real form, prevails in every form of Chinese art.

Regardless of this focus on the spirit of an object, or perhaps because of it, the early Chinese were keen observers of nature. Many classical Chinese sages recorded their observations and their differentiation, classification, categorization, and characterization activities. For instance, in one case, early Chinese farmers classified eighteen types of soil and their suitability for farming in particular regions. These classifications were further divided into three classes and seven grades, according to potential productivity.

This example highlights many anecdotal observations that Chinese people enjoy numbers and ardently group items into classes and categories, such as fifteen types of plateaus, thirty-six types of tactics, and so forth. Many books, covering a broad range of fields such as metallurgy, medicine, astronomy, military, and agriculture, demonstrate that the Chinese are dedicated recorders and classifiers of nature. In addition, Chinese legends are populated with stories such as that of Shen Nung, the legendary folk hero credited with teaching people the art of agriculture. He tasted one hundred plants in a day and found that seventy were poisonous, unfit for human consumption. Indeed, despite their mythological nature, these stories are credible if we interpret "Shen Nung" to be a representative group, whose name means roughly, "experience accumulated by groups of herbalists through the ages." As we witness even today, Chinese medicine relies heavily on herbs, chemicals, minerals, animal parts, insects, and plants for its remedies. Some components are mildly poisonous on their own, but they serve a desired function in formulation. Deep understanding of both the independent and combined properties of these ingredients is, of course, crucial for their successful application. Much of this type of knowledge is tacit in character, accumulated simply by trial and error.

Chinese people are generally practical and utilitarian. So characterization of an element or an object in terms of its usefulness and application is common in Chinese thinking. This tendency carries over to Chinese philosophies and Chinese legends and mythologies, which are quite different from the Greeks or the Romans in the sense that the Chinese stories are always practical. Graham (1964) commented:

> If we can make a safe generalization about the whole of Chinese philosophy, it is that interests have always centered on human needs, on the improvement of government, on morals, and on the value of human life.

The Chinese legendary heroes or heroines are all ethical characters who earned their fame with deeds that served humankind. In another sign of this pragmatism, no classical literature in any civilization paid more attention to the recording and honoring of ancient inventors and innovators than that of the Chinese. No other culture probably went so far in the veritable deification of these figures. As one travels around China today, large numbers of beautiful modern votive temples dedicated to these folk heroes or heroines serve as a testament to their importance. In fact, many schools of Chinese philosophy, such as Confucianism, simply refuse to deal with the supernatural, insisting on more human priorities. In *The Analects of Confucius*, it states:

> How can we serve the spirits of the dead before we are able to serve the living? Before we know what life is, how can we know what death is?

It can be argued that the Chinese are too practical and too involved with everyday life to be religious.

The early Chinese, keen in their observation of nature, were also zealous students of the sky. According to Joseph Needham, the Chinese were the most persistent and accurate observers of celestial phenomena in the world before the Renaissance. Although geometrical planetary theory did not develop among them, they conceived an enlightened cosmology, mapped the heavens using our modern coordinates (not the Greek ones), and kept records of eclipses, comets, novae, meteors, sunspots, and so on that today's radio astronomers use.

The early advancement of Chinese astronomy is not surprising. It is very practical, given that China was one of the first regions of the world to develop agriculture, the success of which depended heavily on an understanding of nature. Additional motivation for the study of astronomy was found in the Chinese political climate of the time. In ancient times, a success in the prediction of a heavenly event provided a confirmation of a government's mandate to rule. Predictably, Chinese astronomers were frequently government officers.

Structured Chinese thinking depends on a type of analogy or metaphor, which may be called correlative thinking. The earliest documentation we have indicates the Chinese noticed that their world and the plants they gathered for their food came and went in cyclical patterns, according to the changing weather of the four seasons. They also became aware that the two extremes, which they called yin and yang, were complementary. Any single polarity alone lacked meaning in the absence of the other. In the view of the Chinese, the elements and events of the world always appear in pairs. Cold and hot, low and high, the moon and the sun, night and day, left and right, complete and one-sided, genial and overbearing, yin and yang are all symmetrically related and reliant upon their complement for meaning. Yin does not transcend yang, and night does not transcend day. Every element in the world is simply relative to every other. More significantly, in nature's order, night always turns into day, and day always turns again to night. The world is a dynamic organism in which every element and every event is interrelated. The Chinese approach to problems, whether personal, social, or political, is to strike a dynamic balance between the extremes. This is the rule of the golden mean.

The concept of polarity, which holds the key to understanding Chinese thinking, contrasts with the concept of dualism that has long occupied Western thought. Traditional Western ways of thinking look at polar extremes as conflicting or differentiating, as opposed to the more Chinese conception of complementarity. The originality of the Chinese lies in their indifference to the notion of a final end. They seek instead to interpret reality solely through its own manifestation. Reality is the phenomena of the myriad of things, including ourselves.

The holistic and tacit thinking of the Chinese also diverges from the more abstract, yet atomistic and explicit thinking, of the West. In everyday living, all of us essentially function in an integrated way with little awareness of particular aspects or details. Whatever knowledge of the aspects we employ, we do so tacitly, that is, in an implied or understood manner that is not openly expressed. Even though we might focus our attention on a single object, we are open to and aware of the context of that object. For example, a reader may concentrate on a book, but be simultaneously aware of events and conditions around him, such as his wife cooking or children playing. This is similar to the notion that philosopher Michael Polanyi introduced in *The Tacit Dimension* (1967). We make use of tools or knowledge without realizing we are doing so. They become part of us in a very real way. Knowledge regarding our functioning has been compiled into our minds, and we function without awareness of the details of what we are doing. This example of everyday functioning is increasingly successful the more we integrate the aspects of our actions with our intuition. The resulting thinking is integrative and may be said to allow us knowledge of the whole.

Chinese thoughts are also dynamically inclined, emphasizing from an early date the concepts of change and motion that are applied to both space and time. Change is a marked feature in this conception of thinking, but it is neither a haphazard nor causal concept. The Chinese approach to thinking follows a certain pattern of polar oscillation or cyclical return. The world is envisioned as a theatre with a limited playbill of tragedies and comedies running in repertory. The Chinese people believe in infinity and the cyclical nature of time. History, whether personal, societal, national, global, or cosmological, repeats itself in many different ways. Thus, if we are attuned to the lessons of history, we can see the future through both the present and the past.

Section Four:
Space-Time and Chinese Cosmology

Where the Western conception of nature necessitates a discussion of science, the correspondingly central concepts for Chinese focus on space-time, metaphysics, and cosmology.

Chinese Space-Time

The Chinese word for the universe is *yuzhou* 宇宙, in which *yu* means space and *zhou* means time. When these terms are combined, they express the interdependence of time and space. The Chinese characters for the "world" are *shijie* 世界, which combines the word *shi*, meaning "a generation," with the word *jie*, meaning "a boundary." Thus, shijie is literally "the present world," representing the fluid boundaries between past and future generations.

For the Chinese, with their ready acceptance of change in the world, the concept of space and time is very real and distinct. Sima Qian (202 BC–AD 220), a renowned historian in the Han dynasty and author of *Shiji*, wrote, "Explore and understand the boundaries between man and heaven, explain all transformations between the past and the present, so as to establish one school of thought."

In a tradition that perceives a trinity of heaven, earth, and human, conceptually, there are no fixed or discernable boundaries between any of the three. Heaven, earth, and human therefore encompass the totality of space, which is the universe. At the same time, because the past world continually transforms into the present world, understanding and explaining the nature of such transformations, which depend on the interrelationships between heaven, earth, and human, can lead to the establishment of our own school of thought on space-time and human relationships.

Libai, a poet in the Tang dynasty, must have had a similar notion of space-time in mind when he wrote, "What is heaven and earth? It is all the active journeys for the ten thousand things. What is time? It is the passage, the trajectories of the hundred generations."

Again, in the Chinese mind, the processes and activities of the ten thousand things that constitute the notion of space. History, configured by the passage of time and the transformation of events through generations, constitutes the notion of time.

As a tradition that emphasizes respect for the continuity of change and the passage of time, Chinese thinking is particularly concerned with processes or phenomena that create history and humanity's place within it. Ames and Hall (2003) pointed out that, for ancient China, time is not independent of things. It is a fundamental aspect of them. In the absence of the Western ideal of objectivity that objectifies and thus makes objects of phenomena, the Chinese tradition does not have any separation between time and entities that allow for either time without entities or entities without time. There is no possibility of either an empty temporal corridor or an eternal anything. Hence, each phenomenon is some unique current or impulse within a temporal flow. In fact, the actual meaning of time is the pervasive and collective capacity of the events of the world to transform continuously.

Space-time is therefore a continuum of events, as the Chinese perceive it, in sharp contrast to the Western metaphysical tradition. For the Chinese, history is simply a record of this continuum. Again, this is contrary to the Western conception of history. As articulated by Hall and Ames (1983), in the development of Western thought, which is based on a strongly atomistic and essentialistic commitment traceable to the early Greeks, the prominence of a historical figure is usually a function of the degree to which that figure reflects discontinuity with what has gone before. A Descartes, Newton, or Einstein is most visible because of the extent to which he challenges the status quo. Western historians perceive such figures as being responsible for setting their respective disciplines on a new track. This historical paradigm is reflective of the act/agent distinction usually presupposed in the Western interpretation of human experience. Moreover, it is consistent with a perception of historical research as being primarily concerned with identifying agency and imputing responsibility for past events. By contrast, the Chinese intellectual tradition is generally characterized by a commitment to continuity. It would be much easier for a philosopher to gain a hearing and win support for a new concept by reinterpreting the existing and popularly accepted vocabulary than it would for him to advance his own original set of categories. This same commitment to continuity meant that the authority one's ideas might gain by operating within the bounds of an existing tradition would far outweigh the pride of authorship. It is for this reason that much in the revolution of philosophical ideas tends to be expressed in a process of organic growth, not through a dialectical process of thesis and antithesis. Thus, the difference between the Chinese and Western approaches seems to be evolutionary versus revolutionary.

The Chinese people often say, "History repeats itself." From this perspective, the Chinese understanding of time sounds cyclical. Needham (1981), however, asserted that linearity of time has actually dominated the Chinese culture, even though elements of both linear and cyclical time were present. This emphasis on the linearity of time in Chinese history does not imply a progressive world.

Confucians insist on looking back with envy at the ideal society of past times. Conversely, a vision of time as cyclical can be progressive. As contemporary philosopher Tang Junyi (1986) indicated, cosmology for the Chinese is not simply a linear zero-sum victory of order over chaos driven by some external cause. Rather, the endless alternation between rising and falling, emerging and collapsing, and moving and attaining equilibrium is occasioned by its own internal energy of transformation. This cosmic unfolding is not cyclical in the sense of reversibility and replication. Instead, it is a continuing spiral that is both continually recursive and continually renewing. This process is analogous to the four seasons of nature, in which spring returns each year but every spring season reveals itself uniquely.

Chinese Cosmology

Our discussion of space-time gives way to an examination of cosmology. Broadly speaking, cosmology is the theory of the universe and includes the science, study, philosophy, and understanding of the physics and metaphysics of both the macrocosmic and microcosmic. We will limit this section to Chinese metaphysics. We addressed science in the first two sections.

In the Western understanding of the cosmos, religious beliefs are central. This is not the case for the Chinese. In fact, adopting the practice of Hall and Ames, we use the term "cosmology" here only for consistency because we have already characterized Chinese thinking as "acosmo" due to its lack of a single order vision of the world. For Chinese cosmologists, as well as their counterparts in most other premodern cultures, the key to understanding order in the universe was correlative thinking.

In general, correlative thinking draws systematic correspondences among various orders of reality or realms of the cosmos, such as the human body, the body politic, and the heavenly bodies of the universe. Correlative thinking assumes these related orders are homologous; they correspond with one another in number, kind, structure, or some other basic respect; and they form a continuum. When the space-time relationship, or change, is also taken into account, we are looking at a dynamic correlative cosmology. Based on this dynamic correlative cosmology, the ancient Chinese interpreted humans, their relationships with other humans, the natural world, and, in particular, the astronomical heaven.

According to contemporary Chinese philosopher Cheng Chung-Ying (Allinson 1991), the search for cosmological becoming in the Chinese philosophical tradition was presented and preserved in the two primary texts, the *Yijing* and the *Daodejing*. These texts represent a cosmological outlook not confined to cosmology and address ethics and philosophical anthropology. The *Daodejing*, a classic canon of the Daoists written by Laozi between the third and fifth century BC, was previously cited in this volume. Although we do not know precisely who composed the texts of *Yijing* or *I-Ching*, which are thought to have been in existence as early as the late Neolithic period, both are historic and of great historical significance, providing deep insights into the minds that composed them and the collective wisdom of the Chinese experience of reality. The *Yijing* deals with the cosmological philosophy of the reality of change. In this work, metaphysics and symbolism are often used for divination. Cheng located the origin of the *Yijing* way of thinking in the response of a person first finding himself or herself in the primordial existential situation of a network of relationships, encountering manifold worldly phenomena, including many that can not be understood, and puzzling over events occurring both in heaven and on the earth. We know the Chinese have accepted the only constant in the world to be change. *Yijing* is the very book that understands and deals with change, as signified by *yi* in its title.

Cheng Chung-Ying further pointed out that, in the Chinese philosophical tradition, knowledge centers on the harmonization of self and world. In mainstream Western philosophy, the purpose of knowledge is overcoming the world. In the Buddhist philosophical tradition, the purpose of knowledge is overcoming the self. Chinese philosophy fosters a holistic outlook on both the universe and humanity within the universe, realizing the dynamic unity of all things and experiencing the dynamic source of all things. To use the term "dynamic" is to accentuate the importance of movement and creativity as a universal nature of things, not only as a universal phenomenon. Dynamic implies getting behind the phenomenon and identifying the ultimate reality of all phenomena without denying the individual reality of the specific phenomenon. Concurrently, it is discerning the substance of things through the functioning of things. This penetrating insight into the nature of things led Cheng to call the cosmological understanding of the world the "ontological" understanding of things. His conception of ontological must not be confused with the notion of being found in Western philosophy. The Chinese word, *benti* 本 體, or original substance, unifies the meaning of origin, *ben*, with the character for base or substance, *ti*. On one hand, ti is the unchanging base and framework for a system of activities. On the other hand, it is the source and origin of the system of activities. When used as an object, ti also implies comprehension of integration and harmonization. Cheng argued that, in the expression and the consideration of reality, it is possible to make a union of the object, ti, and the subject, ti, resulting in a dynamic concept suggestive of embodiment, integration, and harmonization.

Cheng proposed the new terms "cosmo-ontology" or "onto-cosmology" to represent the dynamic unity of the cosmological and the ontological, the Chinese notion of Dao. As the cosmo-ontological reality, the Dao is revealed as the dynamic force in the cosmological activities of things. It is the ti (body) of the universe. It is things going back to their origin and source. As the onto-cosmological reality, Dao is the process of presenting things in the universe. Hence, it is the process of presenting the universe.

It is, therefore, the origin and source at work toward the differentiation of reality. Dao is not separable from the concrete and the visible at work, which is called the *q'i* 器 (utensil) in the *Dazhuan* of the *Yijing*, but it does not interfere with the functioning of things within shape. When *Dazhuan* says, "What is above shape is called the Dao; what is within shape is called the q'i," it does not mean that Dao and q'i are separated as two distinct entities. It means the same entity is Dao when seen as above shape and is q'i when seen as within shape. Dao is spoken of as the ti 體 of things; q'i is spoken of as the *yong* 用 (functioning) of things.

In this sense, the Dao is radically different from being in the Western metaphysical tradition, especially as represented by Parmenides. Whereas being separates itself absolutely from the changing phenomenon of nature, the Dao never leaves things behind or aside. Instead, it always embraces them in change. Whereas being denies reality to things in change and therefore condemns becoming to unreality, the Dao imparts both being and becoming to things. As such, it becomes the essence of both being and becoming, thus making being and becoming equivalent. Whereas being transcends the world by being self-identical, the Dao immerses itself in the world by producing difference and variety. Whereas being is the object of pure thinking, the Dao is the effect of a process of profound experiencing, including feeling and perception. Thus, being becomes the exclusive subject of ontology by excluding cosmology whereas the Dao bridges the gap between ontology and cosmology by including both. The integration of being and becoming, the inclusion of cosmology and ontology, and the comprehension of both thinking and feeling are based on the comprehensive experience of things in the universe as a whole. This experience is one of unity in variety and variety in unity. It is specifically one of polarity of opposition and complementarity, unity of oneness and difference at the same time.

This conception of Dao found in the *Yijing* is also called *taiji* 太 極, the creative unity of heaven and earth, being and becoming, difference and identity, rest and motion, completion and beginning, constancy and change, and yin and yang. Before taiji, existence was void of time, space, and matter. It was a point of unknown, or *wuji* 無 極 (ultimate nothing), which, just like the big bang of modern cosmological theory, was a single event whose occurrence created taiji. Hence, taiji is the origin of all things. The trinity of heaven, earth, and humanity, when integrated with the unities of knowledge and practical action, substance and function, and fact and value, form a system that embodies "an infinite possibility of understanding and interpretation as well as an inexhaustible source of meaning and value" (Allinson 1991).

The *Yijing* also provided a framework for the innovative and continuous development of the Daoist philosophy of Laozi and Zhuangzi, which, when combined with Confucian *Yizhuan* 易 傳 metaphysics, has formed the basis of the Chinese metaphysical and philosophical tradition. The essence of the *Yijing* is found in its dealing with change, which is the nature of Dao, and consists of infinite productive transformations of things in the world. This is how reality is ultimately conceived within this framework, that is, the infinite creative becoming in the being of the totality of things and the oneness of the Great Ultimate as the primordial source, where being and becoming cannot be separated. With the Great Ultimate, taiji, it gives birth to two norms: yin and yang. Two norms give birth to four forms. Four forms give birth to eight trigrams and sixty-four hexagrams, representing the *Yijing*, symbolic universe, and metaphysical thinking. Since ancient times, the Chinese have been using these elements for divination, fortune-telling, guiding wisdom, principles for daily action and decision-making, and, on the highest intellectual level, gaining mystical insight into the nature and workings of the cosmos. Cheng maintained:

> The most important characteristic of this way of thinking is that nothing in the experience of reality is left out in understanding reality. In fact, the experience is that of total reality and reality is that of total experience. The basic motif in Chinese metaphysical thinking is to preserve and present this totality of experience of reality and this reality of total experience in a comprehensive system of symbols, language, and undertaking. (1991)

Clearly, the Chinese pursuit of the way, the Dao, through the conception of reality as a unity of polarities, yin and yang, engaged in creative interaction and transformation, is in contrast with the Western precept of metaphysical thinking as a quest for being, which amounts to the elimination of becoming from "being." The Daoists later developed *Yijing* metaphysics into a cosmology that continues to impacts contemporary Chinese thinking and attitudes.

In their philosophical translation of *Daodejing*, Ames and Hall (2003) argued that the defining purpose of the text is bringing into focus and sustaining a productive disposition that allows for the fullest appreciation of those specific things and events that constitute one's field of experience. According to these authors, the Daoist agenda is the furtherance of each person's ability to extract maximum consciousness from their own unique experience. Daoism endorses making this life significant and getting the most out of one's capability. Ames and Hall wrote:

> The reality of time, novelty, and change; the persistence of particularity; the intrinsic, constitutive nature of relationships; the perspectival nature of experience. Taken together, these several presuppositions that ground the Daoist worldview and provide Daoism with its interpretative context set the terms for optimizing our experience. Or said in a more metaphorical way, there is a strategy in the *Daodejing* for getting the most out of the ingredients of our lives. (2003)

For the Daoist, heaven can be found on earth through the efforts of people, not in an afterlife allotted through supernatural agency.

Particularly impressive is Ames and Hall's description of the Daoist cosmology, wherein the field of experience is always construed from many different perspectives:

> There is no view from nowhere, no external perspective, no decontextualized vantage point. We are all in the soup. The intrinsic, constitutive relations that obtain among things make them reflexive and mutually implicating, residing together within the flux and flow. This mutuality does not in any way negate the uniqueness of the particular perspective ... A corollary to this radical perspectivism is that each particular element in our experience is holographic in the sense that it has implicated within it the entire field of experience. This single flower has leaves and roots that take their nourishment from the environing soil and air. And the soil contains the distilled nutrients of past growth and decay that constitute the living ecological system in which all of its participants are organically interdependent. The sun enables the flower to process these nutrients, while the atmosphere that caresses the flower also nourishes and protects it. By the time we have "cashed out" the complex of conditions that conspire to produce and conserve this particular flower, one ripple after another in an ever-extending series of radial circles, we have implicated the entire cosmos within it without remainder. For the Daoist, there is an intoxicating bottomlessness to any particular event in our experience. The entire cosmos resides happily in the smile on the dirty face of this one little child. (2003)

This passage vividly describes the Daoist view of humans as part of a universal ecosystem. It is *ziran*, the natural way, free of artificial interference.

Ames and Hall further pointed out that this aesthetic perspective of the Daoists, as opposed to a rational or logical one, involves experiencing the world in a relatively unmediated fashion. While mediated experience requires one to grasp or comprehend the essence of a thing, the unmediated aesthetic experience is simply had as lived experience. The achievement of order and harmony in nature and human relations, the effective way-making of Dao, is a multifaceted effort dependent on the exercise of imagination and creativity within our environmental or social contexts. The *Daodejing* encourages a comprehensive, process-oriented view of experience, requiring a full understanding of the larger picture and the ability to locate and appreciate the particular events within it. This broad view of the field of experience allows one to contextualize particular events like everyday routines and provides the peripheral vision necessary to stay focused at the center while simultaneously anticipating future turns. These patterns of experience are endlessly manifold and diverse. Their ever-changing novelty makes them constantly unique and distinctive. The *Daodejing* directs us to cultivate those habits of awareness that allow us to measure and appreciate the magic of the ordinary and the everyday. Our habits, traditions, and roots are the background to spontaneous, creative actions. The disposition these habits constitute is indeterminate in the sense that these novel interactions are constantly reshaping and redirecting it. Indeed, by enchanting the routine, we are on the way to making this life truly significant. These habit-informed interactions between persons and environments occur within customs and the broadly construed notion of culture. This ecological sensibility is what gives Daoist philosophy its profoundly cosmic dimension.

In contrast with the Daoist ideal of Dao and *De*, Confucian cosmology is embedded in a nature that is moral and just. For Confucians, cosmology involves the moral self-cultivation of humans in order to reveal our natural goodness through education and harmonize our relationship with others, nature, and the universe. For historical reasons, the Confucian notion of virtue has often, regretfully, been misunderstood as ethical dogma. In fact, Confucius was the greatest humanitarian who ever lived. Most of his teachings were rooted in *Yijing*, the book of change. Confucius's students frequently asked him to define his virtues in *Analects*. He repeatedly avoided doing so, focusing on specific situations and leaving ample room for spontaneity and creativity in their application. Confucianism did become dogmatic during the Ming and Qing dynasties. However, as a result of governmental policies, the results of this change provide a topic for discussion in a later chapter.

By combining the basic concepts of Daoism and Confucianism, which were further incorporated with Zen Buddhism at a later date, the ancient Chinese have created a consistent, reasonably accurate, and uniquely harmonious view of the universe. Succeeding Chinese thinkers perceive the universe as a dynamic organism with humanity, society, earth, heaven, and nature fully integrated in dynamic equilibrium. The universe is a seamless whole. It has no beginning and no end, and it is infinite and evolutionary. Although individual objects and elements of that whole exist, they obtain meaning only through their spontaneous and harmonious participation as individual chords in a great symphony of nature. Because motion and change are essential properties of things, the animating force is found as an intrinsic property of the constituent matter, not outside the objects. Space-time is a wavelike continuum with every moment of existence and every process or phenomenon constantly renewed, novel, spontaneous, and creative. The human role in the world is participatory. We are to follow and harmonize with the natural way of the Dao.

The Dao is infinite and eternal, and it immerses itself in the world by producing difference and variety through *Qi*, the animated energy and vitality of all things. The dynamic correlative cosmology and resonance of human and nature organizes the world into a highly regular and predictable system. Change and transformation as well as evolution and decay remain, to use Needham's term, organic.

The "ten thousand things" in the world and the sum of all phenomena and processes, that is, all aspects of our experience, can be understood in terms of correlative cosmology by combining Dao, Qi, yin and yang, the four seasons, eight trigrams, sixty-four hexagrams, and the five phases. The principal characteristic of Dao is the cyclical nature of its ceaseless motion and change. When a situation develops to its extreme, it inevitably turns around and becomes its opposite. The five phases of water, fire, wood, metal, and earth must not be misconstrued as mere physical substances. Rather, they are a set of fivefold aspects, also complementary, of configurations or processes.

The aesthetic experience of humanity is a reflection on the aesthetic order of nature, which is neither supernatural nor preordained by principles. The field of experience is metaphorically holographic. It is always interpreted from many different perspectives. Because each particular perspective is unique, particular events can be understood only in context. The essence of this worldview is the awareness of the unity and mutual interrelation of all things and events, that is, the experience of all phenomena in the world as manifestations of a basic oneness. All things are understood to be interdependent and inseparable parts of the cosmic whole and as different manifestations of the same ultimate reality.

Section Five:
Religious Thinking

Chaos and Order: Cosmogony, the Origins of the Universe

Hall and Ames (1995) attributed the disparities of Chinese and Western thinking and philosophy to their different beliefs in cosmogony, that is, the origins of the universe. They summarized the presuppositions of the dominant style of Western causal thinking, which they call "second problematic thinking," as follows:

1. The construal of the beginning of things in terms of chaos as either emptiness, separation, or confusion

2. The understanding of cosmos as a single-ordered world

3. The assertion of the priority of rest over change and motion (alternatively expressed as the preference for being over becoming)

4. The belief that the order of the cosmos is a consequence of some agency of construal such as *Nous*, the *Demiourgos*, the Unmoved Mover, the Will of God, and so forth

5. The tacit or explicit claim that the state of affairs comprising the world is grounded in and ultimately determined by these agencies of construal

In significant contrast with second problematic thinking is analogical or correlative thinking, which Hall and Ames called "first problematic thinking." Favored by the Chinese, the presuppositions of correlative thinking are:

1. No presumption of initial beginning

2. No presumption of the existence of a single-order world

3. Acceptance of the priority of change or process over rest and permanence

4. No ultimate agency responsible for the general order of things

5. Seeks to account for the states of affairs by appealing to correlative procedure rather than by determining agencies or principles

These divergent perspectives have characterized the essential ways in which the two cultures interpret their respective relationship with nature.

Western Cosmogony: Chaos and Order

Western cosmogonies presuppose a foregoing time characterized by a basic irrationality, or nonrationality. They thereby remind us that, beyond the conception of an ordered and harmonious universe, lie emptiness, alienation, and confusion. The first state of the universe is thus chaos, traditionally associated with an irrational, unprincipled, and anarchic world. Western thought then contrasts chaos with cosmos, the ordered or harmonious world. The idea of forming cosmos out of chaos is at the very root of the Western conception of beginnings. Ancient Greek arguments of the one and the many, being and becoming, and rest and motion were all concerned with the very nature of the cosmos. Causal thinking favors the view that there is only one world order with relatively stable laws prevailing from the beginning to the end of that order. Belief in a single-ordered universe assumes the many phenomena comprising the world are defined in accordance with unifying principles, which, in turn, determine the essential reality of things of the world. This kind of thinking led to the development of modern science, as described previously. Hall and Ames argued that:

> The description of the source or origin as a formless, dark, void is similar to the characterizations of chaos in terms of the "primordial waters" in Egyptian and Mesopotamian creation myths. Such a cosmogonic process tells of a victory over the forces of chaos. God's command in Genesis, "Let there be light," established order and command. It is logical to argue that creating cosmos out of chaos required some form of "agency," such as "God." The Western preference of rest and permanence over motion and change, being over non-being or becoming, has determined that subsequent cosmological speculation must involve the search for beings or principles which, as transcendent sources of order, account for the orders experienced or observed. (1995)

So God created the universe, the creatures that populate it, and all the things that exist within it. This Western dualism of "God the Creator" and "Man the Creation" is perhaps one of the most significant notions separating Western and Chinese cosmogony.

Chinese Cosmogony

In contrast with the Western belief of Creation, the classical Chinese are primarily acosmatic thinkers. By acosmatic, we mean they do not assume that the totality of things (*wan-wu* or *wan-you* 萬 有, "the ten thousand things") has radical beginnings or these things constitute a single-ordered world. According to Hall and Ames, in classical Western metaphysics, the equivocation between unity and uniqueness is resolved in favor of unity. Thus, in any of the various conceptions of a single-ordered universe assumed by the early systematic philosophers, the many phenomena comprising the world are defined in accordance with unifying principles that determine the essential reality of the things of the world. In classical Chinese reflections on world order, the equivocation between unity and uniqueness is resolved in favor of the unique. Hence, the nameless Dao engenders an individual one that then proliferates. The natural philosophy of classical China does not require a single-ordered cosmos. Instead, it invokes an understanding of a world constituted by the ten thousand things. In ancient Greece, the preference for rest and permanence over process and becoming entails the need for a causal agency accounting for change. The Chinese "world as such" (ziran 自 然 or natural), a process of spontaneous arising, requires no external principle or agency to account for it. Indeed, the Chinese acosmatic, noncausal, analogical, pragmatic, and correlative thinking resulted in their aesthetic attitude toward nature rather than the more religious views of the West.

In a culture such as that of the Chinese, which is grounded in deontological, nontranscendental, and nondualistic philosophy, the aesthetic immanent order is sought. In contrast, Western culture seeks rational or logical order. According to Hall and Ames (1987), aesthetic order begins with the uniqueness of the one thing and assesses that particular element as a contributor to the balanced complexity of its context. Aesthetic order focuses on the way in which a single, specific detail contributes to a harmony comprised of many individual details acting in relationship to one another. On the other hand, a rational or logical order consists of a pattern of relatedness, which is, in principle, indifferent to the elements whose mutual relatedness comprises the order. The direction of logical or rational construction is always away from the concrete particular toward the universal. Thus, in the quest for truth, goodness, and beauty, the Chinese value goodness and beauty while the West favors truth.

A detailed description of Chinese cosmogony is found in *Huainanzi*, an ancient text compiled by Liu An (180–122 BC), king of Huainan and a grandson of the founding emperor of the Han dynasty, Liu Bang. Although well-known, the text has always been considered as a miscellaneous or eclectic Daoist work, never achieving the status accorded to the classics in the Confucian tradition. Recently, however, many scholars in the West and in China and Japan have taken a fresh look at the *Huainanzi*. They see it now as an attempt, largely successful in its own time, to define the dominant currents of thought in the early Han. It is a syncretism of Confucianism, Daoism, Legalism, and other schools in the Warring States Era. *Huainanzi* covers a wide range of topics with chapters on cosmology, cosmogony, sciences, military affairs, politics, social philosophy, and the art of rulership during the formative period of imperial Chinese history. Modern Chinese editions and translations of *Huainanzi* by Cao (1990) and English translations by Major (1993), Ames (1983), and Le Blanc (1985) represent excellent introductions to this work.

On the subject of Chinese cosmogony, Major wrote:

> *Huainanzi* Chapter 1, 2, and 3 offer different, but not necessarily incompatible, accounts of the coming-into-being of the cosmos; these accounts are supplemented by additional cosmogonic passage found in other chapters of the text. Together they paint a picture of a cosmos that begins in formlessness and chaos, goes through a process of differentiation governed by principles inherent in the system itself (that is, without the intervention of a Demiurge or *deus faber*), finally producing the world-as-it appears. This, however, persists for an unspecified duration in a mythic state of timelessness before entering the realm of time and history.

Major further summarized the *Huainanzi* cosmogony:

> Heaven and Earth are inchoate and unformed: The Great Inception.
> The Dao begins in the nebulous void.
> The nebulous void produce space-time.
> Space-time produces primordial Qi.
> Qi divides; the light and pure forms Heaven, the heavy and turbid forms Earth.
> Heaven and Earth produce yin and yang.
> Yin and yang produce the four seasons.
> The four seasons produce the ten thousand things.
> Yin and Yang Qi produce the heavenly bodies.
> The fight between Gong Gong and Zhuan Xu causes heaven to tilt to the northwest.
> Yin and yang cause the heavenly bodies to shine and produce meteorological phenomena.
> All things respond to yin and yang according to their kind.

The concepts of Dao, yin and yang, and Qi take on complementary meanings in *Huainanzi* and remain central in Chinese cosmogony and cosmology throughout history. The Dao is the unity of yin and yang, a continuity of being that links inorganic, organic, and human life forms. The linkage is through Qi, the constituent of all matter. These concepts are conceptualized as processes, not substances. We will elaborate on this distinction later.

Chaos and Creativity

There is an interesting exposé on power and creativity in Ames and Hall (2003), wherein the authors follow A. N. Whitehead in questioning the appropriateness of using creativity in the familiar *creatio ex nihilo* (created out of chaos) model that we associate with Judeo-Christian cosmogony. Whitehead argued that any robust sense of creativity requires creativity itself to be more primordial than God. Ames and Hall argued that God, as the omnipotent other who commands the world into being, is Maker of the world, not its Creator. In the presence of the perfection that is God, nothing can be added or taken away. There can be no novelty or spontaneity. Thus, all subsequent acts of creativity are actually secondary and derivative exercises of power. Power is construed as the production of intended effects determined by external causation. Real creativity, on the other hand, entails the spontaneous production of novelty not caused by any external force. Power is exercised with respect to and over others. Creativity is always reflexive and is exercised over and with respect to self. Because self in a processive world is always communal, creativity is contextual, transactional, and multidimensional. Thus creativity is both self-creativity and co-creativity. Either everything shares in creativity, or there is no creativity. The term Dao, like building, learning, and work, entails both the process and the product. When Zhuangzi observed, "We are one with all things," this insight is a recognition that each and every unique phenomenon is continuous with every other phenomenon within one's field of experience.

This is an insightful perspective, explaining the aesthetic character of Chinese culture and providing the reason why traditional Chinese thinkers and philosophers emphasize arts and ethics rather than religion. It also explains why there was a sudden explosion of Western creativity when, after the European Renaissance and the Age of Enlightenment, freedom from religious dogma became a reality for many people. This burgeoning creativity ultimately resulted in the Industrial Revolution.

The experience of Dao is something without borders. There is no sense of the unity of the world, no feeling that all things are one. The fundamental sense of things is of "this" and "that". Where a Daoist celebrates his or her oneness with all things, the meaning of oneness is continuity with other things, not identity.

Continuity makes Dao one. Difference makes Dao myriad. For the Daoist, the question is that of the difference between an (*ad hoc*) whole and the part that construes it, the indiscriminate field and its particular focus. In a radical processive acosmology of the sort we claim, Daoism represents "only becoming is." Dao may be construed as becoming itself, the process of each instance of becoming. The boundless, boundary-less world of the "ten thousand things" is the subject of the mystical intuition underlying Daoist philosophy.

Chaos and Science

Contemporary scientists study chaos as an inquiry into the irregular, discontinuous, and nonlinear laws of nature. Science has historically suffered from a lack of understanding of disorder. This ignorance previously limited our knowledge of the occurrence and the dynamics of:

- Tornados and typhoons

- Wave particle interactions in a turbulent sea

- Mechanisms controlling the fluctuations of wildlife populations

- Complexity in the oscillations of the heart and brain

- Apparent unpredictable trends of the stock market

- Nonlinearity in a differential equation

The irregular side of nature, that is, the discontinuous, erratic, and nonlinear, has puzzled mathematicians, physicists, biologists, chemists, economists, meteorologists, and oceanographers for some time.

Since the 1970s, many surprising answers have been found. Research into chaos, aided by powerful computers that allow a glimpse into the delicate structure underlying its complexities, has shown promise in many laboratories across a variety of disciplines. The advent of new computers and sophisticated, nonlinear mathematical techniques help modern scientists understand chaotic, complex, emergent phenomena that have resisted analysis by the reductionist methods of the past. Researchers are now beginning to employ computers in simulating selected aspects of the natural world. To name just a few applications, these include weather simulation and prediction, the investigation of turbulent fluid flows, exploration of the global topology of biological systems, models of the growth patterns of crystals in ice and metal alloys, and even the study of the evolutionary history of the universe. As technology advances, there seems to be no limit to what this new science may offer.

Another product of computer science that has captured our imagination is Benoit Mandelbrot's invention of fractals, a direct outcome of research in chaos. Fractals are patterns that recur at increasingly finer scales with amazing simplicity. The so-called Mandelbrot Set has become a kind of laboratory in which mathematicians can test ideas about the behavior of nonlinear (chaotic or complex) systems.

It is not our intention to detail the important new topic of scientific research into chaos. It is worthy of mention that one of the most passionate advocates of this new science has gone so far as to say that twentieth-century science will be remembered for just three things: relativity, quantum mechanics, and chaos. As a physicist once said, "relativity eliminated the Newtonian illusion of absolute space and time; quantum theory eliminated the Newtonian dream of a controllable measurement process; and chaos eliminated the Laplacian fantasy of deterministic predictability."

Section Six:
Thinking Western vs. Thinking Chinese

The key classical philosophical and religious attitudes and preferences of the Western and Chinese cultures described previously can be summarized by the following comparisons.

What vs. Where

Ancient Westerners ask "What?" and become truth-seekers. Truth-seekers look for rest, permanence, and substance in things (being). They seek unifying principles or a transcendent agency to rationally account for reality. They look for clear definitions, specifically a separation of body and soul, hearts and mind, and human and nonhuman. Individuals are independent, rational beings. True knowledge is a kind of know-why.

Ancient Chinese ask "Where?" and become way-seekers. Way-seekers accept the fact that the only permanence in the world is change and look for ways (Dao) to accommodate this phenomenon or apparent reality. Everything in the universe, including humanity, is understood to be interdependent as inseparable parts of the cosmic whole and as different manifestations of the same ultimate reality. Knowledge to them is a kind of know-how.

Permanence vs. Change

Ancient Westerners believe permanence (truth, true reality, and unifying principles) is the rational, logical, eternal, and immutable one, unity, and being (ontology) that exists behind the apparent phenomena and changes (many, plurality, and becoming). Metaphysics is the most general and fundamental aspect of all knowledge. True knowledge must be eternal, universal, and objective. Sensory experience or empirical knowledge cannot provide access to universal truth. A transcendent agency (the will of God) is needed to reconcile the logical order of cosmos emerging out of the initial state of chaos (emptiness, alienation, and confusion).

To the ancient Chinese, the Dao (the way) is an infinite and constantly productive transformation of things in the world. The experience of Dao is ziran, which means "natural and unmediated." An infinite, immanent aesthetic order requires no external principle or agency to account for it. There is no one behind many, no unity behind plurality, and being and becoming cannot be separated. Ancient Chinese metaphysical thinking is to preserve and present the total experience of reality. Far from being a means for lifting oneself out of the world of experience in an attempt to achieve objectivity, thinking for the Chinese is fundamentally integrative, not a process of abstract reasoning.

One vs. Many

The idea of forming the cosmos out of chaos is at the very root of the Western conception of beginnings. Ancient Greek arguments of the one and the many, being and becoming, and rest and motion were all concerned with the very nature of the cosmos. Causal thinking favors the view that there is only one world order with relatively stable laws prevailing from the beginning to the end of that order. Belief in a single-ordered universe assumes the many phenomena comprising the world are defined in accordance with unifying principles, which, in turn, determine the essential reality of things of the world. True existence of reality must be continuous, unchanging, timeless, and indivisible unity. It must be a finite, single-ordered world defined in accordance with unifying principles for perfection and completeness. This Western dualism of "God the Creator" and "Man the

Creation" is perhaps one of the most significant notions separating Western and Chinese views on the beginning of the universe.

The Dao of the Chinese culture is the unity of yin and yang, a continuity of being that links inorganic, organic, and human life-forms. The linkage is through Qi, the constituent of all matter. All of these concepts are conceptualized as processes, not substances. The nameless Dao engenders an individual one, which then proliferates to a world of "ten thousand things." When a Daoist celebrates oneness with all things, the meaning of oneness is continuity with other things, not identity. Continuity makes Dao one; difference makes Dao myriad. Dao may be construed as becoming itself, the process of each instance of becoming. The universe is a dynamic organism with humanity, society, earth, heaven, and nature fully integrated in dynamic equilibrium. The boundless, boundary-less world of the "ten thousand things" is creative, novel, diverse, and plural.

Transcendence vs. Immanence

The Western traditional concept of transcendence means that God is completely outside and beyond this world. This meaning originates both in the Aristotelian view of God as the prime mover, a nonmaterial, self-consciousness that is outside of the world. In the Jewish and Christian idea of God as a being outside of the world, God created the world out of nothingness (*creatio ex nihilo*). In worship, a believer in immanence might say that one can find God wherever one seeks Him.

The Chinese traditional concept of immanence is a notion complementary to transcendence, minus the religious connotation. It is a continuum connecting the inside and the outside. Immanence is the tendency to introspect, examine one's own thoughts and feelings, and self-cultivate. The notion of immanence is common to the various currents of Chinese thought. Whether through a moral influence or natural propensity, it is the tendency of realizing oneself of one's own accord in relation to all the outside factors.

As a result of this contrast, Chinese people are more inward-looking, inward-relating, and self-cultivating in their thinking. Westerners, in contrast, are more outwardly inclined and liable to challenge limits, resulting in significantly different perceptions and dealings with themselves, their society, the world, and the universe.

Western humanistic psychologist Abraham Maslow's hierarchy of needs goes from basic human needs to end with self-actualization. Modern transpersonal psychology continues this sequence by exploring the next level of self-transcendence beyond Maslow's socially constructed bounds. The contemporary notion of self-transcendence encompasses the common mystical experiences of all the world's spiritual paths. Thus, these relatively new disciplines see the human saga as one that reaches from solely personal achievements of well-being and success through to transpersonal achievements of universal wisdom and compassion, spiritual insight, and enlightenment. The gap between Chinese and postmodern Western philosophies is narrowing.

Logical vs. Aesthetic Order

Western culture seeks rational or logical order that consists of a pattern of relatedness, which is, in principle, indifferent to the elements whose mutual relatedness comprises the order. Logical or rational order is inclined toward universality, generality, and absolute substitutability, which is away from the concrete particular.

Chinese culture seeks aesthetic immanent order, which begins with the uniqueness of the one thing, and assesses that particular element as a contributor to the balanced complexity of its context. Aesthetic order focuses on the way in which a single, specific detail contributes to a harmony comprised of many individual details acting in relationship to one another. Aesthetic order presses in the direction of particularity and uniqueness away from universality.

The concepts of aesthetic and logical order are inversely related. A complex of elements reaches the maximum of aesthetic disorder with the realization of absolute uniformity. But this is the highest degree of rational order.

Division vs. Integration

Analytical Western thoughts are atomistic, divisive, and exclusive. Concepts, rules, and ideologies are well-defined, specifically logical, rational, and explicit. Ambiguities are to be avoided wherever possible. The contrasting higher abstraction practiced in the West involves isolating one aspect from all others (and from its context) and focusing attention solely upon that object or aspect. This type of isolation of an aspect is sought when we wish to study a particular aspect and discover the laws that govern it, free from other influences. This is a key concept of the scientific method. Studies in classical science require the maintenance of consistency among dependent variables in order to accurately examine the effect on an independent variable when change in a specific parameter is introduced.

The Western logical experience of humanity has resulted in a dichotomy of man and nature, body and soul, individual and society, individual and state, space and time, and so forth. Separate, independent, individual parts compose the whole, which is the single-ordered world.

The not-so analytical Chinese thoughts are holistic, integrative, and inclusive. They dislike definitions. Concepts, rules, and ideologies are often tacit, implicit, and allow plenty of room for interpretation. The universe is a dynamic organism with humanity, society, earth, heaven, and nature fully integrated in dynamic equilibrium. It is open and has no ends and no boundaries. Every element of the universe is interrelated to every other element; every element thinks inclusively and not exclusively. Space-time is a wavelike continuum with every moment of existence and every process or phenomenon constantly renewed, novel, spontaneous, and creative.

The Chinese aesthetic experience of humanity is a reflection on the aesthetic order of nature. They emphasize unification and integration of the sensual and rational, mind and body, transcendental and immanent, human and nature, and supernatural and natural aspects of human existence, the seen and unseen.

Dualism vs. Yin and Yang

In classical Western philosophy, dualism is any of a narrow variety of views about the relationship between mind and matter, which claims that mind and matter are two ontologically separate categories. In particular, mind-body dualism claims that neither the mind nor matter can be reduced to each other in any way. In a given domain of knowledge, dualism involves the existence of two fundamental principles (or concepts), often distinct from and in opposition to each other. There is religious dualism of monotheism, moral dualism of good and evil, scientific dualism of subject and object, and so forth. The contemporary fundamentalism in religion and economics is an outcome of dualistic thinking, which still impacts all of us.

In Chinese philosophy, the Dao engenders yin and yang, for example, cold and hot, low and high, the moon and the sun, night and day, left and right, correct and one-sided, genial and overbearing, and women and men. All are symmetrically interrelated and reliant on their partner for meaning. Yin does not transcend yang; night does not transcend day. Every element in the world is relative to every other. More significantly, night will always become day, and day will always become night. This reflects the cycle of nature. The world is a dynamic organism where every element and every event is interrelated. Between the two polarities, a full spectrum of perceivable realities is found, that is, novel patterns that reflect the aesthetic order of events. The Chinese preference for handling problems, whether personal, social, or political, is to strike a dynamic balance between these extremes. This is called the rule of the golden mean.

In recent years, after European imperialism, the distinction between Eastern and Western philosophy has been less significant than in previous times. In the wake of these changes, new religious and philosophical movements have drawn freely upon many of the world's religions to attract new initiates. Along with ideas of oneness and wholeness, dualism is often cited within these groups.

Abstract vs. Correlative Thinking

Abstraction is the process of generalization by reducing the information content of a concept or an observable phenomenon, typically to retain only information that is relevant for a particular purpose. Western abstract thinking is a process wherein ideas are distanced from the object, which is a process of simplification wherein formerly concrete details are left ambiguous, vague, or undefined. The way that physical objects, like rocks and trees, have being differs from the way that properties of abstract concepts or relations have being. That difference accounts for the ontological usefulness of the word "abstract." The word applies to properties and relations to mark the fact that, if they exist, they do not exist in space or time, but that instances of them can exist, potentially in many different places and times.

Correlative thinking is a species of spontaneous thinking grounded in informal and *ad hoc* analogical procedures presupposing both association and differentiation. The regulative element in this type of thinking is shared patterns of culture and tradition rather than common assumptions about causal necessity. Correlative thinking is the primary instrument in the creation, organization, and transmission of the classical curriculum in China. Chinese thoughts are correlative and metaphorical, observing patterns and classifying differences and similarities. There is an emphasis on properties, processes, interrelationships, and structures of matter, elements, or aspects instead of on the individual elements themselves. Yin and yang is a good example of correlative thinking. Such correlative schemes orient human beings in a very practical manner to their external surroundings. The application of analogy and metaphor is pervasive in ancient Chinese philosophy. The constant appeal to historical incidents and models provides concrete instances of conduct, which then serve as a resource for organizing and articulating present experience. In the broadest terms, an immanental view of reality that does not subscribe to absolute and objective principles must employ models rather than norms as the means of evoking appropriate behavioral responses. The establishment and cultivation of these modeling relationships is effected through analogy.

Revolutionary vs. Evolutionary History

In the Western notion of history, the prominence of a historical figure is usually a function of the degree to which that figure reflects discontinuity with what has gone before. That is a revolutionary view of history. A Newton or Einstein is most visible because of the extent to which he challenges the status quo. Western historians perceive such figures as being responsible for setting their respective disciplines on a new track. This historical paradigm is reflective of the act/agent distinction usually presupposed in the Western interpretation of human experience. Moreover, it is consistent with a perception of historical research as being primarily concerned with identifying agency and imputing responsibility for past events.

Chinese intellectual tradition is generally characterized by a commitment to continuity, that is, an evolutionary view of history. It would be much easier for a philosopher to gain a hearing and win support for a new concept by reinterpreting the existing and popularly accepted vocabulary than it would for him to advance his own original set of categories. This same commitment to continuity meant the authority one's ideas might gain by operating within the bounds of an existing tradition would far outweigh any pride of authorship. For this reason, much in the revolution of philosophical ideas tends to be expressed in a process of organic growth, not through a dialectical process of thesis and antithesis.

Summary

Let us tabulate these differences in Western and Chinese thought preferences:

WESTERN THOUGHT PREFERENCES	CHINESE THOUGHT PREFERENCES
Highly Abstract, Theoretical, Analytical	Practical, Empirical, Pragmatic
Atomistic, Divisive, Exclusive	Holistic, Integrative, Inclusive
Rational, Explicit	Tacit, Implicit
Dualist, Logical	Yin-Yang, Complementary, Synthetic, Dialectic

Causal, Absolute, Rational	Analogical, Correlative, Metaphorical, Aesthetic
Static, Searching for Permanence, Substantial	Dynamic, Accepting of Change and Motion, Processive

One should not overgeneralize these points. They merely represent trends in the psychological preferences or sensibilities of people in either given culture, Chinese or Western. In the end, the occurrence of either preference is incidental, an outcome of environment and history as described previously. In fact, these preferences need not be mutually exclusive. We ourselves frequently think in both modes. Historically, there were certain Greek schools of philosophy, such as those of Heraclitian and Anaxagoras, that thought in a manner very similar to the Chinese. Nevertheless, the majority of Greeks did not prefer to think in this manner. In a similar nonconformist fashion, the schools of China's Later Mohists, Zhuangzi, or Gongsun Long developed fairly sophisticated logic and analytics that did not appeal to the general Chinese temperament. For the Chinese, the Greek style of disputation seemed like frivolous quibbling, playing with words rather than contributing to solutions for practical problems.

From another perspective, there are actually numerous coinciding elements in both cultures. According to Reding (2004), these similarities include the discovery of the axiomatic method, the art of definition, principles of contradiction, logical syntax, and categories. Ultimately, it could be argued that Greek and Chinese rational thinking are simply different facets of the same phenomenon. Notwithstanding such similarities, cultural distinctions in thinking do exist. Even to casual observers of our contemporary societies, they are fairly obvious, both inside and outside China. The following chapters expand upon this distinction by examining cultural differences that stem from diverging Chinese and Western thinking preferences and account for different cultural attitudes in our life pursuits, psychological or philosophical inclinations, artistic appreciations, moral judgments, and our relationships with nature, ourselves, other people, our communities, and human institutions.

Part Two

Human Relationships

We now proceed with an understanding of the fundamental worldviews already presented, recognizing they evolved from human responses to divergent natural environments in the prehistorical China and West.

The following three chapters are organized according to the two main inter-related facets of the Chinese tradition, as founded by Confucius:

- The qualities and modes of conduct necessary to be a full and worthy human being

- The foundation of good government and proper social order

Chapter four focuses on how Chinese perceive themselves from moral, philo-sophical, and psychological viewpoints and, wherever possible, makes comparisons with Western perceptions on the same areas. Chapter five discusses differences in interactions with family, the people on which an individual can exert the most influence and be influenced. Chapter six evaluates the interactions of people with their society and state in order to meet sometime different requirements of good government and proper social order.

CHAPTER FOUR

Being Human

How one perceives oneself is probably one of the most important issues in modern psychology because it ultimately impacts all other relationships.

Section One:
A Microcosm of Nature

We have seen that Western science has embarked upon a dramatic exploration of the subatomic and astronomical worlds. While we have also seen that the Chinese tradition has not developed a similar focus on science, there is, nevertheless, a similarity to the macrofocus of modern physics. A Chinese person views his or her own body as a microcosm of nature, mimicking in miniature the functioning of the universe. Thus, the correlative, metaphorical, tacit and holistic thinking preferred by the Chinese described in chapter three can be further explained by examining how Chinese people perceive themselves. We will also examine some related notions embedded in the way Chinese people heal themselves through traditional Chinese medicine (TCM).

In the Chinese tradition, each person is a unified body and soul, a landscape that embodies the energies of nature called Qi, the life energy that permeates and constitutes the whole universe. The human body combines two kinds of Qi. Coagulated Qi is manifested as various visible or structural components of the body, such as viscera, body figure, sense organs, blood, body fluids, and essence, which includes eggs, sperm, and genetic material. Diffused Qi is manifested as the Qi that flows in the body, but it does not take any certain form. The term "sense organs" commonly used in TCM is similar to, but not the same as, the physical organs in Western medicine.

TCM has four main clinical classes of Qi: primordial, pectoral, nutritive, and defensive. Primordial Qi is inherited from the parents, manufactured by kidney essence, and functions as the primary motive force for the growth and development of the human body. Pectoral Qi, or great Qi, is generated by the combination of the food essence transported by the spleen and transforms the fresh air inhaled by the lungs. Its main functions are to assist the lungs and serve as the force for breathing and voice. Nutritive Qi is the nutrient-rich Qi flowing in the blood vessels. In TCM, blood consists mainly of nutritive Qi and body fluids. Finally, defensive Qi defends the human body and warms and nourishes the viscera organs. In this scheme, health implies that the animated power of the Qi in our body is clear and flowing smoothly like a stream. Sickness means that the Qi is polluted, turbid, stagnant, and blocked or flowing in the wrong direction. The objective of TCM is to clear the Qi by removing blockages.

Chinese medicine is primarily physiological and only derivatively anatomical. That is, health is to be found and encouraged in the way in which the various parts of the body interact. For instance, Western medicine asks, "What is the heart's role in human anatomy?" TCM asks, "How does the heart function as part of the whole system in the most productive way?" TCM, like much of ancient Chinese culture, is based on yin and yang and five phases models.

Yin and yang order all experience into one of two categories. Like fire, yang is hot, dry, and active. Like water, yin is cold, moist, and passive. An imbalance of yin and yang causes sickness. Symptoms of too much yang and inadequate yin include feeling hot and restless, dry skin, scanty urination, constipation, and a rapid pulse. Symptoms of too much yin and not enough yang are feeling coldness, lack of thirst, low energy, edema, frequent urination, loose stools, and a slow pulse. Yin and yang is an empirical model based on clinical observations and monitoring of a client's pulse.

The five phases of water, wood, fire, earth, and metal represent processes that express the relationship between nature and the human body. In this model, water, wood, fire, earth, and metal correspond to winter, spring, late spring, summer, and autumn, respectively. Each phase, in turn, corresponds to body organs and Qi, moisture, blood, essence, and *shen* 神, or spirit, which embodies consciousness, emotions, and thought. In the body, fire corresponds to the heart, which stores the shen and moves the blood. Metal corresponds to the lungs, which circulate the Qi. Earth corresponds to the spleen, which distributes moisture. Wood corresponds to the liver, which stores the blood and ensures smooth movement of Qi. Water corresponds to the kidneys, which store the essence. The five phases are hence created through the generating cycle. Fire produces earth, which then produces metal. The metal creates water, which produces wood. Then the cycle returns to its beginning as wood produces fire.

The interrelationships of the five phases mirror the cycles of functional control within the human body. Because fire melts metal, so the blood of the heart helps control the Qi of the lungs. Because wood breaks up the earth, the Qi of the liver helps control the digestive functions of the spleen. As earth dams water, so the Qi of the spleen controls the kidney's ability to concentrate moisture. Because water extinguishes fire, the essence of the kidney keeps the yang fire of the heart in check.

The yin and yang and five phases models are so dominant that every aspect of TCM is built upon their understanding of herbal remedies, symptoms of illness, clinical diagnoses, and so forth. These models are effectively an organizational scheme compiled from an accumulation of more than five thousand years of detailed observations and clinical trial-and-error experiences on actual human beings. Even though there is no theoretical justification for such an empirical model in the modern sense, numerous case histories have demonstrated its workability. It has helped the Chinese medical professional by facilitating further experimentation, assisting in visualization and abstraction of medical conditions and appropriate remedies, communicating, and teaching.

Just as Western thought is inclined to seek truth, modern Western medical practice often attempts to find a single cause for an illness, such as a bacteria, virus, or genetic defect, and prescribe an exact remedy, cure, or medication to eliminate illness. If no bacteria, virus, or genetic malfunction is found, Western doctors may be unable to find a cure. Drugs and surgery are then used to suppress the symptom, often with undesirable side effects. This system may excel in the treatment of acute, traumatic, or life-threatening situations, but it can be helpless if a single cause is difficult to find or too complex to be diagnosed. TCM, on the other hand, emphasizes healing and prevention and searches every patient's situation for an imbalance in the emotional, social, and physical realms. Disease and symptoms are understood as the body's attempts to restore harmony and equilibrium. Chinese treatments such as acupuncture, herbs, and *Qigong*, a form of meditative exercise, all aim to restore balance in the body. The practice of medicine is viewed as the cultivation of health, wholeness, and harmony with the doctor and patient working in partnership. Ideally, remedies may change daily according to the current assessment of the patient's conditions. TCM is a much slower process than Western medicine and preferred for prevention and treatment of chronic disease conditions. Chinese and Western medicine, as with most aspects concerning the two cultures, are complementary, and they should be used as such for our benefit.

Section Two:
Body and Soul, Heart and Mind, and Self

In contrast to the more unified Eastern notion of the human as a microcosm of the universe, polarities and separateness characterize the major formative ideas of self as advanced in the West.

Body and Soul, Heart and Mind

Abraham Maslow, one of the founding fathers of modern psychology, introduced the renowned Maslow's Hierarchy of Human Needs in the early 1900s. This system chronicles the progress of human self-consciousness in life through the stages of need-directed (survival and belonging), outer-directed (self-esteem), and inner-directed (self-actualization). Maslow pointed out that our first need and first priority is survival. The most basic constituents of which are food and shelter. Once basic survival needs are met, people focus on belonging to a group, family, community, tribe, or country. Again, once people attain the security of belonging, they aspire to stand out, that is, become outer-directed as achievers. This is an urge toward individuality, but the prevailing values and acceptable behaviors of the group or community limits it. The highest level of conscious development is self-actualization, which is inner-directed. These people have achieved self-esteem and material success. Therefore, they choose to shape their own destinies. By developing skills in critical thinking and introspection, they understand their own needs, strengths, and weaknesses. As a result, they become capable of setting their own direction for life and managing their own path of development and learning.

The important notions characteristic of the Western mind, soul, self, and self-consciousness are vague in the sense that they are open to rich and diverse interpretations. Hall and Ames (1998) argued that, in the Western tradition, the cosmogonic motivation of construing order from chaos has influenced our cultural self-understanding. This motivation has operated to shape our myths, religions, laws, and institutions. Thus, one way of recounting the narrative of our developing intellectual culture is by examining the manner in which humans established the meanings of important notions such as God, nature, power, law, freedom, and, of course, self. They believe that, broadly speaking, there have been four primary semantic contexts—the materialist, formalist, organicist, and volitional models—that have shaped terminology such as individual, human being, personality, and self. Western culture interprets the human condition through a materialistic-mechanistic lens. The neurophysiologist understands human behavior in terms of neuronal firings. The sociobiologist characterizes genetic determinants. The behaviorist explores human individuality by appealing to contingencies of reinforcement in local environments.

On the other hand, traditional Western ontology entails a separation or dualism that presupposes incorporeal and non-mechanistic elements—body and soul and heart and mind—where the body represents the physical constituents, including anatomical heart, and the soul harbors the non-physical elements, including the mind and perhaps rationality and conscience.

Aristotle's organic naturalism conceived of the human being as a language-bearing creature whose experience is constituted of interactions with other persons. The chief defining characteristic of this organism is its principal aim, which Aristotle conceived to be happiness. This social view is found in a variety of forms in sociology, social psychology, and political science. The political version of a contextualized self is the Sophistic tradition that persists in the twentieth century through the characterization of knowledge as a function of rhetorical persuasion and personality as a function of self-creativity and persuasive power. This perception is political to the extent that it promotes hierarchical relationships as the context within which meaningful human existence is to be found.

Self-perception

Descartes' mind-body distinction also remains fundamental to contemporary discussion, even though few contemporary philosophers and scientists are substance dualists. On the one hand, we have the mind, sometimes called mental events, states, or properties. On the other, we have body or matter, that is, events in, states of, or properties of the brain. The mind-body problem is encountered in the attempt to conceptualize, describe, and account for the evident relationship between these two categories of phenomena.

Contemporary writers study the notion of self and consciousness mainly from psychological perspectives. Psychiatrist Arthur Deikman (1996) claimed the core of subjectivity, that is, the I, is actually identical to awareness. Introspection reveals that this I should be differentiated from the various aspects of the physical person and its mental contents, which form the self. He pointed out that we seem to have numerous versions of I. There is the I of "I want," the I of "I wrote a letter," and the I of "I am thinking." But there is another I that is basic, which underlies our desires, activities, and physical characteristics. This I is the subjective sense of our existence. It is different from self-image, the body, passions, fears, social categories. Each is an aspect of our person that we reference when we speak of the self. They do not refer to the core of our conscious being. They are not the origin of our sense of personal existence. Deikman claimed that most discussions of consciousness confuse the I and the self.

Awareness is different than that of which we are aware: thoughts, emotions, images, sensations, desires and memories. Awareness is the field in which the mind's contents manifest themselves. According to Deikman, awareness may vary in intensity as our total state changes, but it is usually a constant. Awareness cannot itself be observed. It is not an object and not a thing. Indeed, it is featureless, lacking form, texture, color, and spatial dimensions. These characteristics indicate that awareness has no intrinsic content, form, and surface characteristics. Thus, experience is dualistic. It is not the dualism of mind and matter, but it is the dualism of awareness and the content of awareness. In other words, experience consists of the observer and the observed. Our sensations, our images, our thoughts, that is, the mental activity by which we engage and define the physical world, are all part of the observed. In contrast, the observer, that is, the I, is prior to everything else. Without it, there is no experience of existence. If awareness did not exist in its own right there would be no I. There would be me, my personhood, and my social and emotional identity. There would be no I or transparent center of being.

This misunderstanding of I has apparently created some confusion among psychologists regarding awareness and content. Deikman maintained one can read numerous psychology texts and not find any that treat awareness as a phenomenon in its own right, something distinct from the contents of consciousness. Nor do their authors recognize the identity of I and awareness. Instead, the phenomenon of awareness is usually confused with one type of content or another. According to Deikman, William James made this mistake in his classic, *Principles of Psychology*. When he introspected on the core "self of all other selves," he equated the core self with "a feeling of bodily activities," concluding our experience of the I, the subjective self, is really our experience of the body. Beginning with behavioral psychology and continuing through our preoccupation with artificial intelligence, parallel-distributed processing, and neural networks, the topic of awareness has received relatively little attention. When the topic does emerge, consciousness in the sense of pure awareness is invariably confused with some type of content.

Deikman also observed the same confusion arising in philosophy. For example, after Husserl, nearly all modern Western philosophical approaches to the nature of mind and its relation to the body fail to recognize that introspection reveals I to be identical to awareness. Furthermore, most philosophers do not recognize awareness as existing in its own right, different from contents. Owen Flanagan, a philosopher who has written extensively on consciousness, sided with James and spoke of "the illusion of the mind's I" (Flanagan 1992). C. O. Evans started out recognizing the importance of the distinction between the observer and the observed, the subjective self, but then retreated to the position that awareness is "unprojected consciousness," the amorphous experience of background content (Evans 1970). However, the background is composed of elements to which we can shift attention. Deikman pointed out that this is what Freud called the preconscious. I/awareness has no elements or features. It is not a matter of a searchlight illuminating one element while the rest is dark. It has to do with the nature of the light itself.

Consciousness and Awareness

It is interesting that Deikman eventually found companions in the Eastern philosophers, Buddhist literature, and Western mystics like Meister Eckhart and Saint John of the Cross. Each of these philosophies, based on introspective meditation, emphasizes the distinction between awareness and content, but they favor awareness as the real I, deeming that all contents are illusionary. Deikman also contended that the failure of Western psychology to discriminate awareness from content and the resulting confusion of I with mental content may be due to a cultural limitation. Most Western scientists lack experience with Eastern meditative disciplines. Carl Jung may be one of the exceptions. His work was geared largely toward the nature of symbolism. Armed with the knowledge of the symbolism of complex mystical Eastern traditions, Jung was trying to make sense of the unconscious component of the human conscious.

In contrast, Chinese cultural tradition, in a manner similar to other Eastern philosophical traditions, seeks unity and parity of all things, including body and soul along with heart and mind. Tellingly, the Chinese language uses the same character, *xin* 心, to mean both heart and mind. For this reason, some authors use "heart/mind" as the denotation of xin. The Chinese use of the word "soul" does not have the religious connotation embedded in the Western tradition, and it often shares meaning with xin, the heart/mind. As described previously, TCM views the human body as a microcosmos, a unity of body and soul. A person's physical well-being is a necessary, but insufficient, condition for good health. The well-being of both mental and physical states is required for a vital life, one in which the body's Qi flows clearly and without blockage. Body, soul, heart, mind, and even self are often indistinguishable in Chinese traditions.

The primary schools of Chinese philosophy—Confucianism, Daoism, and Zen Buddhism—all use specific techniques of meditation to communicate or introspect with one's own consciousness. Scientifically, even today, very little is known about the state of a mind involved in meditation. Potentially mystical experiences, such as meditation, may represent a simple form of human consciousness. Our minds are an enormously complex stew of thoughts, feelings, sensations, desires, pains, daydreams, and, of course, consciousness itself. Adding to the complexity of this stew, one of its ingredients, consciousness, is essentially aware of all this complexity. Thus, to understand consciousness in itself, the obvious thing would be to clear away as much of this internal noise as possible. The techniques that most mystics use, such as meditation or contemplation, seem to be doing precisely that. According to Robert Forman (1998), in a work delivered at the 1996 Tucson Conference, *Toward a Science of Consciousness*, the state of meditation can be described as follows:

> During meditation, one begins to slow down the thinking process, and have fewer or less intense thoughts. One's thoughts become as if more distant, vague, or less preoccupying; one stops paying attention to bodily sensations; one has fewer intense fantasies and daydreams. Thus by reducing the intensity or compelling quality of outward perception and inward thoughts, one may come to a time of greater stillness. Ultimately one may become utterly silent inside, as though in a gap between thoughts, where one becomes completely perception-and-thought free. One neither thinks nor perceives any mental or sensory content. Yet, despite this suspension of content, one emerges from such events confident that one had remained awake inside, fully conscious. This experience, which has been called the pure consciousness event, or PCE, has been identified in virtually every tradition. Though PCEs typically happen to any single individual only occasionally, they are quite regular for some practitioners. The pure consciousness event may be defined as a wakeful but contentless (nonintentional) consciousness. These PCEs, encounters with consciousness devoid of intentional content, may be just the least complex encounter with awareness per se that we students of consciousness seek. (1998)

It is interesting to see contemporary scientists begin to pay attention to mystical experiences, which, in the case of the Chinese experience, have been well documented in Confucian and Daoist literature for thousands of years. We hope that contemporary psychologists will choose to utilize this literature to further enrich our self-understanding.

Following his vivid description of the meditation experience, Forman continued to refer to Buddhist literature regarding this type of content and attribute-free consciousness, such as during meditation, and stated, "I, though abiding in emptiness, am now abiding in the fullness thereof." He also quoted W. T. Stace:

Suppose then that we obliterate from consciousness all objects physical or mental. When the self is not engaged in apprehending objects it
becomes aware of itself. The self itself emerges. The self, however, when
stripped of all psychological contents or objects, is not another thing, or
substance, distinct from its contents. It is the bare unity of the manifold
of consciousness from which the manifold itself has been obliterated.
(1960)

In the end, Forman summarized the implications from which we can draw
about the nature of human consciousness from the pure consciousness event as
follow:

1. The phenomenon of PCE is not an artifact of any one culture. It is something
    closer to an experience that is reasonably common and available in a variety of
    cultural contexts.

2. Consciousness does persist even when one has no perception, thought, or
    evaluation. This suggests that consciousness should not be defined as merely
    an epiphenomenon of perception, an evaluative mechanism, or an arbiter
    of perceptual functions. Rather, it is something that exists independently of
    them.

3. Binding, to tie together perception and thought, is something done by or for
    consciousness, not something that creates consciousness.

4. We should conceptually and linguistically differentiate merely being aware or
    awake from its functional activities.

Reports of PCE suggest that, despite the absence of mental content, the subjects were somehow aware that they remained aware throughout the period of
PCE. Apparently, they sensed a continuity of awareness through past and present.
If they did, even though there was no content, then they must have somehow
directly recalled they had been aware despite the absence of remembered content.
This implies human awareness has the ability to tie itself together and know intui-
tively that it has persisted. This provides a fascinating description of the sense of
expansion beyond the borders of one's own body and even of transcending time,
what Freud called the "peculiar oceanic feeling."
    Forman continued:

The phenomenology, simply put, makes room for the suggestion that
consciousness is not limited to the body. Consciousness is encountered as something more like a field than a localized point, a field that

transcends the body and yet somehow interacts with it. This mystical phenomenon tends to confirm William James' hypothesis in his monumental *Principles of Psychology* that awareness is field-like. This thought was picked up by Peter Fenwick and Chris Clarke in the Mind and Brain Symposium in 1994, that the mind may be non-localized, like a field, and that experience arises from some sort of interplay between non-localized awareness and the localized brain. (1998)

As a result of further studies into this phenomenon, Forman conceptualized the experience of awareness as some sort of field, allowing for the theory that consciousness is more than a product of the materialistic interactions of brain cells. A field may not only transcend our own bodily limits, but it may indeed interpenetrate or connect self and external objects. This is, of course, strikingly parallel to our earlier discussion of physical energy fields and the quantum mechanical field understood to operate at the most basic level of matter. These fields, too, are both immanent within and transcendent of their object. The perception of unity holds out the possibility that the field of awareness may be common to all objects and, however implausible it may seem, all human beings as well. It implies that our own consciousness may be somehow connected to a tree, the stars, a drizzle of rain, or a blade of grass. Ancient Chinese sages have long adhered to this concept. Might this be the same field that Hall and Ames postulated in their focus-field model of Chinese relationships? This whole field of awareness theory is also very similar to the Neo-Confucian theory of human nature and the self, a topic of discussion in the next few sections.

Section Three: Focus-Field Model

The convergence of Western science and Eastern cosmology seen in the last section provides us with a model for examining Chinese thought. The Western-originated focus-field model is a highly descriptive and intuitive lens for the understanding of how the Chinese view themselves as individuals and their relationship to others, society, nation, and the universe.

In physics, we often use the terms "particle" and "field" to describe an object and the force it exerts on a point across empty space. The concept of field and particle, the focus of the field lines of force, is very useful in modern physics. We often hear references to quantum field, gravity field, or electromagnetic field. All of these concepts are significant from the small scales of subatomic physics to the grand scale of astronomy and astrophysics.

Hall and Ames wrote an insightful book, *Anticipating China*, in 1995 in which field and focus were used to describe Chinese relationships. The authors saw the focus-field model of order as a constituent that appears fundamental to Chinese conceptualizations. In "Ritual, Role, and Family: The Confucian Synthesis," they introduced the Latin words *locus* and *focus*:

Whereas the Latin term locus means simply "place," the term focus means "place of convergence or divergence." Originally, the term meant "hearth" or "fireplace." It came to mean "burning point"—identifying the place at which the sun's rays pass through a lens to converge with intensified heat. Kepler was apparently the first to use the term in its geometrical sense as focal point of a curve. We mention the term in this bit of etymology only to point out something of the richness of the word focus, which has its original association with hearth and home. This humanizing sense of focus ought to be factored into our extension of the term to characterize the Chinese sense of family and society. Field likewise has original domestic associations which we do not wish to abandon, though we shall be using the term in the sense of "sphere of influence." By sphere of influence we shall indicate the area within which the influences of and upon an agent may be discernibly experienced and perceived. (1995)

Hall and Ames described the use of these concepts:

It is important to recall that fields and foci are never finally fixed or determinant. Fields are unbounded, pulsating in some vague manner from and to their various transient foci. The notion of field readily contrasts with one-many and part-whole models. The relations of human beings to their communities, for example, are not established by the presumption of "essences" or "natural kinds" defining membership in a set of such kinds, nor by presumption of the contextually defined mereological sets wherein the parts constitute the wholes in an additive or summative manner. (1995)

In fact, the model assumes a vague, unbound field, both constituting and constituted by its discernible foci. Alternatively, there are a variety of shifting foci, the influences upon which and from which are resourced in a vague and unbounded field. Thus, our model is neither one-many nor is it a nominalized version of the part-whole model. The focus-field perspective employs a this-that model.

The similar focus-field model can be applied in attempting to understand how the Chinese view themselves as individuals and in relationship to others, society, their nation, and the universe.

Each individual possesses a force of morality that exerts influence upon his or her environment. A strong, highly principled person exerts a more powerful field of force, influencing people in the surrounding environment. Every person is a focus, having been born with innate goodness, a strong potential force. But personal desires and greed mask some people. Their innate nature can be restored only through education and self-cultivation. In this context, goodness means a person can only exert a positive influence when his or her actions harmonize with the laws of nature. In the absence of harmony, he or she must contest against the laws of nature, resulting in suffering. This is what contemporary philosopher Tu Weiming called the "anthropocosmic" nature of Confucianism as an inclusive humanism rooted in the regenerative rhythms of the cosmos.

A person's initial sphere of influence is the family, where family ethics is the combined field of the individual family members. Again, a family with strong-shared ethics would exert a strong field on first the immediate community and then the region, nation, world, and, ultimately, the universe. At each level of the sphere of influence, a member contributes as well as receives. The degree of his or her contribution and the degree of received influence depends on his or her own immanent moral persuasion. Humanity's moral persuasion, of course, is always grounded in behavior, expressed through principled actions rather than words. Thus, each hierarchy within this system and, consequently, the overall whole of this perspective embodies the ideals of a natural, ethical, and just cosmology in which everything and every person performs to his or her ultimate capacity.

This model will represent the Chinese notion of order in the remaining chapters. It can be clearly seen both in the following section and subsequent chapter with its focus on the moral suasion, or field, that exists within the Chinese family.

Section Four:
An Ethical Self

Karl-Heinz Pohl must have shared views comparable to those articulated in the preceding sections. He wrote:

> If we understand "self" as an individual in its modern atomistic sense as an autonomous entity, marked by its ability and right to choose freely

between equal alternatives as well as its potential for unconstrained self-fulfillment, then there is no equivalent in Chinese tradition to the modern Western notion of the individual. And yet we find in Confucian thought the individual person standing at the very beginning of all social and moral considerations. The Confucian "self" is not an "unencumbered self," it is rather a relational self, defined through social institutions and relationships. According to Tu Weiming, the Confucian self stands in the midst of partly concentric, partly overlapping circles of relationships—family, seniors/juniors at work, friends, community, country, universe (2003).

Pohl's discussion bears many similarities to the focus-field relationship and the contemporary psychological studies on consciousness presented in the preceding sections.

Human Nature

A major Chinese classic *Zhongyong*, or *The Doctrine of the Mean*, opens with this verse:

> What *tian* 天 (nature, heaven, or macrocosmos) imparts to man is called *xing* 性, human nature. To follow one's nature is called Dao, the way. To cultivate the way is called education.

Since the time of Confucius in the fifth century BC, and in the Warring States period that followed, known as the time of "the Hundred Schools of Thought," Chinese philosophers of all schools have debated the notion of human nature. The Xunzi (310–220 BC, approximately) believed human nature was essentially bad. The Kaozi believed human nature was neither good nor bad. Mengzi, or Mencius (approximately 372–289 BC), the dominant school of Confucianism, believed in the innate goodness of all humans. Mencius held that human nature is good because, when guided by innate feelings, a person will do what is good and develop into a full moral being. Like many early Chinese thinkers, Mencius believed that to cultivate oneself according to one's true nature is to follow the way, which fulfills a design inscribed by nature upon our human hearts. The microcosmos would naturally follow the laws of the macrocosmos, or nature. The same view is supported by Laozi, who took the emulation of the natural Dao as a vehicle for achieving identity with the constant Dao as his project. In the Daodejing he states:

The human being emulates Earth; Earth emulates heaven; Heaven emulates the Dao; and the Dao emulates that which is natural to it.

For the Chinese, nature is always moral and just. If humans do not do what is good, their instincts are not to blame. Instead, they have lost some of their original power to do good, but they nevertheless retain the potential to do good. The great problem confronting humanity is therefore that of preserving and cultivating those good feelings that are our birthright.

Self-cultivation

According to Mencius, there are four nascent moral senses: the feeling of compassion (benevolence), shame (righteousness or a failure in one's desire for goodness), reverence (respect or deference), and discrimination (judgment) between right and wrong. One of his examples was imagining the feeling of compassion that would be instinctively aroused if one were to see a child about to fall into a well. We react spontaneously because we are endowed with a heart that cannot endure the suffering of fellow human beings, especially the suffering of an innocent child. It is not because of distress at the child's cries or possibly winning favor with the child's parents. If Mencius is right, contemplating this hypothetical scenario as a moral thought experiment will cause a stirring in our heart that testifies to our own feeling of compassion. Mencius urged his followers to discover their own moral self-cultivation, what Ivanhoe (2000) called a discovery model.

Mencius further developed his case by arguing that there is a natural structure to the self and each of our parts has a natural function to fulfill. Of critical importance is the role played by our heart-mind, the governor of the self. He argued that, if we monitor and assess our reactions to our thoughts and behaviors by engaging in an internal act of reflection or concentration, we will be guided toward good actions and away from bad. The contemplation of good acts produces a special feeling of joy in us, which reinforces the moral sense and enables us, through a process of extension representing a moral field, to aspire to increasingly complex actions. In Mencius's own terms, such joy nourishes the moral sprouts. It provides them with a special kind of Qi, or energy and vitality. This is the same Qi we described previously. It is the Qi that nourishes life. Mencius contended it is also the energy of moral courage. How well one followed the proper course of human development depended upon how well one's heart/mind realized the way of nature. Mencius said in The Book of Mencius:

Fully realizing one's heart/mind is the way to know one's nature. One who knows one's nature knows Nature (or Heaven). To preserve one's heart/mind and develop one's nature is the way to serve Nature. When dying young or living long do not cause one to be double minded, cultivating oneself and awaiting whatever is to come—this is the way to establish one's destiny.

Mencius used metaphors to illustrate how we should cultivate and nourish these moral sprouts. First, we must neither neglect our shoots nor force them to grow. The former course of action will result in a lack of progress; the latter will do them harm. Moral development is a long and difficult process that depends more on the steady accumulation of simple acts rather than a grand display of goodness. It requires the cultivation and constant nurturing of one's knowledge, sensitivities, and dispositions through patient and persistent application. The desire to do good without proper resources can sometimes be harmful because improper moral cultivation causes one's moral sprouts to wither rather than flourish. Proper moral cultivation also requires the appropriate environment. As in the planting of seeds, a good environment favors while a harsh one spoils. When Mencius was young, his mother moved the family three times before she was settled and satisfied with the living conditions for her son's moral growth. In order to realize nature's design and become fully human, one must work to develop one's nature. This development requires the acceptance of and adherence to the way of nature. Although Xunzi's notion of human nature was opposite to that of Mencius, that is, believing human nature was full of desires and thus bad, Xunzi had his similarities, suggesting humans could develop a second nature that was good and could counter the inherently negative nature of our desires.

From the four nascent senses, if properly cultivated and nurtured, will spring the four great virtues of Confucianism, respectively: *ren* 仁 (humanity, benevolence, authoritativeness, and human-heartedness), *yi* 義 (righteousness and appropriateness), *li* 禮 (propriety and ritual practice) and *zhi* 智 (wisdom and realization).

Ren, cultivated from the nascent sense of compassion, the central virtue of Confucianism, asserts the relational character and interdependence of human beings. For Confucians, ren is the reality of the universe. Confucius considered ren the most valuable seed of humanity, the quality that made us human and distinguished us from animals. Confucius endorsed a simple moral and political teaching. Love others. Honor one's parents. Do what is right instead of what is of advantage. Practice reciprocity, that is, do not do to others what you would not want done to yourself. Rule by moral example (de 德) instead of force and violence.

Confucius said in The Analects, "Authoritative persons establish others in seeking to establish themselves and promote others in seeking to get there themselves."

In the Confucian tradition, the concept of maturing to a great self, or authentic person, from a small self comprises metaphysical notions explicated by Pohl:

> For it is precisely the "Way of Heaven" to be authentic, that is, great, all inclusive, and true to itself. Confucian authenticity thus puts man into a sequence of responsibilities which finally lets him or her partake in the process of self-fulfillment of the entire universe. (2003)

Through the process of self-cultivation, the individual self becomes part of a "fiduciary community" (Tu Wei-ming 1989) in which all members must transcend their respective and still-limited self (the self representing family, clan, community, and nation in addition to the individual) in order to "realize the deepest meaning of humanity."

According to Tu, the ideal of individuation in Confucianism is self-transcendence in addition to self-fulfillment. The influence of the Chinese intellectual elite of other philosophies, such as Daoism and Zen Buddhism, furthered this ideal.

During the Han dynasty (206 BC–AD 220), the classical core of Confucianism was effectively synthesized with elements of what were originally other schools of thought, most notably the cosmological speculations of the yin and yang and five phases philosophies. Individual, society, and government were woven together with the cosmos in a complex system of correspondences that described an all-encompassing underlying order, a fitting reflection of the unity of the great Chinese empire of Qin.

Han Confucians also incorporated some of the doctrines from other schools, such as Daoism, Mohism, and Legalism, into their own teachings. While earlier Confucians were concerned mainly with ethical issues, Han Confucians emphasized the unity of human interaction with nature and the resulting resonance. This integration of human and nature is also evident in the early Han syncretism of Confucianism, Daoism, and Legalism as witnessed in *Huainanzi* (Major 1993), wherein people are enjoined to use the sphere of nature as a model for natural conduct. By understanding the process of spontaneous development and their ecological dependency on their environment, an understanding of the true nature of reality could be accomplished. For Han syncretists, Dao is the highest and most primary expression of universal potentiality, order, and potency, as expressed in the cosmic order, which embraces both the natural and human world. Human order is a subset of natural order, and both are moral and good.

But the vision reflected in the success of the Han dynasty became less plausible when the dynasty entered a decline, and Chinese society again slid toward chaos. In the minds of many, the malfunction and disorder that marked the final decades of the Han dynasty discredited, not only the government, but also the ideology that had been sponsored by the government and legitimated its rulers. China was ready for something new. This was when Indian Buddhism competed for dominance with a resurgent Daoism. The schools of Buddhism regarded the very notion of the self as the ultimate illusion. This belief challenged orthodox Confucian teachings. Philip Ivanhoe (1990 and 2000) has followed the development of Neo-Confucianism in the Song/Ming/Qing dynasties and claimed that development of this new approach was a reaction of the Confucians of that time in meeting challenges from Daoism and Zen Buddhism. In particular, Zhu Xi (1130–1200) and Wang Yanming (1472–1529) developed new views on human nature and the mind, views that enabled them to provide solutions to what was a perennial Confucian problem of reconciling the claim that human nature is good with the evidently corrupt behavior of large numbers of people.

Early Buddhists believed that all suffering and the imperfect aspects of the world ultimately arose as a result of mistaken views about the self and the nature of reality. People believe that we, and the things we desire, endure, but the Buddhists would tell us that, in reality, all things are in a constant state of coming into and passing out of being. Nothing lasts. Our failure to realize the fundamental emptiness of both material things and ourselves inevitably results in continual and unending dissatisfaction, deepening our damaging ignorance. The escape from this descent is found in developing right views about the self and the world, that is, seeing the true nature of reality. In Zen Buddhism, the Chinese version of Buddhism, to accomplish this development, we must pare away the selfish desires and false views that obscure our innate Buddha nature, which is lively and perfect. Just as dust may obscure one's mirror, self-generated, self-imposed, and self-sustained delusions may obscure the true reflection of ourselves. This obscuring dust is empty and unreal in the sense that it is unnatural. Even the mirror is illusionary because it is also materialistic. Such distortions and delusions will simply disappear if we can fully engage and bring our true and fundamental nature into spontaneous play.

Built on this affirming foundation, Buddhism reached a creative and flourishing peak during the Tang dynasty (618–907). The Song dynasty (979–1279), however, reacted to this foreign religion and initiated a revitalization of the stagnant Confucian tradition. In the political world, this was manifested by a reform movement, which attempted to address the pressing socioeconomic problems of the day by a creative reinterpretation of ancient Confucian institutions. Of more lasting importance than the political outcome was the intellectual and spiritual reshaping of the tradition that returned to a sincere regard for the Confucian classics. Not surprisingly, the people of the time found what they were looking for, an ancient doctrine dealing with the cultivation of the inner life of mind and a metaphysics that framed this inner journey within a philosophical account of sagehood, self-cultivation, and connection with the universe.

Neo-Confucianism

This return to Confucianism is heralded in a passage of the *Book of Documents, shujin,* "The human mind is insecure, the mind of Dao is subtle; be discerning, be undivided (One or unity). Hold fast the Mean."

This passage became the keystone of the understanding of the heart-mind in the school of Cheng Yi (1033–1107) and Zhu Xi, renowned as the Cheng-Zhu school. They believed the human mind has two components:

- The mind of the Dao embodied the innate goodness of human nature referenced by Mencius and enshrined philosophically in doctrine that equated human nature with *li* 理 (principle, pattern, and process).

- The human mind was equated with a manifestation of physical nature.

The spirituality and consciousness of the heart-mind are one and undivided. Yet there is a difference between the human mind and the mind of Dao because some aspects of human mind arise through the individuality (or selfishness) of the physical form while the rest originate in the rectitude of the natural Mandate. The consequent types of consciousness are not the same. Therefore, the one is perilous and insecure. The other is wondrously subtle and difficult to perceive.

This dichotomy of the human mind and the mind of Dao can explain historical events of how ancient sages such as Yao and Shun governed by the principles of Dao and Confucian values of ren and yi and the tyranny of some emperors governed by force. It can also explain diverse human behavior. Because all humans have physical form, even the wisest cannot leave behind the human mind. Likewise, we all possess this good nature. Even a criminal possesses the mind of the Dao. These two are mixed together within the heart-mind. If one does not know how to control them, the perilous will become even more perilous, and the subtle will become even more subtle. In the end, the impartiality of the principle of heaven will not be able to overcome the selfishness of human desire. This passage also offers a solution. By adherence to the rule of the golden mean, maintain the rectitude of the original mind and not become separated from it.

The Cheng-Zhu school, as Ivanhoe described, further believed that the li gives form and meaning to all things, but it is itself without perceptible form or meaning. Both of which must instead be embedded in Qi. Qi is that of which the world is made. It is not inert matter, and it comes in various grades of impurity. The Qi of different things, to varying degrees, obscures the li within them and only allows some of it to shine through. While all things equally possess all the li, their different endowments of Qi make them different because each thing only manifests certain of the li. Moreover, given that Qi exists in different grades of purity and is constantly churning around, their endowments naturally differ in purity when people are generated out of Qi. One's individual endowment is called one's *cai*, or capacity and talent. This determines, at least to begin with, how aware one is of the various principles in the world. Those with a better endowment of Qi are naturally clearer about how things are. The purer one's Qi, the more li shines forth and the more one understands. Because each thing possesses all the li, in theory at least, each and every thing is innately endowed with perfect knowledge. But human beings are unique among things in that we alone have the ability to realize this knowledge completely by refining our Qi to a highly tenuous state that allows all the li to shine forth. Most important, this allows us to realize complete and perfect knowledge of moral patterns or principles. This endowment, something like a complete set of innate ideas, is our basic *xing* 性, or nature. There are two distinct aspects of nature: original nature and material nature. In relation to these, Zhu Xi has described two aspects or modes of mind: the mind of Dao or the way and the human mind.

Ivanhoe (2000) called Zhu Xi's theory a "recovery model" of self-cultivation, which can be viewed as having two primary aspects and a mediating state that unites them. The first aspect consists of "preserving the mind" by "honoring the virtuous nature." Meditation was the primary method for carrying out this half of the task of self-cultivation. It is notable that this method is in agreement with our account of the modern psychological approach. The goal of meditation was to gather together and calm one's mind, thereby protecting it from the obscuring effects of agitated emotions and desires. However, meditation alone could not advance one's grasp of principles. Sitting quietly could become an obstacle to moral progress if allowed to become an end unto itself. Therefore, to supplement this practice, Zhu Xi advocated a second component of self-cultivation that was "pursuing inquiry and study." This process involved studying the classical texts of Confucianism and investigating the various events and phenomena one encounters in the course of daily life. The purpose of this step was the effort to understand the ruling li behind the objects of investigation. Self-cultivation required uniting both tasks through the correct attitude of *jing* 敬 or "reverential attention," an attitude of calm perseverance, seriousness, and reflection in the midst of the ongoing activity of self-cultivation. This state of mind was to be maintained throughout self-cultivation, whether engaged in the task of preserving the mind or pursuing inquiry and study.

Zhu Xi relied heavily on his interpretation of Neo-Confucian texts in providing clear criteria to students of the way, and he arranged these texts into a systematic course of study. A student was first to study the *Four Books*: the *Daxue*, *Zhongyong*, *Mengzi*, and *Analects*. A study of the original *Five Classics* followed. The three stages of Zhu Xi's curriculum were thought to represent specific aspects of his program of learning. Theory was first. Paradigmatic cases was next. More general and extensive applications was last. His basic concept was the need to study extensively in order to fully appreciate the nuance and texture of a given moral principle. At the same time, throughout this extensive study, one must continually strive to discern and embrace the underlying and unifying principle at work.

Wang Yangming (1472–1529) represented another school of Neo-Confucianism that believed Zhu Xi had the right aim but the wrong approach. Wang insisted we must concentrate on our inherent intuition from the earliest moment. Failing this, we would never bring this capacity into full play. There were three aspects to Wang's general theory of moral self-cultivation. The first is the "unity of knowledge and action." Wang argued that knowledge of right action resulted in right action. Therefore, if someone failed to do the right thing, he or she simply lacked complete knowledge of the good. This aspect of Wang's theory contended that our selfish desires, feelings, and emotions often interfere with our rational knowledge of what is right and prevent us from acting accordingly. By extension, one cannot possess real knowledge, that is, knowledge that is self-activating in the same way as genuine virtues until one has actually acted in the appropriate way. For example, Wang believed we cannot know what courage is until we have acted courageously. By extension, whenever courage is called for, someone who really knows courage will spontaneously act in a courageous manner.

The second aspect of Wang's theory relates to sincerity, a trait Wang held to be in opposition to selfishness. According to Wang, people delude themselves and lose sight of their innate moral mind in the process. He promoted the maintenance of constant inner scrutiny over every thought and vigilance against the intrusion of selfishness. If we could sustain a state of uninterrupted inner vigilance, he believed our innate moral minds would recognize each and every selfish thought as it arose. Such awareness in itself had the power to eliminate the selfishness, provided that our self-knowledge was sincere.

The final aspect of Wang's view on self-cultivation is what Ivanhoe (2000) called the "existential flavor" of his teachings. Wang's beliefs about the innate moral mind and the need to pursue self cultivation in the affairs of one's own life led him to see moral choice as extremely context-sensitive and the moral life as an intensely personal and rather isolated affair. In Wang and his disciples, we see a strong commitment to and confidence in the power of the innate moral mind. They regarded this phenomenon as a faculty, akin to seeing or hearing, that allows the discernment of right and wrong in each situation we encounter. If one kept selfish thoughts from clouding the moral mirror of one's innate mind, it would spontaneously and accurately reflect the true dimensions and precise features of every situation that came before it.

Daoist Self-cultivation

To this point, we have focused on the views of Confucianism and the Chinese tradition regarding the ethical issues of self-cultivation. The naturalistic tradition of Daoism that has, in complement with Confucianism, shaped Chinese life for more than two thousand years offers a different perspective. With its emphasis on individual freedom and spontaneity, *laissez-faire* government and social primitivism, mystical experience, and techniques of self-transformation, the Daoist heritage represents the antithesis to Confucian concerns with individual moral duties, community standards and governmental responsibilities in many ways. Daoism encompasses both the Daoist philosophical tradition associated with Laozi and Zhuangzi, which was established during the Warring States Period (481–221 BC), and a religious tradition that arrived in the second century with the Late Han dynasty, which was identified by organized doctrine, formalized cultic activity, and institutional leadership. We shall limit the present discussion to the philosophical aspect of the Daoist teaching.

The text central to all expressions of Daoist spirit is the *Daodejing*, a classic of a scant five thousand Chinese characters, dealing with topics ranging from the origin of the universe to the liberty of the individual. The Daoist notions of humanity and the universe have been treated in some detail previously. To recapitulate, Dao is the way of nature, or the path, the way in which all things happen, including both advance and decline, growth and decay, activity and passivity, and motion and rest. It is the law of change, the sum total of all that changes. It is the space-time continuum of beings that change and the beings themselves. De is the manifestation of the Dao within all things. Thus, to possess the fullness of De means to be in perfect harmony with one's original nature. To help manifest our De, Laozi gave us his "three treasures" that assist in developing our perception of the unity of life and cultivating a way of being that is harmonious with the Dao. The first treasure is compassion, the second is frugality or balance, and the third is humility, daring not to be ahead of others.

To highlight a contrast, in Confucianism, action begins in balance, but with an emphasis on the active principle (ethics and rituals) that originates from heaven. Action is thus represented as yang. In Daoism, action also begins in balance, but with an emphasis on the receptive on earth. It is passive. Action is yin. The Daoists stress noninterference because too much activity interferes with the creative process. Too much planning kills spontaneity. Too much unnatural interference from elements, such as moral principles, jeopardize both nonhuman and human nature. Water is used to signify Dao because water always seeks the path of least resistance. Water does not compete, but it spiders out, finds the easiest path, and follows it. But there is nothing stronger. Water can carve through rock and steel, cut deeply through canyons, and overcome any resistance if given no other path around, under, or over an obstacle. It does this simply by obeying the natural laws of hydrodynamics and gravity.

According to Zhuangzi (fourth century BC), an individual in harmony with the Dao comprehends the course of nature's constant change and fears not the rhythm of life and death. By following practices such as fasting the mind, embracing the opposites, and becoming receptive, Daoists entreat us to surrender to the larger order of the universe in quest of the goal of real self-actualization and self-realization. Confucianism and Daoism both require an understanding of one's nature relative to one's context and a restructuring of one's values to accommodate the natural order. In both traditions, ego-self and human desires are the source of our disharmony with nature, and they must be minimized through education and self-cultivation. The Chinese notion of education is to learn to be human, which is to engage oneself in a ceaseless, unending process of creative self-transformation, both as a communal act and response to nature. The purpose of learning is always understood as being for the sake of the self, but the self is never an isolated individual. It is rather a center point of relationships, which is the topic of the next two chapters.

CHAPTER FIVE

The Individual and the Family

By applying the focus-field model, a self-cultivated individual exerts high moral influence on others and vice versa. Obviously, the strongest influence one can exert is upon one's immediate family. Here, we begin our examination of the individual in context.

Section One:
Familial Relationships, Western and Chinese

Western Family

The Bible holds that, to have a right relationship with one another, we must live in obedience to God's ordained principles. The Word teaches us these specific principles, ordained by God with knowledge of our capability and needs, to bring love and harmony to the family. These rules are understood to be the way to joy, happiness, peace, love, and a rich life. The Christian ethic not only tells of the wife's obligation to the husband. It tells us of the husband's obligation to the wife. It not only lists the child's obligation to the parent. It lists the parent's obligation to the child as well. This reciprocity differs from the ethics of the Greek philosophies, Roman culture, and even traditional Jewish culture. All of which lack an emphasis on reciprocal obligations between members of a family.

Christians also believe in interplay of submission and love, pointing to God's rule that the husband be the head of the house and the wife should submit to the husband. At the same time, there is one place in the Scriptures where the wife led the husband—in the Garden of Eden. And women have been blamed ever since for humanity's banishment from the Garden.

Naturally, an order is involved in these relationships of love and submission. In the traditional Christian order, the husband submits unto Christ, even as Christ willingly submitted himself unto the Father. Because the husband submits to Christ and the wife submits to the husband, the wife therefore submits to Christ through the husband. Similarly, under the law of God, children were commanded to honor their parents, showing respect and obedience. Parents, in turn, must bring up their children in the discipline and admonition of the Lord. These Christian ethics have dominated the Western world for a long time. Thus, it can be argued that Western family ethics are often associated with religion and, by extension, the supernatural.

In the liberal tradition of the modern West, the family is no longer the basic building block of society. The individual has instead assumed this role. Family is usually seen as a part of a private sphere wherein religion has little part to play, except in families united by agreement to adhere to ethics based in Christian doctrine. The state does not interfere with the family, except in the case of family members acting violently toward one another or harming their dependents. By the same token, families, as units of a community, generally do not interfere with affairs of the state. Civil society is therefore the proper arena for citizens to interact within a democratic state, as opposed to doing so from within natural society, which primarily consists of the family.

A healthy civil society is one consisting of many widely varied groups of free-willed individuals with balance constantly shifting between these multiple interest groups, providing society with both freedom and stability. Emphasis is placed on the rights of the individual in the society. The focus on individuality in modern Western culture results from the domination of the liberal ideal relating the modern version of civil society to the liberation of individuals from rigid primordial loyalties, such as the feudal family system reinforced by dogmatic religious institutions. The modern family is thus a voluntary association based on a contract between consenting adults, who may rescind the contract when it is no longer in their mutual self-interest. Family ethics are normally not an issue because the individual has freedom to depart an inefficacious situation. This is simply a sketch. Contemporary considerations on the individual, family, community, and state will be presented in greater detail subsequently.

Chinese Family

In contrast to the ethics predominant in Western societies, religion has played only a small part in the ethical tradition of the Chinese. Religious beliefs contribute to the ethical principles of the Chinese people mainly in their belief in karmic retribution and reward or punishment of behavior by the supernatural (Overmyer 2003). The traditional Chinese family, as concisely described by David Jordan (2003), was a patrilineal, patriarchal, prescriptively virilocal kinship group, sharing a common household budget and normatively extended in form.

Some definitions may be helpful here. Patrilineal societies determine descent through the male line. Thus, one inherited family membership from one's father. China was extremely patrilineal in that a woman was quite intentionally removed from the family of her birth and affiliated instead with her husband's family, a transition always clearly symbolized in local marriage customs. Patriarchal families are hierarchically organized with the prime institutionalized authority being vested in the most senior male. This was a tradition dating back in China more than three thousand years. However, in practice, the system was not totally rigid throughout history. Virilocal societies are those in which there is a strongly held preference and expectation that a newly married couple should live with the groom's family. This preference was indeed commonly prescribed in China. The kinship groups in China were formed of family members who were related genealogically, either through common ancestry or marriage. They had known boundaries and shared activities or resources with each other while excluding outsiders. The possessions, income, and expenses of all family members were pooled. Decisions about resource distribution were the legitimate business of all family members, although decisions were ultimately made via the patriarchal authority structure of the family.

The Chinese word for family, *jia* 家, uses the same character as home, school, or lineage, suggests the family was central to Chinese philosophical thinking about life, and actually serves as a model for understanding the nature of reality itself. Family, rather than the individual, is the core unit of traditional Chinese society. Family solidarity is the most important goal. It is not an exaggeration to say that, in the Chinese world, all relationships are familial. Chinese culture is often described as "the culture of filial morality" because the family is the center of Chinese culture and philosophy. For the Chinese, the family is the most important aspect of a person's life, the foundation of one's identity, one's morality, and the source of the meaning of life. Individuals can be understood as the centers of webs of relationships with the webs themselves being as real and important as any single person, such as in our focus-field model.

The ideal Confucian five relations, namely between ruler/subject, parent/child, husband/wife, older/younger sibling, and between friends, are considered the basis of all social connections between persons. Sometimes, the additional relationship of teacher/student is included to make six. At least half of these relations are found within the family, a testament to the importance of family in China. Yet a relation to God is not considered here because Confucius felt one should not deal with God or any supernatural until one first learns to deal with human beings on earth. Ironically, there are, nevertheless, distinct similarities between Confucian and Christian teachings. The focus-field model described in the third section of chapter four provides a model for this interpretation. In an ideal situation, Confucian teaching holds that the superior member of each of the relationships (ruler, parent, husband, older brother, older friend, or teacher) has the duty of benevolence and the role of provision of guidance and loving care for the subordinate member (subject, child, wife, and so forth). The subordinate member, in turn, has the duty to obey and reciprocate with, not only support, but also love and respect.

The relationship with the utmost significance in Chinese tradition is that of parent/child. This relationship is the most necessary part of the Chinese social structure, and it has implications relevant to the entire human context because family is ultimately the model for the empire. Ideally, the father, as the head of the family and husband, is responsible for setting the moral standard for the whole family through his own strong moral suasion cultivated via Confucian or other virtues. The father's teachings and actions become a model for other family members to aspire to and emulate. In terms of the focus-field model, focus, characterized by a strong moral force, radiates a powerful field of influence. Of course, the morality of the family can easily be compromised if the father and other members fail. An uncultivated father can easily turn into a tyrant, which bodes ill for the rest of the family.

The wife's role in the family is also essential, both to her husband and her children and in private and in public. Her role actually serves as a model for the emperor, whose success as a leader depends, not only on his own virtue, but also on his authority in the ruling family and his responsiveness to the needs of his people in much the same way that a woman must respond to the needs of her family. Chinese culture envisions the wise and virtuous woman empowering her husband and her children for social leadership. From which, the family and state will benefit. With the support of his mother, the eldest son, being heir apparent to the father as a leader, has an important role to play. The son must also set a high moral standard for his brothers and sisters to follow.

Giskin and Walsh quoted Roger Ames in summarizing the importance of the family in Chinese culture:

> All of the institutions of community, from religion to education to polity, are constructed around and function on the model of the family. Government, for better and for worse, has been largely patriarchal, appealing mostly to those virtues which, when adequately cultivated,

make families work: credibility and trust, obligation and deference, contribution and privilege. (2001)

Filial Piety

Of all ancient virtues in China, *xiao* 孝, or filial piety, the almost-religious respect that children owe to their parents, their grandparents, and the aged, is one of the most important. Xiao often determines how one is judged by society at large, not only by other members of the family.

The Classic of Filial Piety teaches, "Filial piety is the unchanging truth of Heaven, the unfailing equity of Earth, the universal practice of man," and "It is filial piety which forms the root of all virtues, and with it all enlightening studies come into existence."

Chinese people believe that human love toward one's parents is innate, as children all love the parents who carried them in their arms.

The Confucian virtues of filial piety and benevolence, ren, are closely related, forming the foundation of all benevolent actions. In the case of little children, the inherent love and respect toward parents is the natural starting point of ren. In order to protect the durability and expansion of benevolence, cultivation of filial piety is indispensable. In the complicated relations among humans, filial piety forms the primary and most fundamental unit of all good and moral conduct, the fountainhead for universal love and compassion toward others. Thus, genuine and comprehensive love toward one's own parents teaches Chinese people to be benevolent to all living creatures, affectionate toward humankind as a whole, loyal to their country, successful in the duties of a free citizen, faithful in keeping obligations, righteous in action, peaceful in behavior, and just in all dealings. Each of these eight virtues—and many others—emanate from filial piety. Filial piety, xiao and ren, as with most important virtues, must be genuine, respectful, spontaneous, and transcend economic circumstances. Poor children often practice filial piety better than rich children because the latter may be preoccupied with their own materialistic pursuits.

An example of filial piety in practice could be seen during the Han dynasty when governmental officers were recruited to the court from among filial sons highly recommended by the local communities. This system was the prototype of the renowned merit-based bureaucratic system of the later dynasties when governmental officers were recruited, placed, and evaluated for advancement through rational, merit-oriented techniques of scholastic examinations.

In practice, many high ideals such as those described previously are extremely difficult to realize except in the case of a small minority who are very well self-cultivated. In ancient China, society was so close-knit that enormous social pressure was exerted on all members of society to conform to these norms so harmony within the family could at least be attained, even if only superficially. In addition, obedience to the precepts of the five relations was contingent on the superior member actually observing his duty to be benevolent and caring. The highest Confucian obedience was to do what was right. As a result, true obedience to a ruler, parent, or husband might involve refusing to obey any orders to do that which is wrong, which would eventually be regretted. The rule of the golden mean applies here in the quest for harmony. All Confucian virtues, such as ren, yi, li, zhi, or xiao, must not be dogmatic doctrines. Rather, they are guiding principles that depends heavily on the specific situation. This is why Confucians never attempt to clearly define such virtues. Instead, they use examples and metaphors to characterize them. In *Analects*, Confucius was asked about ren 104 times and, for this very reason, supplied a different answer each time.

The almost-religious respect accorded to elders in China extended even beyond death. Ancestor worship is an extension of filial piety, one of the most important and perhaps unique traditions of the Chinese. It is traceable all the way back to Neolithic times. Ancestor worship provided all the essentials of a religion for the Chinese, providing spiritual comfort and support for members of the family. In addition, it served as a method of repayment. Yu-wei Hsieh stated:

> The main sentiment of Chinese ancestor-worship lay in commemoration of one's origin—the fountain of his life—and in repaying the debt that he owes to his ancestors … Confucian ancestral worship did not conceal the desire for blessings from some supernatural force or forces, on the one hand, and the desire to avoid calamity, on the other. When facing some critical moment—for example, prior to waging war or making important decisions on state affairs—ancient Chinese emperors or kings appealed to their ancestors for oracular revelations and blessings. (Moore 1968)

Later, the Chinese geomancy practiced by the common people as another form of ancestral worship laid even more emphasis upon the seeking of blessings from the supernatural power through the intermediary grace of ancestors, who, in certain respects, were looked upon as identical to Buddhist or Daoist deities. The doctrine of filial piety played an even greater role in the search for emotional consolation through ancestral worship. Because human beings cannot avoid death, practically all religions have been built upon the sentiment that, even after passing into the unknown world, some supernatural force will take care of the human soul with deserved reward or punishment. However, if there is another way to dispose of the soul without the need of the help of such abstract faith, there is no need to seek help from any religious sect. Thus, ancestor worship, together with a belief in karmic retribution and reward or punishment of behavior by the supernatural, fulfilled both the spiritual and the psychological needs of the ancient Chinese.

The Chinese conception of generations existing along a space-time continuum also manifests itself in filial piety. To Confucians, offspring represent perpetuity of lineage. The ancestors' lives are consequently perceived as immortal. Through reproduction, one passes along one's family name, one's blood, and, hence, life to later generations. Therefore, anyone who severed the flow of continuity would be condemned as having committed the gravest sin of being unfilial.

To preserve this crucial existence, a filially pious son is cautioned to take good care of his body and his mental and moral attainments.

The Classic of Filial Piety reminds its readers, "The body with its limbs and hair and skin comes to a person from father and mother, and it is on no account to be spoiled or injured."

Thus, looking after oneself and one's children becomes a form of repayment to one's parents. This cycle contrasts sharply with the Christian morality founded in the notion that "God makes Man." We, therefore, live to please God.

Unsurprisingly, in ancient China, the lineage shrines dedicated to ancestor worship were always the clan's community center where the records of every birth, death, and significant achievement of clan members were kept. Even today, the genealogy of names and records of tens of generations can still be found in some villages, especially in the cases of families with high prestige, such as those of the families of Confucius or Mencius. These records claim the present head of the descendents of Confucius represent the seventy-fourth generation of that family.

Extended Family

Kin relations have been the nucleus of all social and political organization in China, predating the beginning of written history in 1612 BC. The family hearth has defined the basic dynamics of Chinese society up to the present day. The ideal family was a large group, primarily held together by filial piety and its expression through the religious sanctioning of ancestor worship, making the family an indefinitely perpetuated corporation whose living members were accountable both to forebears and descendants. In addition, the socioeconomics deriving from the fact that the family head controlled and was answerable for the activities of all family members also served to bind the family together. The extended family consisted of a male head, his immediate family, and the families of all his male descendants with several generations living together in a cooperative household. When the family head died and his property was divided, his sons became the heads of their own extended families. Thus the nuclear family, that is, a married couple and their children, were ideally part of a larger living and working unit, the extended family. Moreover, closely related extended families considered themselves related and obligated to all other clans sharing the same surname, who were thought to constitute a common descent group.

Exogamy was practiced within the patrilineal lineage. A man might marry a first cousin on his mother's side because she bore a different surname, but he could not marry a woman of the same surname, even if the two families had lived at opposite ends of the country for centuries and had no traceable blood relationship. Indeed, such distinct differentiation between the father's side and the mother's side extends to the use of different titles for grandparents, uncles, aunts, and even cousins from maternal and paternal sides. The relation between any two members of the extended family is well-defined. Although increasing social complexity diluted blood bonds in later times, society continued to use real and fictitious kinship as fundamental building blocks for networking purposes. Each kinship role came with elaborate rules and expectations. By acting out these roles, individuals and families defined their identities and created opportunities for self-actualization and self-realization. This form of the family corporation persists up to the present and is commonly found in Hong Kong, Taiwan, the Chinese mainland, and countries of Chinese cultural heritage such as Singapore, Korea, and Vietnam.

> In an article on ethics and the family entitled "China/West," Richard Madsen wrote:
> In classical Chinese, there are no words that correspond to Western terms of "civil society." There is not even a word for "society" in the modern sense, as a realm of life institutionally differentiated from economy and polity ... For the Western liberal, even the family in a truly modern society should become like a voluntary association, whose members have easy exit and the ability to affiliate or not if they so please. For the Confucian, even voluntary associations, like learned societies or guilds, should be like families—their members should be bound by loyalties that make exit difficult. In the Confucian perspective, then, freedom does not consist of choosing which group one will belong to. It consists in creatively contextualizing those commitments which fate has assigned. It involves ever deeper understanding of the meaning of one's role as father, son, husband, wife, sibling, friend, subject, so that

one can flexibly reconcile them with all of the other roles one must play in a world that is complex and changing, but in the end capable of achieving a harmonious integration among its major institutions. (Pohl and Muller 2002)

Madsen's description highlighted the distinction between Western and Chinese conceptions as described by Z. S. Bai (2000)—the difference and the subsequent reconciliation between a society of rights versus a society of responsibilities and obligations.

Section Two:
Feminine Roles in Traditional China

The identities and roles of women in both traditional and contemporary China have been topics of meaningful research interest for some time, particularly in the West. The stereotypical image of the Chinese woman is docile, submissive, subservient, or mysterious. Seeking a more objective point of view, Robin Wang (2003) surveyed and explored Chinese perspectives on women and gender, cosmology and human nature, and women's social roles and virtue. Wang used an anthology of fifty-four Chinese texts forming the earliest writings of women from the Pre-Qin period (1200 BC) through the Song dynasty (AD 1279). She found that the images of women in China have changed throughout history.

By studying the ancient texts, Wang concluded that traditional images of women, especially pre-Ming-Qing, were indeed different from the stereotype. According to Wang, the cosmological identity of women is not simply an important fact defining her physical appearance or psychological dispositions, any more than it is for man. Her cosmological identity, as is also true for man, is first of all her Dao, the way by which she is to achieve her own distinctive fulfillment as a human being. Chinese women's social roles as daughter, wife, and mother are the embodiment of their Dao. Each role has its own specific virtues. The task of self-cultivation proceeds differently in each of these clusters of relationships. Through the practice of self-cultivation, women, like men, make valuable contributions to human life and society. The cosmic vision thus entails a systematic and conceptual negation of the kind of dualistic thinking that has warranted misogynistic prejudice, as if woman were merely an incomplete man and, hence, his biological and social inferior in most important respects. In the context of Chinese conceptual understanding, woman's cosmological identity guarantees that women are equal and complementary to men—at least at the metaphysical level.

The Role of a Woman

One primal pattern is woman as mother. According to Wang, because the Dao, to the extent that it can be named, is fittingly named "Mother," motherhood is seen as a privileged way of following the Dao. The second primal pattern is woman as wife. Marriage is the appropriate institution in which the complementary of yin and yang, woman and man, is lived out. The third primal pattern is woman as daughter. Within the family, a woman cultivates the central virtue of filial piety out of respect for her parents and ancestors and in preparation for her entry into her husband's family. Taken together, these three roles are the source of woman's power through which she achieves her own metaphysical dignity.

Apart from metaphysical considerations, the primary Chinese texts that Wang presented celebrate different female virtues. They show the way in which women contribute to the overall harmony of the family and to society as a whole through the family. There is no distinction among spiritual, moral, intellectual, emotional, or aesthetic concerns. All are seamlessly woven into a single fabric, one in which there is no room for a patronizing dichotomy between women's beautiful virtues and the noble virtues reserved for men. While the ensemble of women's virtues remains socially significant, women and men follow the path toward self-cultivation in their own unique way.

Implicit in all three roles (mother, wife, and daughter), Wang discerned another pattern, that is, the aesthetic image of woman as lover, the inexhaustible source of artistic inspiration. In Chinese writing, women are not identified with lust or blamed as the root of evil in the world. In diverse ways, women were admired as aesthetic objects and cherished for their intrinsic beauty, which was honored and cultivated as an expression of virtue. Thus, women's beauty ultimately resides in virtue, but beauty itself is a sign of virtue. Beauty and goodness, explains the Dao, are intertwined and complementary. Beauty is simply an externalization of a woman's inner goodness.

Roles through Time

When one talks about the roles of a traditional Chinese woman, one must indicate clearly which period of Chinese history is under examination. Prehistoric Chinese legends did not discriminate against women. For example, the highest goddess, Hsi Huang Mu 西 王 母, or Queen Mother of the West, was portrayed as compassionate and powerful at the same time. Another goddess, Nu Wa 女 媧, was credited with repairing a hole in the heavenly sky, allowing the present universe to be formed. Some of the earliest poetry quoted by Hanson (2000) in

The Book of Songs, Shijing, and dating to 1000 BC, was well-known for its free and vivid description of the expression of love and affection given and received by both sexes. Some of the songs give full voice to the emotions of women, expressing their joy in dating and their sadness in an unhappy or unfaithful marriage. There are hints that girls may engage in premarital sex, although at their own risk.

Another story concerning a powerful woman among the ancients is detailed in Hansen's description of the discovery of oracle bone inscriptions at the tomb of Lady Hao 侯 夫 人 at Anyang, Henan Province. Lady Hao lived sometime around 1200 BC and was one of sixty-four consorts of the Shang king known as Wu Ding. Inscriptions reveal she led her own armies into enemy states, took captives from other tribes, possessed her own lands outside the capital, and conducted certain sacrifices, including those of captives. According to Hansen, this formidable woman is the first person among those mentioned in the oracle bones whose remains have been positively identified. Lady Hao's tomb contained, among other items, three ivory carvings, close to five hundred bone hairpins, more than five hundred jade objects, and nearly seven thousand cowry shells, which were used as money. Sixteen corpses, including those of men, women, and children, were buried in different places in her grave. A spectacular bronze collection included five large and eighteen small bronze bells, more than two hundred bronze ritual vessels, and over one hundred and thirty bronze weapons. Lady Hao herself may have used some in battle. Clearly, proscriptive roles did not limit her activities.

In traditional Daoism, women were able to seek spiritual fulfillment beyond their family duties. Some joined convents. Others gathered with men to discuss philosophy and religion. A few became Daoist adepts. After Buddhism was introduced to China, such traditions were continued, and women were given some new areas of empowerment. Women went on pilgrimages to Buddhist temples, retreated to nunneries, sometimes gave public lectures, and became lead priests. Wu Zetian (Tang dynasty, 625–705) achieved even greater success, becoming the only female emperor in Chinese history. With her reign, Chinese Buddhism reached its height. She promoted the religion and even justified her rule by claiming she was the reincarnation of a female Buddhist saint. During her reign and throughout the early to mid-Tang period, women enjoyed relatively high status and freedom. Tang arts often depict women on horseback and as administrators, dancers, and musicians, all indicating the openness and freedom of Tang culture. The years of the Tang dynasty were also one of the periods in which China was the most open to foreign cultural influences.

According to a Chinese book 古 道 俠 風 by Pang Wai 彭 衛 (1999), women living in the Han dynasty (206 BC–AD 220), however, were even freer than those of the Tang. Both Han men and women loved singing and dancing. These activities were available for both rich and poor, regardless of social status. As illustration of his argument, Pang documented many artifacts and paintings from archaeological finds and from ancient literature, which all demonstrate sexual and social freedom among both Han men and women. His research also found the Han people emotional, crying freely for sadness and joy, possessing a strong sense of right and wrong, and having an inclination to exact vengeance to right wrongs. Many stories substantiate Pang's finding. Most Chinese people know the love story of Sima Xiangru 司馬相如 and Zhuo Wanjun 卓文君 in which the widowed Wanjun was first touched and impressed by Xiangru's *qin* music and his literary ability and ultimately paired with him in defiance of Confucian ethics. There is no moral condemnation in the telling of this story. In fact, it is a beloved tale. These findings do not suggest that the Han people were inadequate Confucians. For example, female historian班昭 Ban Zhao, also of the Han dynasty, wrote *Lessons for Girls* 素女經, a prescriptive advice manual specifying proper behaviors and instructing women to defer to others, as would a true Confucian woman. Indeed, in the Han dynasty, Confucianism became the state orthodoxy for the Chinese court. Despite this, it is fair to conclude that women enjoyed reasonably high status and freedom in the early imperial period of the Han, Tang, and even the earlier Song dynasties.

During the Northern Song (960–1127) dynasty, while men prepared for examinations, women often took on the role of breadwinner in order to "help their husbands and educate their sons, some peddling medicine, some running little restaurants" (Tsai 2000). According to Tsai, the Northern Song was a relatively liberal age. It was not until the Southern Song (1127–1279) that the conservative orthodoxies of Neo-Confucianism really took hold. During the Northern Song, for example, women were still allowed to remarry, and they had the right to inherit property. When the statesman Fan Chongyan was a child, his surname was changed to Zhu upon the remarriage of his mother. He didn't change it back to Fan until he became prominent in later life. When the son of the reformer Wang Anshi died young, Wang allowed his daughter-in-law to marry another man.

Motherhood was the most powerful social role available to the majority of women in the early imperial period. According to Bret Hinsch (2002), the mother's monopoly over procreation was a major source of female power, pride, and identity within the family. Ancient poetry and art extravagantly celebrated the life-giving ability of the woman. While Christians believe God created humankind, the Chinese emphasize we are born of our parents. Given the terrifying dangers of childbirth in ancient times, it is not surprising that praise of maternal bravery, kindness, and compassion frequently elevated the ideal mother to the level of sainthood.

The mother plays numerous demanding roles, including providing love and care for her children, love, and support for her husband. As a daughter-in-law, she served the elders of her husband's family. Tragedies have resulted throughout Chinese history when the self-interests of a couple or daughter-in-law conflict with those of their parents or mother-in-law. In such cases, Confucian ethics and their focus on the virtue of filial piety demand the younger generation sacrifice his or her own interests voluntarily and spontaneously. The offspring's unconditional love and deference is not simply natural or normal. It is a social obligation, as one must love one's mother as repayment for her sacrifices. Family tensions and tragedies also surface when the husband is absent due to travel, sickness, or death. The mother then becomes the head of the family. If she has experienced a traumatic subjugation in the family, her role could become an excuse for tyranny of her own, which would ultimately perpetuate a harmful cycle when her son brought home a wife.

Nevertheless, motherhood is a method of self-actualization for women in Chinese society. Glorification of motherhood proliferates in Chinese literature throughout history. Extremely intense mother-child bonds seem to have been an ideal in traditional China, shaping both personal psychology and group morals. The importance of reciprocity in the bond between mother and child continues to influence present-day Chinese morality. These unique social conditions form a psychology within the individual that differs significantly from that described by Freud and other Western psychologists. When replicated throughout Chinese society, this characteristic individual psychology is manifested in the collective mentality underlying major social roles. It is still identifiable even today.

Most textbook accounts report a decline in the status of Chinese women around the eleventh century in the late Song, Ming, and Qing dynasties, signaled by the advent of foot binding, increases in widow chastity and suicide, and the selling of unwanted daughters. Many writers attribute this decline to the reinterpretation of Confucian teaching in a set of tenets called Neo-Confucianism, augmented by ideas of wifely fidelity and husband worship that the Mongols imposed at that time.

From the sixteenth century onward, China began to experience important social and economic changes, including rapid economic expansion, population growth, urbanization, expansion of printing and literacy, and increased social mobility. These changes significantly impacted women's issues. Recently, many Western scholars have turned their attention to these Chinese women and the gender-related issues of this late imperial period. Since 1986, Paul Ropp (1994) has reviewed highlights of this rapidly expanding field and discussed many topics, including the evolution of kinship patterns and marriage institutions, women as commodities, widow chastity and suicide, women in religion, women in historical and philosophical discourse, and women's cultural opportunities, literacy, and involvement in publishing. He asserted that, despite the relatively small size of Chinese studies in the West, there has been too little communication in the China field between scholars of the late imperial era and the modern and contemporary periods. Western specialists in twentieth-century China easily accept the anti-traditional biases of twentieth-century Chinese scholars and/or the somewhat different, but no less, real anti-traditional biases of our own society. As a result, they tend to condemn Confucianism and traditional society with caricatures that miss much of the complexity and ambiguity of the past. As a result, Chinese women are too easily seen as passive victims of the traditional society. Their participation in the system's perpetuation is too easily dismissed as a result of false consciousness and/or powerlessness. The work discussed by Ropp goes far to undermine such simplistic views, but it has yet to exert a strong influence on most studies of twentieth-century China.

Ropp's review ranges broadly with deep insight on historical women topics and concludes with a recommendation for further research. His material is worthwhile reading, but it is too detailed for our purposes here. Yet we mention this work because we feel strongly that contemporary historians, both inside and outside China, should critically review the stance on traditional Chinese issues, particularly gender-related issues that the writers of the May 4th Movement cultivated. The depth and breadth of ancient Chinese culture is due far more credit than the intellectuals of the Movement give. It is time to put things back into proper perspective.

CHAPTER SIX

Individual, Society, and State

We continue our exploration expanding outwards from the individual to examine the individual's role in their society and state. This examination begins with a modern theory of particular relevance to the Western context.

Section One:
On Moral and Social Development

Jean Piaget is among the earliest psychologists whose work remains directly relevant to contemporary theories of moral development. In his early writing, Piaget focused specifically on the moral lives of children. By studying the way children play games, he sought to learn more about children's beliefs about right and wrong. Based on observations of children's application of rules while playing, Piaget determined that morality could also be considered a developmental process. This contemporary cognitive psychological model of moral and social development is quite different from certain moral relativist, value-neutral theories that some postmodernists endorse. This cognitive model is equally descriptive of the social development of an individual, a society, and a state. It is grounded in pure human terms without appeals to tradition, metaphysics, or religion.

Moral Development

Children begin in a heteronomous stage of moral reasoning, characterized by a strict adherence to rules and duties and obedience to authority. At this stage, children are unable to reconcile their own view of things with the perspective of someone else. This stage is also associated with a unidirectional view of rules and power affiliated with heteronomous moral thought and various forms of moral realism. The objective responsibility of moral realism is characterized by valuing the letter of the law above the purpose of the law. The second major contributor to heteronomous moral thinking in young children is their relative social relationship with adults. In the natural authority relationship between adults and children, power is handed down from above. The relative powerlessness of young children, coupled with childhood egocentrism, feeds into an heteronomous moral orientation.

Through interactions with other children during play, children develop toward a second stage of an autonomous moral reasoning, characterized by the ability to consider rules critically and selectively apply those rules based on a goal of mutual respect and cooperation. The ability to act from a sense of reciprocity and mutual respect is associated with a shift in the child's cognitive structure from egocentrism to perspective-taking. Piaget viewed moral development to be the result of interpersonal interactions through which individuals achieve a mutually agreed-upon resolution. This autonomous view of morality as fairness is more efficacious and leads to more consistent behavior than the heteronomous orientation that younger children hold.

Lawrence Kohlberg modified and elaborated Piaget's work by proposing that children form ways of thinking through their experiences, which includes understanding of moral concepts such as justice, rights, equality, and human welfare. On the basis of his research, Kohlberg identified six stages of moral reasoning that he grouped into three primary levels. In 2004, Mary Elizabeth Murray of the University of Illinois at Chicago summarized them in three levels where each level represented a fundamental shift in the social-moral perspective of the individual.

At the first level, the preconventional level, a concrete, individual perspective characterizes a person's moral judgments. Within this level, children focus on avoiding breaking rules that are backed by punishment. It is obedience for their own sake and avoiding the physical consequences of an action to persons and property. As in Piaget's framework, egocentrism and the inability to consider the perspectives of others characterize the reasoning of the first stage.

At the second stage, there is the early emergence of moral reciprocity. Its orientation focuses on the instrumental, pragmatic value of an action. Reciprocity is of the form, "you scratch my back, and I'll scratch yours." The golden rule becomes, "If someone hits you, you hit them back." At this stage, one follows the rules only when it benefits his or her immediate interests. What is right is what is fair in the sense of an equal exchange, deal, or agreement. At the second stage, there is an understanding that everybody has his or her own interests to pursue. These sometimes conflict, so what is right becomes relative in the concrete, individualist sense.

At the third stage, the conventional level of reasoning, individuals have a basic understanding of conventional morality and reason with an understanding that norms and conventions are necessary to uphold society. They tend to be self-identified with these rules and uphold them consistently, viewing morality as acting in accordance with what society defines as right. Within this level, individuals are aware of shared feelings, agreements, and expectations that take priority over individual interests. Persons at this stage define what is right in terms of what is expected by people close to one's self and in terms of the stereotypic roles that define being good, for example, a good brother, mother, or teacher. Being good means keeping mutual relationships, such as trust, loyalty, respect, and gratitude. The perspective is that of the local community or family. There is not as yet a consideration of the generalized social system.

The fourth stage marks the shift from defining what is right in terms of local norms and role expectations to defining right in terms of the laws and norms that the larger social system established. This is the member of society perspective in which one is moral by fulfilling the actual duties defining one's social responsibilities. Except in extreme cases in which the law comes into conflict with other prescribed social duties, one must obey the law. Obeying the law is seen as necessary in order to maintain the system of laws that protect everyone.

Finally, reasoning based on principles, using a prior to society perspective, characterize the post-conventional level. These individuals reason based on the principles that underlie rules and norms, but they reject a uniform application of a rule or norm. While two stages have been presented within the theory, only one, the fifth stage, has received substantial empirical support. The sixth stage remains as a theoretical endpoint that rationally follows from the preceding five stages. Essentially, this last level of moral judgment entails reasoning rooted in the ethical fairness principles from which moral laws would be devised. Laws are evaluated in terms of their coherence with basic principles of fairness rather than upheld simply on the basis of their place within an existing social order. Thus, there is an understanding that elements of morality, such as regard for life and human welfare, transcend particular cultures and societies. They are to be upheld, irrespective of other conventions or normative obligations. Findings from longitudinal and cross-cultural research have empirically supported all of the stages (Power et al. 1989).

Moral Education

Turning to the topic of moral education, Murray summarized the work of Kohlberg:

Kohlberg rejected the focus on values and virtues, not only due to the lack of consensus on what virtues are to be taught, but also because of the complex nature of practicing such virtues. For example, people often make different decisions yet hold the same basic moral values. Kohlberg believed a better approach to affecting moral behavior should focus on stages of moral development. These stages are critical, as they consider the way a person organizes their understanding of virtues, rules, and norms, and integrate these into a moral choice. (Power, Higgins, and Kohlberg 1989)

In addition, Kohlberg rejected the relativist viewpoint in favor of the view that certain principles of justice and fairness represent the pinnacle of moral maturity. He discovered that these basic moral principles are found in different cultures and subcultures around the world (Kohlberg and Turiel 1971).

The goal of moral education is to encourage individuals to develop to the next stage of moral reasoning. Initial educational efforts employing Kohlberg's theory were grounded in basic Piagetian assumptions of cognitive development. In this model, development is not merely the result of gaining more knowledge. Rather, it consists of a sequence of qualitative changes in the way an individual thinks. Within any stage of development, thought is organized according to the constraints of that stage. An individual then interacts with the environment according to his or her basic understanding of the environment. However, the child will eventually encounter information that does not fit into his or her view, forcing the child to adjust his or her view to accommodate this new information. This process is called equilibration. Through equilibration, that development occurs. Early moral development approaches to education sought to force students to ponder contradiction inherent to their present level of moral reasoning.

While Kohlberg appreciated the importance and value of such moral dilemma discussion, from very early on, he held that moral education required more than individual reflection. It also needed to include experiences for students to operate as moral agents within a community. In this regard, Kohlberg reconciled some of the differences in orientation that existed between the theories of moral growth that Piaget and Durkheim held. In order to provide students with an optimal context within which to grow morally, Kohlberg and his colleagues developed the just community schools approach toward promoting moral development (Power, Higgins, and Kohlberg 1989). The basic premise of these schools is to enhance students' moral development by offering them the chance to participate in a democratic community. Here, democracy refers to more than simply casting a vote. It entails full participation of community members in arriving at consensual rather than the majority rules version of decision-making. It is believed that, by placing the responsibility of determining and enforcing rules on students, they will take prosocial behavior more seriously. However, this is not to say that a just community school simply leaves students to their own devices. Teachers play a crucial leadership role in these discussions, promoting rules and norms that have a concern for justice and community and, ultimately, enforcing the rules. This role is not an easy one because teachers must listen closely and understand a student's reasoning in order to help the student to the next level of reasoning. This requires a delicate balance between letting the students make decisions and advocating in a way that shows them the limits in their reasoning. A primary advantage to the just community approach is its effectiveness in affecting students' actions, not just their reasoning. Students are, in effect, expected to practice what they preach by following the rules determined in community meetings.

Ethico-political Order

Indeed, if we substitute "member of society" for "student," "leader" for "teacher," and "state" for "community" in this school model, we then have a functioning participatory democracy with positive moral values and norms, based on the humanitarian precepts of reciprocity, justice, fairness, rights, equality, and other social virtues. Ideally, this system incorporates ethico-political orders, as described in Tan (2003). Ethics has a critical role in politics and vice versa. Ethics answers the question, "How should one live?" Politics answers the question, "How should we live together?" Although these questions may be distinct from one another, the answers involve one single ethico-political order in which individuals live together in harmony and personal fulfillment.

Harmony is a dynamic, rather than static, concept. It is ordered change. The principle of community, that is, achieving harmony through a communicative process, incorporates diversity, resistance, tension, and focus. It promotes growth with its accompanying freedom, but it remains without ultimate closure. This process of bringing about a sustaining community does not oppress the individual. Personal fulfillment similarly occurs in the context of social and ethical dimensions, although it is personal and more dependent on culture and value. As we know, both social and ethical dimensions depend on culture and values. The emphasis that a leader, community, or individual places on a particular value remains arbitrary and often subjective, depending on one's societal, cultural, and personal beliefs. In order to address this issue of ethical relativity, some have adopted the value-clarification approach to moral education, which is based on the assumption that there are no single, correct answers to ethical dilemmas. Nevertheless, there is value in holding clear views and acting accordingly. In addition, this approach values tolerance of divergent views. Most Western postmodern thinkers commonly adopt such an ethical stance.

The European Enlightenment promoted three archetypal ideals of liberty, equality, and solidarity, that is, brotherhood and sisterhood or shared humanity. Solidarity is comprised of the humanitarian dynamics that we have already covered. Liberty is what humans have striven for since our advent on the earth. We first strove for physical survival, that is, freedom from hunger, cold, the threat of other animals, and the calamities of nature. In doing so, we began to interact with other people and developed social consciousness and morality as a result. Hence, we became members of societies and states. Society was manifested as a response to the need for cooperation, mutual interdependence, and security, specifically physical, emotional, and spiritual. The state, or nationhood, is a relatively new concept in the world, appearing only in the last two to three hundred years. Politics deals with an individual's relationship to the state, which determines how a society is ordered.

Equality is perhaps the most confounding of the three archetypical ideals. Its enactment has been far from self-evident, even among those who share the belief that God created all humans. In fact, the belief in a natural, divinely ordained, hierarchical order in the cosmos has been used to justify the divine rights of kings and rigidly stratified societies. Democratic equality should be based on individuality. It denotes an effective regard for what is distinctive and unique in each individual, irrespective of physical and psychological inequalities. In practice, effective regard denotes equal treatment that maintains respect for the uniqueness of each person. Democratic equality then means equal opportunity for growth where resources and goods are distributed based on needs and capacities that contribute to growth.

Social Order

Edward Crane, a president of the Cato Institute, a nonprofit public policy research foundation based in the United States, contended in a speech delivered to the Shanghai Conference of 2004 that there are ultimately two fundamental ways to order society. The first is voluntarily through the private interaction of individuals, associations, religious organizations, businesses, and so on, which is termed "civil society." Or it can be coercively through state mandates, which is termed "political society." Crane argued that certain elements of a political society are required because we need protection against crime at home and threats from abroad. But the civil society is desirable from both economic and political points of view. He said:

In civil society, as we define it, you make the choices about your life. In political society, someone else makes those choices. Do you choose the career path that you desire, or does someone else assign that career to you? Do you choose the literature you read, or does someone in authority limit your choices? Do you spend the money you earn or does someone else spend it for you? The opportunities for political society to intervene in our lives are as great as the infinite choices a free individual faces in civil society.

According to Crane (2004), the twentieth century has been a long, bloody experiment in political society. The great nations of the world have, to one degree or another, all experimented with what the great Nobel Laureate economist and social philosopher F. A. Hayek called the "fatal conceit," believing one or a few very smart people could order societal affairs in ways that were somehow going to yield results superior to those that would spring from the spontaneous order of a free society. Hayek himself described the enormous economic benefits that resulted from the unplanned, spontaneous order of the marketplace. But his thinking about economics and civil society, while original in many ways, reflected the insights of the great thinkers throughout history who have understood the dangers of giving political power to a few to rule a multitude.

Crane elaborated, quoting the Chinese philosopher Laozi from some 2,600 years ago as one who has provided a solid intellectual basis for civil society and demonstrating the unintentional convergence of Western science-based thought with Eastern philosophy:

> Because it is in the nature of man to be free, Laozi described how much better off society is—not just economically, but spiritually—when politics plays as small a role as possible in societal affairs ... But it is not just empirical observation that leads us to appreciate the importance of getting politicians and bureaucrats out of economic decision-making. The great economists of the twentieth century—Ludwig von Mises, F. A. Hayek, Milton Friedman, George Stiegler and others—have shown that the market is not a machine, but more like an organism. It does not have rigid input and output relationships, but instead involves a constant discovery process. What is more, the entrepreneurial spirit that drives an economy is based on knowledge that is not centralized, but widely dispersed. Not only is it widely dispersed, but also most of it isn't even articulated. It is tacit, local knowledge that is the essence of any economy. Only freedom can allow that knowledge to be coordinated in a manner that will yield dynamic economic growth (2004).

Crane maintained that the essence of such a free economy is competition and cooperation. The tremendous complexity of a highly integrated free market economy is the greatest example of human cooperation the world has ever known, contrary to what its critics may claim. But civil society is much more than economic. Political society does not just stifle economic growth. It ultimately denies the sense of human fulfillment that can only come from having lived one's life in freedom, that is, making our own decisions and pursuing our own values, so that, in the end, our life's achievements, for example, raising a family of many children, inventing a new computer chip, or helping those in need, are something we can take pride in for having been our achievements, not merely activities others have imposed on us. Thus, political freedom, that is, the freedom to make decisions about one's life not just in the economic sphere, but regarding all of life's choices, is of paramount importance if we are to have a true civil society.

The concept of a civil society, in combination with a minimally invasive political society and the humanitarian notions of reciprocity, justice, fairness, rights, equality, and so forth, may represent the ideal society toward which we can aspire. This model can even be extended to a civil state instead of a political state, serving as a template for our one and only global village.

Many cultures of the world share the value of aspiration to freedom from coercion. In ancient China, this value is called *wuwei*, a term often seen in Chinese philosophy and political theories. The unique meaning of wuwei in the political context is a topic of special discussion in section three.

Section Two:
Western Social and Political Ideals

This section explores the development of Western social and political thought, delving into the concept of rights as a cornerstone of the Western conception of the individual's relationship with their society and state.

Karl-Heinz Pohl (2003) provided an excellent summary of the current state of Western ethics. According to him, during the age of Enlightenment, when an absolutism of reason replaced the religious absolutism of the Christian faith, there was a development toward excessive legislation. Codified law, which went back to the Roman tradition, and a language of rights, beginning with John Locke, increasingly became a substitute for unwritten rules of moral conduct. Pohl quoted Charles Taylor as saying, "Instead of saying that it is wrong to kill me, we begin to say that I have a right to life." The language of rights was reinforced at the time of the French Revolution when rights were understood as claims of the citizens against the state. Because of the history of the *ancien régime*, the state (government) was—and still largely is—conceived as being a potentially evil force that the citizens had to be protected against with rights. Today, we have reached a status in which everything is permissible that is not explicitly prohibited by law. In other words, in terms of minimalist ethics, this means, "I can do whatever I want, so long as no one gets hurt." Morality as an unwritten code has dissolved into written rights and laws and has essentially become superfluous.

In the field of Western moral philosophy, we can observe a development from virtue ethics over a formalistic deontological ethics to a utilitarian ethics. Today, we have discourse ethics and ethics of rights. The realization of the good now means not to limit the possibilities for self-realization of the other. Thus, to guarantee unforced procedures, according to which, people can negotiate their respective self-interests and problems.

Pohl maintained that procedural rules and laws are necessary in order to safeguard a complex, pluralistic polity comprised of individuals who are regarded as standing in contractual relationship with one another. The problem is that the good gets minimized in an ethics of rights. If there still is a common good, it consists only in the guarantee that each individual interest is being treated fairly. Such ethics might guarantee a minimal (thin) ethical standard under which a society may not fall. In contrast to this, there would also be a virtue ethics aiming for a high (thick) standard.

Pohl's brief and descriptive account outlined the present state of the Western postmodern ethics of rights, which governs human relationships with society and other persons. In contrast with the ethics of responsibility that the ancient Chinese advocated, modern Western theory has evolved only within the past few hundred years.

Individuals and Society

The feudal world of the Western medieval period conceptualized the interconnections of material, human, and divine existence in the notion of the great chain of being. This doctrine, endorsed and promoted by the Christian religion, ranked the physical, human, and divine in a hierarchy with inanimate matter at the bottom, God at the top, and humans occupying a space just below the angels. This ordering of the material and divine universe, with the ultimate subservience of all objects and beings to a universal God, remained an important concept until the age of the Enlightenment in the eighteenth century. The first tentative changes in this view began in the Renaissance of the fifteenth century with a shift from the idea of God as the supreme creator of nature to the belief that God was expressed in the laws of nature.

René Descartes (1596–1650) was one of the first to systematically examine the idea that science and mathematics, not religious dogma, formed the basis for control of the physical world. The scientific method, as exemplified in the work of Sir Isaac Newton (1642–1727) and many others, has facilitated the discovery that regularities and relationships in the physical world rest on observation rather than abstract, theoretical reasoning. (For more information, see chapter three.) Enlightenment thinkers applied this approach to the investigation of society.

Society did not emerge until relatively recently as the key concept for understanding relations between individuals and groups. John Locke (1632–1702) was the first who contrasted society with the state. Just as Newton had learned that order was observable in the physical world, careful observation also led to the discovery of order in the social world. This led to the development of a new science that Auguste Comte (1789–1857) termed "sociology" at the beginning of the nineteenth century.

Comte was one of a group of social theorists who developed a model of good society, subjecting society itself to scientific scrutiny. In Comte's view, applying scientific objectivity to the social world would produce order and progress. At the core of Comte's new science was the idea that society has a real existence with properties separate and different from those of individuals. Relying on four methods for learning about social phenomena (observation, experimentation, comparison, and historical analysis), Comte formulated his social theory.

Since Comte's time, the Western world has experienced four profound revolutions (the French, American, Communist, and Industrial) and three wars on a global scale (World War I, World War II, and the Cold War). All of which were massive events requiring rational explanations and political and social interpretation. It is partially through the application of Comte's broad integrative processes to these events that sociology and political science have matured into important disciplines of the contemporary social sciences. However, before engaging in the study of social science, it is first necessary to ascertain a crucial difference between the individual and society.

This distinction appears deceptively simple, but it has been the source of enduring debate among social scientists. Clearly, the identities of the individual and the society are interdependent, but the exact nature of this relationship has eluded most theorists, leaving the question unanswered of whether society is a collection of individuals or individuals are components of society. Among the philosophers who have contributed their perspectives to this debate are Thomas Hobbes (1588–1679) and John Locke.

Locke believed people are, by nature, good, rational and tolerant, entering into society in order to preserve and regulate the rights to own and enjoy property. In contrast, Hobbes believed humankind is, by nature, evil. In this state of penury, all people are governed by natural laws consisting primarily of justice and equity. He contended that living in this natural state is so horrible that we join together and agree to be ruled by a common leader. Hobbes first established the principle that the legitimacy of government stems from the rights of those governed rather than from the divine right of kings or the natural superiority of those who rule. Thus, society came about because of a social contract that was based on the fundamental agreement that, in return for the preservation of their physical existence, that is, the most basic right of nature, individuals give up their unjust desires, such as unearned pride and vanity. Furthermore, people had a right in a civil society to a protection of the right of the industrious and rational to create abundance for all people through the institution and protection of private property, not just to the preservation of social peace. Beyond establishing these rules for mutual self-preservation and the protection of basic rights, liberal societies would not attempt to define any positive goals for their citizens or promote a particular way of life as superior or desirable. Hobbes's ideas of society significantly influenced Western thought, as did those of his philosophical successor, Jean-Jacques Rousseau (1712–1778).

Rousseau is best known for the social contract, notions regarding the state of nature, and his often-quoted statement, "Man is born free; and everywhere he is in chains." His notion of individual liberty and his convictions about political unity helped to fuel the romantic spirit of the French Revolution. In a manner perhaps similar to Mencius (see the fourth section of chapter four), Rousseau began with an optimistic view of human nature, believing humanity is perfectible and individuals are equal and have sympathy for one another. These are the prerequisites for the creation of a better society.

Rousseau was very critical of the pitfalls of the existing society, but he also thought that appropriate change could unite individuals and simultaneously promote freedom and equality. He was looking for "a social order whose laws were in greatest harmony with the fundamental laws of nature." In fact, Rousseau's ideas were forerunners of modern sociology because he understood the notion of culture, that is, what people acquire from society.

According to Rousseau, concern for private property gives rise to civil society. His reasoning proceeded thusly. As the fundamental social unit, the family is designed to secure the necessities of human life. Therefore, the well-being of all society's members is served by reliance on each other in the basic patterns of cooperation that characterize the family. However, the very success of this cooperative effort produces time for leisure and leads to productive agriculture and industry. These developments, in turn, require ownership of land and promote acquisition of wealth. Both require the protection of a stable government. Thus, Rousseau held that a body politic must be established by means of a contract that unites many wills into one. That established government is always provisional and temporary and subject to a continual review by its citizens. Because the legitimacy of the social contract depends upon the unanimous consent of those governed, the general will can be expressed only via an assembly of the entire populace. Rousseau argued that any partial effort, such as establishing a representative legislative body, is an illusion because the general will can only be determined by each for all.

In the late nineteenth century, Max Weber (1864–1920) added his insight to this discussion of society. He believed the individual was a representative unit of the larger society and social behavior could be studied through this unit. Weber believed individuals interact subjectively in society, that is, all people assign meaning and value to objects and actions. That it is the interpretations of these special meanings that define our social relationships. Furthermore, he recognized that not all actions have meaning. Some have different meanings at different times. Some actions have meaning only some of the time. Our ability to act on the basis of subjectivity rather than by pure instinct makes us human and separates us from animals.

Weber believed the individual, not the society, acts in the world. Labor, production, economy, and politics are all the actions and ideas of individuals, and these elements formed the basis of his studies in society. He contended that society fosters the existence of individuals and it is within society that people succeed or fail. Weber felt the main goal of the individual is to obtain power, that is, overcome the subjectivity of others. The more complex a society becomes, the more it is necessary to have people with power to provide rational authority over the individuals within the society.

Karl Marx (1818–1883) and Emile Durkheim (1858–1917) were proponents of a notion on the individual and society that was completely different from that of Hobbes, Locke, and Weber. These later sociologists moved toward the theory that society forms the individual rather than the reverse.

Marx believed the nature of the individual is an explicit representation of the nature of contemporary society. He believed people are inherently good; however, the individual's disposition often becomes confused with the state in which he or she lives. He argued that individuals depend on society for survival, an idea antithetical to Weber's argument that society depends on the individual. Marx posited that, if the economy does well, the society will do well, and the individuals will prosper. If the economy falls, society will deteriorate, and the individuals will suffer. He stated that this is true because society is bound together by scientific laws of matter, not individuals. The rudimentary basis of society is material production. This notion formed the basis for Marx's most famous work on class structures.

Similar to Marx, Durkheim also believed that society defines the individual. He theorized that individuals are built on the sense of belonging, needing a connection to and a knowledge of the norms of a group. That society provides that belonging. This need was so great that people would actually commit suicide if their needs were unfulfilled. Durkheim hypothesized that the collective conscience of its members holds together this crucial social network. Each institution carrying out its specific role in promoting cohesion and order stabilizes it. In this way, the institutions of society define the structure of its individual members. Durkheim identified collective consciousness or the "totality of beliefs and sentiments common to the average members of a society" as the basis for social solidarity.

Clearly, we have two conflicting views on the nature of the individual and the society and the boundaries between the two. The relationship of the individual with his or her immediate society can also be perceived as a microcosm of the overall picture. Because humans identify objects by their simplest attributes and people are distinguished by the nature of the societies in which the individual participates as a member, the nature of the society becomes one of the rudimentary attributes of that particular individual. It is true that society is composed of individuals, but it is equally true that individuals are comprised of attributes specific to their societies.

The relationship of the individual person to the larger society is a key issue in many spheres of thought, including ethics, political and legal theory, psychology, and religion. Obviously, the individual is the primary unit of human existence. Consciousness, as we experience it, is ultimately personal, regardless of empathy and relationships we may share with others. At the same time, we are basically social animals. We depend on each other in myriad ways. Nowhere in the world do human beings live on an ongoing basis without sophisticated social and political structures to guide their thoughts and actions. Human association distinguishes itself from other forms of association when it becomes communicative. Without communication, there can be no community. The quality of communication rather than exclusionary boundaries creates and sustains communal bonds. In fact, community is simply a form of society where people feel they belong.

Democracy and Liberalism

Based on this type of human rationale, many twentieth-century philosophers and social scientists, including John Dewey, J. S. Mill, and John Rawl, conceptualize society as an organism. Individuals are related to one another and the social whole. This is similar to how cells are organized into organs, which are then organized to form an organism.

John Dewey, renowned for his pragmatic philosophy, offered an alternative view of the individual and society. Dewey's view of society focuses on the characteristics of interactive processes in which individuals participate, rather than on the maintenance of the boundaries of social entities. Individuals develop in connection with one another, not in a remote entity called "society" at large. He provided an account of how human beings form society as "association, coming together in joint intercourse and action for the better realization of any form of experience, which is augmented and confirmed by being shared" (Tan 2003). Here, the meanings of "society" and "community" converge into a way of living together that fosters personal and social growth. A Deweyan community does not have rigid boundaries because it is held together by the process of communication, not homogeneity. It is not about creating a single, overarching horizon that amounts to everyone developing God's view. It is about creating and deepening an infinite number of overlaps among countless changing horizons. Such a non-exclusionary community is not intolerant of differences. It needs differences to flourish. This Deweyan view of community, society, and individual is comparable with the early Confucian view depicted earlier. In our concluding remarks, we will present an attempt by Sor-Hoon Tan to synthesize early Confucianism with John Dewey's pragmatist philosophy in order to form what she calls a "Confucian democracy" of the future.

Western liberalism, which rejected conceptions of the social individual because it implied an organic model of society, dominated the twentieth century. From the perspective of a liberal, such organic conceptions sacrificed individuality. Francis Fukuyama, in *The End of History and the Last Man* (1992), declared the total triumph of liberal democracy after the end of the Cold War and the fall of the Soviet Empire in Eastern Europe in 1989, marking the end of authoritarianism and socialist state planning economies. Two hundred years after they first animated the French and American revolutions, the principles of liberty and equality had proven resurgent as well as durable. Fukuyama, nevertheless, is careful to distinguish liberalism and democracy as closely related, but separate, concepts. According to Fukuyama, political liberalism can be defined simply as a rule of law that recognizes certain individual rights or freedoms from government control.

While there can be a wide variety of definitions of fundamental rights, he uses the one contained in Lord Bryce's classic work on democracy, which limits them to three: civil rights ("the exemption from control of the citizen in respect of his person and property"), religious rights ("exemption from control in the expression of religious opinions and the practice of worship"), and what he calls political rights ("exemption from control in matters which do not so plainly affect the welfare of the whole community as to render control necessary"). The latter includes the fundamental right of press freedom. Democracy, on the other hand, is the right that all citizens hold universally to have a share of political power, that is, the right of all citizens to vote and participate in politics. The right to participate in political power can be thought of as yet another liberal right. Indeed, it is the most important one. For this reason, liberalism has been closely associated historically with democracy.

In its economic manifestation, liberalism is the recognition of the right for free economic activity and economic exchange based on private property and markets. Because the term "capitalism" has acquired so many different connotations over the years, it has recently become fashionable to speak of the free-market economy instead. Both are acceptable alternative terms for economic liberalism. What is emerging victorious is not so much liberal practice as the liberal idea. By the same token, it is not the democratic system or the practice of multiparty election. It is the democratic ideal that makes liberal democracy so irresistible. Hence, according to Fukuyama, for a very large part of the world, there is now no ideology with pretensions to universality that is in a position to challenge liberal democracy and no universal principle of legitimacy other than the sovereignty of the people. Fukuyama further argued that the victory of liberal democracy and the market economy around the world signifies the end of a period where an attempt was made to accommodate modernity. During which, we saw the aftermath of industrialization.

Some critics, including most communitarians, are dissatisfied with liberalism's neglect of community and shared values. They are concerned with civic virtues, which they believe liberalism cannot accommodate. Liberalism is not usually so individualistic that it denies the importance of society. What concerns communitarians is that the liberal's conception of the autonomous self as a moral agent is concomitant with an atomistic understanding of society as a collection of preformed individuals. This mechanical conception of society underlies social contract theories, which are still closely associated with liberalism today. Thus, there is a need to find a balance between liberalism and communitarianism.

The universality of liberalism and liberal democracy is the subject of discussion in different regions of the world today. Sor-Hoon Tan introduced the "end of history" claim that has two parts, specifically what will happen and what should happen: "At the end of history, it is not necessary that all societies become successful liberal societies, merely that they end their ideological pretensions of representing different and higher forms of human society" (2003).

She found Fukuyama's contention unpersuasive that liberal democracy is the only universally valid norm because it fundamentally resolves the contradiction involved in the human struggle for recognition by ensuring universal and equal recognition. Fukuyama's conception of a universal human nature underlying his claim that the struggle for recognition is the basic driving force of history is open to challenge. Even if there is general human desire for recognition, it could take many forms. Some, for example, the desire to be superior instead of equal to others, may find better fulfillment in an undemocratic society. Fukuyama's claim notwithstanding, no consensus has developed in the world concerning the legitimacy and viability of liberal democracy. Instead, voices of doubt and outright challenges are getting louder. Asians have been defending their departure from the liberal democratic mode on normative grounds. They need not lay claim to higher forms of human society or an alternative universal model. All they need to establish and reject Fukuyama's thesis is that their particular historical and cultural circumstances make Western-style liberal democracy inappropriate, even harmful, for their societies. Nonliberal alternatives offer better solutions to their problems.

As discussed in section one, human fulfillment is very personal and depends on culture and values. Thus, all people may not share belief in the universality of liberalism.

Humankind's progress will not end with the rapid advancement of microelectronics, computer sciences, and information technology in the latter part of the twentieth century. We stand again on the edge of "a new synthesis," as futurist Alvin Toffler suggested in his book *The Third Wave*. In all intellectual fields, from the sciences to sociology, psychology, political science, and economics, we are likely to see a return to large-scale thinking, general theory, and the merging of the pieces. We are beginning to understand that our obsessive emphasis on quantified detail in the absence of context and progressively finer measurement of smaller problems leaves us knowing more about less. Toffler said:

> We should look for those streams of change that are shaking our lives, to reveal the underground connections among them, not simply because each of these is important in itself, but because of the way these streams of change run together to form even larger, deeper, swifter rivers of change that, in turn, flow into something still larger. (1980)

Under the illumination of this new light, we see a pressing need for Chinese and Western people to learn from each other, especially in fields such as ethics, social sciences, and politics, where the ideals of the two traditions are either complementary or supplementary.

Section Three:
Wuwei, A Chinese Social and Political Ideal

One of the most important concepts in traditional Chinese philosophy is wuwei 無 為. Variously characterized as non-action without effort, noninterference, creative quietude, and pure effectiveness, it describes the most efficient and natural way of acting. A person of wuwei operates in a natural, free, and spontaneous flow of Dao without forcing or self-consciously achieving objectives. This process is described in the *Daodejing*:

> Eternal Dao doesn't do anything, yet it leaves nothing undone.
> If you abide by it, everything in existence will transform itself.
> When, in the process of self-transformation, desires are aroused, calm them with nameless simplicity.
> When desires are dissolved in the primordial presence, peace and Harmony naturally occurs, and the world orders itself.

Here, wuwei refers to the practice of noninterference with the natural tendencies of events, which is one way of understanding the notion of Dao. Human desires interfere with natural processes. A self-realized person in the Daoist tradition, through a mode of living patterned on and in concert with the natural Dao, achieves integration with nature and contributes to cosmic harmony. Roger Ames and David Hall said, "In Zhuangzi, wuwei is associated with the 'spiritual rambling' quality of the enlightened person who has overcome the distorting influence of ego-self and is able to experience the totality of things" (2003).

To the renowned Daoist Zhuangzi, wuwei is not merely a way of acting. It is a way of approaching the world, that is, matching attitude to circumstance. This requires a willingness to shift contexts and see things from novel or different perspectives, continuously finding new possibilities.

Using Watson's 1968 translation, Alan Fox explained the notion of wuwei in Zhuangzi by quoting the story of Cook Ding. The story goes like this:

Cook Ding was cutting up an ox for Lord Wen-hui. At every touch of his hand, every heave of his shoulder, every move of his feet, every thrust of his knee—zip! Zoop! He slithered the knife along with a zing, and all was in perfect rhythm, as though he were performing the dance of the Mulberry Grove or keeping time to the Jingshow music ... Cook Ding laid down his knife and [said], "What I care about is the Way, which goes beyond all skill. When I first began cutting up oxen, all I could see was the ox itself. After three years I no longer saw the whole ox. And now—now I go at it by spirit and don't look with my eyes. Perception and understanding have come to a stop and spirit moves where it wants. I go along with the natural makeup, strike in the big hollows, guide the knife through the big openings, and follow things as they are. So I never touch the smallest ligament or tendon, much less a main joint. A good cook changes his knife once a year—because he cuts. A mediocre cook changes his knife once a month—because he hacks. I've had this knife of mine for nineteen years and I've cut up thousands of oxen with it, and yet the blade is as good as though it had just come from the grindstone. There are spaces between the joints, and the blade of the knife has really no thickness. If you insert what has no thickness into such spaces, then there's plenty of room—more than enough for the blade to play about in. That's why after nineteen years the blade of my knife is still as good as when it first came from the grindstone." (Cook 2003)

Fox explained that true mastery and skill in life as well as in cooking involves a knack, not a formula. The ideal is to follow things as they are and never confront obstacles, just as water flows around a rock in the stream. The spirit or daemonic (shen 神) to which Cook Ding refers can be seen as the autopilot that guides us in the absence of conscious intention. A mundane example of this would be walking through a crowd of people without noticing the many various adjustments our bodies make to avoid hitting anyone. But this kind of response can hardly be planned. It must occur spontaneously and be completely integrated into whatever situation is at hand. S. C. Graham said:

People who really know what they are doing, such as cooks, carpenters, swimmers, boatmen, do not go in much for analyzing, posing alternatives and reasoning from first principles, they no longer even bear in mind any rules they were taught as apprentices; they attend to the total situation and respond. (Cook 2003)

Cook Ding does not decide where he wants to cut. He finds freedom of movement in the space between the bones using the blade of a knife that has no thickness. His natural, tacit, intuitive, and holistic thinking guides him through the space between the bones. This comes from knowledge harmonized through the practice of cutting up thousands of oxen over the years. Fox explained the lesson of this story in human terms:

> Zhuangzi's privileging of the unobtrusive allows us to conclude that for him, inappropriate action might be defined as that which is unnatural and "sticks out," that which leads to conflict, friction, frustration, and "disease"; while appropriate, natural, or spontaneous (ziran) action leads to a condition of ease and contentment. Such "frictionless activity" (wuwei) leads to greatest contentment. (2003)

For Zhuangzi, the most effective mode of human experience is to blend or fit into any given situation in such a way as to allow ourselves to respond effortlessly and spontaneously. This mode of nonobtrusive experience is what we might call wuwei. Zhuangzi actually encourages us not to remove or distance ourselves from the day-to-day world by identifying with some transcendental Dao. Rather, we are to immerse ourselves in the world, understand ourselves as a part of it, and seek to fully and completely integrate within it. Thus, the concept of wuwei is participatory and applicable in both the social and political domains.

Ames (1983) has outlined the disparate interpretation of wuwei as political theory in the Confucian, Daoist, Legalist, and *Huainanzi* traditions. The political postulates of these traditions use wuwei to represent an ideal posture for the ruler. The interpretations of wuwei, seen in the context of their respective systems, are fundamentally at variance. Confucius advocated the principle of government by moral suasion and dynamic example as the core of his political philosophy. The ruler, adhering to the principle of wuwei, emanates morally potent virtue, de 德, which influences his people and encourages them in the cultivation of their own moral nature. Thus, while seemingly doing nothing, he is able to bring about social harmony.

Wuwei is also the main precept behind the Daoist conception of government as a peculiar anarchism. According to Ames, this type of political structure results in a minimum amount of external interference being projected from those in power onto the individual as well as resulting in an environment most conducive to the individual's quest for personal fulfillment. As in Confucian political theory, the existence of a ruler and his position in society are taken as natural conditions. As long as he functions to facilitate the orderly operation necessary to sustain social living, he is authoritative rather than authoritarian in his relationship to the people. His position in the state is best seen as an analogy to the role of father within the family. In actualizing his natural role as ruler, he creates a fertile situation for the self-realization of his subordinates.

According to Ames (1983), another political philosophy, the Legalist, might be described as "government of the ruler, by the ruler, and for the ruler," the opposite extreme to Daoism. Legalism is a technique used to buttress a highly structured totalitarianism. The Legalist theorists conceived of an administration structured on self-regulating systems as the most effective means of achieving the purpose of the ruler. The first of these systems is the codification of an objective and universally applicable body of laws. From the ruler's perspective, the elimination of the human element and the reduction of litigation to a machinelike process guarantees order within his borders. Once established and set in motion, the laws arrest social irregularity and function automatically to ensure swift, severe punishment for anyone bold enough to challenge the system. The ruler, having structured the empire's administration on the basis of these systems, controls the state rather than administering it. With this model of rulership, the positions and occupations of ruler and minister are clearly defined. Yet, even while maintaining an attitude of wuwei, clever people who can anticipate the ruler's reactions cannot deceive him. Rather than trying to second-guess the ruler, these people look to the laws and their responsibilities of office as their standards of conduct. In Legalist political theory, wuwei and related strategies of rulership were intended to prevent any insight into the ruler's personality because such awareness might interfere with the operations of governmental machinery.

In *The Art of Rulership*, Book Nine of *Huainanzi*, the concept of wuwei is essentially an unlikely synthesis of the political philosophies of Confucian, Daoist, and Legalist traditions. This is unlikely because, given the obvious disparity in their interpretations of wuwei, an internally consistent and practicable compromise is really quite hard to envision. As Ames (1983) explained in *The Art of Rulership*, wuwei is constructed upon a basically Legalist framework using Legalist terminology and metaphor. It borrows certain supporting features in Legalist tradition, specifically an objective and universally applicable system of laws, a bureaucratic organization governed by an objective system of accountability, and a wuwei posture for the ruler. As a consequence of this posture, the ruler remains in solitude and seclusion, keeps his own counsel, encourages a personal mystique, refrains from overriding objective standards with subjective preferences, and disdains to make a display of personal attributes, opinions, and ambitions. At the same time, *The Art of Rulership* modifies the Legalist interpretation of wuwei in such a manner that the ruler is actually deprived of coercive authority over others. While the formal aspects of wuwei might appear Legalistic, the degree to which a spirit of

Daoist-influenced anarchism has replaced that of Legalist totalitarianism is strik-ing. The spirit is apparent inasmuch as the ruler, while himself remaining wuwei, orchestrates the natural development of individuals and enables them to also assume a wuwei posture. He follows nature in accepting from subordinates those things that keep with their individual aptitudes and are easy for them to achieve. While retaining the Legalist conception of law, it removes the element of coercion by grounding these laws in what is congenial to the people. While retaining the Legalist bureaucracy, it removes the element of coercion by encouraging the use of broad human talents in accordance with individual aptitudes. While retaining a seemingly Legalist conception of the ruler, it removes the element of coercion by insisting his interests coincide with those of his subjects and are best served by devotion to the well-being of his people. While retaining a Legalist conviction in the efficacy of a solid political structure, it removes the element of coercion by insisting that intervention is necessary only when natural order breaks down.

The concept of wuwei, as interpreted in *The Art of Rulership*, represents the kind of political ideals to which the ancient Chinese aspired for centuries. We will explore this idea in greater detail in the final section of this chapter.

Section Four:
Chinese Precepts of Harmony in Diversity

Various concepts are at the core of an understanding of Chinese relationships. This section examines some of those concepts.

The virtues of Confucianism endorse a strong humanitarian and pragmatist focus, a focus that subsequently typifies Chinese culture as a whole. These virtues place an emphasis on cooperation, tolerance, reciprocation, and deference in deal-ing with other humans and on how to achieve harmony among people and all matters within the universe. These concepts have perennially been a significant consideration for Chinese thinkers.

Harmony in Diversity 和而不同

Harmony in diversity is one of the most important teachings of Confucian tradi-tion. This is the aesthetic order discussed in chapter three, as opposed to rational or logical order. In the Western tradition, belief in a single-order cosmos rein-forces the search for natural and social uniformities. This is the rational or logical order. In contrast, the aesthetic order that the Chinese sought is found in the harmony of the ten thousand things, the myriad unique particulars, including human beings themselves, that constitute the universe.

The original meaning of the word *he* 和 (harmony) originally applied to harmonizing in singing, but it was later extended to describe the unity of any non-identical objects. In a famous passage in the *Guo Yu*, a description of harmony is given in the *Sayings of Zheng* 鄭 語:

> Harmony fulfills living things; but identity does not lead to growth. Putting the objects on the same level is harmony; therefore it is able to promote abundance and growth and things revert to it. If identity is used to put down identity then in the end one will dismiss the object. Therefore the former kings mixed together earth, metal, wood, water and fire so as to form the hundred things. Therefore they harmonized the five tastes so as to please the palate; fashioned the four limbs so as to maintain the body; harmonized the six tonic notes so as to attune the ear; rectified the seven internal organs so as to serve the heart; leveled the eight elements to form human beings; affirmed the nine threads so as to establish pure virtue, united the ten numbers so as to instruct the hundred units.

Harmony is depicted as the acceptance of diversity rather than a reduction to uniformity.

A similar passage is found in the *Analects*: "The gentleman *jun zi* 君 子 pursues harmony rather than agreement; the 'small' person pursues the opposite." Confucius repeatedly described social and political participation in terms of pursuing a harmony among diversities and differences. Hall and Ames said:

> The difference between he, translated here as "harmony" and *t'ung* [同], "agreement," is the difference between "attuning" and "tuning." Attuning is the combining and blending of two or more ingredients in a harmonious whole with benefit and enhancement that maximizes the possibilities of all without sacrificing their separate and particular identities. "Tuning" is finding agreement by bringing one ingredient into conformity and concurrence with an existing standard such that one ingredient is enhanced possibly at the expense of others. (1987)

Harmony in diversity is traditionally a Chinese political ideal. In the *Analects*, Confucius specifically condemned factionalism in political service, such as that seen in the forming of political cliques, parties, or caucuses. He instead advocated a social and political harmony that can take the disparate opinions of its participants into account. Tolerance is therefore a necessary condition in this conception of sociopolitical order, which strives to allow the fullest possible disclosure of particularity. Supreme harmony is the state in which each thing abides in its correct place. All things are free from interference. Harmony is dynamic rather than static. Tan stated:

> Energies are channeled so that there is a cumulative carrying forward, with each successive stage emerging from and temporarily completing the preceding stages. In a harmonious process, each participating element anticipates the one that follows, and the latter is born in response to the former. (2003)

A State of Ritual: Li 禮

Harmony in diversity is one ideal of the ancient Chinese tradition. Another is ritual, particularly a state of ritual li, which further enhances harmony. The primary function of li is to prevent human conflict. It is a set of constraints that defines the negative limits of self-regarding activities. In addition, li also has supportive and ennobling functions. Given that Confucius's program for building character presumes the disciplining of oneself and the practice of ritual li, attitudes such as respect, tolerance, and deference are preconditions required for the emergence of one's personhood within a community. The disposition of the society and the state accordingly unfolds in a dialogue between inherited tradition and present circumstance and between inherited meaning preserved in ritual structures and the contribution of the present participants. All are aimed at preserving social harmony. As a generic term, li focuses on a traditional ritual code that is essentially a set of formal prescriptions or procedures for appropriate behavior. In the classic Confucian text, *Liji* 禮記, the subject matter ranges from ritual rules concerning mourning, sacrifices, marriage, and communal festivities to guidelines for conduct toward others on more common occasions. In every case, li is spontaneous and never dogmatic. The ability to adapt to changing circumstances may be called for, depending on the needs of the time denoted by yi 宜, the appropriateness.

Herbert Fingarette contextualized li for the modern Western reader:

> I see you on the street; I smile, walk toward you, put out my hand to shake yours. And behold—without any command, stratagem, force, special tricks or tools, without any effort on my part to make you do so, you spontaneously turn toward me, return my smile, raise your hand

toward mine. We shake hands—not by my pulling your hand up and down or your pulling mine but by spontaneous and perfect cooperative action. Normally we do not notice the subtlety and amazing complexity of this coordinated "ritual" act. This subtlety and complexity become very evident, however, if one has had to learn the ceremony only from a book of instructions, or if one is a foreigner from a non-handshaking culture. (1972)

These complex, but familiar, gestures are characteristic of human relationships at their most human. They are free of conceptions of each other as physical objects, animals, or even creatures that can be driven, threatened, forced, or maneuvered. Looking at these ceremonies through the lens of li, we realize that explicitly sacred rites can be seen as emphatic, intensified, and elaborated extensions of everyday civilized interaction. Consequently, not only does ritual li profoundly demonstrate the harmony and beauty of social forms and the inherent and ultimate dignity of human interaction, it also accentuates the moral perfection implicit in achieving one's ends by dealing with others as beings of equal dignity, as free co-participants in li. In this beautiful and dignified, shared, and open participation with others who are ultimately like us, we realize ourselves.

Confucius's recognition of the value of models as guiding norms is illustrated in his comparison of ritual action (li 禮) and penal law (fa 法) as a method of achieving social order. Hall and Ames stated:

> Ritual action li permits the spontaneous exercise of harmonizing actions. Law (fa) only controls external behavior. The existence of law, particularly penal law, however necessary it might be, suggests the failure of ritual action. Ritual actions (li) are models for Confucius. They are objects of imitation ... What is principally at issue here is the character of social harmony, and that leads us back to the contrast of aesthetic and rational order. (1995)

Indeed, law becomes coercive force when necessitated by the loss of spontaneity in ritual action and the consequent substitution of dogma, as witnessed in the disorder of the late imperial era in China.

Masayuki Sato (2003) studied the Confucian quest for order and ritual action (li 禮) by focusing on the origin and formation of the political thought of Xunzi (310–220 BC; dates uncertain), the founder of the naturalist and rationalist school of Confucianism. In a famous debate with Mencius, Xunzi maintained that humans are evil and the state needs to control and guide its populace in becoming good citizens. Xunzi argued that desire is the main cause of our evil nature. Unbounded desire is inimical to the state. Any person who follows his or her nature and indulges his or her emotions, such as a fondness for profit or feelings of envy and hate, will inevitably violate the norms and rules of society and end up a criminal. Xunzi suggested we defer our desires via rituals. If people concentrate upon fulfilling ritual principles, they may satisfy both human desires and the demands of ritual. If people concentrate only upon fulfilling their desires, then they will end by satisfying neither. Thus, under proper government control, desires can be channeled to the benefit of the state. For Xunzi, the successful state effectively controls human desire through the self-enforced mechanisms of morality and external pressures, which he calls "environment."

According to Xunzi, humans differ from animals in their ability to form societies and the division (*fen* 分) of roles within that society. Through a sense of morality and justice (yi 義), humans divide (fen) themselves and distribute resources to social constituents according to designated social roles. Li is the embodiment, or operation, of morality (yi), a prescription for self-controlling human desires. Sato (2003) attempted to elucidate various meanings and characteristics of the ritual principles of li according to Xunzi and claimed that Xunzi used the term li to describe relatively concrete rituals and social norms, as opposed to the psychological or mental condition that Mencius seems to have envisaged. The practice of li by all participants in a social structure would ultimately lead to social order and harmony, which could be associated with the providential process of heaven and earth. Therefore, li, in the broadest sense, can be paraphrased as the manifestation of the way as well as the means for attaining order, Xunzi's highest theoretical goal. Sato concluded that Xunzi's concept of li contains nine aspects, each important for an understanding of li:

1. The expression of moral value (yi)

2. The manifestation of social distinction and distribution of resources (fen)

3. Manifestation of order and harmony in the human world

4. Nourishment of human life

5. Ornamentation and refinement of human life

6. Modification of human heart-mind and vital breath

7. The method by which an individual steps up to sagehood

8. The method by which a ruler can recruit an appropriate minister

9. The ultimate origin of proper political order

In various discourses, Xunzi explored the practice of li as the ultimate solution for major issues that preceding thinkers had not persuasively answered. Xunzi's concept of li supplemented analytical discourse with a firm, ethical foundation. By synthesizing both ethical and analytical insights, his theory of li led pre-Qin Confucianism to its consummation and provided Han Confucianism with a decisive edge over other schools of thought, leading to its acceptance as the official curriculum of the Han court.

Although the benefits of ritual li are many, there are occasions when conflict can no longer be resolved through ritual li alone. When states encounter these types of situations, they may resort to war for resolution. Indeed, the Chinese have been involved in warfare from the beginning of their statehood. Words of wisdom regarding the philosophy of war and peace abound in Chinese literature.

Warfare and Propensity of Things: Shi 勢

One of the most renowned Chinese texts, written by a General Sunzi 孫子 sometime in the third or fourth century BC, is entitled *The Art of War* 孫子兵法. This classic text contains only 5,600 Chinese ideograms, or words, organized into thirteen chapters. The ideogram for war in Chinese is more complex than its English designation suggests, implying combat, maneuver, weapon, conflict, and other related notions. It does not, however, connote negativity, as do Western interpretations of conflict. For the Chinese, a conflict in ideas leads to growth and change. Thus, the word "conflict" in *The Art of War* has both positive and negative connotations. It can be used to characterize conflict with oneself, between individuals, between armies, and between political organizations or countries.

Sunzi valued moral, political, social, economic, and environmental factors when electing to wage war. He seriously considered the potential sacrifices of this course of action when he said that "weapons are ominous tools to be used only when there is no alternative." The best way to win a war, he contended, is to fight no battles. He said, "Those skilled in war subdue the enemy's army without battle." To achieve this objective, Sunzi's philosophy embraced the notion that it is easier to win a war when that war is just. Sunzi believed that moral strength and intellectual faculties were decisive factors in warfare. If these factors were properly applied, war could be waged with certain success.

According to Griffith (1963), war was never to be undertaken thoughtlessly or recklessly, and it should be preceded by measures designed to make it easy to win. The master conqueror frustrated his enemy's plans and broke up his alliances. He created cleavages between sovereign and minister, superiors and inferiors, and commanders and subordinates. His spies and agents were active everywhere, gathering information, sowing dissension, and nurturing subversion. The enemy was isolated and demoralized. His will to resist was broken. Thus, without battle, his army was conquered. His cities were taken, and his state was overthrown. Only when the enemy could not be overcome by these means was there recourse to armed force, which was to be applied so that victory was gained in the shortest possible time, at the least possible cost in lives and effort, and with infliction on the enemy of the fewest possible casualties. Sunzi deemed national unity to be an essential requirement of victorious war. This could be attained only under a government that was devoted to the people's welfare and did not oppose them.

When a situation necessitating battle arose, information and strategy became of critical importance. Sunzi contended that all warfare is based on deception. He said:

> Know the enemy and know yourself; in a hundred battles you will never be in peril. When you are ignorant of the enemy but know yourself, your chances of winning or losing are equal. If ignorant both of your enemy and of yourself, you are certain in every battle to be in peril.

Therefore, timeliness and the accuracy of information gained the utmost importance. Griffith (1963) stated:

> A skilled general must be master of the complementary arts of simulation and dissimulation; while creating shapes to confuse and delude the enemy he conceals his true dispositions and ultimate intent. When capable he feigns incapacity; when near he makes it appear that he is far away; when far away, that he is near. Moving as intangibly as a ghost in the starlight, he is obscure, inaudible. His primary target is the mind of the opposing commander; the victorious situation, a product of his creative imagination. He creates conditions certain to produce a quick decision; for victory is the object of war, not lengthy operations however brilliantly conducted. He knows that prolonged campaigns drain the treasury and exhaust the troops; prices rise, the people are hungry.

The discussion of ancient Chinese conceptions of warfare dovetails with a discussion of the propensity of things. In the context of military strategy, the dispositions and maneuvers central to the strategy of Sunzi may be expressed by the Chinese word of shi 勢, "a potential born of disposition." Shi is a very interesting word. French philosopher and sinologist Francois Jullien wrote an entire book regarding this one word. Jullien explained that shi "oscillates between the static and the dynamic points of view; it provides us with a thread to follow, sliding between different levels in which our own analysis is trapped" (1995).

Shi represents the propensity of things, the natural tendency or potential born of one's disposition. Thus, by extension, it is a word reflective of culture as well.

Shi construes diverse modes of conditioning reality, modes that may be strategically deployed or arranged to one's advantage. According to Jullien, the use of the crossbow, a Chinese invention dating to circa 400 BC, significantly contributed to revolutionizing the conduct of warfare through both the accuracy of its straight trajectory and its formidable force. The activation of its mechanism thus naturally served to symbolize the sudden unleashing of an army's energy. Shi is like a "crossbow stretched to its maximum." Apart from its pertinence to the theme, the image of the bending of the bow being used to convey potential, the technological innovation that the crossbow represented reflected progress comparable to the capacity to exploit shi rigorously at the strategic level. In fact, it is possible to develop this image more precisely. The advantage peculiar to the crossbow is that:

> [W]hile the point from which the bolt departs is very close (between the shoulder and the chest), one can kill people more than one hundred paces away, without their companions realizing from where it was fired. (Jullien, 1995)

The same applies to the good general who, by using shi, manages with minimum effort to achieve the maximum effect from a distance, either temporal or spatial, by simply exploiting the factors in play without common knowledge of how the result was achieved or by whom.

In the twentieth century, even Mao Zedong (Mao Tse-Tung) resorted to this concept to explain the tactics most appropriate to a war of resistance, the long war, against Japan. This was a tactic of alertness and spontaneous reaction to all occasions and situations. This strategy became all the more effective because it precluded immobilization or being blocked in a predetermined disposition from which there would soon be no escape. The perspective operative here is of a process that can evolve to our advantage if we make opportune use of its propensity. The combined use of shi and Sunzi's *The Art of War* was actually the thinking behind Mao's renowned guerrilla tactics, which was successfully used against the Japanese and in Vietnam and many parts of the world.

Reading the ancient Chinese literature on strategy, one begins to realize the extent to which the type of representation it embodies is opposed to any heroic or tragic vision and why ancient China remained so disinclined to such a vision. Confrontation lies at the heart of that vision. A confrontation carried to the crisis point in a situation offers no escape. In contrast, anyone who knows how to exploit strategically the potential born of disposition can lead the antagonism to revolve itself, thanks to this perfectly controllable internal pattern. Whereas tragic man clashes irrevocably against superior powers, resisting all surrender, the Chinese strategist prides himself on his ability to manage all the factors in play because he knows how to go along with the logic behind them and adapt to it. The former fatally discovers, all too late, his destiny. The latter knows how to anticipate the propensity at work so he has it at his own disposal.

Indeed, effective strategic exploitation of shi is one of the ways that the ancient as well as the contemporary Chinese avoid conflict and maintain harmony, not only in situations of war, but in those of a political or social nature as well.

Section Five: Traditional Chinese Dreams and Ideals

Traditional Chinese dreams and ideals start with social harmony and harmonious ethical-political order, that is, the governance of wuwei and ren 仁 政.

Social Relationships and Harmony

In Confucian cultural tradition, the family is not a private sphere. Rather, the boundaries between public and private are fluid, porous, and indistinct. Both are within and outside the family and akin to the continuum of the focus-field model described previously. Family is thus an extension of the individual; social groups are related in a continuous, interactive process that forms networks of families. Community and state are simply broader extensions of the family model. Thus, the first social objective in Confucianism is to achieve harmony in family relationships. From the family, social harmony is then extended until it embraces all human relationships in the ideal of "bringing peace to all under heaven."

Instead of an emphasis on the rights of an individual, prominent in the preceding discussion of Western sociology and politics, the Confucian tradition of order stresses the obligations or duties of individuals to their family, community, and nation. Theoretically at least, this notion of responsibility applies equally to both the ruler and the ruled. The familial and political realms were not the only application of this tradition. Chinese social life was also an expansion upon the family with social loyalty reflective of the filial piety described previously. Again, family, rather than the individual, was the basic unit of community.

Hsieh Yu-wei (Moore 1968) reminded us that, in the Chinese community, kinship was formed through the marriage relationship, clans were established through blood relationship, and villages were built up through the regional relationship in which one was born and brought up. One's ancestors, tutors, and friends were linked together through academic pursuit or mutual attraction or other causes. All revolved around the center of gravity of the practice of filial piety. In Confucian ethics, the position of the tutor was particularly respected, ranking next to the father's position in every household. On a simple tablet in the family alcove, there were "Heaven, Earth, Sovereign, Father, Tutor," 天 地 君 親 師 listing the order for worship. Even though parents gave birth to the physical body of a child, the teacher had the most to do in formulating the pupil's spiritual and cultural life. By expanding the view that one must honor his physical life-giver, one must also honor his cultural life-giver. Using the same reasoning, one treats his bosom friends with high respect, too. Confucius's disciple Zengzi 曾 子 said, "The superior man on grounds of culture meets with his friends, and by their friendship helps to establish his virtue." Together with friends, the closely knit patterns of relatives, clansmen, fellow countrymen, and tutors were all interwoven around a filial axis in the Chinese community. Such a condition still prevails in some conservative groups of overseas Chinese residents.

This brings us back to the ideal six relations 倫 of Confucianism: ruler/subject, parents/children, husband/wife, older brother/younger brother, teacher/pupil, and the relationship between friends. Most of these relationships are located in the family, which was previously described. Confucians also place significant emphasis on friendship and learning from friends, especially of high moral suasion whom we can emulate, as an effective method of self-cultivation. Indeed, one of the Confucian dreams is to make friends with the ancient moral sages from whose wisdom one could then learn how to be human.

Traditional Governance of Ren and Wuwei

The ruler/subject relationship is laid out in the famous opening passage of *The Great Learning* (500 BC), one of the four essential Confucian classics:

> The ancient who wishes to illuminate "brilliant learning" all under Heaven first governed their state.
> Wishing to govern their states, they first regulated their families.
> Wishing to regulate their families, they first cultivated their personal lives.

Wishing to cultivate their personal lives, they first rectified their heart/minds.

Wishing to rectify their heart/minds, they first authenticated their intentions.

Wishing to authenticate their intentions, they first refined their knowledge.

The refinement of knowledge lay in the study of things.

This passage emphasizes that a ruler, an emperor, for example, who rules with a "Mandate from Heaven," must nevertheless cultivate his own moral character if he wishes to effectively govern the state. As a mediator between heaven and the people, he should use his own potent moral suasion, which heaven endowed, to induce order in his own family. Furthermore, he must always act in the interest of the people, whose happiness will provide the final judgment of his mandate. This application of moral suasion is equally necessary in ordinary people who strive for excellence.

Hence, individuals should aspire to the personal qualities described in this ancient text, attaining knowledge first and then authenticity, rectification of the heart-mind, and moral cultivation before he or she can take responsibility for family, community, state, and nature. To Confucians and the ancient Chinese, every social and political relationship began with self-cultivation 內聖外王, just as described in our discussion of the focus-field model.

Although these Confucian aspirations begin with individuals, they rarely look at the human as an individual isolated from the surrounding context. Rather, the identity of the individual and the family is defined in terms of relationships with community and country. This kind of thinking, which each social entity is organically related to every other and cooperates on differing levels to achieve the integrated functioning of the total organism, is an expression of the same organicist world view that Joseph Needham so often stressed in his writings about China.

The Confucian view of society considers family to be fundamental in the family-state relationship. Each family is viewed as the microcosm, and the state is the macrocosm. Under Confucian social hierarchical order, good polity follows when the "ruler rules, minister ministers; the father fathers, [and] son sons" when everyone conducts themselves well within their appointed sphere.

Though Confucian ethics call for the discharging of the duties of the individual to the community, they do not overemphasize the community to the detriment of the individual. In fact, the individual is considered to be even more important than the community. Confucians regard individuals as the metaphorical roots, comprising the foundation of society, while communities are the leaves that form a protective roof. They also often describe the relationship between people and state as akin to water and a boat. Water can float a boat, but it can just as easily sink that boat, depending on the water's turbulence and the boat's stability. Thus, while asserting the duties of the individual to the community, Confucian ethics are contextual and not dogmatic. When conflicts arise between the individual and the community, the individual must maintain his or her own responsibility for independent decision. In such cases, the individual determines if the authority of the community is obeyed or is set aside by the adjuration of conscience, heart-mind, or ren. For Confucians, the individual's relationship with the family and the community is actually one single relationship of mutual dependence and equal importance.

As we move from Chinese notions of family toward Chinese conceptions of community and state, it is worthwhile to note that ancient Western and Chinese thinkers had quite different notions of rulership. Divergence was first evident in their respective views of prehistoric, Stone Age humans. Traditional Western thinkers accepted these humans as independent, rational individuals. Chinese counterparts viewed these ancient ancestors as primitive groups of animal-like beings.

Zunzi wrote, "Men are weaker than cows, run slower than horses, why are they superior? The answer lies in that men are social beings, animals are not."

Chinese thinkers further contended that, even if primitive humans were social beings, they were no better than animals because they fought one another until such time as virtues and morals were cultivated. In the Chinese view, it was not until the arrival of a strong moral leader, the so-called sage king 聖王, that humans attained civilization, established proper social order, and distinguished themselves from animals. Mohists believe nations were built from the top-down as the sage king appointed ministers of high moral suasion who were capable of leading the people. In contrast, a renowned philosopher of the Tang dynasty (618–906), Liu Chong-Yuan 柳宗元 believed in a bottom-up model of nation building with men of wisdom leading small groups and sage kings assembling these small groups into nations. Regardless, men of merit and strong moral conviction would lead people in social organizations for the benefit of the larger group, not the ruler's own benefit.

Julia Ching (1991) described the sage kings as either "cultural heroes," a position held in Confucianism and Legalism, or "wise rulers," the belief of the Confucians and Mohists. Legendary characters such as *Fuxi* (animal tamer), *Sui-ren* (fire maker), and *Shen-nong* (divine farmer) were the first type of sage kings. The wise rulers (*Yao, Shun,* and *Yu*) were a later type. In the *Analects,* Confucius seldom described the attributes of sagehood, but he occasionally referenced those ancients he admired, particularly Yao and Shun, who were apparently deemed to be sages or persons of superior virtue. Both were regarded as model rulers whose devotion to their people, political wisdom, personal integrity, family loyalty, and filial piety were singled out for special praise. This commendation was an expression of an ancient Chinese tradition anchored in humanism, which admires rulership, "For the people, by a ruler of merits." This contrasts with the Western notion of democracy, which is "For the people, by the people." Chinese rulers are judged by how well they have served their subjects, not their popularity.

An ideal Chinese ruler was also a man of wuwei, as described previously. Confucians, Daoists, Buddhists, and even Legalists all shared this view. Ames (1983) maintained, in the ideal Confucian administration, the ruler does not personally attend to matters of government. He leads by setting a positive example. Through the charismatic influence of his virtue (de), the people are led into a manner of conduct through which they seek moral achievement: "A ruler who governs by virtue can be compared to the pole star which merely lodges in its place while the other stars pay it homage." (The Analects)

The Confucian ruler, by regulating his conduct so his activities reflect a commitment to the expression of his moral nature, can influence his subordinates and transform his people. This is the political principle of guiding and transforming the people through moral example. The ruler who does nothing inasmuch as his high level of personal cultivation, possible only through interaction with his people, does not require the projection of arbitrary demands on his subjects. His relationship with these subordinates is characterized by a total absence of coercion, the essence of wuwei.

Similarly, in the *Daodejing*, the Daoists hold that "the best ruler is one whose existence is scarcely noticed by the people." They reflect that "the Dao does nothing, yet leaves nothing undone."

The *Daodejing* is primarily a political treatise directed at the incumbent ruler. Laozi seeks to convince the sitting ruler that policies, especially those that are aggressive, authoritarian, rigid, and violent, will not succeed in achieving the ruler's goal, that is, political control. To Laozi, "The natural Dao benefits without injuring; the Dao of the sage does without contending" (*Daodejing*). The best government, paradoxically, is nongovernment. The difference between the Daoist notion of wuwei and its Confucian counterpart is that Daoism is unwilling to interpret cosmic activity in terms of human moral categories. Confucianism insists a correlation between human moral achievement and cosmic harmony

According to John Wu's (1968) reading of the most ancient of Chinese documents, *Shujin* 書 經 or *The Book of Documents*, the sources of all political authority are three: the mandate of heaven, the people's good will, and the ruler's virtue. The mandate of heaven is a trust conferred upon the government for the welfare of the people. This doctrine is rooted in religious notions that the Zhou (1116–249 BC) introduced into the Chinese mainstream. Specifically, they believed an impersonal, but all-powerful heaven, dominated the cosmos and no one rules except by the mandate of heaven. If a ruler is less than virtuous, heaven will withdraw its mandate. The people will then rise against the ruler. Thus, the government is created for the people rather than the people for the government. Both Daoism and Confucianism draw upon *The Book of Documents* as a common source of political wisdom. Both emphasize the role of the ruler's humility toward the people. Consider, for instance, the following song recorded in *The Book of Documents*:

> The people should be cherished,
> And should not be downtrodden.
> The people are the root of a country,
> And, if the root is firm, the country will be tranquil.

As Wu pointed out, both Confucius and Laozi agreed that punishment must not be relied upon as a governmental policy and the ruler must guard against luxury, the lust for power, giving arbitrary rein to his will, engaging in violence and extreme measures, and especially pride and self-complacency. Both also stress the necessity of self-denial by the ruler, although there are some differences in their notion of altruism. Confucius thinks of reality in terms of the will of heaven; Laozi thinks of it in terms of the way of heaven or the way of nature. Because Confucius and his followers had a clear view of the true foundations of political authority, they never lost sight of the well-being of the people. They never regarded political authority as an end. It was only a means to an end, the development of the human personality and human civilization for the benefit of the people. *The Great Learning* stated, "When a prince loves what the people love, and loathes what the people loathe, then he truly deserves to be called the parent of the people." Here again, the emphasis is on benefiting the people. Thus, to the Chinese people, even democracy is only a mean to the end, not the end itself.

The Art of Rulership

Recently, students of ancient Chinese rulership have evidenced a renewed interest in *Huainanzi*, a political treatise of the early Han dynasty that synthesized many different schools of thought on governance. (Huainanzi was introduced previously.) The early Han periods were a time of astonishing intellectual fertility and creativity in China. Major (1993) best provided the background of Huainanzi in the setting of this verdant period. From the Daoism of Laozi and Zhuangzi came the ideas of the primacy of Dao and the existence of an ancient condition of primitive harmony before human schemes and contrivances brought disorder to the world. The astronomers, astrologers, and natural philosophers of the naturalist school used their star maps and almanacs and observations of the natural world to develop an elaborate system of correlative and categorical reasoning, so sense could be made, philosophically, of the organic, cyclical, self-created universe in which they lived. At the same time, a school of statesmen sometimes known as the Technocrats blended the ideas of Laozi and other sage government achieved through oneness with the Dao with Legalist ideas about how to organize an army and a bureaucracy and make them serve the purposes of the state. Added to the mixture were the theories of astrologers, especially those of the yin and yang militarist school, who observed configurations of the celestial bodies to predict military success or failure. From these various strands of thought was produced a theory of statecraft. According to which, an enlightened ruler could align his own actions with those of the universe and rule in accord with natural rhythms and harmonies.

This synthesis was subscribed to by a growing number of thinkers and came to be called the Huang-Lao 黃 老 school, joining the political, cosmological, and magical arts of Huangdi 黃 帝 (the Yellow Thearchy) and the sage rulership of Laozi. This Huang-Lao school was renowned as the Jixia Academy of Qi 稷 下 之 學 in the fourth century BC. It was the predecessor of the academy of Huainan under the patronage of Liu An, king of Huainan. *Huainanzi* is the treatise that follows this tradition.

Our examination of governance in ancient China must include Roger Ames's translation of Book Nine, *The Art of Rulership*, in which he focused on five issues concerning the Huainanzi ideal of governance: wuwei, shi (strategic advantage/political purchase), fa (penal law), *yong zhong* 用 眾 (utilizing the people), and *li min* 利 民 (benefiting the people). Ames's quote is our favorite passage of *The Art of Rulership*:

The art of the ruler is to deal with things through nonaction and to disseminate wordless instructions.

> Limpid and still he does not move; even when moved he is not agitated:
> taking advantage of the course of things he delegates responsibility to subordinates and, holding them to account, he does not wear himself out. Even though he is aware of how things should be done, he allows himself to be guided by the imperial tutors; even though he himself is able to speak, he allows his diplomats to proclaim the ceremonial

words; even though he himself is able to hear, he allows the administrators to select the right advice. (1983)

This description of rule by wuwei predates the modern management by objective and management through delegation. The antiwar sentiments in both the traditions of Daoism and Confucianism, and Chinese culture generally, emphasize defense over offense and display a preference for nonviolent solutions to security problems. Sunzi stated that the acme of military excellence is to subdue the enemy without fighting. Mencius maintained that the truly virtuous ruler, by means of his moral suasion, can bring his enemies to submission voluntarily and without recourse to physical coercion. Thus, Confucianism is pacifist in nature and clearly yin, leaving no place for the ideas of conquest, expansion, and military rule, ideas that were driving forces in, for example, Roman and Ottoman Turkish history, traditions that were clearly yang.

With respect to shi, there were two attempts to blunt radical Legalist theory with Confucian humanism. First, the ideal ruler/minister relationship was interpreted as a symbiosis. Each position was responsive to and dependent upon the other. Second, the acknowledgment of the effectiveness of shi was used as an instrument of political influence to impact the Confucian objective of transforming and elevating the people. It was understood that one, only through the use of shi, could grasp the disposition and propensity of events prior to their occurrence. This process was very real to the people of the time and comprised a fundamental element of good governance.

This revised interpretation of shi stands in sharp contrast to its function as a tool of political repression in the Legalist system. The purport of *The Art of Rulership* is one of harmony rather than control and cooperation rather than contention. The intent of this book is to serve as a theory of political efficacy. In politics, one must clearly understand and follow the crucial nature of hierarchical positions and their attendant shi. Shi signifies both a particular situation and the tendency expressed through it and orienting it. According to its shi, anything that appears to result from circumstance acts as a force and is endowed with efficacy. Understanding of any situation's shi allows reconciliation and appropriate anticipation with a dynamic perspective that can accommodate the ongoing evolution and flow of events.

The third concept of governance espoused by *The Art of Rulership* is fa 法, or penal law, which accepts some characteristics from the Legalist tradition, thereby giving the system structure. The direction, disposition, orientation, and political philosophy presented in *The Art of Rulership* introduces some radical modifications. The will of the ruler becomes subordinate to the rule of law. The law is asserted to have been established to contain the political authority of the ruler.

The ruler is obliged to abide by the law and be exemplary in his personal conduct. The ultimate authority of the law is transferred from the will of the ruler to that which is congenial to the people, thus grounding law in rightness. The formal structure of government is regarded as a framework within which the ideal of godlike transformation (*shen hua* 神 化) can be cultivated and the people guided to a thorough and lasting transformation. By insisting that penal laws have their basis in the moral achievements of the people, a principle found at the core of traditional Confucianism, the absolute power of the ruler characteristic of the Legalist doctrine has been considerably reduced. Not only does this law dictate that the ruler's will is superseded by the will of the people, the ruler himself is answerable to the law. Perhaps of even greater significance is the assertion that laws were originally devised to limit the arbitrary powers of the ruler. Thus, the concept of fa is fundamentally a synthesis of ideas, making its own contribution to a developing theory of government and seeking to temper high ideals with sensible pragmatism.

The Art of Rulership's interpretation of yong zhong (utilizing the people), tempered with the notion that each element seeks to achieve that which is appropriate to it, recognizes the vital importance of allowing each particular to express its own naturalness and uniqueness. It advocates full use of the spontaneous contribution of each participant in an organization committed to the nonmediated action of personal initiative. Essentially, much here points to Daoist anarchism. In early Confucianism and Daoism, personal realization is coextensive with familial, social, and political structures outlined in *The Art of Rulership* and seems to provide a framework for the collective realization of all members in the society to the extent that this is practically possible. The function of this political apparatus focuses on organization rather than authority. Yong zhong is knit into an integrated program of government and strongly influences the disposition of the other components in the overall political theory, consistent with the correlating concepts of wuwei, shi, and fa.

The final and most important concept of governance explained in *The Art of Rulership* is the concept of li min (benefiting the people), which endorses the notion of government for the people. This notion represents the essence of Chinese political philosophy. Ames explained that li min encompasses two principles. First, the ruler can organize the people by manipulating their instinct for self-interest. Second, the ruler can consolidate and expand his influence by benefiting the people. The first principle takes advantage of the fact that personal profit or self-interest motivate people. The ruler can use this insight into human nature to manipulate the energies of his people for his own purpose. This application is essentially the central Legalist concept of reward and punishment. The second principle is typically Confucian.

The traditional concept that the people are the foundation of government was absorbed into the Confucian doctrine at its inception and became the foundation of Confucian political philosophy. Acknowledging this basic principle of the supersession of the people. The Confucians then insisted that government must function for the sake of its people. Moreover, the ruler's power and stability are correlative to the degree of his success in advancing the people's interests. While the first assertion is purely Legalist, the second synthesizes the Legalist's preoccupation with the ruler's interests and the Confucian belief that the ruler's interests and those of the people are one and the same. Confucians believe any government concession to the interests of the people reinforces the strength and stability of the government itself. Thus, it ultimately benefits the ruler.

Because the political philosophy outlined in *The Art of Rulership* in Huainanzi was intended to delineate what a Chinese ruler needed to know to govern his kingdom properly, it would seem that some of this philosophy would retain modern relevance. Unfortunately, around 124 BC, Emperor Wu, under the influence of the leading Confucian scholar of the time, Tung Chungshu, pronounced Confucianism as the ideological basis of his imperial court. The emperor banned all but professed Confucians from state service and founded a national university where officials were trained in a wholly Confucian curriculum. As a result, no further original development of political philosophy occurred until very recently.

Dreams and Utopia

Questions of political and social philosophy were at play when Sir Thomas More coined the term "utopia" in 1516 and applied it to an ideal community on an imaginary island in America that ordinary, flawed individuals inhabited. In this work, More explored the French Revolutionary ideals of equality and reform and provided a lens through which to study the aspirations of a culture or tradition, that is, its utopian ideals. Hsu Cho-Yun (Ching and Guisso 1991) studied the concept of utopia as it appears in the Chinese tradition and found three kinds of utopian models: the Confucian bureaucratic welfare state, the Daoist isolated community, and a self-governed community that essentially bridged the Confucian and Daoist models.

The Confucian welfare state model is best elucidated in a famous passage from the *Book of Rites* called 禮 運 大 同 篇 the "Great Community," which has inspired Chinese people for generations:

When the Great Way was in practice, a public and common spirit ruled everything under Heaven;

Men of talent, virtue, and ability were selected; sincerity was emphasized and harmonious relationships were cultivated.

The men did not love only their own parents, nor did they treat as children only their own children.

A competent provision was secured for the aged till their death, employment was given to the able-bodied, and a means was provided for the upbringing of the young.

Kindness and compassion were shown to widows, orphans, childless men, and those who were disabled by disease, so that they all were sufficiently maintained.

Men had their proper work and women had their home.

They hated to see the wealth of natural resources unused (so they developed it, but) not for their own profit.

In this way selfish schemings were thwarted and did not develop.

Bandits and thieves, rebels and troublemakers did not show themselves.

Hence the outer doors of houses never had to be closed.

This was called the Great Community.

The Great Community was a spontaneously organized community representing the epitome of the Confucian idealized society. It modeled the type of simple egalitarian welfare community that people in agricultural societies, such as the ancient Chinese, could aspire to build.

Carrying the Confucian ideal one step further by suggesting a practical application, Mencius (372–289 BC), presented his own dream, the "well-field" system, a term that survives to this day in the Chinese theory of land distribution. Mencius suggested a square block of land should be divided into nine equal, smaller squares, like in a tic-tac-toe game. Each would measure 100 *mou* (Chinese acres) in size. A household was to cultivate each of the eight peripheral plots. The central plot was designated as a public field or "field for the lord." The income from this public field was for the state, and no other tax was to be levied. On the occasion of death or moving from one dwelling to another, there would be no quitting of the district. Those who belonged to the same block of nine squares rendered friendly assistance to one another, helping to maintain the land and sustaining one another in sickness and tribulation. Thus, the people would live in affection and harmony. Such a small basic community would then serve as the foundation of the state, which was comprised of a farming population in the field and an urban population in the capital, who would pay to the state as tax, one-tenth of their income, as assessed by themselves. Mencius's idealized Confucian society, a liberal community requiring little government involvement, subsequently inspired another land reform movement in the Sung dynasty a thousand years later.

The popular story and poem, "Peach Blossom Source," by T'ao Yuanming 陶淵明 (365–427) characterized the Chinese ideal of an isolated Daoist society. The narrative follows a fisherman who accidentally enters a community after he had gone astray through a grove of peach trees and then penetrated a small opening in a hill. In this isolated place, the fisherman found people who had been cut off from communication with outsiders for some five hundred years. The peaceful, undisturbed life in the community was self-sufficient and did not require the intervention of state authority to regulate or sanction it.

In his study of utopian societies in China, Hsu suggested this story represents another idealized society, one totally cut off from the outside world with no tax or government. Even knowledge was unnecessary. This Daoist utopia served as an ideological alternative to the Confucian version of an idealized society. Traditionally, if a Chinese person is doing well, he or she espouses Confucianism, adopting the positive attitude and outlook of a Confucian. However, if one is out of favor or facing desperate circumstance, Daoism provides a convenient escape into a secluded, peaceful life, like that led by the poet T'ao himself.

The third utopian model described by Hsu, the self-governed community, represents a compromise between the Daoist and Confucian utopias. A counterpart to the community envisioned in the "Peach Blossom Source" was allegedly found in a small village during the twelfth century, as documented by K'ang Yuchih. The setting of K'ang's idealized community was also in a hidden valley reached through an opening in the hill, which could be blocked for the purpose of cutting off communication with the outside world. In this idealized community, people who were not kinsmen lived harmoniously together. They were self-sufficient in producing basic necessities for themselves. Money or precious commodities, such as fine silk, were to be destroyed if brought in. Each household was assigned land for cultivation according to the number of household members. Oxen, other domestic animals, implements, clothing, and even food were to be shared and not possessed. New members were welcomed to join the community, provided they were productive and useful to others. When the outside world was suffering from foreign invasions, people in the hidden valley simply sealed the entrance to keep themselves in safety. The operation of this society in a hidden valley bears great similarity to the "Peach Blossom Source." There are two significant differences. First, the community could collectively enforce the destruction of valuable items for the sake of preventing trouble caused by greed. Second, the community had a collective authority to assign a share of cultivated field to each according to the per-capita principal. In other words, K'ang's utopia did not exist in a state of benign anarchy as in the "Peach Blossom Source." A certain type of self-government was seemingly regarded as necessary. The autonomous government was at the community level.

Each of Hsu's three models is distinctively different from the idea of utopia found in the West. The Western utopia is often a city-state; the Chinese are always small rural communities, uncomplicated and representative of the Chinese longing for natural simplicity. Second, the Chinese utopia is depicted as either a blueprint for a fairer order or a hidden place where people could control their own destiny without outside interference, thus representing the aspiration for equality and freedom. These ideals were not mere wild dreams or intellectual games. They often appeared to the ancient Chinese to be within their reach. Thus, they were ideals that captured people's imagination for generations.

These Chinese dreams contrast sharply to the ideals of the late and contemporary period in the West, which focus on themes of achievement, advancement, expansion, and progress. An explanation for these differences can be found in the contrasting agricultural and nomadic backgrounds of the two cultural histories as well as in contrasting cultures, philosophy, and thinking preferences guided by the notions of yin and yang. For this reason, we would like to return to the study of history in the next few chapters and examine the formation and development of the Chinese nation, drawing comparisons with European history. We will see that agrarians are tied to their land and are usually more conservative in outlook. Nomadic herdsmen are generally colonists and traders and usually more progressive. In addition, we must acknowledge that, thus far, we have been dealing only with ideals and theories. History offers us a reality check as we examine how Chinese and Western societies and nations actually developed in light of their differences in culture, philosophy, and thinking.

Part Three

Mega History, China and the West

To this point, we have dealt primarily with theoretical and cosmological aspects of human existence, including thoughts, interpretations of nature, and our relationship with family, society, the state, and ourselves. We are now ready for a reality check. The history of Europe, in combination with that of the Near East, and China furnishes a record of events that allows us to compare the unfolding processes of history in the West and East. These actual events can be held up for examination in the light of the worldviews elucidated in the preceding chapters.

A reminder is warranted before we proceed. While history provides a story or record of important events that happened to a person or a nation, the writing of history usually reflects the conceptualizations and interpretations of the writer as well as the events themselves. Thus, all historians should take responsibility for understanding and clarifying their unique biases as researchers and authors. In our case, the materials upon which we have based our cultural comparison represent only a small selection culled from the vast literature of history. They are presented with only the background verification we have personally been able to collect. But we hope that awareness of our own shortcomings allows us to share our conclusions with a minimum of cultural or ideological partiality. In addition, because of the breadth of the topics involved both in space and time, we can only sketch the big picture at this time. For readers interested in studying further, many reputable history books are available.

In the upcoming six chapters, we will present mega events in history and concentrate on, by way of comparison between cultures, different forces that were behind the occurrence of these events, such as technological, cultural, economic, sociological, and political. These specific forces provide a method of organizing our exploration because they are ultimately offshoots of human thinking and relationships, topics profiled in the previous chapters.

CHAPTER SEVEN

The Neolithic Times
(~8000 BC–500 BC)

In chapter two, we discussed the Paleolithic era and the impact of the Ice Age on thinking. During the immensely long period of time marked by the Ice Age, the use of tools led to the evolution of the concept of culture. In this chapter, we will examine the subsequent Neolithic era. During which, we will see cultures further develop into civilizations as Neolithic villagers create cities that became increasingly larger as better technology, organization, and management became available. Urban communities that shared a common ethnic heritage grouped themselves into nations; nations ultimately fused into empires.

Advances in stone-working technology, precipitated by the development and spread of agriculture around ten thousand years ago, marked the Neolithic era of eastern and western Eurasia. During this era, our ancestors' means of survival slowly transformed from food gathering to food cultivation, leading to increased independence from nature. Many of the foundational structures of civilization resulted from this important transformation. Languages, customs, traditions, forms of government, and many of our fundamental solutions to the uncertainties of the world emerged during this period in Europe, the Near East, and China.

As documented previously, the civilizations that arose from the agricultural revolution varied according to their unique environmental and climatic conditions, adaptation to specific environments, thinking preferences, and worldviews. Yet, in most cases, the agricultural revolution fostered increases in both productivity and population as a square mile of cultivated land could support many more people than could the same land area were it used merely as a resource for food gathering. According to L. S. Stavrianos (1983), in the period between ten thousand and two thousand years ago, global human population jumped from 5.22 to 133 million, a twenty-five-fold increase within just eight thousand years. Those groups who switched to agriculture the earliest grew the fastest. Those who remained food gatherers the longest were left behind. Population pressure soon built up in the villages, leading surplus populations to migrate to nearby uncultivated lands. Food gatherers using these lands were forced to flee to areas that were unsuitable for farming. In other cases, agricultural immigrants and local food gatherers intermarried and produced a new hybrid people. As population pressure built up again, the new hybrid population migrated into fresh lands where further interbreeding took place with native peoples. In this way, agricultural techniques and crops were transmitted long distances. The descendents of the original food cultivators could be of an entirely different racial type from their ancestors.

In this section, we shall first look at conditions that prevailed when agriculture was introduced to Europe, the Near East, and Chinese regions. The similarities and differences between these regions act as precursors to the divergent development of Europe, the Near East, and Chinese nations over this period.

Section One:
Neolithic Civilizations of Europe and Mesopotamia

According to Price and Feinman (2001), the story of European prehistory during the Neolithic era is one of spectacular growth and change. From the appearance of the first farmers to the events of the Roman conquest, it is a story of the spread of agriculture, technological innovation, and the development of economically and politically powerful groups. This story chronicles the evolution of society from small bands of hunter-gatherers in the late Pleistocene through the first hierarchical societies of the early Neolithic to the Bronze and Iron Ages.

Many major innovations, including domesticated plants and animals, pottery, metallurgy, and writing, and so forth, arrived in Europe from the Near East, appearing initially in the southeast shortly before 7000 BC and moving gradually to the north and west until about 4000 BC.

Following the domestication of the first plant in the Near East, various plants were adapted over a period of many centuries to a wide variety of environmental conditions. In the process, such plants have spread to other areas, thereby creating a regional complex of multispecies agriculture. Stavrianos (1983) maintained that this advanced type of agriculture had two great advantages: a high level of productivity and subsistence security. If one crop failed for climatic reasons, another with different climatic requirements could survive. Thus, multispecies agriculture first provided the dependable food supply essential for dense populations and later for the civilizations such density produced.

Farming required more intensive labor, better organization, and better discipline than had been prevalent in earlier societies. Thus, the transition from the earliest domestications to the agricultural revolution, which is defined here as a full dependence on agriculture, was very gradual and prolonged. This period is known as the phase of incipient agriculture. In the Middle East, this phase lasted from roughly 9500–7500 BC, when the ancestors of modern wheat, oats, rye, and barley as well as those of modern goats, sheep, cattle, and pigs were domesticated. Incipient farming communities appeared first in the Aegean area and Greece around 6500 BC, utilizing domesticated plants and animals, architecture, and ceramics brought from the Near East. The indicative characteristics of pottery, mud-brick houses, and domestic plants and animals were then spread to other areas via the Danube and other rivers of the Balkan Peninsula. By 3000 BC, farming had penetrated to the coasts of western Europe and reached its climatic limits in northern Scandinavia and Britain. In the third millennium BC, these initial Neolithic societies became regionalized, following distinctive trends toward increasing warfare, wealth, trade, and colonization.

In the meantime, technological advancement continued in Mesopotamia with the gradual development of new and more productive irrigation-based agriculture. In combination with new social institutions, this set off a chain reaction that eventually culminated in the first civilization of western Eurasia.

As the ancient Mesopotamians moved from the hills to the riverside lowlands, they encountered problems of inadequate rainfall, searing heat, periodic floods, and a lack of stone for building materials. Irrigation was arrived at as the necessary solution, allowing these pioneering farmers to cultivate the rich, alluvial soils by digging short canals leading from the river channels to the fields. The rewards for this extra output in human energy far outweighed the effort because the resultant crops were incredibly productive compared to those that had previously been wrested from the stone hillsides. Documents dating to 2500 BC indicate that the average yield of a field of barley was eighty-six times greater than the seed required for sowing. Food was now more abundant, varied, and assured, which resulted in more people, irrigation canals, new fields, and food.

While the techniques of irrigation were being worked out, the new craft of metallurgy was also being mastered. By 3000 BC, bronze, an alloy of copper and tin, became available. This catalyzed several major changes in technology and transportation, including the manufacture of bronze weapons and jewelry, the widespread adoption of the plow and the wheel, and the use of draft animals such as oxen and horses to pull carts and chariots. The ox-drawn plow and the wheel was significant because people could use something other than their own muscles for motive power for the first time. Again, these improved technologies enhanced production and created more food for a larger population.

The introduction of agriculture resulted in major changes in European societies and economies throughout the six millennia before Christ. Far-reaching technological advances went together with significant institutional changes. Increases in population enabled some villages to grow into towns, which attracted a new elite of religious, military, and administrative leaders. Resulting urban communities that shared a common ethnic heritage grouped themselves into nations. Subsequently, nations fused into empires through trade, colonization, and military conquest. The ancient world aspired to the formation of a universal state encompassing all civilized communities, so small empires merged and grew bigger. Large urban communities or nations could then support a growing newly independent class of priests, soldiers, and bureaucrats.

Priests, the successors of the earlier tribal shamans, became the first elite group responsible for the growing managerial functions essential to an increasingly complex society. Decisions regarding the proper operation and construction of irrigation facilities were often included in these responsibilities. In addition, it is now believed that the earliest writing was actually a priestly invention born of the need for keeping records essential to their administrative responsibilities. Priests also provided the main stimulus for crafts, which were initially designed as temple decorations rather than secular market trade goods. As towns grew increasingly complex, priests with a purely religious sanction became increasingly ineffective as more professional management skills were needed. This led to the shift of power from the priesthood to a new secular elite and bureaucracy.

As the territories of contiguous communities encroached upon one another, warfare increased in frequency. War leaders often became permanent military chiefs and even kings. Palaces began to rival temples. Working partnerships between the priesthood and secular powers eventually evolved. The priests normally retained their great landholdings and continued their sacred services while palace officials constructed walls around their cities and raised large armies, which they employed against neighboring cities and eventually in building empires.

The third and second millennia BC in western Eurasia witnessed the appearance of early states and empires in Mesopotamia, the Nile Valley, and the Aegean. Stavrianos (1983) described the style of the pioneer civilization of Mesopotamia as urban with its first center at Sumer, which consisted of twelve separate city-states by 3000 BC. These cities continually fought each other. Indo-European invaders from the north and Semitic invaders from the south easily conquered them. The history of Mesopotamia then became a centuries-long struggle between the Indo-European and Semitic invaders for control of the fertile river valley.

State-level societies also emerged in the Aegean, Crete, and Greek mainland before the literate civilizations of classical Greece and Rome. The Minoan palaces and Mycenaean citadels were the urban centers of these civilizations and the focal points of industry, commerce, religion, military power, and central accumulation. Stavrianos referred to the style of the Minoan civilization on the island of Crete as *thalassocracy*, a Greek word meaning "sea civilization." The prosperity of Crete depended on its trade with countries throughout the basin of the Mediterranean Sea. The single-masted trading ships of the Minoans carried foodstuffs, ivory, and glass of Egypt; the horses and wood of Syria; the silver, pottery, and marble of the Aegean Isles; the copper of Cyprus; and the Minoans' own olive oil and pottery. From Stavrianos's writings and research, the Minoan civilization evidently flourished long before that of the Greeks on the mainland and was actually very sociologically advanced.

The mainland Greeks created two very divergent civilizations: the Mycenaean and the Hellenic or Classical. The Mycenaean civilization was the product of monarchies whose bureaucratic institutions resembled those of the older eastern nations. The Hellenic evolved in cities where popular governments promoted humanistic values.

Despite their evident prosperity, these civilizations were not immune to hardship. During the second millennium BC, many ancient civilizations were collapsing under pressure from nomads, including the Semitic tribesmen from the southern deserts and the Indo-Europeans from the Eurasian steppes to the west. In addition, scarcity and costliness of copper and bronze, used in making weapons and tools, contributed to the eventual downfall of the Mycenaean and Hellenic civilizations.

The Indo-Europeans were a cultural, rather than racial, group originating in the region of the Caspian Sea. Primarily farmers, they tended their herds of cattle and cultivated some crops. Yet, two occurrences vaulted these nomads into a commanding military position that threatened the very existence of other great civilizations: the domestication of the horse in the second millennium BC and the smelting of iron later.

The first wave of invasion by the Indo-Europeans came between roughly 1700 and 1500 BC with relatively small numbers of nomadic invaders in horse-drawn chariots wielding bronze weapons. Yet, the use of horses clearly tipped the balance in favor of the invaders:

> The first military use that the nomads made of their horse was to harness it to a light-bodied chariot with two spoked wheels, which they developed as an improvement on the clumsy Mesopotamian cart with four solid wheels. The combination of the large horse and easily maneu-

verable chariot gave the nomads a formidable weapon—the war chariot. The first wave of nomadic invasions in the second millennium BC were invasions of charioteers. They rode hard into battle with one warrior in the chariot in charge of the horses and the others shooting arrows from their powerful compound bows. Few infantrymen could stand up for long to the volleys of arrows, let alone to the massed chariot charges that followed. Toward the end of the second millennium the nomads further increased their military effectiveness by shifting from chariot to cavalry warfare. Their horses were now large and strong enough to bear the direct weight of the rider. Also the nomads developed the bridle and bit for guiding the horse, and the horned saddle and stirrup, which enabled them to ride with both hands free and to launch a shower of arrows at full gallop. Hence the Eurasian nomads had unprecedented mobility, and were able to outride and outfight armies defending the urban centers. The riding process was the basis of nomadic military power through the Classical and Medieval ages, and culminated in the extraordinary conquests of Genghis Khan in the thirteenth century (Stavrianos 1983).

The discovery of the technique for smelting iron ore further enhanced nomadic military strength. Iron ore, in contrast to copper and tin, was very widespread and relatively cheap. By 1200 BC, the nomadic warriors enjoyed, in addition to superior mobility, iron weapons that were as good and as plentiful as those of the soldiers guarding the civilized centers.

The second wave of invasion between 1200–1100 BC was launched by Indo-Europeans wielding iron weapons. The end result was the uprooting of civilizations everywhere with the exception of the Middle East. Empires rose and fell in rapid succession. According to Stavrianos, by the end of the first wave, three powers—the Hittites in the north, the Egyptians in the south, and the Semitic Assyrians in the east—controlled the Middle East. During the second wave of invasion, a long series of wars between the Hittites and Egyptians weakened both empires. Three Semitic invaders moved into the vacuum: the Phoenicians to the Mediterranean coast; the Arameans to Syria, Palestine, and northern Mesopotamia; and the Hebrews to Palestine and Syria. About 1100 BC, the powerful second Assyrian Empire began to expand with its iron weapons, disciplined army, efficient bureaucracy, and iron-battering rams mounted on wheels. By the seventh century the Assyrian empire with its capital at Nineveh included all Mesopotamia, Asia Minor, Syria, Palestine, and Egypt. But overextension of the empire and the deep hostility of its subject peoples finally led to disaster. In 612 BC, a coalition of enemies destroyed Nineveh and forever ended the role of the Assyrians in history.

The Persians, who now organized the greatest empire to that date, followed the Assyrians. Under King Cyrus (550–529 BC) and using Assyrian military techniques, the Persians conquered all the lands from the Nile River in the west to the Indus River in the east. For the first time, the entire Middle East was under one rule. The barbarian invaders were firmly shut out.

The first invading Indo-European Achaeans were fighters, but their general level of development was far behind that of the Minoan Cretans. By 1600 BC, the newcomers had absorbed much of the Minoan culture that had been transplanted to the mainland by then and established a number of small kingdoms from Thessaly down to the southern tip of the Peloponnesus. Mycenae was the outstanding center of the Peloponnesus, and it lent its name to the emerging civilization.

In contrast to the cities of Crete, settlements in Mycenaean Greece were strongly fortified. Massive hilltop citadels were constructed where the king and his retainers lived. The commoners built their dwellings outside the citadel, but they sought refuge within its walls in time of danger. Even with their existing strength on land, the Mycenaeans took to the sea after the fashion of the Minoans and developed a formidable maritime power. They raided or traded as opportunities dictated and founded overseas colonies in Rhodes, Cyprus, and the west coast of Asia Minor. By the fifteenth century BC, they were raiding the great island of Crete itself. Its unfortified cities, including the capital of Knossos, were taken and destroyed. In combination with a series of devastating earthquakes, this conquest led to the virtual extinction by 1150 BC of the formerly great Minoan civilization. Meanwhile, in 1200 BC, the Mycenaeans were experiencing a similar fate at the hands of new invaders, the Dorians, who were armed with superior iron weapons.

The Dorians captured the Mycenaean citadels and towns one by one and returned them back to an agrarian and pastoral economy. A Dark Age descended and obscured Greece until the rise of the city-states in about 800 BC, a topic we will examine in section three.

Section Two:
Neolithic Civilizations of China and the Formation of the Chinese Nations

As the Neolithic civilizations of Europe and the Near East were experiencing fission, diffusion, expansion, conquest, counterconquest, barbarian invasion, and colonization culminating in the formation of the powerful Roman Empire of the first century BC, the Chinese Neolithic civilizations were marked by economic, cultural, and political fission and fusion, assimilation, kinship linkage, intermarriage, and integration, which eventually resulted in the equally powerful and vast Chinese Qin/Han empires. In what way these differences in history are the result of divergent worldviews, cultural philosophies, and thinking preferences, as described previously, is a judgment that readers will ultimately have to make for themselves. The historical record suggests that there is indeed a relationship.

In contrast to the beliefs of Stavrianos and other Western writers who view Chinese Neolithic civilizations to be the result of the eastward expansion of Western civilizations, new archaeological finds in China over the past few decades have convincingly suggested an indigenous nature to China's Paleolithic and Neolithic cultures. In fact, at some time around 10000–8000 BC, domestication of animals and cultivation of plants, mainly millet in the north and rice in the south, occurred independently in several areas of China. Using the regional systems and cultural type (*quxi lexing* 區 系 類 形) approach first proposed by archaeologist Su Bingqi 蘇 秉 琦 in 1979, there were evidently at least six independent regional systems of macroscale, each with many cultural types. Chinese civilization, rather than being the end result of a process radiating from the core (the Central Plain of the Yellow River) to the land of the barbarians, as we used to believe, is now known to have had multiple origins, which were diverse, plural, and mutually influencing with the degree of influence depending on the time and local conditions. Eventually, every region and local culture contributed in its own way and to varying degrees to the Chinese-ness of the integrated culture that we now know.

Natural borders within settlements that were established usually define regional cultures in China, including river valleys, mountain valleys, coastal plains, and other ecological enclaves. The early Chinese were comprised of very diverse groups of people who were scattered in valleys around the feeder channels of its many great rivers, among which the largest are the Yellow, Yangtze, and Pearl Rivers.

In comparison with the relatively small basins around the Mediterranean and in Mesopotamia, basins near the great Chinese rivers are much larger in scale and more self-sufficient and abundant in water. They also have more fertile soil and climates more suitable for farming. They are less dependent on trade. The loess deposits of the Yellow River Plateau, in particular, were loose sediments rich in organic nutrients and suited to the use of stone plows, one of the reasons for the early development of organized farming in China.

In all areas of China, farming started with just a few families grouping around a feeder channel of a river. As more food became available due to the result of technological advancements in farming, populations grew and spread through a process of contact, fusion, assimilation, intermarriage, and integration. The whole village, valley, and region became populated. Warfare was only a resort when natural integration failed. Increasing density led to the further supplementation of agriculture by the home industries of arts and crafts as well as other nonagricultural industries while fishing and hunting continued to thrive. This development process repeated over and over again as the communities grew increasingly larger and networks of communities and markets of trade appeared.

We know now that several traditions developed simultaneously in the Neolithic China of the third millennium BC (Chang 1998) and they interacted with each other when geography allowed. In addition to such communal expansion, the hydraulic work required to tame the mighty rivers and allow human survival demanded effective leadership, productive technology, and genuine cooperation from people who lived by the waters. This interaction stimulated and enriched the content of life and made fusion necessary and inevitable. The competitive stimulus between communities created conditions from which emerged an organized political entity, the state. With this evolution, China stepped into civilization.

As examples of this emerging civilization, we would like to provide a rough sketch of three geographical areas of great significance in the prehistory of northern China, areas that were typical of Neolithic development and neatly tie together legends, written historical essays and literature, and new archaeological finds. The first area, the valley of the Liao River 遼 河 in Manchuria, was occupied by a succession of three cultures: the Xinglongwa 興 隆 洼 (8500–7000 BC), the Xinle 新 樂 (7000–5000 BC), and the Hongshan 紅 山 (3000–2500 BC). The second area, the middle Yellow River valleys, was home to the Yangshao culture 仰 韶 (5000–3000 BC). The third region, the hills and lakeshores of the Shandong highlands of the lower Yellow River, was occupied by the Dawenkou culture 大 汶 口 (4300–1900 BC). Materials abound on the Neolithic cultures of these regions, so we will sketch only a rough outline here. We will also skip over the similar, but independent, developments found along other river valleys, such as those of the Yangtze and Pearl Rivers, where the same dynamics apply with the exception that rice was the main crop under cultivation.

The Liao River 遼 河

The Liao River of northern China originates in the eastern part of the Mongolian plateau, flows east into the southern Manchurian plains, and then takes a sharp turn south, draining finally into the Bay of Bohai. Around 8500 BC, this river valley was heavy vegetated, providing cover and sustenance for a great variety of animals and plants. Because of the lush vegetation and proximity to the river, the ancient peoples of this area were hunters, fishers, and farmers at the same time. Millet farming and domestication of cattle and sheep were common.

Recent research has associated the Hongshan culture (the successors of the Xinglongwa and Xinle cultures) in this area with the ancestral home of the legendary sage, the Yellow Emperor, Huangdi 黃 帝, the symbolic father of all Chinese people. The name "Huangdi" may not refer to a person at all. Instead, it may be a tribal identifier or an assemblage of many tribes over a period of time. According to the *Book of History* (*Shiji*), Huangdi cultivated himself morally, excelled militarily, administered the five types of Qi, grew five crops, pacified ten thousand people, and exerted an influence that extended in all four directions. He is also allegedly the father of what is now known as the Huang Lao school of Daoism and Legalism, the institution of family names and family life. Among other inventions, he was the creator of the compass and the wheel. For her part, his wife is credited with the invention of silk. If he existed, the Huangdi of tribal legend must have been simultaneously a brilliant military, religious, and cultural leader. Some Chinese writers suggest that China's history as a nation actually begins with Huangdi in approximately 2698 BC.

Recent archaeological finds substantiate the story of Huangdi. Many outstanding art objects have been brought to light in the Liao River area. The materials and motifs of these objects anticipate later elements of southern China. Foremost among these are a variety of jade objects, which are sacred for divination, and the dragon motif. Apparently, bears and dragons were the important totem symbols of the tribes in these areas. The most characteristic pottery is rocker-stamped flat-bottomed vessels in the earlier period and red-striped bowls and tubes in the later period.

The Yangshao Culture 仰 韶 文 化

The Yangshao was the first Neolithic culture for which Swedish geologist Andersson found evidence in China in 1920, and it is perhaps still the best known. The Yangshao was a culture of millet and vegetable farmers, planting both *Setaria* and *Panicum* millets. These crops were highly drought-resistant and particularly suited to the northern Chinese climate, especially in the period before irrigation became common. More than a thousand archaeological sites distributed in the Yellow River Valley show evidence of this culture, from Chengzhou in the east to the river's upper reaches in Gansu and Qinghai in the west. Within this vast area, the culture can be divided into several phases on the basis of ceramic styles, which are of reddish color and painted with various designs in black or dark brown. Major vessel types include the bowl, water bottle, jar, and urn. This red-based pottery is polished. The best-known style painted with geometric designs and an occasional representational image has given Yangshao the name "painted pottery" culture. In addition to pottery, artifacts from Yangshao sites include many agricultural implements, such as chipped or polished stone hoes, spades, harvesting knives, stones for grinding grain, and artifacts indicating continued activities of fishing and hunting in certain areas.

The Yangshao area, which used to be called the Central Plain (*Zhongyuan* 中原), comprised the valley of the Wei River in Shaanxi near the foothill of Mount Hua. It is particularly interesting because it was the ancestral home of another legendary hero, Shen Nong.

Beginning his reign in 2737 BC, Shen Nong 神農 was the legendary leader of the Hua people. Even today, Chinese people refer to themselves by this name. His rule was legendary for its peacefulness, but he was simultaneously renowned as an herbalist, the progenitor of Chinese medicine, the inventor of the stone plow and hoe, slash and burn agriculture, and the domestication of animals. Again, Shen Nong was likely not actually one person, but a composite of many leaders of various tribes.

In contrast to the bear and dragon totem symbols of the Hongshan, the Yangshao culture used flowers, such as the rose, as totem symbols.

The Yangshao culture covered a large area as a result of population growth, and the steady fission and fusion of settlements eventually pushed the communities of this culture out across a broad area. Despite their size, they remained farming communities and were no match for the nomads from the north when it came to warfare. With a few exceptions, this was actually a general rule throughout the history of China.

The Dawenkou Culture 大汶口文化

The third emerging civilization in Neolithic China during the third millennium BC was the Dawenkou culture. With a long tradition of millet farming, this culture was located in a broad area from Pohai Bay on the Shantung Peninsula that extended west into the eastern parts of the loess plain and south to the periphery of the Yangtze delta. Although Dawenkou pottery, or "black pottery," is distinctive, there is clear evidence of mutual influence shared with Yangshao to the west, Hongshan to the north, and Hemudo 河姆渡 to the south, suggesting a dynamic communication among all these cultures. A remarkable archaeological discovery in Dawenkou is the graphs etched onto the sides of some black pots, representing the earliest known script in China. These scripts, dating to the second half of the third millennium BC, are identifiable and decipherable according to the etymological principles of Chinese writing during the Shang and later dynasties.

Racially, people of the Dawenkou area belonged to the diverse Yi 夷 people of eastern and southern China. Here, they were called Dong Yi 東 夷, or Eastern Yi. They were known to be brave seafarers. According to Louise Levathes (1994), it is thought that the Yi people from the mainland of Asia crossed the Taiwan Strait and settled in Taiwan around 9000 BC. From 7000–5500 BC, some moved from Taiwan to the Philippines. Around 4000 BC, they moved on to the Malay Peninsula and the Moluccas and east to the Bismarck Archipelago. By 1300 BC, they reached Fiji. Being at the crossroads of many cultures, the Dong Yi are more advanced technologically than others of the Dawenkou time. They were the forefathers of the Longshan cultures and the subsequent founders of the powerful Shang kingdom.

The Longshan Culture 龍 山 文 化

The archaeological record of these three cultures provides clear evidence of the indigenous nature of China's Paleolithic and Neolithic cultures. According to Chang Kwang-chih, discoveries related to the Longshan cultures that then followed these three are among the most significant that archaeology has made during the twentieth century. These rich finds are also of great importance in the comparative study of Chinese cultures of the third millennium BC, providing tangible and reliable clues to why and how civilizations and states first came into being. The most important of these clues include the settlement patterns of the Longshan towns excavated in Shandong and Henan. Items found include the gradations of furnishings and spatial distributions of graves in Shanxi, Shandong, Jiangsu and Zhejiang provinces and the remains of ritual objects, especially ritual jades. The archaeological evidence clearly shows that societies in China had become stratified by the Longshan period and the existence of a large number of ordered communities known as the ten thousand states (wan guo 萬 國) was a prerequisite for stratified societies. The manner in which societies became stratified in China offers an explanation for the characteristic animal designs that decorate jade and bronze ritual objects.

Excavations of Longshan graves make it clear that political power in ancient China derived from the concentration of shamanic paraphernalia as the principal means to accumulate and divide material wealth. Among these items of shamanic power, the most important were made of jade, a rock that is both geologically rare and required political power to quarry. This political power manifested itself in two aspects of ancient Chinese life, ritual and war, as emphasized in the classic text,

Zuo zhuan 左 傳, "Ritual and war are the affairs of the state." Archaeologically, the most conspicuous aspects of the lives of the Longshan elite support such an emphasis. Wars were relatively small in scale during the time of Longshan culture and often fought in a gentlemanly manner. These wars are not to be confused with the cruel, large-scale wars of the later Warring State period. The Longshan elite and their followers lived in clusters with power woven through their networks. The late Longshan period during the latter part of the third millennium and the earlier part of the second millennium was the period of the ten thousand states. During which, many such clusters of power were competing for political survival. The surge in interactions among these many states made the Longshan one of the most active periods in ancient Chinese history. Not only did political chiefdoms, hierarchical settlements, and high shamanism begin in this period, it may have been witness to the invention of true writing as well.

According to Z. Wang (1998), the Longshan period was marked by a distribution and density of villages in the valleys of north China that approached a level of saturation similar to that of today. Armed with advanced technology in irrigation, drilling of water wells distant from rivers, building cities and palaces, the development of an effective bureaucracy, the textile industry, and making bronze, Longshan culture was poised at the threshold of statehood. In fact, this was the era of Yao 堯 and Shun 舜, the two sages that Confucius singled out as models for those who would aspire to governance. (For more information, see chapter six. It was the best era of antiquity to emulate). It was also the final reign in which merit, rather than inheritance, determined succession.

The Three Dynasty Period 三代

Around 2083 BC, the Great Yu 大 禹, a legendary hero whose successful water works project tamed the flood of the mighty Yellow River, met with an assembly of state-chiefs of the ten thousand states. At this meeting on Mount Tushan 塗 山, Yu was proclaimed the Overlord of Hsia 夏. Following his reign and upon his death, Yu's son contended with a lieutenant already designated as a successor in a struggle for the position of leader. According to legend, the Hsia people chose to support the legitimate son of the Great Yu as their leader, thus creating a precedent that decisively moved the Hsia toward the status of a dynasty. The Hsia succession then lasted for 471 years to 1612 BC.

Archaeological data have confirmed literary sources that state the legendary worlds of the Hsia and later the Shang were multiracial alliances of many tribes. Many local cultures developed at that time into nations or groups of people with a defined identity. Interaction among them allowed the transfer of bronze technology, effective communication, and the organization and management of the important hydraulic projects. These frequent interactions signaled a change that finally pulled these local cultures, or nations, into a common area dominated by a single political entity, the Hsia.

The Hsia culture was probably partially descended from Erlitou culture 二里頭, which originated in the western Henan and eastern Shanxi provinces. Four cultural levels excavated at Erlitou, between the Luoyang and Zhengzhou areas, were highly sophisticated with evidence of early-stage bronze making found in the third in the form of casting molds, bronze tools, and weapons. In addition, there were pottery workshops, bone artifacts, jade and stone ritual objects, and musical instruments. The foundation of a large house, which the archaeologists called a "palace," was discovered. It is the oldest such building excavated in this area so far.

The Three Dynasty period refers to the contemporary existence of the Hsia 夏, Shang 商, and Zhou 周 dynasties. The Hsia was situated in the middle between the Shang and the Zhou, around Henan and Shanxi. The Shang was more to the east, and the Zhou was located to the west. These three were not actually dynasties in the popular sense. Rather, they were more like chiefdoms or confederations.

When the Shang began to dominate northern China in the second millennium BC, they adopted many features of the Hsia as well as other cultures. According to Chang Kwang-chih (Loewe and Shaughnessy 1999), the organizational potential of the state gave rise to bronze production and urbanization. Both required the mobilization of human and natural resources. When used to make weapons, bronze allowed the utilization of resources to buttress the power of the state. Therefore, even stronger controls developed through bureaucratization and adoption of unified symbols of authority and communication, for instance, a state art and a state writing system. Advancements in agriculture brought a surplus of food, one due to increased efficiency resulting from clever organization of workers who were mobilized to increase the capacity of the land through reclamation. The Shang, as a consequence of cultural and commercial exchange between the regions, cultivated both northern and southern crops. Shang architecture combined the use of stamped earth, a northern tradition, and wooden superstructures in the style of the south. The Shang writing system, which had its origins in the Dawenkou script being used to the east of the Shang lands, was the foundation for all later written Chinese. The Zhou inherited and elaborated these conditions and models to shape the basic patterns of Chinese civilization during the first millennium BC.

Using advanced technology, Shang civilization developed well-documented large and multifunctional cities with populations that were differentiated and stratified by rank, status, and occupation. One example of documents chronicling these developments are the archives at An-Yang, which have yielded more than one hundred thousand oracle bones 甲 骨 文, from which we have gleaned most of what is now known about Shang history, administration, culture, and religion. As Charles Hucker (1975) summarized, large cities, horse-drawn chariots, a high-order bronze technology, and a fully mature version of the Chinese writing system are special developments differentiating Shang civilization from the preceding Neolithic cultures.

From oracle bone records and scattered references in classical literature, it is now believed that the succession of kings in the Shang was patrilineal as well as fraternal. Chang Kwang-chih has theorized that there was a rotation system in which kingship passed among members of ten segments of the Shang ruling class. Of which, three dominated the majority of shares of the throne. Interrelationships among these segments also figured importantly in decisions about marriage alliances. If Chang's hypothesis is true, we can conclude that Shang state institutions heavily relied on the kinship system, favoring lineal descendants. In this case, the kings were in the main line of descent over the collateral line. As Chang indicated, the location of the Shang capital shifted frequently because of the system of rotating power between segments of the ruling class. After Pan Geng 盤 庚 moved the court to Anyang in 1300 BC, the Shang kings ruled from there until the very end of the succession, thus providing physical stability for the state.

At the time of Wu Ding 武 丁, who reigned in the early thirteenth century BC, the area under Shang control extended in all directions. Even with fluctuations in the extent of its domains, more than five hundred Shang sites have been identified in, among others, the provinces of Henan, Hebei, Shanxi, Shaanxi, Anhui, Shandong, Jiangsu, Zhejiang, Hubei, Jiangxi, Hunan, Sichuan, Inner Mongolia, and Liaoning. Clearly, this widespread presence explains the traditional view that the Shang state was extensive.

At this time, larger-scale wars began to occur, such as Wu Ding's series of major campaigns against the Tufang and Gongfang. Beyond the boundaries of Shang were other states. The Shang were either friendly to these states or subordinated them. Others were independent or even hostile. Conflicts as well as peaceful interactions between the Shang and these neighboring states were commonly reported in the oracle bone inscriptions discovered in the archives at An-Yang.

We know the Shang was chiefly an agricultural society with a mastery of many aspects of technology. There are many controversies concerning the nature of the Shang social system. The argument arises over whether or not the Shang system was feudal, involved slavery, or was a so-called Asiatic Mode of Production (AMP), as Karl Marx postulated. Li Jun, in his well-researched book on the topic

(1996), supplied some of the answers to these questions via his interpretation of the Chinese word *zhongren* 眾 人, used in the oracle inscriptions to denote the main labor force of the Shang period. After a lengthy analysis of the word, Li wrote:

> *Zhongren* were mobilized for most of the activities in the Shang time. From this perspective *zhongren* were what Marx called the "general slaves" of the state. But strictly speaking, they were not slaves of the ancient Greek or Roman type, since the definition of a slave requires not only absolute control of the slave by the slave-owner in production activities, but also the right to transfer his ownership to another owner "by sale, barter, gift, or in some other way" (Wilbur 1943: 62). The Shang *zhongren* clearly did not satisfy the requirement of the above definition of a slave ... Can we then define *zhongren* as serfs like laborers in medieval Europe ... Serfdom was a particular phenomenon belonging to Western feudalism. Since there was no landlord in the Shang, it is difficult to define *zhongren* as serfs. Although no record of transfer of *zhongren* from one owner to another is found, oracle bones do reveal that they were mobilized from one area to another to set up new towns and that they were frequently organized to wage wars against other tribes to expand the Shang territories. (1996)

Li then quoted from both archaeological finds and contemporary literature to suggest that zhongren were ordinary members of different lineages or sublineages. Thus, they could not be defined either as slaves or serfs. Nor could they be called "free men" by the Western standard. The economic and social dynamics of the Shang manifested themselves somewhat differently than in the traditional Marxist notion of AMP.

Section Three: Comparisons

Agriculture developed simultaneously in China and Mesopotamia before 8000 BC. However, agriculture did not spread from Mesopotamia to the Aegean area and Greece until around 6500 BC and Western Europe until 3000 BC. Hence, by the end of the Neolithic era, China was already heavily populated in comparison with Europe. Thus, many problems encountered by the early Chinese, such as flood control of its big rivers, population explosion, and other problems associated with the development of intense agriculture, were less problematic in Europe. Also, in comparison with the relatively small basins around the Mediterranean and Mesopotamia, basins near the great Chinese rivers are much larger in scale and are more self-sufficient and abundant in water. They also have more fertile soil and climates more suitable for farming. They are less dependent on trade. The loess deposits of the Yellow River Plateau, in particular, were loose sediments rich in organic nutrients and suited to the use of stone plows and the early development of organized farming. Therefore, in comparison with the smaller city-states of Europe, China could be developed along the agricultural path further and earlier in the Neolithic period. Instead of intense agriculture, the relatively smaller city-states around the Mediterranean flourished with trade, seafaring, warfare, and colonized settlement.

This summary clearly demonstrates that the processes influencing the origins of both European and Chinese civilization were diverse, plural, and multicentered. But the dynamics of their integration into larger polities were very different. Neolithic Europe was marked by the events of warfare, especially conquests by Indo-European and Semitic invaders; innovations and developments in trade, agriculture, technology, and religion; and the establishment of city-states. Regional integration in China, on the other hand, was catalyzed by technological innovation and exchange, intensive cultivation, cooperation on large hydraulic projects, mutual support in times of natural calamity, ancestor and nature (*tien* 天) worship, ritual and music, the development of a common system of writing, inter- as well as intramarriage, blood lineage and warfare, which, according to ancient Chinese tradition, was deployed only as a last resort. The larger and higher density of the Chinese Neolithic population, in comparison with Europe, required more social accommodation, cooperation, and harmony from everybody. Large urban centers existed in the Neolithic period, but all local Chinese cultures were nevertheless essentially agricultural, supplementing their production with trade and other industries.

While Europeans distinguished between racial groups, the Chinese were cultural rather than racial in their distinctions. The tradition of the Chinese people emphasized human similarities rather than differences. As described in chapter two, early Chinese thinking preferences were practical, holistic, integrative, tacit, aesthetic, and dynamic. Early Chinese civilizations functioned under a similar set of values. As was further outlined in chapters three to six, ancient Chinese views of relationships with nature, families, communities, states, and oneself were practical and processual, moral-based but principle-free, dynamic and spontaneous, creative, constitutive and transformative, sensitive and tolerant, respectful and deferent, distinctive and harmonious, unique but interdependent, evolutionary but committed to continuity, humanistic and nonreligious (in the Western sense), and intrinsic and immanent. Again, these characteristics apply equally to early Chinese civilizations. These cultural characteristics certainly dominated later historical development and have actually continued to do so until the present day. On the other hand, Western thinking preferences were abstract, analytical, rational, logical, divisive, and static. We will see that, in the classical periods of Greece and Rome, European civilizations were further characterized by many specialized disciplines, such as religion, philosophy, metaphysics, mathematics, and science. For a long time, European societies have remained identifiable by their divisiveness and individuality.

CHAPTER EIGHT

The Great Empires

(500 BC–200 BC)

This chapter examines the next phase in the development of civilizations—the formation of empires, both in Europe and China, beginning around the early part of the first millennium BC. This is an important page of human history. Just before the formation of the two great empires, around 500 BC, was the period known as the Axial Age. A time of great social, political, and cultural advancement happened simultaneously around the world. It was the Classical Age of Greece, China, and India.

Section One:
The Greco-Roman Empire

The last chapter concluded with the descent of Greece into a Dark Age subsequent to the arrival of the Dorians in about 1200 BC. The chaotic movements of tribes in these Dark Ages lasted for two centuries. However, in the eighth century BC, the Dorian's rule declined, and the Greek tribal states began to reemerge.

The Classical Hellenic Civilization

Through trade contacts, Greek tribes adopted the Phoenician alphabet and other technological innovations, which accelerated Greek cultural, economic, political, and military development. A growth from tribal communities to that of the city-state, the *polis*, characterized this period in Greek history. At the same time, various social classes had risen to challenge the nobility. Industry and commerce had come to play an important role. Greek colonies were scattered across all the Mediterranean shores.

According to Stavrianos (1983), a basic factor behind these developments was the geography of the Greek landscape. Greece did not have any rich natural resources or fertile river valleys or broad plains that, when properly developed and exploited, could support elaborate empires. In addition, in Greece and on the coast of Asia Minor, successive mountain chains restricted agricultural productivity and compartmentalized the countryside. Consequently, the Greeks did not have any natural geopolitical center that could provide a basis for regional integration. Instead, scattered by the invasions of various Indo-European groups, most recently the Dorians, they settled in isolated villages, usually located near some easily defensible high point that provided both a refuge in times of danger and a location for a shrine to the gods. If the polis were strategically situated near fertile lands or communication routes, it would have attracted correspondingly more settlers and thus become the leading city of the region. This fateful individualism in political development was also a reflection on the Hellenic temperament, according to Stavrianos. As a result, these city-states were tightly knit. They were self-governing political and religious communities whose citizens were prepared to make any sacrifice to maintain their freedom. Among the dozens of polis that emerged, Sparta, head of the later Peloponnesian league, was the first city-state that organized itself with a rigid social structure and government, including an assembly with representation for every citizen. As a result, Sparta excelled militarily. In the meantime, an even larger polis had appeared, Athens, which had a social system based on wealth rather than aristocratic birth.

The Hellenic civilization of the polis, as Sparta and Athens exemplified, reached the peak of its power during the fifth century BC. In 478 BC, following the Greek defeat of the Persian invasion, Athens assumed leadership of an alliance known as the Delian League, which was formed to provide collective security against the possibility of further Persian attacks. The league was theoretically an alliance of equals. The constitution provided each member with only one vote in the periodic meetings. From the start, Athens provided the executive leadership. Soon, the entire Mediterranean basin, including the Black Sea, was ringed with prosperous Greek colonies that were overseas replicas of the mother cities, most notably Athens. In what is now known as the Classical Golden Age of 500–336 BC, Athens became the preeminent power in the Mediterranean. It was in total control of the Aegean and had 172 tribute-paying states. By 450 BC, the league had become an empire.

Almost inevitably, the preeminent sea power of Athens clashed with the dominant land power of Sparta. The fighting between these two polis dragged on indecisively for ten years. The Spartans raided Attica each year, but they could not penetrate the long walls that joined Athens to the sea and protected its supplies. In 415 BC, the fatal decision was made to send the Athenian fleet to capture Sicily, a campaign from which no ships returned. Athens's allies seized the opportunity and revolted. The Spartans finally destroyed the long walls, and Athens was starved into capitulation in 404 BC. Soon after, in 371 BC, the Thebans inflicted the first major defeat on the Spartans in two hundred years. Finally, in 388 BC, Philip of Macedon smashed the combined armies of Thebes and Athens at Chaeronea, only to be later assassinated in 336 BC. His successor was his world-famous son, Alexander the Great.

The enormous wealth amassed during the Golden Age permitted Athens to flourish in the fields of art, architecture, philosophy, and politics to such an extent that the culture and thought of this age remains a source of inspiration all over the world today.

The Hellenistic Age

The remarkable achievements of Alexander the Great trumpeted the end of the Classical Age of Hellenic civilization and the beginning of the Hellenistic Age (331–31 BC). The shift from the Hellenic to the Hellenistic in the Mediterranean world represents a shift from a culture dominated by ethnic Greeks, however scattered geographically, to a culture dominated by Greek speakers of disparate ethnicities and the political dominance of the city-state to that of larger monarchies. Furthermore, in this period, the traditional Greek culture is altered by strong Middle Eastern, especially Persian, influences. Alexander and the Macedonians conquered the eastern Mediterranean, Mesopotamia, and Iranian plateau and invaded India. His successors held on to the territory west of the Tigris for some time and controlled the eastern Mediterranean until the Roman Republic took control in the second and first centuries BC.

A new system of colonization, fashioned after the Greek prototype, spread as far as the Indus city-communities. Greek education and language came to be of consequence in the world at large. Following the death of Alexander, a struggle for the succession continued until 281 BC, resulting in the establishment of three large territorial states: the Ptolemaic dynasty in Egypt based at Alexandria, the Seleucid dynasty in Syria based at Antioch, and the Antigonid dynasty in Macedonia and on the Greek mainland. Although Alexander's empire proved short-lived, the succeeding states essentially survived intact for three centuries. During which time, the Middle East became Hellenized. Thousands of Greek merchants, administrators, teachers, professionals, and mercenary soldiers emigrated from their city-states to Egypt and the Asian provinces, attracted by the unprecedented opportunities that those rich lands afforded.

The historical significance of the Hellenistic Age lies in its bringing together of the East and West, breaking the separate cultural molds that had been formed through history to this point. Under Hellenism, people, for the first time, thought of the entire civilized world of western Eurasia as a single unit. At first, the Greeks and Macedonians traveled east as conquerors and rulers, imposing a pattern of Hellenization. In the process, they themselves were changed, so the resulting Hellenistic civilization was a blend rather than transplantation. Subsequently, Eastern religions traveled as well, making their way west and contributing substantially to the transformation of the Roman Empire and medieval Europe.

The Roman Empire

Meanwhile, the city-states in Greece continued to fight among themselves, as they had in the past. They totally ignored the rising power of the Romans. According to Percival Turnbull (2004), the Romans built up their empire through conquest or annexation between the third century BC and the third century AD. At its height, the Roman Empire stretched from northwestern Europe to the Near East and encompassed all the lands of the Mediterranean. The control of an empire of this scale depended on a tightly controlled system of administration, a strong and disciplined army, and excellent communications. Thus, Roman governors appointed by the emperor controlled provinces of the empire. Troops of the Roman army and their strategically placed forts ensured the empire was defended against hostile local peoples. An efficient network of roads was built to allow troops to move swiftly within the empire and facilitate trade. The levying of taxes and control of valuable commodities such as grain, minerals and slaves enriched Rome and financed its army. The many diverse peoples and cultures whose countries became part of the Roman Empire were, to varying degrees, united by Roman culture and Roman ideals of government and citizenship.

Around 509 BC, the last king of Rome was defeated, and Rome started on the road to becoming a populist republic. The Roman constitution was structured with a Senate, magistrates, and popular assemblies. Political power was in the hands of the patrician class, the wealthy landowners, who governed through the Senate. From 499 BC onward, Rome was a democracy with two political parties: the plebeian and the patrician. Each held a relatively equal balance of power. An effect of this balanced democracy was the very stable expansion of the republic. Actually, there were many similarities between the temperate early histories of the Greeks and the Romans. For one, both were of the same ethnic stock. Just as the Indo-European Achaeans and Dorians filtered down the Balkan peninsula to Greece, the Indo-European Latins filtered down the Italian peninsula to the south bank of the Tiber River.

Rome's strategic location made the city more mercantile and open to foreign influence than other Latin settlements. The development of Rome diverged from that of the Greek city-states when Rome, aided by fortuitous geography, accomplished what was beyond the capacity of the Greek cities, that is, the conquest and unification of the entire peninsula. The Greeks had to contend with the jumbled mountains of the Balkans, whereas, in Italy, there are only the Apennines, which are not as difficult to cross and run north and south without transverse ranges. The Greeks could not build a Balkan counterpart to the system of Roman roads that eventually knitted Italy into one unit. Consequently, the far less compartmentalized Italian peninsula was easier to unite and keep united.

Another reason for the success of the Romans was their enlightened treatment of the other Italian peoples. Athens had levied tribute and never extended its citizenship. Rome, on the other hand, granted full citizenship to about one-fourth of the population of the peninsula. The remainder was granted Latin citizenship, which carried substantial, although not complete, privileges. In addition, all enjoyed autonomy. This farsighted policy saved Rome because its Italian allies remained loyal during the critical years when Hannibal rampaged up and down the length of the peninsula. Finally, the Romans prevailed through the development of superior military force and strategy. The Roman legions were trained to disperse and fight in small units. By 295 BC, the Romans had won central Italy and pushed south against Tarentum, the prosperous Greek city in the instep of the peninsula.

The transformation of Rome from an Italian republic to a great empire was sudden and spectacular, rather like the conquests of Alexander (Stavrianos 1983). The parallels between Greece and Rome help to explain the explosive expansions of both Macedon and Rome. Each had evolved superior military instruments and techniques, and each enjoyed the vital advantage of social vigor and cohesion greater than that of other Middle Eastern states or empires.

Rome's great rival, Carthage, had started as a Phoenician colony around 850 BC and became rich and powerful because of its near-monopoly of the transit trade in the western Mediterranean. Struggling to solidify their dominance, the Phoenicians fought three Punic Wars from 264 to 146 BC, via which Rome found itself pulled into a chain reaction of conquest leading to further conquest, subsequently becoming the leading power in the Mediterranean. These conquests were manifestly profitable to Rome, as plunder, slaves, and tribute poured in from each new province. Finally, Rome took advantage of the inevitable commitments and challenges created by the far-flung imperial frontiers of other nations. As a result, the Romans overran and, in quick succession, annexed Macedonia, Greece, the Asia Minor states of Pergamum, Bithynia, and Cilicia, Seleucid Syria, and, finally, Egypt in 31 BC. In this manner, the Romans occupied all of the Hellenistic succession states of the East. In Asia, they only acquired the provinces along the Mediterranean coast. The entire interior had fallen to Parthia. Meanwhile, Julius Caesar had gained fame by conquering all of Gaul between the English Channel and the Mediterranean in 58–49 BC. Finally, Rome achieved the permanent occupation of Britain in the first century AD. This marked the limits of Roman rule in Northern Europe. Sadly, this period was also marked with internal strife. Stavrianos pointed out:

> Rome did not treat its newly acquired provinces as generously as it had its earlier Italian allies. The Senate appointed governors who were given a free hand so long as they kept sending back home an adequate flow of tribute, taxes, grain, and slaves. The result was shameless exploitation and extortion ... These policies affected the Roman homeland almost as adversely as it affected the subject territories. Many of the small farmers in Italy had been ruined by the ravages of Hannibal's campaigns and by the long years of overseas service during the following wars. The peasants were forced to sell out to the new class of the very rich, who were eager to accumulate large estates because agriculture was still considered the only respectable calling for gentlemen. Thus the second century BC saw the growth in Italy of large plantations worked by slaves and owned by absentee landlords. The dispossessed peasantry drifted to the towns where they once again had to compete with slaves for such work as was available. (1983)

In addition to the economic suffering, the imperial expansion reversed the earlier trend toward democratization and disrupted traditional Roman culture. A program of reform through a moderate policy of land distribution was attempted, but it was to no avail because the oligarchy resorted to violence to gain its ends. Generals competing for power tore apart the empire at the top. From below, there were slave revolts. The final victor was Julius Caesar, the conqueror of Gaul, who had built up a powerful and devoted army. In 49 BC, in a series of brilliant campaigns, he defeated the forces of the Senate led by his rival Pompey. He became the undisputed master of the empire until his assassination in 44 BC by representatives of the old oligarchy. After another thirteen years of strife between Octavian, his adopted son and heir, and Mark Antony, a political adventurer, Octavian finally won power.

In 27 BC, the Senate conferred the titles of Augustus and Imperator upon Octavian, symbolizing the transformation of Rome from republic to empire. By Stavrianos's account, Augustus created an efficient administrative system that ensured the empire's prevalence for two centuries to come. But the four emperors following Augustus were unworthy of their high office. The empire weathered their misrule and blossomed under a succession of five capable emperors from 96 to 180. During this time, the Roman Empire reached its height, both in geographic extent and the quality of its civilization.

At its greatest extent, the Roman Empire included all the lands bordering on the Mediterranean Sea and reached far into northern Europe and the Near East. Various factors contributed to the flourishing imperial economy during these centuries, including honest and efficient administration, monetary stability, large-scale public works, and extensive trade, both within and beyond the empire. In the cultural field, a basic achievement of the Romans was the extension into central and western Europe of urban civilization with all it entailed.

Section Two: The First Unified Chinese Empire, the Qin/Han Dynasties

At the same time that the second wave of invaders in the West, the Phoenicians, were moving to the Mediterranean coast in the twelfth century BC, the Zhou people of western China were conquering the powerful Shang state.

The Western Zhou 西 周

The Zhou were not barbarous invaders. They were Chinese-speaking descendants of the Longshan Neolithic culture located in the Wei River 渭 河 valley of modern Shanxi province. In preconquest times, the Shang king conferred the title "Chief of the West" on one of the Zhou leaders. According to tradition, a Shang noblewoman was given to him in marriage. In addition, the Zhou developed an early alliance and probably intermarried with proto-Tibetan tribesmen called the Qiang 羌. Some credence is given to legends explaining the origin of the Zhou. A tribal chief led his people away from barbarian pressures into the heart of the Shanxi basin, began to develop Shang-style agriculture, and built a city in an area called the Plain of Zhou 周原, whence comes the name of the state. Despite the many achievements of the Zhou, they were technologically inferior to the Shang.

In the face of these unlikely odds, King Wen 文王, who appeared in early writings as a paragon of benevolence and wisdom and was a favorite Confucian sage-king, paved the way for conquest. Wen made alliances with neighboring chiefs. Upon which, his son, King Wu 武王, capitalized in leading a coalition of tribes that successfully overthrew the Shang state. In subsequent years, numerous military expeditions took place. The Western Zhou state expanded its territorial control further south and east. Eventually, it occupied approximately half of the area of present-day China. As the longest dynasty ever, enduring almost nine hundred years, the Zhou has served as a guiding paradigm for governmental, intellectual, and social development throughout the length of Chinese history. Part of the great success of the Zhou was due to their ability to absorb divergent populations, whether Zhou or non-Zhou, and integrate their beliefs into a grand, centralized schema, which later generations of Chinese still share.

Traditional Chinese history says the Zhou were able to take over the Shang because the latter had degenerated morally. The Western Zhou justified the conquest of the Shang by citing superior moral grounds, first regarding the will of heaven and, subsequently, via the new ideology of the Mandate of Heaven 天命 being reflected in the will of humanity. The Zhou aristocracy claimed heaven 天 was a universal being, concerned with the welfare of all the world's people and operating on a stage beyond the limits of any nation. The Zhou kings reigned because they had received the mandate of heaven, and they could equally lose the throne if their performance did not satisfy heaven. Zhou kingship was thus founded on a conception of legitimacy, which depended on accountability to a universal heaven that guided the world of human beings on a moral course.

According to Hsu and Linduff (1988), this was humanism in its incipient form. This type of thinking determined the subsequent orientation of Chinese thinking, both politically and philosophically. Not only did the Zhou ideology provide the cornerstone for their own political legitimacy, it also opened the way for the long Chinese tradition of humanism and rationalism. The Zhou provided an explanation for their new order. Ever since, the Chinese have held, almost religiously, that legitimate political authority is the manifestation of high moral principles that serve the well-being of the people. They believed society should be organized to maintain a secular order that would allow people to live together under the guidance of a morality ensured by the mandate of heaven.

The Zhou adopted much of the Shang lifestyle, often importing Shang families or communities to their new towns in order to utilize the knowledge of the Shang artisans. The bronze vessels of the Zhou are nearly identical with those of the Shang. The Zhou adopted much of the Shang writing system, many of their rituals, and their administration techniques.

From the time of the Zhou onward, the Hua-Xia 華夏, or Chinese, geographical world occupied the central plain, uniting the east and the west and proclaiming its central role relative to others with the name of "middle kingdom 中國." The Hua-Xia order was based on an agricultural economy in a single complex that likely encompassed more population and land area than any other Axial Age civilization of ancient times. Nevertheless, its cultural coherence outlasted its political institutions. According to Hsu and Linduff, the ability of Hua-Xia attitude to tolerate a variety of new members from non-Zhou cultures demonstrates its durability. Apparently, the universalism of the Hua-Xia order made it receptive to foreign elements. The Zhou supposedly morally guided "the world under heaven," or *Tien-hsia* 天下, rather than a great city, as had the Shang. The Hua-Xia order did not exclude anyone who came into contact with it and aspired to join its ranks. Later, Confucius would hold that we should not discriminate against anyone involved in the mission to teach the civilized way of life. Thus, the emphasis upon kinship and mandated morality survived the Zhou and became the center of Confucianism.

Not only did the universalism of the Hua-Xia order owe much to the concept of the mandate of heaven, but the rationalism derived from it was significant. Solidarity within the Chinese population and the Hua-Xia tolerance of others were the chief supports of Chinese culture. China survived other Axial Age civilizations and lasted three thousand years while repeatedly incorporating non-Chinese nations. The Western Zhou period was the cradle of the beliefs and procedures that made possible this integrative process.

Kinship groups or lineage systems structured much like a family organized and ran the Zhou state. After the conquest of the Shang, the Zhou kings parceled out territories to members of the principal lineage, favorite generals of the conquest, and certain local leaders, thereby forming subordinate states, or earldoms. The rulers of these subordinate states were treated very much like relatives, even when there were no real ties of blood. Descent was patriarchal, from father to son, rather than from eldest brother to youngest brother, as the Shang practiced. A complex *zongfa* 宗法制度 lineage system, wherein each person theoretically knows his exact position, determined succession. The total number of people who received appointments from the kings is not known, but the kinship appointment, called fengjian 封建, meaning "to award and to establish land and state," was the hallmark of the Zhou culture, dominating the society until the Qin dynasty replaced it in 221 BC.

The idea that the country is merely an extension of the king's family explains both the nature of the Zhou fengjian and its great influence on the traditional Chinese mentality. To a great extent, the success of the Zhou expansion was in its ability to intermingle with the local people. Through intermarriage and mutual cultural influence, the non-Zhou people were gradually integrated into the Zhou social, political, and economic sphere. Consequently, the Zhou established a vast empire from its roots in an obscure Neolithic background. A common Chinese identity also evolved out of this process, in sharp contrast to the often divisive conquests of the proto-Roman and Greek empires.

After the first two centuries of the Western Zhou, its royal power began to decline. Aristocratic families of many vassal states also underwent a decline. Ministers and senior officials or even household officials then usurped political power in the states. As a result, ministers gained control of some vassal states. In some cases, because the power of several ministerial families was comparable, the states were divided into several polities. The kings took less interest in maintaining strong government, and their vassals became increasingly disaffected. Pressure from nomads on the northern steppes and in the west manifested in conflicts with the Zhou.

A major attack was mounted on the Zhou royal domain in the Xi'an area in 771 BC. According to Stephen Haw (1995), the attacking forces included both disaffected vassal states and non-Zhou tribes. The fighting apparently resulted in the loss of large segments of the west to the independent tribes. The Zhou king, You 幽 王, was killed, and the surviving aristocratic lords set up his son Ping 平 王 as the new monarch. Ping ruled from 770–720 BC in the eastern capital at Chengzhou, the present-day Luoyang, in the province of Henan. From this time forward, the Zhou kings held only nominal authority over their vassals.

The Eastern Zhou 東 周

The end of the Western Zhou period in 771 BC signified the end of the real power of the Zhou kings and the beginning of an age of powerful regional states. Smaller and weaker states were conquered and absorbed by stronger ones, so only a few large states eventually remained to struggle for ascendancy. The Eastern Zhou (770–256 BC), as it is commonly known, refers to this period, stretching from the reign of King Ping 平 王 to the centuries-later death of King Nang 赧 王 in 256 BC. Most scholars, however, extend this period to 221 BC, when Emperor Qin united China.

The Eastern Zhou is further subdivided into the Spring and Autumn period (*Chun Qiu* 春 秋) of 722–481 BC, and the Warring States period (*Zhan Guo*

戰 國) of 476–221 BC. Together, these well-documented periods of the Eastern Zhou represent a time of rapid social, political, economic, and ideological change in Chinese history. Their many changes brought about the emergence of a single Chinese state that included large areas south of the Yangtze River. Within which, almost all of the essential features of later China were already present in embryonic form. In many respects, these few centuries are the most interesting and important in the whole, long history of China.

The decline of royal authority throughout the Eastern Zhou effectively left China in a leadership vacuum. The states struggled to maintain the status quo, but none was powerful enough to defeat all the others. Several were dominant enough to disrupt the existing order. This set the stage for a long period of political divisiveness, marked by frequent warfare between states and social and intellectual turmoil.

At the beginning of the Eastern Zhou period, there were some 170 states represented in the area characterized as culturally Chinese. Most were small, but a few, especially around the borders of the area where there was room to expand through the assimilation of non-Zhou states, were large. Some of the formerly non-Zhou states gradually absorbed Chinese culture and gained acceptance into the Chinese sphere. Ultimately, there were about a dozen major states during the Spring and Autumn period, vying with each other for supremacy and gradually conquering and absorbing the smaller and weaker states.

By the sixth century BC, ancient China had developed a multistate system and seen the establishment of the *ba* 霸, or hegemon, system of recognized leadership among the states. At the same time, cultural pluralism among the states gained increasingly widespread acceptance. The nine major powers, the states of Zheng, Lu, Jin, Chu, Qi, Qin, Song, Wu, and Yue, had each acquired their own areas of influence as the status of the Zhou royal house had correspondingly diminished. The renowned five hegemonies were the most powerful lords of the Hua-Xia states of the Central Plains. Among those powers, the Chu, Wu, Yue, Qi, Jin, and Qin were still regarded as barbarians.

This precariously balanced system of power meant frequent wars in which chivalry, honor, loyalty, fair play, and sportsmanship—military and agrarian virtues in origin—reached their highest development. A gentleman of the period would prefer death to dishonor of any kind. Suicide was justifiable escape from dishonor. Ironically, compared with later periods, state politics during the Spring and Autumn period were generally civil, gentle, and respectful. The great states struggled for hegemony or a rebalancing of power, but they eschewed attempts to conquer rivals. Trust among the nobility was the rule rather than the exception. Agreements among states, primarily on matters of mutual interest and defense against barbarians and the expansion of the barbarous house of Chu in the south, were still possible.

As larger states continued to expand their influence and power through absorption of smaller ones, the downfall of many noble families was an ongoing consequence. Simultaneously, successful warriors of humble origins were exalted. In 552 BC, the ruler of the Qi established a system of conferring honorific titles on those who were valorous in battle. Later, grants of land or official positions were bestowed upon good soldiers in the central state of Jin.

The wars of this time were gradually breaking up the old social system. The old nobility was losing its prestige, and they could no longer expect to automatically receive preference because of hereditary status. Some of the former elite became responsible for the dissemination of knowledge to the public. A new social class, shi 士, constituted of scholars with high capability and great character, was then formed. This new cultural elite brought a renewed consciousness of their responsibility to serve the world and uphold virtuous behavior by death, if necessary. Three ritual works, the *Li-ji* 禮記, *Yi-li* 儀禮, and *Zhou-li* 周禮, were said to have set up an elaborate system of administration, ceremonies, official ranks, methods of communication, and behavioral standards, which also supposedly formed the model for the Zhou Empire. While these works may have existed in some form during the early Zhou, they are now generally conceded to be later fabrications. In any case, it was increasingly common that appointments of advisors, officials, and ministers in the Eastern Zhou were based on the talents of this group of shi, who were commoners, instead of ancestry. Accomplishments were evaluated by merit. This was another significant step toward government bureaucratization. This era was also the time of Confucius (551–479 BC) and the beginning of Confucianism, an effort to restore some of the lost traditions. One of many private teachers of the day, Confucius had three thousand student followers living and traveling with him, and he offered advice to rulers in various states. He taught by example, both his own and those of other people, historical and contemporary. His focus was ethics, but his priority was instruction in the practice of becoming truly human.

The Spring and Autumn period was also a time of economic and technological advances. Bronze casting had a long history in ancient China. Shang and Zhou bronze vessels were cast in a great variety of sizes and shapes, decorated with ornamental designs, and inscribed with lengthy texts. In the Spring and Autumn period, bronze casting advanced in several ways. The lost-wax technique, for example, facilitated the production of different shapes, including new bronze weapons. These advanced bronze casting techniques required very high temperatures, a prerequisite as well for iron casting, whose later invention reduced the cost of farming and other implements (Li June 1996). The subsequent widespread use of both draught animals and iron ploughs and many other improvements in agriculturally related techniques made intensive cultivation possible. Resulting increases in both productivity and population then encouraged individual farming, which ultimately constituted one of the most significant factors in the eventual breakdown of lineage-based communities. The gradual emergence of private land ownership was the call of the time.

These advances in agriculture and basic industries were associated with the rise of an active market economy. Bronze money began to circulate in the late Spring and Autumn period, and its distribution around the Zhou capital and around Jin suggests these areas must have been busy centers for a brisk exchange of goods. Frequent wars among the states, as well as equally frequent court visits and conferences, made interregional transportation commonplace, which a road system that had already been well developed in the Western Zhou period facilitated. The vassal states were expected to maintain and provide security for the highways. One of the items in an interstate agreement of 579 BC was a promise not to impede travelers.

All these changes and conditions stimulated the ambition of sublineages to expand their territorial control. As a result, constant warfare between those allegedly descending from the same ancestor accelerated the dissolution of the time-hollowed fengjian system. Local lords of the Spring and Autumn period city-states started to enjoy *de facto* sovereignty in the areas under their control. By the onset of the Warring States period, fully fledged states had emerged out of the bloodshed and continued to dominate the political scenario for more than two centuries.

These early political, social, economic, and ideological changes continued and further accelerated during the Warring State period, which is considered the Classical Age of China. This cultural flowering is reflected in the alternative name sometimes given to the time, the One Hundred Schools period. Confucianism 儒, Daoism 道, Legalism 法, Moism 墨, and many other different schools of philosophy, politics, and practical sciences developed, along with the emergence of a large intellectual class and the practice of private teaching. Some of the most memorable Chinese poetry and prose was written during this time. Fundamental changes in arts, such as in the decorative designs of bronze, jades, and lacquered objects, took place, signaling a trend toward rationalization, eloquence, freshness, and worldliness instead of focusing entirely on ritual. Other advances included the transcription of laws, an increase in commercial activities seen in marketplaces functioning with a money economy, and an increase in social mobility. The appearance of large commercial cities indicated the flourishing state of commerce.

In the Spring and Autumn period, cities were mostly political centers or military fortresses. The fall of a city meant the fall from influence of the noble household that ruled the city in question. In the Warring States period, within its walls, a city included a large population representing a large variety of professions, not just political institutions. These cities were usually located at a crossroads or on an important waterway. As states attempted to strengthen their positions in the contemporary power struggle, the more developed cities were chosen as new political capitals.

Further developments in technology, especially those related to iron and tools made of iron, greatly increased agriculture. Thus, the population exploded. This was, however, an explosion that was countered by frequent wars. Private land ownership and a tax system based on productivity replaced the well field system, described in chapter six, and the zongfa system, based on blood relationships. Chinese society then comprised four classes of people, ranked according to their relative social value as follows (in descending order): shi or scholar-officials, farmers, artisans or technicians, and merchants. We will discuss the four Chinese social classes in section three.

According to Lewis (Loewe and Shaughnessy 1999), the new style of polity that appeared in the Warring States period was both an expansion and a contraction of the old Zhou model. It was an expansion because it developed a full-blown territorial state in place of the city-based state of the Zhou world. It was a contraction because it concentrated all power in the court of a single monarch, who commanded a large number of dependent officials. The reforms that occupied a prominent position in the political history of the time were legalist in philosophy, which the centralization of governmental power characterized. The ruler was thus vested with the power of administrator, military leader, judge, manager of the economy, priest, educator, and moral exemplar. His responsibility was total. By the time of the Warring States period, the system of *jun* 郡, or commanderies, and xian 縣, or prefectures, had begun to prevail in all states. The central government made merit-based appointments of officers for commanderies and prefectures instead of relying on kinship and blood succession. Additional officers were employed to register and mobilize the individual peasant households, primarily for the sake of imposing universal military service. The mass peasant armies of the period catalyzed the emergence of military specialists who were masters of the theories and techniques of warfare. At the same time, the requirements of diplomatic maneuvers produced theorists of stratagem and persuasion who formulated new models of interstate relations. The Zhou world was also reinvented as a geographic entity, both through expansion to the south and the southwest and new patterns of physical mobility that marked differences of status.

The transition from the Spring and Autumn to the Warring States periods represented a change from an age of relative peace to one in which war became large scale and brutal. According to Haizong Lei (1943), all military weapons before this time had been made of bronze, but iron swords of unprecedented keenness began to appear now. The introduction of cavalry to the ranks of the traditional infantry and war chariots refashioned military tactics and strategy. Rapidity in movement and unexpected maneuvers became both possible and necessary. With these developments, war indeed became a business of wholesale slaughter, even of annihilation.

The Warring States world was dominated by seven major states 戰 國 七 雄. Primarily, it was Qin in the west, Qi in the east, and Chu in the south. Secondarily, it was the Yan was based in modern Beijing and the three states that had formerly constituted Jin in central China, Han, Zhao, and Wei. Although the central and lower Yangtze regions had become important in the Spring and Autumn period, the drainage basin of the Yellow River still primarily defined the Warring States world. The history of interstate rivalry among these seven major Warring States may be divided into four periods: before 351 BC, 351–311 BC, 311–272 BC, and 272–221 BC. During the first period, most of the states had not yet resolved their internal difficulties, but Wei seemed to be the strongest military power. The Qin state started to reform and rapidly rose to dominate the second period. Individually, the states declared independence during this era, and their rulers assumed the title of king. The century between the universal assumption of the royal title and the final victory of Qin in 221 BC is known as the age of alliances and counter-alliances, *hezong* 合 眾 and *lianheng* 連 環. Hezong was the international policy of Qi and Chu, resulting in a north-south alliance and cooperation of six states against Qin. Lianheng was the international policy of Qin, pursuing the subordination of the six eastern states to the sole state of the west, Qin itself. This century was one of a triple contest for world supremacy among the three dominant powers. The remaining four states were comparatively too feeble to have a really independent policy of their own. The third period of international politics was to witness the downfall of Qi and the sole supremacy of Qin. Between 230 and 221 BC, all six major states succumbed successively to the might of Qin. With the exception of Qi, all fought to the last with grim determination.

The First Empire

In 221 BC, King Zheng 秦 王 政 of the now-ubiquitous Qin state proclaimed himself to be the first emperor. For the first time, China was a unified empire, ruled by the Qin dynasty from 221–207 BC. The First Emperor's domestic programs emphasized unification, standardization, and centralization. According to Milton Meyer (1975), Emperor Zheng erected a huge palace at the capital, measuring some 2,500 feet in length from east to west and 500 feet in width from north to south. It housed 10,000 people. He was in constant fear of assassination, so he constructed a network of secret tunnels throughout the palace that led to subsidiary palaces. He oversaw large construction projects, including the initial 1,400 miles of what we now know as the Great Wall; a giant tomb for himself with its now-famous army of 7,500 terracotta warriors, each life-sized and distinctly individual; and artificial waterways that linked two tributaries in southern China, establishing a continuous transport route between the Yangtze and West river systems. Under Zheng's rule, irrigation networks were expanded, and canals funneled grain taxes to the capital. An efficient network of roads radiated out from the capital. Drastic domestic measures included the shifting of whole populations according to labor needs and military necessity. State monopolies were imposed on salt and iron. Currency was unified. Weights and measures were standardized. Axles on carts were also standardized, mainly to reduce ruts on the loess roads in northwestern China. Going to great lengths to organize routines and customs, the emperor formalized written Chinese into a basic script, which has persisted to this day. Emperor Zheng defined and expanded China's frontiers, mobilizing large armies of conscripts. The Great Wall was built to shut out the nomads. By 214 BC, his troops had penetrated Vietnamese valleys in the northern and central regions and coastlines in the south. For the first time, foreign conquests and expansion rounded out the map of China proper until the empire approximated the borders that exist today.

Yet the Qin dynasty lasted for only eighteen years. In 210 BC, the emperor died while on a trip away from the capital. In 202 BC, Liu Bang 劉 邦, the founder of the Han 漢 dynasty, overthrew the short-lived ascendancy of Zheng's heir. The brevity of Qin rule provided an object lesson to the first sovereigns of Han, who anxiously recognized that, while military force was sufficient for conquering other states, the maintenance of power depended on a rule of virtue. The Han dynasty adopted the political structures that the Qin first erected, but, without the terror and oppression of the former empire, the Han dynasty lasted for more than four centuries.

Around the same time, the Roman Empire peaked during the reign of Augustus (27 BC–AD 14). The Western Han Empire was mere decades into its own peak period, signaled when the Chinese generals under Emperor Wudi 武 帝 (circa 141–87 BC) successfully fought the Xiongnu, who had been a continued menace in the north and west since the establishment of the Qin/Han dynasties, and advanced some two thousand miles from their capital city of Chang'an.

The Xiongnu 匈奴 were nomadic Huns who emerged in Mongolia during the Zhou period. The latter group's annals mention the Huns as early as the fifth century BC. The periodic failures of already-limited food supplies in their homeland made the nomadic Xiongnu restless and aggressive. Despite agreements made with Liu Bang, founder of the Han, the nomads continued to raid Chinese territory. In 166 BC, they had penetrated to within one hundred miles of the Han capital. It was not until 127 BC and after great loss of life that the Chinese finally managed to drive the Huns out of the Ordos and back across the Gobi deserts. A period of uneasy coexistence followed between the opposing forces. By the middle of the first century, the Xiongnu had declined in power. By then, other barbarian groups rose to plague the Chinese.

Wudi's reign was the high point of Han power, prestige, and morale, but the emperor paid a correspondingly high price for this success. As Stavrianos pointed out (1983), Wudi overstrained the imperial resources. He resorted to a variety of measures to cope with the crisis, including currency debasement and minting of coins, the sale of ranks, and the reinstatement of government monopolies on salt, iron, and liquor. Although he managed to remain solvent for the duration of his reign, his successors sank deeper into trouble as the results of protracted warfare diminished the number of taxpaying peasants.

Essentially, Wudi's successors were undistinguished. The emperor's immediate successor was a minor. Pending his adulthood, power was held by a triumvirate headed by Huo Guang 霍光, who actually retained power throughout this emperor's reign, and eventually played a key role in the selection of a grandson of Wudi to become Emperor Xuandi 宣帝 in 74 BC. The ascendancy of a minor to the role of emperor did not necessarily weaken the dynasty. Emperors rarely played an active part in the administration of the state. On the other hand, the excessive influence of a great family such as Huo Guang's was undoubtedly a threat. After Huo Guang's death in 68 BC, the emperor ordered the elimination of the leading members of the Huo family. After Xuandi's death, the characteristic features of dynastic decline multiplied. In Charles Hucker's (1975) view, Wudi's successors allowed most of their domestic controls to lapse and fell under the influence of powerful eunuchs and imperial in-laws. Nepotism and cronyism flourished at court, and rapacious landlordism went unchecked in the countryside. The imperial family lost its prestige and its nerve. A succession of young emperors who died without natural heirs finally convinced the court that the Liu family had lost its heavenly mandate as well as its earthly one. After AD 6, the investiture of an infant emperor meant that a regency council governed China until AD 9, when a prestigious minister named Wang Mang 王猛 was induced to take the throne and established the new one-ruler dynasty of Xin 新 (meaning "new"), which lasted for only fourteen years.

Wang Mang came into power endorsing a program of reviving Confucian doctrines. He sought support from the Confucian bureaucrats, but they despised him because of the illegality of his mandate. Once in power, he revived the Legalist tradition of strong authoritarian rule, strengthened the bureaucracy, created more monopolies, reinstated the traditional granaries, and extended agricultural loans to peasants. He debased the currency by introducing coins of different denominations and stipulated that gold be exchanged for bronze and copper coins. He also nationalized land ownership. In AD 9, he decreed the end of the great, private, tax-free estates that had evolved over the previous century. He parceled out land among taxpaying peasants and abolished domestic slavery. These vigorous reforms cost Wang Mang the support of the bureaucracy and the rich families, and his measures had never been implemented. In addition, natural disasters resulting in poor harvests, an internal peasant rebellion by the so-called red eyebrows, lack of administrative experience, and renewed Xiongnu invasions all contributed to the downfall of his brief dynasty. In 23, rebels killed Wang Mang. After two years of ensuing civil strife, Liu Xiu 劉 秀, a cousin of the last emperor of the Western Han, emerged victorious. Liu's rule from 25–57, approximately contemporaneous with Augustus's rule of the Roman Empire, witnessed the relocation and rebuilding of the capital at Luoyang, the former center of Eastern Zhou power. The period delimited by the reign of Emperor Liu Xiu is now known as the Eastern or Later Han, an era that Chinese historians view as the model of dynastic restoration.

During the reigns of Liu Xiu, or Guang Wudi光 武 帝, and his successors Mingdi 明 帝 (circa AD 57–75) and Zhangdi 章 帝 (circa AD 75–88), many of the administrative practices of the Western Han were continued. All three emperors tried to assert Chinese influence on the periphery of the empire. The outcome was short-term success and longer-term problems with nomads remaining a threat.

As Stavrianos summarized it, the history of the Later Han (AD 25–222) was basically the same as that of its predecessor. During the lengthy war, many of the old aristocrats and landowners had been wiped out. Tax returns were adequate at the beginning of the revived dynasty. Again, the taxpaying peasantry began to be squeezed out, and the downward spiral once more was under way. Great rebellions broke out, and the situation resembled that of the last days of Rome. The decimation of the small peasants had also destroyed the original peasant draft army. Professional troops, whose first loyalty was to their generals, replaced them. The generals, therefore, could ignore the central government. Great landowners also defied the government by evading taxes and enlarging their holdings by various legal and extralegal means. Helpless peasants, fleeing the barbarian invaders or government tax collectors, became the virtual serfs of these landowners in return for economic and physical security. The great families converted their manors into fortresses, virtually taking over the functions of government in their respective localities. Their estates were largely self-sufficient, so trade declined and cities shrank correspondingly. Thus, the Han dynasty disappeared in AD 222 from the stage of history in a swirl of peasant revolts, warlord coups, and nomadic raids. China then entered a prolonged period of disunity and disorder similar to that in the West following the collapse of the Roman Empire.

Section Three:
Contrasts between the Roman and Qin/Han Empires

The Roman and Qin/Han Empires, amassed independently at opposite ends of the Eurasian continent, nevertheless often invite direct comparisons because they were broadly comparable in terms of area, around four million square kilometers each, and population, approximately more than sixty million apiece. Both even largely coexisted around the same time (200 BC–AD 395 for the unified Roman Empire and 221 BC–AD 220 for the Qin/Han Empire). In addition, both empires resulted from gradual conquest or absorption of a large number of smaller polities into a handful of large imperial states, which were subsequently unified as an empire and ruled by authoritarian emperors.

As we have seen, the two empires formed their own distinctive characteristics, politically, sociologically, economically, and culturally. At the same time, both empires enjoyed the fruits of similar technological advancements, including the revolution from bronze to iron tools, agricultural adaptation and large irrigation and flood control projects, new architectural designs and techniques in building roads, and the construction of large political and commercial city centers. Hence, the differences in their eventual historical outcomes may best be attributed to other factors, such as divergence in the development of their individual thinking preferences, worldviews, and cultural and historical heritage. Some of which were outlined previously, and all of which contribute to the prevailing theme of this book.

Roman Politics

Even though both empires were the result of military conquests achieved by a powerful state, the basic constituents of the Roman and Qin/Han Empires were quite different. Historian Joseph Strayer described the Roman Empire as a union of people who shared a common Mediterranean civilization under a single, powerful ruler.

Military conquest played a key role in the formation of the empire. Romans were fierce soldiers. The Roman army was the largest and, by far, the most effectively organized power grouping in Roman politics. The ancient Romans were very different from the ancient Greeks. Romans were down-to-earth realists, not idealists. The power of the emperor was based on the army. The empire was practically a military dictatorship. Rome was a realm of quasikings, magistrates, and senators whose power varied with the efficacy of the governing emperor. The Roman fighting force combined disciplined training with a clear, hierarchical command structure, regular pay, flexibility in unit size, and aggressive persistence in the pursuit of fixed objectives. It did not have any rival or imitator that could approach its effectiveness in civilian politics.

The administration of Rome was the responsibility of a broad range of magistrates. The Senate was a council comprised of three hundred members chosen from among the leaders of the people, such as former judges. The role of the Senate was to receive foreign ambassadors and sign treaties with the former foreign countries, appoint provincial governors, and control public administration and the making of laws. Thus, the Senate was the main organ of the republican government. In order to avoid abuses, magistrates held office for only a single year. Censors held a term for eighteen months. Both were then replaced through election. The consuls (advisors), two in number, presided over the Senate and the Comitia. These two advisors introduced bills and commanded the army in war. Praetors were charged with the administration of justice. Censors took the census of the citizens, both to register them in the electoral rolls and enforce payment of taxes. They also supervised the citizens' morality and drew up a list of candidates for the Senate. From which, they could expel those who were found unworthy to hold the appointment.

There were three popular assemblies where censors could pass or reject bills introduced by the consuls, although they could not discuss or introduce new bills. The *comitia curiata* confirmed the appointments of the magistrates elected on other committees, such as the *comitia centuriata*, which elected the consuls, praetors, and censors; decided issues of peace or war; and judged criminal cases that potentially involved death sentences for Roman citizens. In the *comitia tributa*, citizens met according to their tribe without discrimination. Each tribe included patricians and plebeians who voted together. In the operation of these committees, the majority vote ruled. More distant from the eyes of Rome herself and more autonomous than anyone holding office within the capital, the provincial governors enjoyed the most latitude and the least scrutiny of their power.

The establishment of the Roman Empire and its military expansion had actually reversed the earlier trend of Rome toward democratization and disrupted traditional cultures. Augustus reigned over the Roman Empire from 27 BC to AD 14 with what was effectively absolute power. While he desired to maintain the form of the Roman republic, he nevertheless fundamentally transformed the government by assuming almost full executive authority. He reestablished political and social stability after the civil war and launched two centuries of prosperity called the Roman Peace (*Pax Romana*). Augustus laid the foundation for *Pax Romana* by encouraging trade, building roads that linked the cities of the empire, and establishing an efficient civil service. Occupants of the Roman provinces streamed to Rome, where they became soldiers, bureaucrats, senators, and even emperors.

However, Augustus never established rules for the succession of emperors. Thus, the death of an emperor led to civil war and assassination as different groups struggled for power. In this climate, the army became the central institution of the Roman Empire. Under the reforms of Marius, a Roman general, the army became an occupying force, serving the needs of its commander rather than those of the state. The emperors who followed Augustus varied in their abilities. Some were intelligent and able. Others were corrupt, cruel, and even insane. Nonetheless, the empire continued to function because of the systems that Augustus had established.

Qin/Han Politics

In contrast with the powerful military dictatorship of the Roman Empire, the Qin/Han dynasties of China were family-based agrarian states. China's governing central and local bureaucracies, intensive agriculture, and market network and economy that the Chinese had been building for many centuries matured during the Han dynasty and flourished during the Tang and Song dynasties. In addition, most ancient Chinese shared the common ideology of Confucianism and the concept of a legitimate rulership working for the benefit of people under the mandate of heaven. Compared with the expansive nature of the Romans, these states are defensive in nature with the building of the Great Wall to shut out the nomads as a testament to this contention. Unlike the Romans, the ancient Chinese were terrible soldiers. They won very few wars, losing many encounters with the nomads.

Fortunately, because of geographical isolation, they did not have fierce enemies from the south and east.

One of their few successful engagements was a series of grand campaigns against the nomadic Xiongnu during the reign of Wudi in 133 BC in which the Han split the Xiongnu into two rival leagues. In 51 BC, the chieftain of the southern league came to the Han capital, Chang'an, to submit as a Han vassal. His counterpart in the north retreated westward, only to be killed in 36 BC by a Han force venturing far beyond the Pamirs into the Samarkand region, where it defeated a coalition reportedly including some Roman legionaries. The reason for their success was the adaptation of similar military tactics as the Xiongnu. With this victory, the Han influence was extended all the way westward to the Caspian Sea. The fleeing Hun traveled so far that they disturbed the peace of Gaul and Italy. Successes such as these were rare for the Chinese military. More often, the Han allied with one barbarian group to defeat another, practicing divide-and-rule tactics. They fought the enemy and then married into their ranks or bought them off. Somehow, despite their limited martial facility and pacifist attitude, the Han successfully contained foreign threats for centuries. In fact, under Emperor Wudi, the Han frontiers were greatly expanded in all directions. Tribal territories in the south were conquered, and local peoples were assimilated. New immigrants came from the north. In the west, Chinese expeditions drove across Central Asia, vastly increasing trade along the Silk Road.

The success of the Han dynasty in its dealings with nomads, using both military and nonmilitary strategies and tactics, highlighted the strength and resilience of the Chinese culture. In chapters three and six, we characterized Chinese culture as inclusive, thriving on social harmony and cohesion, which can be attained through the achievement of a dynamic equilibrium of yin and yang. The use of military force, such as applied by the mighty Roman Empire for conquest, is pure yang. The various pacification and assimilation tactics, such as those that the Han and succeeding Chinese dynasties used to compensate for its many military weaknesses, are definitely yin. For many centuries, the stability of the Chinese empire was achieved through the proper balancing of yin and yang. Thus, the Chinese empires remained essentially cohesive through good times and bad. On the other hand, Western culture is known to be exclusive. Once the mighty Roman Empire was divided into many nations, it remained unable to reestablish unity.

Historically, the word "Oriental" often had negative connotations of despotism and was associated with the kind of tyrannical power seen in eastern empires such as the Persian, Turkish, Egyptian, or Ottoman cultures. The ancient Chinese empires in the Far East have also been painted with this brush. However, if we more deeply examine the Chinese case, we find that the Qin dynasties established their empire according to a Legalist framework built upon governance by one of the world's largest bureaucracies, not just one ruler. The emperor did possess absolute power, but this power could only be exercised through the governmental bureaucracy. Armed with Confucian political ideology, the bureaucrats constantly combated and restrained the power of the emperors while simultaneously contending for power themselves. Under the first four emperors of the early Han, the philosophy of governance shifted in favor of the Huang-Lao school, espousing the Daoist ideal of rule by wuwei, as described previously.

Charles Hucker described the Han bureaucracy of the central government as follow:

> the top-echelon of ministerial dignitaries comprised a chief counselor, a grand marshal, and a censor-in-chief. [三 公] The chief counselor directed the national government as a kind of chief of staff or prime minister for the emperor. He presided over a number of central government agencies. Notable among them were the offices of "the nine chief ministers [九 卿]," as the high-ranking dignitaries who constituted a kind of imperial household administration. In less prestigious but more substantially functional roles, thirteen department heads [十 三 曹] were responsible for routine administration of the government; their duties were divided quite rationally into fiscal affairs, judicial affairs, military affairs, and the like. Important policy questions were often submitted to court conferences of all the chief ministers and other court dignitaries. Such conferences were assembled on the emperor's order and were presided over by the chief counselor, who reported both majority and minority views to the emperor. Although final decision-making power rested with the emperor, the tradition called for emperors to heed their advisers; the chief counselors were particularly prestigious and influential as the acknowledged leaders of the spokesmen for the officialdom in general. (1975)

Indeed, the position and prestige of the office of chief counselor 宰 相 persisted through all later dynasties until its abolition in the Ming dynasty. The power and longevity of this position greatly influenced ancient Chinese politics. In addition, the censor's 御 史 duty was to criticize the policies and actions of imperial ministers and even the emperor himself. Such criticism carried weight because later historians' judgment of the true merit of an emperor's reign was based heavily on the preserved records of censors, particularly the censor-in-chief 御 史 大 夫. Earning a favorable place in history is a common obsession of many emperors. Local government, likewise, was divided into a large number of political bodies, first into thirty-six and later forty-one military regions or commanderies (jun). By the time of Wudi, there were 110. A triad of top officials in each of these included a civil commandery governor, a military commandant, and a supervisory bureaucrat. All reported to the central bureaucracy located in the capital. These administrative units were then subdivided into prefectures (xian), districts, and, finally, wards.

Each commandery governor and perfectural magistrate was responsible for all aspects of government in his territorial jurisdiction, accounting for his actions in annual reports to the capital. Each had a staff that normally included a military commandant, and all areas were subject to intermittent inspection tours by investigating censors from the capital. The fourth Han emperor, Wudi, tried to strengthen the central government's authority over the commandery governors by dividing the empire into thirteen circuits or regions and assigning a censor to each who served as circuit inspector. He was charged with checking and reporting on the performance of the commandery governors in his circuit. As time passed, these inspectors became ever more powerful regional supervisors, moving far beyond the limited purpose that Wudi had envisioned, ultimately achieving a still-greater coordination of local governments under the umbrella of the central government.

The founding emperor of the Han dynasty, Liu Bang, was of humble origin. This became the model for the Han bureaucracy. Appointments to government office were based on a system of recommendation from the villages and meritocracy rather than hereditary aristocracy. To promote this practice, a unique system of competitive examinations was subsequently developed for the selection of civil service personnel. In principle, the examinations were open to everyone, but the prolonged study required in preparation for the exams meant that, realistically, only the well-to-do could qualify with the poor relying on occasional endowments available from their village or clan.

By 100 BC, the bureaucracy numbered some 130,285 persons, controlling a population of about sixty million people (Meyer 1994). Such a high ratio of officials to citizens, in this instance one to four or five hundred, was also typical of later empires. In fact, the late Han patterns of organization persisted through the following centuries with minor changes. The Han balance of power between the emperor and his chief counselor and the central and regional administration still served as an important model for later generations and dynasties in China. Yet, what ultimately kept society in bounds was the webs of accepted, unstated social obligations and relationships that typify the Chinese, not a heavy layer of officialdom.

Roman Social Life

Romans were fierce soldiers, wonderful builders, and city dwellers. One of the most striking features of Roman life was that Rome was specifically an urban culture. Roman civilization depended on the vitality of its cities. There were perhaps only a handful of cities with populations exceeding seventy-five thousand. The typical city had about twenty thousand permanent residents. The entire concept of Roman life seemed to center around the city, be it the city of Rome itself or any other town. The countryside was a nice place to retire for a while in order to stay in touch with nature. But it was seen as an unsuitable place for a true citizen. After all, Romans were social creatures, who craved being part of a society. The truly civilized citizen had to be more than educated or successful. In the Roman mind-set, it was necessary to belong, whether to a group of friends, family, or community. There was no better place for this than the city. So, if one was to look at Roman cities as hives of economic life where people settled merely to find jobs, entertainment, and convenience. One would only see a small part of the picture.

The idea of living in cities was a cultural statement in itself. To them, it represented advancement from the mere existence as a peasant living off the land. One might say they saw themselves as taking a next step in the evolution of man. The barbarian tribes still lived dispersed all over the countryside. In the Roman mind, cities formed its inhabitants into greater, abler, nobler beings. There is no one more highborn than a Roman citizen. A citizen has to show himself a worthy person, respectful to his parents, loyal to his patrons, able in raising his family, and just toward his slaves. Just as the Roman craved society, so was he made to prove himself worthy of membership in it.

Traditionally, Roman society was extremely rigid. By the first century, the need for capable men to run Rome's vast empire was slowly eroding the old social barriers. The social structure of ancient Rome was originally based on heredity, property, wealth, citizenship, and freedom. It was also based around men. The social status of fathers or husbands defined women. Women were expected to look after the houses. Very few had any real independence.

Institutionalized in what is called the patron-client system, Roman society was really a network of personal relationships that obligated people to one another in a legal fashion. A man of superior talent and status was a patron. He could provide benefits to people of lower status, who then paid him special attention. These were his clients who, in return for the benefits bestowed upon them, owed specific duties to the patron. Of course, because we are talking about a network of relationships, a patron was often the client of a more superior patron.

Similar to Chinese society, in Roman society, confirmation by others was sought as well as required. Be they the elders of his family, his patron or clients, army comrades, or even the people of Rome in an election, no Roman could be his own judge. He could see himself only through the eyes of others. They looked to others, not inward, to understand themselves. The opinion of others dictated how the Roman ultimately viewed himself. A good man was hence a man deemed worthy by others, a man deemed honorable. But honorable was only that which was actually honored. Glory or honor was measured only in the recognition it drew from others.

At the heart of the Roman family was the father of the family. The father's power made him the sole owner of all property acquired by his sons, regardless of his son's age. A son would work hard and acquire wealth, but that wealth was not his, but his father's. By law, a father could kill his wife if he found her in bed with another man. Not only could he sell any of his children into slavery, he could kill them as well. The Romans are even known for practicing infanticide.

The Roman household was quite large and could include the father, his wife, his sons with their wives and children, unmarried daughters, and slaves. The household then could be considered to be a small state within a state.

The number of slaves increased dramatically during the reign of Augustus and continued to increase for almost two centuries. Slaves were obtained during warfare. A bankrupt citizen could sell himself into slavery. As a result of this increase, slaves were highly visible during the Roman Empire. The homes of the rich were filled with slaves. The more slaves a man owned, the greater was his status and prestige in Roman society. Roman slaves served as hairdressers, footmen, messengers, accountants, tutors, secretaries, carpenters, plumbers, librarians, and goldsmiths. Some slaves even possessed high-status jobs and served as doctors, architects, and business managers. Many educated slaves were members of the imperial bureaucracy.

Societal issues unrelated to religion, such as taxes, crime, and commerce were addressed through civil law that the Romans developed. Roman law in the republic was often based on custom, and it was one of the most original products of the Roman mind. Perhaps the single most important intellectual contribution of the Roman Empire was the body of law based on reason rather than custom. Their original laws, as set down in the *Twelve Tablets* around 450 BC, were simple and conservative, typical of a peasant people. With the growth of commerce and empire, however, life became more complicated. The Romans formulated a new body of law, the law of the people, which they applied both to themselves and others. The Romans also evolved the legal concept of natural law, which stemmed from the Stoic notion of a rational god ruling the universe, not judicial practice.

The basis for Roman civil law was the notion that the exact form of words or actions, rather than their intention, produced legal consequences. Ignoring intention may not seem fair from a modern perspective, but the Romans recognized there could be witnesses to actions and words, not intentions. Roman civil law allowed great flexibility in adopting new ideas or extending legal principles within the complex environment of the empire. It was not until much later in the sixth century that Byzantine emperor Justinian I began to publish a comprehensive code of laws, the *Corpus Juris Civilis*, or Justinian Code, which constitutes the basis for modern legal systems in the Latin countries of Europe and Latin America and Quebec and Louisiana in North America.

Qin/Han Social Life

The Qin/Han societies were mainly agrarian with a small family industrial supplement and highly developed marketplace. Only ten percent of the population in the Han dynasty lived in the city. The rise of agriculture, craftsmanship, communications, and trade that coincided with the military expansion of the reign of Wudi helped to bring about a radical transformation of society. Farming methods adopted in the Western Han dynasty imposed a great influence on China's agricultural civilization. During the first two centuries of the Han era, a gulf began to open between a peasant proletariat, who had been brought abject poverty and dependence after the formation of the great estates, and a class of landowners of mounting power and independence. This societal deterioration culminated in great popular insurrections that weakened the central power, caused conflict at court, and brought about the downfall of the dynasty and the splintering of the empire.

Therefore, the Han dynasty was all at once an age of consolidation, change, and experiment. In four centuries, the immense effort devoted to agriculture, the improvement and diffusion in the field of technology, and the great movements of population totally transformed the economic scene. Autocratic government, the desire to centralize power, the ascendancy of Confucian ideology, and social revolution all brought a change in outlook. After a while, those in control realized they had to give up a little in order to hold on to a lot. But that little was enough to allow a vibrant middle class to emerge, one comprised of farmers, merchants, craftspeople, and middle ranks of the military, constabulary, judicial, and religious establishments. As institutions developed, relative power and wealth percolated down through the masses.

Any examination of the Han period must also note the traditional Chinese hierarchy of four major social classes: shi, *nong, kong,* and *shang* 士 農 工 商. In other words, these are scholars, farmers, artisans or technicians, and merchants. They are listed here in descending order of prestige according to Confucian values. Notice that, among the four major social classes, the shang, or merchants, rank last in importance. Central to the Confucian tradition was a belief that, although commerce and finance should be nourished, they should neither be allowed to dominate society nor control the political system, whether centrally or locally. Unsurprisingly, this belief had a profound effect on the social and economic development of ancient China. Peter Nolan (2004), in providing one answer to the Needham question of why China failed to achieve an industrial revolution despite a high level of technical development, contends that in China:

> ... markets were so highly developed that any local bottlenecks could almost always be met through the market mechanism, across the great Chinese "free trade area." The state stepped in where markets failed, not only regarding immediate growth issues, but also in relation to the wider issues of social stability and cohesion. It nurtured and stimulated commerce, but refused to allow commerce, financial interests and spec-ulation to dominate society. (2004)

This traditional Chinese hierarchy of social groups omits at least four other groups that would have been significant at the same time in the West, specifically clergy, nobility, military, and slaves. The absence in China of the clergy raises the issue observed by Derek Bodde (1991) that the very nature of religion in China is particularly difficult for Westerners to visualize because so much of it differs so sharply from the biblical religions with which they are familiar. In addition, schol-ars often disagree over what actually constitutes a religion in China. For example, the question of whether or not Confucianism is a religion remains controversial. Buddhism and Daoism were respected more as philosophies than religions. The open, polytheistic attitude of the Chinese toward all religions may be difficult for Western traditions to comprehend. The institution of Confucianism as the state political philosophy in the early Han encouraged prestigious Confucian scholars to maintain a low opinion of the Buddhist and Daoist clergy with the result that institutional religions remained very weak in traditional China. However, if we look upon Confucians as practitioners of a Confucian ethical religion, then the class of Confucian shi 儒 士, or scholars, could be considered the Chinese equiva-lent of Western clergy or perhaps of the knights of the Middle Ages. In any case, the absence of a well-organized priestly class in ancient China distinguishes it from many other early civilizations.

On the other hand, the omission from the Han of a social class of hereditary nobility is not surprising because, although noblemen were all-important in pre-imperial eras such as the Shang and Zhou, nobles in the Han Empire, aside from the emperor himself, were rarely allowed to hold much political power. They were supposed to be men of virtue, not power.

The exclusion of the military from the traditional listing of Chinese social classes undoubtedly reflects the age-old Confucian antipathy to warfare and violence as well as the Confucian conviction that a military class does not properly belong in a truly well-ordered state. A further pragmatic consideration was that Chinese military forces were inherently impermanent because they were usually made up of short-term peasant conscripts rather than long-term mercenaries. On the other hand, military leaders 儒 將 were often Confucian scholars.

Finally, slavery, if it existed, was not economically significant and, in proportion to the total population, would usually have been quite a small class. Slaves were, like the military, anomalies in the well-ordered Confucian state.

Chinese society has long been criticized for emphasizing human relationships over written codes. But many critics do not realize that, during the Han dynasty, China had a comprehensive set of laws that was every bit as impressive as the renowned imperial civil code of Rome. Though the government of the early Han was mainly *laissez-faire*, the dynasty's longevity depended on a comprehensive legal code. In *Nine Chapters* 定 律 九 篇 by the esteemed Han minister of state, Xiaohe 蕭 何, there were 906 volumes under more than sixty separate legal headings. It covered, among other things, lawsuits, standards for arrest, criminal punishments for robbery and theft, and even marriage laws. If one added to these the supplementary sources of law, such as precedents and debates that legal scholars developed, the Han code could handle virtually every issue covered by modern statute and customary law. The comprehensive legal spirit of the Han was given its fullest development under the chief counselor Dong Zhongshu 董 仲 舒, a Confucian who required that an explanation accompany every legal decision. Moreover, drawing on the essence of classics such as the *Spring and Autumn Annals* 春 秋 繁 露, he introduced a consciousness of the value of the human individual into the law. Hsing Yi-tien, a researcher in the Institute of History and Philology at the Academia Sinica in Beijing, has completed in-depth research into Han dynasty law. He has concluded that the concept of human rights appears in Han dynasty law far earlier than Roman law.

Roman Economics

Farming was the basis of the Roman economy. Republican senators traditionally invested their wealth in Italian land, and they were encouraged to invest abroad. The Romans began to cultivate more land when they brought Mediterranean plants and more sophisticated farming methods farther north into Gaul, the Rhine River valley, and Balkan Peninsula. Vineyards spread throughout Gaul, and olive groves were planted in North Africa. The Romans learned new techniques for farming in wet climates that allowed them to open new lands for agriculture in northern Gaul and Britain, where increasing demands for timber transformed native forests into agricultural estates.

At its greatest extent, the Roman Empire included all the lands bordering on the Mediterranean Sea and reached far into northern Europe and the Near East. Various factors contributed to the flourishing imperial economy during these centuries, including honest and efficient administration, monetary stability, large-scale public works, and extensive trade, both within and beyond the empire. The success of the Roman Empire depended on the distribution of wheat to feed soldiers as well as the populace of Rome.

Rome, an industrial center, was also a city that consumed goods rather than producing them. The government relied on a massive food giveaway program to fulfill the need of feeding the Roman urban population. Beginning with Augustus Caesar, the city of Rome provided bread, oil, and wine to its people. Almost 250,000 inhabitants of Rome consumed about six million sacks of grain per year for free.

The massive giveaway program that the Romans enjoyed was not extended to its provinces. Because only a quarter of the Italian population was Roman citizens, the remainder was granted Latin citizenship with fewer privileges. In many cases, the peasants in the provinces were forced to sell out to the new class of the very rich, who were eager to accumulate large estates because agriculture was still considered the only respectable calling for gentlemen. Thus, the second century BC saw the growth of large plantations in Italy that were worked by slaves and owned by absentee landlords. The dispossessed peasantry drifted to the towns where they once again had to compete with slaves for such work as was available. Chief among structures underpinning the Roman economy was the market for slave labor, especially after the expansion of the empire. Yet, the imperial economy was most profitable to those at the upper levels of the social hierarchy. Most people remained subsistence agriculturalists. Besides the trade in slaves and necessities, an extensive trade in luxury goods, especially those from China, also developed during these years.

Roman forts doubled as granaries designed to hold a year's supply of wheat in case of siege. Supplies of wheat from the provinces, such as Egypt, were maintained via a vast trade network developed throughout the Mediterranean Basin. As the unrivalled metropolis, Rome achieved an absolute lead in the production of luxury goods, particularly in articles of precious metals, such as jewelry and engraved cups. Foreign craftsmen, mostly Greeks, who migrated to the city, created refined masterpieces in their workshops. The building trade naturally became far more developed in Rome than anywhere else. Genoa, Ostia, and Ravenna were Rome's major harbors, providing her with warships as well as benefiting from the rise in shipping trade. Industry flourished elsewhere, including in the iron, bronze, and glass industries as well as cloth making. The policing of the seas and the construction of the famous Roman roads aided trade into the most distant countries. All the while, the vast city of Rome and its massive standing army continued to provide a large demand for goods.

Qin/Han Economics

The Qin/Han empires of China saw further maturing of intensive agriculture, flourishing industry and commerce, and population growth. The Han is also renowned for its prominent family estates as lands were consolidated into a new class of landholding families. Overall, this was a period of economic growth and maturity, especially in agriculture, with gains in reclamation and irrigation, opening of state land to the poor, and improvements in farming techniques. Socioeconomic development also accelerated during the period with more arable land as well as advanced metallurgy, spinning, and weaving technologies.

The Han dynasty saw the expansion of China into a vast territory and prosperous economy. The opening of the Silk Road strengthened links between China and western Asia. Ancient cities, imperial tombs, monuments, and other sites of the Han dynasty testify to the wealth and power of the period. Intricately woven silk fabrics, paintings on silk, and writing on bamboo slips are very important artifact types during this period. Other handicrafts such as bronze, jade, lacquer, and pottery also flourished. Of particular interest are the architectural bricks and stones of the Eastern Han period that illustrate legendary tales, historical events, and daily life.

The first seventy years of the Han dynasty was a period of rest and recuperation for the people. Developments in irrigation brought increased yields. Peace and reconstruction brought general prosperity and an ever-increasing flow of taxes to the government. Thus, by the time of Wudi, China was economically strong enough to fight and win the war with Xiongnu. But Wudi also overstrained the imperial resources. He resorted to a variety of measures to cope with the crisis, including currency debasement and minting of coins, the sale of ranks, and the reinstatement of government monopolies on salt, iron, and liquor. Although he managed to remain solvent for the duration of his reign, his successors sank deeper into trouble as the results of protracted warfare diminished the number of taxpaying peasants. After a brief, unsuccessful attempt for economic reform, the Han declined into economic and political chaos. The Han government, in turn, imposed even more taxes on the remaining independent servants in order to make up the tax losses, thereby encouraging almost all peasants to come under the land-holding elite or the landlords.

Roman Culture

Latins and Greeks were descendents of Indo-European nomads from the steppes of Central Asia. They retained certain traits characteristic of nomadic cultures, such as aggressiveness, adaptability, bravery, cruelty, determination, divisiveness, and destructiveness. Roman culture surely definitely retained such qualities.

The practical Romans achieved little in abstract science, but they excelled in the construction of aqueducts, sewer systems, bridges, and roads. The latter was so well-built that they continued to be used through the Middle Ages and, in some cases, even the present day. Roman architecture was concerned primarily with secular structures such as baths, amphitheaters, stadia, and triumphed arches. New building materials, such as concrete, brick, and mortar, made possible the type of grand-scale vaulting necessary for many of these large buildings.

Rome provided citizens with food. It also provided them with entertainment, including chariot races, gladiator contests, and three kinds of blood sports. This included armed men fighting animals, animals fighting animals, or armed men and women exposed to starving vicious beasts. The latter was usually reserved for criminals. During the reign of Augustus Caesar alone, three thousand five hundred animals died during the days devoted to twenty-six festivals. At the games celebrating the completion of the Coliseum in AD 80, nine thousand were killed. Finally, eleven thousand were killed at the celebration of a military victory in AD 107, a celebration lasting 123 days. By the fourth century, nearly 177 days per year were devoted to the games.

By the time of the empire, the old Roman religion had lost much of its appeal, but religion and philosophy retained their place in Roman society. Greek literature and philosophy gained followers, as did religions from Asia and Egypt. Homer and other Greeks inspired Latin writers. Livy's *History of Rome* is a patriotic account of the city's history from its founding to the rule of Augustus. Virgil's *Aeneid* is an epic poem that traces the origins of Rome back to Aeneas, one of the warriors in Homer's *Illiad*. Not all Roman philosophers praised the empire. Some writers, including the noted poet Juvenal, produced works that mocked the foolish and wicked ways of society. Tacitus, a Roman historian and politician, was also very critical of the imperial government. Epicurus of Athens (270–342) taught that happiness could be found by freeing the body from pain and the mind from fear. Wealthy Romans often used his philosophy to justify their excesses. Greek Stoicism encouraged virtue, duty, endurance, and fairness in law. In response, Roman judges established standards for fairness in Roman law, which endured and formed the basis of later European law.

The people of the Roman Empire followed many different religions, most notably Judaism and Christianity. The areas of Syria and Palestine fell under Roman influence around 65 BC. Jewish monotheism led to many conflicts with the polytheistic Roman rulers. Although Judaism was usually tolerated, many Jews fiercely opposed Roman rule. It took the Roman legions seven years (66–73) to crush rebellions by Jews known as Zealots. In 130, Jews revolted against orders that Jerusalem be rebuilt as a Roman colony. A half-million Jews died before the ensuing conflict ended, expunging the Jewish political state for almost two thousand years, even though Judaism itself endured.

Christianity also challenged the might of Rome. Jesus, a Jew and Roman subject, was born in Bethlehem at the same time that Rome took over Judaea. When Christ was about thirty, he began his work as a wandering prophet and teacher. After three years of ministry, Jesus was arrested because he had described the coming of the kingdom of God in his teaching. He was therefore charged with blasphemy and plotting to be king. Pontius Pilate, a Roman governor, sentenced him to death by crucifixion, a common form of execution in the Roman Empire. According to Christian doctrine, one of Jesus's followers, Mary Magdalene, visited his tomb two days after his burial and found his body gone. Over the next forty days, several of his disciples believed that Jesus appeared to them. They continued his teachings about the kingdom of God and a salvation to be found in love for others and repentance for sin. The disciples and followers of Jesus believed he was the messiah, or savior, whom God had promised the Jewish people. Thus, the religion of Christianity was born, subsequently becoming the state religion of the Roman Empire and later gaining acceptance throughout much of the world.

In short, the Romans, in the process of absorption and adoption that built their empire, perpetuated the art, literature, and philosophy of the Greeks; the religious and ethical system of the Jews; the new religion of the Christians; Babylonian astronomy and astrology; and cultural elements from Persia, Egypt, and other Eastern civilizations. The Romans supplied their own particular talents for government, law, and architecture and spread their Latin language. In this way, they created the Greco-Roman synthesis, the rich combination of cultural elements that has shaped what we call the Western tradition for two millennia.

Qin/Han Culture

The Chinese of the Qin/Han empire, on the other hand, were still very much the progeny of traditional Neolithic agrarian cultures, combining intensive agricultural character with some enduring hunters' instincts. They shared the common traits of most agrarians, including conservativeness, pragmatism, deference, cooperativeness, inclusiveness, and constructiveness. As a result, while Rome's economy relied on slavery, Qin/Han prosperity rode mainly on the backs of free peasants. This labor force was often set to work on projects motivated by a trait the Han shared with the Romans. They were great builders. The Qin/Han built the defensive Great Wall to shut out barbaric nomads in the north and northwest. The central government built a network of roads connecting regional centers and capitals as well as major hydraulic projects, thereby binding the empire together.

One of the distinguishing developments of Emperor Wudi's time was the triumph of Confucianism as the state political philosophy. What emerged at the end of the Han was an eclectic Confucianism, a syncretism that differed in some ways from the tenets that the founding fathers of the Later Zhou period postulated. Meyer (1994) explained that Han Confucianism borrowed a stress on efficient authoritarian administration from the Legalists and appropriated various popular ideas intended to appeal to the masses from the Daoists, including yin and yang, the five phases, concern with signs, portents, unusual natural phenomena, various types of magic, and the search for long life and physical immortality.

The incorporation of a more intellectual Confucianism complemented these popular appeals with scholars reviewing the old classics and as many of the earlier writings as possible. The most notable style of literary writing in the earlier Han was *fu* 賦, free verse or poems in long lines of irregular meter and rhyme that described the capitals and main cities of China, life at the court, imperial activities, and lovely landscapes in rich imagery and with great exuberance. Fu romanticized the themes of love of life and pursuit of pleasure.

However, the most outstanding Han contribution to literature was in the field of historical writing, whose highest intellectual expression was manifested in Sima Qian and Ban Gu. Both considered history to have dual functions in imparting factual information and providing moral instruction. Sima Qian 司馬遷 (circa 145–90 BC) compiled the *Shiji* 史記, or *Historical Records*, a general history of China from ancient times to his day, a volume containing 130 chapters and 700,000 characters. Ban Gu 班固 (32–92) wrote the second great history, the *Han Shu* 漢書, or *History of the Western Han*, carrying on where Sima Qian had left off.

Various other arts flourished during the earlier Han as well, such as the playing of a variety of musical instruments, including a four-stringed plucked lute (*pipa* 琵 琶) derived from Central Asia and a zither of thirteen strings (*Zheng* 箏). Fine pottery glazes were developed, and early porcelains were fashioned. A class of professional painters also arose during this period, although little of their work remains. Han artists and architects are noted for their detailed carvings in jade, wood, or ivory and the building of elaborate temples. They also refined the process of making silk, which set the standard in China for centuries.

According to Meyer (1994), the Han era also made great strides in inventive and technological science. The accomplishments of the time comprise a long list indeed. The Chinese first recorded sunspots in 28 BC. Galileo was the first European to discover sunspots in 1613. They calculated a nine-year elliptical orbit of the moon around the earth, which was very close to the actual 8.85-year orbit. An early form of seismograph was invented to record earthquakes. By 132 BC, its inventor, who was also an astronomer, had enumerated 11,520 different stars. The Chinese utilized sundials and water clocks divided into 100 or 120 equal parts. They continued to note solar and lunar eclipses and officially adopted the lunar calendar in which the four seasons commenced in the first, fourth, seventh, and tenth moons with the equinox noted in the second and eighth and the solstice in the fifth and eleventh. As advanced astronomers, they also created more accurate clocks.

Han scientists wrote textbooks on subjects ranging from zoology to botany and chemistry. Scientists also invented the rudder for use on ships and created other useful devices like the fishing reel and wheelbarrow. The Eastern Han developed the water-powered mill and outfitted their horses with shoulder collars, which increased their efficiency as draft animals. Similar collars were not used in the West for another ten centuries. The Chinese experimented with problem-resistant rice strains, practiced crop rotation, and terraced slopes to grow fruits, vegetables, and bamboo. They also developed iron casting techniques. In an epochal advance, the Western Han developed paper from rags, fibers, and the bark of trees, replacing the bulky and unwieldy wooden and bamboo slips in use until then. Pure paper, dated to around AD 100, has been discovered in former Han outposts located in the dry, Central Asian deserts. In an early form of printing, classics engraved on stone were reproduced on paper by ink rubbing techniques. Because of natural disasters and civil strife, only fragments of these many Han books remain.

Han physicians developed acupuncture to alleviate pain and treat various illnesses. They also made use of certain plants as herbal remedies. They were able to diagnose and successfully treat various illnesses with these techniques. In 16, the Chinese recorded a medical dissection and described the various uses of valuable herbs. In the first part of the third century, a Daoist prepared a medical manual on the manufacture of drugs. At about the same time, the Chinese translated a Buddhist text listing 404 diseases.

The long Han dynasty was indeed a creative one. During four centuries of Han rule, the Chinese achieved political and cultural unity, albeit at the price of philosophical conformity and orthodoxy. Nevertheless, Han society was relatively open and free. The Chinese way of life has radiated into the corners of both China proper and other peripheral areas. Societies in northern Korea, southern Manchuria, northern Vietnam, and the oases along the silk routes leading to Central Asia, all adopted Chinese cultural patterns, either through force or tactical volition. Official scholarship abounded, as evidenced in the first great individual works of history. Inventive technical genius shone, and many arts were developed. Sea routes originating in central and southern Chinese ports promoted trade with Southeast Asia, India, and the Near East. This trade was imbalanced because Chinese goods, predominantly silk, were desired abroad more than foreign-made goods were valued within China. This was not because of any particular prejudice on the part of the Chinese. It is simply because of the greater availability of domestic goods. Each of these advantages played a role in the Han's fashioning of China's first great empire. Modern Chinese actually continue to pay homage to the Han dynasty by choosing to identify themselves as the Han people.

CHAPTER NINE

The Decline of Empires

(200 BC–AD 500)

Clearly from the conclusion of last chapter, the Qin/Han Empire was significantly different from the Roman Empire in development, characteristic, form, and function. These differences then contributed to the subsequent outcomes when the empires faced internal corruption and external pressure from barbarians, the topic of chapter nine.

Section One: The Decline of the Roman Empire

The Roman Empire was at its peak during the reign of Augustus. With Emperor Commodus's rule, beginning in 180, the era of effective leadership ended. Soon, the Roman Empire was laboring under far less able leadership. A century of turmoil began, causing a collapse of political institutions, a weakening of the army, and economic disaster. After the murder of Commodus in 192, a civil war between rival claimants to the imperial throne penetrated every corner of the empire and changed all aspects of Roman life.

Political Successions

Between 193 and 234, a series of rulers known as the Severan dynasty reigned over Rome. For much of that time, civil war raged in many areas. Rome's fatal weakness lay in its lack of a constitution. Without which, all real power derived from the army, which claimed to represent the Roman people. For fifty years, generals caused incredible destruction in their quest for power, but their efforts were largely in vain. Between 235 and 284, the troops acclaimed approximately twenty emperors and another thirty pretenders. These two groups differed only in that the emperors managed, however briefly, to control the city of Rome. Civil war and the collapse of central authority impacted the Roman economy, communication, and trade and caused devaluation of the currency. As Roman money became worthless, much of the empire was reduced to a barter economy. During this period of crisis, emperors were no longer automatically derived from Italy or the Romanized western provinces. They could emerge from Africa, Mauritania, Syria, the Balkans, and even Arabia. These emperors made little use of the Senate, even though the senators retained their prestige and their enormous landholdings. For the first time in Roman history, political authority did not depend on wealth and status. The changes sweeping through the empire impacted every level of Roman society, resulting in the disappearance of the rich freemen and the civil service and the decline of slavery.

During the third century, renegade armies, rebellions, and foreign invasions drove Rome's social and economic systems to the point of collapse. Yet an extraordinary recovery in the fourth century showed that brilliant political leadership could rescue even a seemingly hopeless situation. Emperor Diocletian, a native of Dalmatia on the Adriatic coast, which is part of modern Croatia, ruled from 284 to 306 and instituted reforms that restored stable government and prosperity to the empire. He implemented broad economic reforms in an attempt to restore value to the currency and control runaway inflation and established a new system of taxation to finance the imperial budget. Diocletian was the first Roman leader to try to balance the imperial budget and create a uniform system to evaluate the economic resources of the empire. On his voluntary retirement in 305, he left two Augusti to rule the empire, which was then essentially divided into eastern and western portions. But only a year later, the death of the western Augustus, Constantius I, upset these careful plans.

Constantius's son, Constantine, quickly moved to claim his father's throne. In a dream, Constantine had seen a cross emblazoned with the words, "In this sign you will be the victor." This vision inspired the emperor to adorn the shields of his soldiers with Christian insignia. In 312, Constantine invaded Italy, where he triumphed in the battle of the Milvian Bridge. His victory convinced him to proclaim the Edict of Milan, which imposed tolerance for all religions, including Christianity. Constantine was now master of the western part of the empire. He then launched a decade of civil war, eventually defeating the Eastern emperor and reuniting the entire empire under his sole rule. In 330, for religious and strategic reasons, Constantine dedicated the new capital to be Constantinople, now Istanbul, on the site of the ancient Greek city of Byzantium. The new Christian city became the "New Rome," the center of the East. By his death in 337, Constantine had established Christianity as the favored religion of the Roman state. Other emperors may have had greater political, economic, or military impact, but, when Constantine recognized the humble religious sect of Christianity, he transformed the eventual course of world history.

Theodosius I was the final ruler of the united Roman Empire. At his death in 395, he left the eastern portion of the empire to his eighteen-year-old son, Arcadias, and the western portion to his ten-year-old son, Honorius. In the following years, Constantinople and the Eastern Roman Empire remained strong while the Western Roman Empire began a steady decline in the face of economic disintegration, successive weak emperors, and invading Germanic tribes. The breakdown of communication, commerce, and public order exposed the people of Gaul, Spain, and other provinces to famine and robbery. In 410, the Goths sacked Rome. In 476, Germanic troops in Italy mutinied and elected the Gothic commander Odoacer to the role of king, deposing the young emperor Romulus Augustulus. This date marked the demise of the Western Roman Empire, but the Eastern Roman Empire continued for another thousand years until the Turks finally vanquished it in 1453.

This survey of events and dates outlines what happened as Rome fell into decline, but does not fully explain why. What first led to Rome's decline and, ultimately, her fall?

The Causes of Decline

The most obvious weakness of the Roman Empire was political (Strayer 1991). The republic failed because it could not keep its officials from fighting for the spoils of power. In addition, political office had become a burden rather than an honor because officials were required to pay for circuses and baths. Furthermore, tax collectors were required to personally make up for any shortfall in revenues for their districts. As the republic evolved into the empire, these dangers were avoided by steadily increasing the power of the emperor until no other authority in the state could resist his orders. With an all-powerful emperor on the throne, the great majority of the inhabitants of the empire could not participate in the work of government. But the imperial office was instituted as a temporary expedient, and it was never intended to be held on a permanent basis. The intended lack of permanence in the role of emperor was especially evident when it came to the question of succession. Emperors were made by intrigues in the bureaucracy or plots in the army. Their rivals destroyed almost as fast as they were created. The lack of fixed constitutional principles had turned the Roman Empire into a military despotism. The emperors of the late period were soldiers, anxious to preserve their empire, but they were apt to reduce all difficulties to military terms and use military discipline as their sole solution to all problems.

The military overburden worsened the economic situation. Most of the city governments, many members of the middle class, and the great majority of the peasants were bankrupt long before the fall of Rome. A steady stream of gold and silver flowed from the empire to the Orient for luxury goods, but it still failed to eliminate a large payment shortfall.

Eighteenth-century historian Edward Gibbon discussed various additional causes of Rome's decline in his classic work, *The Decline and Fall of the Roman Empire*. For instance, the long period of peace and the uniform government of the Romans gradually extinguished the industry and creativeness of the people as well as the military discipline and valor of the soldiers. The indulgence in luxury, which originally remained confined to the nobles and residents of the imperial court, was later extended to the troops, resulting in the corruption of their morals. The enrollment of mercenary barbarians in the armies, which served to excuse the Romans themselves from military responsibilities, simultaneously encouraged the barbarians within the empire to grow in power and influence. The rich countered and evaded the multiplication of oppressive taxes. They then shifted the burden to the poor, who, in turn, fled to the woods and mountains and swelled the ranks of Rome's rebels and robbers to dodge the taxes. Notwithstanding the importance of these many contributing causes, Gibbon also considered another two factors to be the most important and decisive in the decline of the Roman Empire: the invasion of the barbarians and the growth of Christianity within the empire.

Every student of ancient Roman history is familiar with the barbarian enemies of the Roman Empire, including the Goths, Lombards, Vandals, Alemannis, Huns, Persians, Turks, and so forth. Each invaded Rome at one time or another, playing their respective role in her fall. However, as Eugene Ho noted in his examination of *The Decline and Fall of the Roman Empire*, it is less easy to understand the role that Christianity played as an accomplice in this downfall. How was it possible that a religion whose humble founder preached love and peace and who later found himself gruesomely nailed to a cross contributed to Rome's collapse? Ho analyzed Gibbon's position on this issue in detail:

> Christianity made for the decline and fall of Rome by sapping the faith of the people in the official (pagan) religion, thereby undermining the state which that religion supported and blessed. To be sure, Gibbon is not blind to the fact that other cults and sects within the Empire were also competing with one another in their attempt to attract believers ... However, Christianity was to be distinguished from other flourishing

sects in its claim to exclusivity, or in other words, in its claim that it alone held the key to "Truth" and to Heaven, and that all its competitors were vicious and damned. Moreover, as the early Christians believed in the imminent end of this world, they all put their thoughts into the "next" world. This other-worldly attitude proved most disastrous to the Empire during the barbarian invasions, since the Christians, instead of bearing arms to serve the state and the public good, diverted men from useful employments and encouraged them to concentrate on heavenly and private salvation. (1994)

Section Two:
The Fall of the Chinese Empire: A Contrast

The Han dynasty disintegrated about two centuries before the fall of the Roman Empire. China fell into a period of political disunity, nomadic invasion, and civil war.

Political Fragmentation

Between 220 and 589, apart from a brief interlude between 280 and 316, no single dynasty ever managed to rule the whole of China (Roberts 1999). This fragmentation is evident from the very beginning of the period. Between 220 and 280, the empire was divided into three kingdoms. The Western Jin briefly and ineffectually reunited the county with a rapid succession of emperors, but, from 316 onward, there was a prolonged division between the north and the south. During this time, the southern dynasties established their capital at Jiankang, modern-day Nanjing. The south succession of the Liu Song, Southern Qi, Liang, and Chen dynasties maintained the Chinese traditions, but they were also joined by large numbers of refugees from the north, sometimes causing tension between the old and new settlers.

In the north, a period of extreme fragmentation caused by nomadic incursions and known as the time of the Sixteen Kingdoms 五胡十六國 lasted until 384. In the first of these incursions, dating to 311, the Xiongnu seized Luoyang. They established the short-lived Earlier Zhao dynasty, which ultimately foundered on the issue that was to perplex all non-Chinese invaders. Should they adopt Chinese culture at the expense of preserving their own identity? The Di 氐 and Qiang 羌, proto-Tibetan tribes from the west, mounted the second major incursion. In

351, the Di established the Earlier Qin dynasty centered in Chang'an. Fu Jian 符 堅, their most famous leader, conquered much of north China. In 382, they invaded the south. But the Eastern Jin, at the famous battle of Feishui 淝 水 之 戰, defeated Fu Jian's army, which was not used to campaigning in the damp conditions of the Yangtze valley. Following the Di came the Toba 拓 跋, a branch of the Xianbei, which established the Northern Wei 北 魏 dynasty with a capital at Luoyang. The Toba conquerors provided the first example of adaptation of Chinese practices, which eventually led the Toba to employ Chinese people as officials, adopt Han names and dress, and abandon the tribal system in favor of a bureaucratic state. Nevertheless, in 534, the dynasty split. A further period of political fragmentation ensued for another several decades.

Cultural Flourishment

Despite the political disorder of the time, Chinese culture did not decline. Instead, it continued to flourish throughout China. In the north, Chinese culture merged with fresh infusions from the nomads and non-Chinese peoples and gained vitality. To the south, population continued to fan out in southward migrations. For the first time in history, the Chinese demographic center shifted from the north to the Yangtze valley. Soon, because of regionalism and civil strife, distinctions began to separate northern and southern life. Yet the ideal of a single unified empire did not die out because the Qin/Han had firmly established the united Chinese identity. Although endemic chaos and change encouraged a widespread pessimism and uncertainty, still progress occurred:

> The Chinese revealed a renewed interest in both the natural world and the realm of spirit. Chinese inventiveness persisted. Paper was now widely used. The wheelbarrow, particularly in South China's hilly and winding narrow paths, came into common use. Water mills were widespread. Suspension bridges were erected, especially across the deep, rushing river courses of southwestern China. Screens, windows, and decorations were fashioned of mica. Flying kites was a popular pastime, and chairs and sedan chairs became widely available. Coal was developed as a fuel. The sciences flourished. In the mid-third century AD one of the greatest cartographers lived; his maps on wood portrayed grid divisions, orientation, route miles, altitudes, bends, and angles. A botanical book, published around AD 300 by a former governor of a southern province, classified four groups of plants into bamboos, herbs, fruit trees, and forest trees. (Meyer 1994)

The quality of life improved for wealthy families. More plants enriched Chinese palates, and tea was recognized for its therapeutic value.

In art as well, the political disorder seemed unable to diminish Chinese culture, as there were the beginnings of the great schools of secular painting, depicting realistic figures rather than traditional landscapes. Both Daoist and Buddhist arts, such as music and painting, were in fashion. Literature was rich in variety and inspired by Buddhist religious tales and wonder stories. This was also the time of China's greatest calligrapher, the scholar and government official Wang Xizhi 王 羲 之 (321–379). Specimens of his calligraphy remain available today. Among many great poets of the era was T'ao Yuanming 陶 淵 明, another scholar-official who abandoned a bureaucratic life in favor of the simple country life of a peasant. Scholarship also flourished, and literary criticism appeared. The earliest encyclopedia was compiled in the third century for the first ruler of the Wei dynasty. The first Buddhist temple was built in Luoyang in 166 after Buddhism was imported from India and the emperor adopted its worship. Daoism also thrived alongside Buddhism.

Contrasting Development

Both the Roman and the Han Empire collapsed under internal pressure from rebellion, corruption, and the breakdown of social order as well as the invasion of barbarians. Yet, this is where the similarities end. The twilight of the Roman Empire signaled a period of chaos and the beginning of a time in history that is now known as the Dark Ages, from which the Roman Empire never recovered as a political entity. As Strayer maintained, the Roman Empire was not a national state. It was a union of people who shared a common Mediterranean civilization under a single powerful ruler. As the empire declined, all these people broke loose. Revival and reconstitution took a new form at a much later date. In contrast, the Han Empire was a national state governed by an efficient and open bureaucracy and code of law with sustainable intensive agriculture within an efficient market network and economy, a common written language and cultural heritage, a shared ideology of Confucianism, and the apparent legitimacy of the mandate of heaven stipulating that the ruler must work for the benefit of the people. The Chinese went through a chaotic period similar to that experienced by the Romans and characterized by the dominion of nomadic peoples, but only the empire itself declined. The Chinese system, on the other hand, prevailed, even culturally flourished, so it was able to unify again and transform itself into an even more advanced and open state manifested in the Sui, Tang, and Song eras of political, cultural, and technological development.

CHAPTER TEN

Divergent Paths

(AD 500–AD 1300)

The Middle Ages of Europe were the centuries between the fall of the Roman Empire and the beginning of modern European civilization. Scholars have argued endlessly as to the exact dates of these two terminal points. There is, however, general consensus that the Middle Ages lasted from the fifth to the fifteenth century. We shall present only from the fifth to the thirteenth centuries in the next chapter because the thirteenth century was an important demarcation point in both European and Chinese histories.

This is the period when Europe and China took a divergent path of historical development. Europe in the Dark Ages was in isolation, immune to new ideas, and reaching its cultural and economic low point. For China, on the other hand, this was a period known for its openness to new ideas while renewing the old at the same time. As a result, it attained new cultural and economic prosperity.

Section One:
Early Medieval Europe/The Dark Ages

The early Middle Ages are often called the Dark Ages because of the then-recent fall of the great civilizations of Greece and Rome. Life in Europe during the Dark Ages was very hard. Very few people could read or write, and nobody expected conditions to improve. The only hope for most people during the Middle Ages was their strong belief in Christianity and the hope that life in heaven would be better than life on earth. Strayer described:

> As the Roman Empire in the West slowly collapsed, the Christian Church emerged as the one stable institution among the ruins. The

ablest inhabitants of the Empire became servants of the Church rather than the state, and they brought with them the Roman genius for administration and law. The men who were still capable of devotion to an ideal gave their loyalty to their faith rather than to their government. As a result, the Church had excellent leadership and strong popular support at a time when the state was weak in both respects. The strength of the early Church laid its uncompromising dogmatism, its ability to give certain and reassuring answers to a bewildered and discouraged people. (1991)

As we now know, Christianity and the Church effectively dominated most of the cultural, political, and economic life of the people and history in Medieval Europe. Because the medieval church supported all of Europe's libraries and schools, and the only literate persons in early medieval society were churchmen of one kind or another, governments had no choice but to staff their bureaucracies with clergy.

The Heirs of Rome

As the Western Roman Empire changed its form and slowly collapsed, other emerging groups contended for power. Several Germanic and Slavic people, the so-called barbarians, as well as the still-powerful regional noble families of the later Holy Roman Empire competed with one another for supremacy in different parts of Europe and battled on their eastern front for the surviving eastern portion of the Roman Empire. Interestingly, the barbarians, whose invasions supposedly caused the Dark Ages, were actually already Christians themselves. The Goths, Vandals, Franks, and other Teutonic tribes of the fifth century did indeed destroy the superstructure of Roman civilization, but Rome herself, which had withstood pressure from barbarians for a millennium, succumbed only after the Christians had held control for almost 150 years. The northern barbarians' legacy left Europe with the nation-states, laws, customs and traditions, and eventually the governments and constitutions that later made up medieval Christendom.

These barbarians were farmers and animal breeders, not stereotypical uncouth louts, except perhaps in the view of urban sophisticates. These northerners had to force their way into the Roman sphere simply because the might of the Huns pressed them from the east. Led by the fierce Attila, the Huns sacked seventy cities of the Eastern empire before advancing on Rome in 452. The northern tribes, on the other hand, were considered barbarians mainly because they did not speak any Latin or Greek and had their own culture, including oral or written literature and mythologies. These barbarians were not so barbaric as some have led us to imagine. They accepted civilization. Some rose to the highest positions in the Roman army and state even before the fifth century. Some were already Christians.

There has never been any deep-rooted racial or cultural antagonism between the Romans and the Germans. Yet the coming of the Germans nevertheless marked the end of Roman civilization in the West, crushed by the strongest kingdom in seventh century Western Europe, the Frankish Empire, which Charles the Great, or Charlemagne, founded. His kingdom is officially known as either the Holy Roman Empire or the Western Empire.

Charlemagne's family, the Carolingian, originated in the borderland between Gaul and Germany. At the time, the Franks held most of Gaul, much of the Rhine Valley in Germany, and an uneasy suzerainty over Aquitania and Bavaria. The Carolingian age saw the establishment of a Western empire strong enough to endure terrific strain, independent enough to keep its identity while in contact with other traditions, broad enough to include all the peoples of Western Europe, and rich enough to develop new forms and ideas from its own resources. By reforming and strengthening the Church, the Carolingians made a nominally Christian Europe truly Christian.

The Frankish kingdom of the Western Empire was strong, but only in comparison with its neighbors. It suffered the same weakness that ruined other Germanic kingdoms, that is, the difficulty of maintaining authority over outlying dependencies. Charles the Great had always intended to divide his empire among his sons, but only one, Louis the Pious, survived to inherit. Louis also chose to divide his empire, but he lacked the strength to keep his sons in line. The empire plunged into civil war, lasting until 843. Obviously, the Germans lacked the political experience and traditions necessary to build a strong state on the ruins of the Roman Empire. In addition, they were equally unable to solve the economic problems of the ancient world. Even more than in the Western Empire, every small district was isolated and self-sufficient. Western Europe continued to be an almost purely agricultural area with few economic ties among its regions. The same decline was observed in other cultural spheres, such as intellectual and literary activities. The Roman tradition had lost most of its vitality, and the German tradition was not sufficiently developed to take its place.

While the Germanic kingdoms of the West clung to the old forms and slowly developed their own unique traits, the East was still united under the emperor at Constantinople, who governed through the old Roman bureaucracy and Roman law. Relations between East and West, while not intimate, were overall amicable. Yet, within the Mediterranean unity, separatist tendencies were developing most strongly in the East, where rival civilizations remained potent despite prolonged suppression. The thoroughly Greek quarter of the empire, centered on Constantinople, could not entirely abandon its old intellectual traditions and still sought to impose them on the rest of the East. Eventually, the wealth of Constantinople, the manpower of Asia Minor, and a sophisticated diplomatic and military tradition gave the East Roman Empire unusual strength and resilience. With a rich heritage of Greek and Christian culture, it developed a remarkable civilization. It was conservative but not decadent, orientalized but not oriental, and profoundly Christian but not theocratic. However, it could no longer claim to be a universal empire,. Though it kept the name of Rome, it was the Empire of Byzantine to most outsiders. Its sphere of influence extended to the Slavs and Russians. Its religion is known as the Greek Orthodox Church, which persists even to this day.

The seventh and eighth centuries also saw the rise of the Islamic religion in the Arabic world, where it triumphed over territories that had been dominated by either Rome or Persia for centuries. The Arabs, like the Germans, were a small, rather poorly organized group of people, who had raided the empire intermittently for centuries without constituting a real military danger. Consequently, nothing more clearly shows the feebleness of the old Mediterranean civilization in its final days than the fact that the insubstantial efforts of these weak border peoples could change the fate of millions.

The Arabs had probably grown in numbers during the sixth century, and Mohammed gave them a better organization than they had previously enjoyed. Mohammed was a man of great ability, who had heard fragments of the Christian story. He had met Arabic-speaking Jews, who told him some of their traditions. He was familiar with Arabic legends, which were not unlike the stories of the Hebrew prophets. Brooding over this material, he became convinced that God had chosen him as the last and greatest of the prophets, the bearer of the final revelation to humanity. The new doctrine, as it finally emerged in Mohammed's sermons and conversation, had enough familiar elements in it to be acceptable to many of the people of the East. He taught there was one all-powerful God, the creator of the world and the protector and judge of humankind. He taught that God had revealed his will to humanity through a series of prophets, the greatest being Abraham, Jesus, and Mohammed. He taught that those who believed his prophets and obeyed his commandments would enjoy paradise whereas the wicked were to suffer endlessly.

After a discouraging start, Mohammed began to gain followers and eventually converted most of the tribes of northern and central Arabia to his new religion. At his death in 632, he was ruler of a large part of the Arabian Peninsula. His followers soon conquered Syria, Egypt, and even the old Persian Empire to become masters of the entire Middle East. With this solid block of territory at their disposal, it was easy for them to push along the North African coast. In 711, they crossed into Spain. By 720, the Arab Empire stretched from the borders of India to the Pyrenees, and Arab raiders were plunging deep into the heart of Gaul. They even developed sea power to challenge the Greeks in the Mediterranean.

By 750, there were three distinct and essentially separate worlds in western Eurasia: the Greek-speaking Byzantines, the Latin-writing Europeans, and the Arabic-writing Muslims. They professed different values, struggled with different problems, and adapted to different standards of living. Yet all three bore the marks of a common parentage. They were sibling heirs of Rome. The Muslims had inherited much of the learning of the Greeks. To this, they added significant material from Persia, India, and even China. On these extensive foundations, the Muslims were able to build a structure of philosophical and scientific thought that made them leaders in these fields for centuries. In addition, they occupied a key position on the ancient trade route between East and West and made the most of this opportunity by building an active commerce and thriving industries.

While the Eastern Roman Empire was not as impressive as the Arab Empire, it was still an important center of civilization and trade for the Muslims. Western Europe was the weakest and poorest of the three western Eurasian areas of the time. It had always been backward, both economically and intellectually. However, in the classical period, it had been able to draw on the East for both supplies and ideas. Now it had to face its own deficiencies with limited resources and without outside aid. In addition, periodic outbreaks of plague had devastated Europe for two centuries, ending only toward the later part of the eighth century. This surely was a low point for Europe.

New Beginnings

The Carolingian Empire began to break up a generation after Charlemagne's death. By AD 900, the empire had little direct authority over the kingdoms, ruling them only nominally. Adding to the confusion, no part of Europe had escaped invasion and civil war, although Germany suffered less damage than other Carolingian realms. New political entities, ranging from weak, local affiliations to strong, united movements, emerged in the wake of these wars and invasions. Everywhere, political reordering brought new military elites to the fore. The great century of the Anglo-Saxon kingdom coincided with the worst period of feudal warfare in France. The German Empire was at the height of its power when Italy was split into quarreling fragments. Somehow, during the hard years of the tenth and eleventh centuries, the people of Europe again learned the secret of effectively working together for the common welfare. Slowly and painfully, they began to form larger social units. By the twelfth century, the difficult period was over, and Europe had started to develop a high civilization of its own. The political developments were associated with the maturing of feudalism. The religious developments were an outgrowth of the reform movement in the Church. The economic developments kept pace with the growth of towns and the increases in commerce. These changes were contemporaneous, equally important, and closely related with each stimulating the others.

In the isolation and chaos of the ninth and tenth centuries, European leaders abandoned attempts to restore Roman institutions and adopted whatever strategy worked. The result was that Europe developed a relatively new and effective set of institutions. Through which, it adapted to a moneyless economy, inadequate transportation and communication facilities, an ineffective central government, and the constant threat of armed attack by raiders such as the Vikings, Magyars, and Saracens. The most renowned of these new institutions were manorialism (the organization of the peasants), monasticism (the organization of the church-men), and feudalism (the institution of the aristocracy).

Manorialism was a political, economic, and social system by which the peasants of medieval Europe were rendered dependent on their land and lord. Its basic unit was the manor, a self-sufficient landed estate, or fief, that was under the control of a lord who enjoyed a variety of rights over it and the peasants attached to it by means of serfdom.

The term "monasticism" describes a way of life chosen by religious men or women who retreat from society for the pursuit of spiritual salvation. However, older, established monasteries were no longer strict enough to satisfy some of the converts to Christianity. Thus, there was a reform movement in the Church, which attempted to free clergy from worldly ties. New religious orders arose and gained great prestige for their fervor and piety. The most influential men in the West during the late eleventh and early twelfth centuries were the abbots of these reformed monasteries. One of the most significant results of this religious revival was the Crusades, which served as a demonstration of papal leadership, a manifestation of popular piety, and an indication of the growing self-confidence of Western Europe. Crusaders went forth with a courage based on the absolute conviction that the Crusade was the will of God. The fact that the Crusades were also a material success for Western Europe was not an unwelcome benefit.

Then there was the institution of feudalism, a term that royal lawyers in Great Britain invented in the sixteenth century. It describes the decentralized and complex social, political, and economic society out of which the modern state emerged. Three elements and their interaction defined the feudal period: lords, vassals, and fiefs. The lord, a noble who owned land called a fief, was responsible for providing military protection for his lands and the vassals who lived on them, organizing agriculture and trade on his lands, and giving military assistance to his liege or king when called upon to do so. Both the lord and the vassal belonged to medieval society's freemen, a broad group comprised of nobles, clerics, soldiers, members of the professions, merchants, artisans, and peasant landowners, with the vassal being simply a freeman who received a fief from the lord. Along with the land, the vassal would receive the serfs inhabiting that land. The lord looked after his serfs and enforced the rules and laws of his manor. In exchange for the fief, the vassal would provide military service to the lord.

The third group of people in medieval society, in addition to freemen and serfs, were the slaves. According to Durrant (1950), the word "slave" derived from "Slav," an etymology occasioned because the Slavs, along with the Muslims, were the most common slaves in medieval Europe. An estimated twenty-five percent of all eleventh-century peasants in Western Europe were slaves. The medieval Church played an important part in the perpetuation of slavery because it permitted the enslavement of non-Christians. On theological grounds, Thomas Aquinas taught that slavery was a consequence of original sin. So, even members of the clergy and monasteries owned slaves. In fact, the eventual decline of slavery in Europe resulted from economic reasons rather than moral ones. Slaves were relatively unproductive, and slave owners began to realize that people work harder if they have a chance to acquire rewards as a result of their work. Thus, serfs, tenant farmers who were tied to the land, gradually replaced slaves in the twelfth century.

Although the obligations and relations between lord, vassal, and fief lie at the heart of feudalism, it was nevertheless practiced differently in different parts of Europe. While feudalism started in Italy and Germany, the most characteristic form occurred in France. For the most part, it came to Great Britain with the Normans after the Conquest in 1066. The feudal system never came of age in northern or eastern Italy, Christian Spain, the Balkans, western Germany, southern France, Norway, or Sweden.

Feudal government was flexible and adaptable to local conditions. Under favorable circumstances, it generated new institutions with surprising rapidity. Eventually, the feudal lordship evolved into the feudal state. As Europe became more peaceful and orderly, population growth and expansion followed. Although this renewed Europe of 1100 was neither orderly nor law-abiding by our present standards, it was so much better than previously. Large-scale cooperation was once again possible. New land was cultivated, urban population increased, commercial activities were enhanced, and the economy improved. Strayer wrote:

A growing network of trade-routes was binding Western Europe into a single economic unit. Some of the elementary principles of division of labor and specialization had been discovered and this increased production and improved quality. Greater mobility of the population gave more opportunities to the individual and supplied the manpower for new activities. For the first time since the great days of Mediterranean civilization there was a surplus of labor and a surplus of food which made it possible to take chances, to try new techniques, to develop new interests. (1991)

In the closing years of the eleventh century, Western Europe had made remarkable advances in social organization, intellectual interests, and the intangible qualities of spirit and conscience that make civilization possible. This improvement continued at an accelerated rate during the twelfth century. The people of Western Europe showed tremendous energy and persistence in all their activities, including religious, political, economic, and cultural. But we will leave that great story to the next chapter and focus now on the contrast between the great Chinese dynasties of the Sui, Tang, and Song, which existed contemporaneously with the depressed state of affairs we have described in Western Europe during the early Middle Ages

Section Two: The Sui, Tang, and Song Dynasties

At the intersection after the fall of Western Roman and Han empires, Europe and China took a divergent path, a significant outcome of their contrasting cultural, social, and political histories. While Europe began its Dark Age, China was at the verge of another golden age, the Sui, Tang, and Song dynasties.

The Sui Dynasty 隋

In 589, the Yang family, under the name of the Sui dynasty, united China again. Their capital in Chang'an, or present-day Xi'an, lasted only twenty-nine years. The founder of the dynasty, Yang Jian 楊堅, or Wendi, was of Chinese stock but married to a Xiongnu wife. He was an effective administrator who centralized the operations of government and restored the centrality of Confucianism with its emphases on stability, ritual, and the importance of the monarch. Although he had scant regard for scholars, during his reign, the essential characteristic of the bureaucratic examination system took shape. Wendi also initiated important legal and taxation reforms. J. A. G. Roberts wrote:

> He promulgated the Kaihuang Code, which synthesized northern and southern legal traditions and abolished some cruel punishments. It defined crimes and their punishments in plain terms and allowed guilty officials to commute their punishment by payment of a fine or by accepting demotion. The Kaihuang Code was to provide a model for all future imperial legal codes. Wendi also overhauled the land and taxation systems, reviving the "equal field" arrangement and the periodic distribution of land to the common people, and revising the tax registers. The common people were required to pay three taxes: a land tax payable in grain, a textile tax payable in silk or linen, and a labor tax requiring 20 days' labor per year from adult males. (1999)

Wendi also reviewed the military situation and reorganized the army under central control. In 590, he demilitarized the population of the North China Plain; recovered control of Champa, or modern Annam; and contained the Turks in the north by establishing military colonies and constructing walls. In many of his actions, Wendi received the advice and encouragement of his consort, the Wenxian empress.

On the empress's advice, their second son, Yangdi 楊廣, succeeded Wendi in 604. Yangdi secured his place in history by building the Grand Canal of China, which connects the drainage basins of the Yellow, Huai, and Yangtze rivers, enabling the resources of the productive land southward to be brought north. Wendi had started this project, but Yangdi ultimately created a network of canals that extended for 1,200 miles. This national system facilitated communications that were to provide the basis for the prosperity of the subsequent Tang period. However, the construction of the canal system required large-scale state intervention in the economy and the conscription of many thousands of men and women laborers, features that earned it the condemnation of Confucian historians.

The collapse of the Sui dynasty has often been attributed to Yangdi's personal failings and his overweening ambition. It has been argued that fortune turned against him when the disastrous flooding of the Yellow River Valley in 611 formed a prelude to the rise of rebellion. However, Yangdi is held personally responsible for the rebellions, which are ascribed to the harsh conscription of peasants for building canals as well as military disasters sustained in the Korean peninsula. Roberts noted that rivalries and power struggles within the northern aristocratic clans, including the Turks, may have been an additional factor in the rebellion.

The Tang Dynasty 唐

The Tang dynasty that followed the Sui, contemporary with Charlemagne's empire in Western Europe, marked another high tide of Chinese politics and culture. It resembled the Han dynasty, but it was on a grander scale with a population of 130 million people at its inception in 618 (Meyer 1994) when the father-and-son team of the Li family, Li Yuan 李 淵 and Li Shimin
李 世 民, inherited the Sui capital of Chang'an to serve as the capital of the Tang dynasty. In 626, the first emperor abdicated to his son, who then eliminated two rival brothers to become Taizong, the most renowned monarch in Chinese history.

The Tang dynasty lasted for almost three centuries to 907. The reign of Taizong 太 宗 himself was regarded as a golden era. Under the Tang dynasty, according to Charles Hucker, China combined prosperity, cultural grandeur, aristocratic sophistication, military power, and supremacy in foreign relations to achieve an age of greatness unseen since the Han. The capital, Chang'an, with a population of two million people, became the world's largest and most brilliantly cosmopolitan city. One in six people was a foreigner. Chang'an was a mecca to which traders, diplomats, and seekers after culture traveled from Japan, Korea, Central Asia, Vietnam, and the South China Sea. Arabs, Persians, Jews, and Christians from the Mediterranean Basin were welcome. As one of the world's earliest planned urban complexes, the city, laid out in a rectangular grid, measured five by six miles and covered almost fifteen thousand acres.

The Tang owed much of its early strength and prosperity to the maturing of institutions that had been developing under the Northern and Sui dynasties. In addition to a stable, centralized administrative structure, these institutions notably included a civil service system that accommodated the hereditary claims of powerful landowning families, but they advanced the bureaucratic principles of recruitment and evaluation that the Han established. Economic inequities were minimized and fiscal stability was ensured by an equal fields system of land tenure. The state claimed ownership of all agricultural lands and then allocated them equitably on a per capita basis for lifetime tenure, collecting taxes, and requisitioning labor services in accordance with head counts. Bureaucratic examinations for the civil service were broadened beyond the customary Confucian topics to include history, law, poetry, mathematics, and even aspects of Daoism. An efficient centralized government operated at the capital, overseeing a country divided into ten provinces (dao 道), 358 prefectures (zhou 州), 634 channels (fu 府), and many more subprefectures (xian 縣). Local princes with Chinese titles ruled over non-Chinese areas. With the renewed stature given Confucianism, the rising bureaucratic class of scholar-gentry, recruited primarily through examinations and now entrenched in political life, began to gain most of their income from holding office rather than landed estates. By the subsequent Song era, this class had further displaced the aristocrats.

The Tang central government manifested the traditional tripartite structure. A staff of generals commanded the imperial armies. There was a consorate that was somewhat more elaborate than its Han antecedent. For general administration, a mature complex of three agencies 三 省 had evolved from mid-Han times: the department of state affairs, the secretariat, and the chancellery. Within this framework, Taizong presented himself as a humble student of the art of civil government and employed a succession of capable ministers who came to epitomize the ideal relationship between an emperor and his advisors.

The department of state affairs was the operating arm of the government. At the core of the department's administrative apparatus was a group of six ministries 六 部, each with an array of specialized subordinate bureaus. These six ministries—personnel, revenue, rites, war, justice, and work—remained the administrative heart of every central government until the end of China's imperial era. With the emergence of these ministries, the Tang central government looked far less like the imperial household administration of its Han predecessor.

By Meyer's account, Tang scholars studied mathematics and astronomy. Gunpowder was used for pyrotechnics. Many new crops from various regions added variety to Tang foods. China imported cane sugar from India and learned how to distill wine from grapes from Central Asia. The porcelain industry continued to develop. In 801, a cartographer created a map, measuring thirty by thirty-three feet, which represented an area ten thousand by eleven thousand miles. On it, he noted seven major trade routes to the known Asian world. Paper reached Central Asia through Chinese people who were captured by Arabs in the Battle of Talas in 751. The prevalence of this innovation later spread to Western Asia and eventually to Europe.

Wood block printing was a significant invention of the Sui and flourished in the Tang, occurring when most of the necessary materials became available. Demand was high because both the examination system and the widespread religious charms and prayer formulas demanded multiple copies of the same text. Printing had precedents in black-and-white rubbings on paper taken from stone engravings and imprints made with large, official seals. By the seventh century, full-page wood block illustrations for texts appeared.

Cultural pursuits also flourished during the Tang era. Tang writers produced many scholarly works. Private and imperial libraries were extensive, and a special Tang archival bureau acquired and cataloged books. Printing advanced the compilation and availability of encyclopedias, which were particularly helpful to students preparing for examinations. Many local gazetteers and collections of excerpts from earlier books were issued, supplementing the dynastic histories as sources of topical information on Chinese politics, economics, and society. The flourishing genre of the short story dealt with both religious and everyday topics. Professional storytellers combined prose and verse. By the eighth century, some of their tales had been written in the vernacular. Drama did not develop during this period, but court jesters produced plays based on short stories. With time, these plays grew longer. On the other hand, poetry (shi) reached its height. Several poetic forms with varying rhyme schemes, line lengths, and tonal emphases were developed. Lyrics of popular songs were recited for their own merit without musical accompaniment. Poets such as Li Bai 李白, Du Fu 杜甫, Bai Juyi 白居易, and others made towering contributions to classical Chinese literature, influencing later generations of Chinese. Secular painting flourished, and Tang music played on indigenous and Central Asian instruments was widespread. Daoism and Confucianism registered marked growth under the Tang, and Buddhism reached the greatest height yet witnessed in China.

On the political front, Taizong pursued a vigorous and aggressive foreign policy, which Meyer described in detail. The emperor regained the Tarim Basin from the western Turks with the help of some newfound Central Asian allies, the Uygurs. In 630, he conquered the now-belligerent eastern Turks and two other frontier groups, the Khitans and the Mongols. Part of his success in this and other campaigns lay in his emphasis on cavalry. Tibet, first unified as recently as 607, came under Chinese suzerainty as well. Upon request of the Tibetan monarch, the emperor sent a princess to marry the king, bringing both the Chinese culture and Tang institutional philosophies with her. Tang contacts extended into northern India, and Chinese Buddhist pilgrimages to India continued on land and sea. All of Korea came under Tang influence when China backed Silla, one of three warring Korean kingdoms, in its defeat of Paekche and Japanese-backed Koguryo in 668, thus unifying Korea and creating a new vassal of the Tang. Thousands of Japanese students streamed to Chang'an to study and return home with whatever they could from the Chinese culture, including philosophy, religion, and language as well as social, political, and cultural ideas and institutions. These returning expatriates built new imperial capitals, first at Nara and then at nearby Kyoto, modeled after the Tang capital of Chang'an. Through these many widespread influences, the imperial court of the Tang became the center of highly developed intellectual and artistic activity for virtually all Asian peoples.

There was one important setback during the Tang dynasty. A Tang army under Xuanzong, the sixth Tang emperor, was lost in 751 to Arab forces at Talas, north of Fergana in present-day central Russian Asia. This defeat marked the end of Chinese expansion in that area and foreshadowed five centuries of steadily diminishing Chinese military prestige, culminating with the Arab conquest of Central Asia and the supplanting of Confucianism by Islam.

An interesting facet of the Tang dynasty was that it boasted the only Chinese empress, Empress Wu 武則天, who ruled from 690–705. She was strong-willed, competent, energetic, and she had an unproven reputation for being lusty. Her grandson, Xuanzong 玄宗, ascended the throne in 712 and ruled for forty-two years, the longest reign of the dynasty. Toward the end of his reign in 755, a young general named An Lushan 安禄山, of non-Chinese origin, rebelled and captured the capital. As the court fled south to Sichuan province, the emperor abdicated. Soon after, in 757, his son killed An Lushan, but the rebellion continued until 763. The dynasty carried on for another 150 years, but times were changing. Never again did China attain the territorial limits of the earlier Tang. During the earlier decades of the Tang, the dynasty resembled the Han in many ways, but the latter decades set the stage for a somewhat different China under the succeeding dynasties.

Chinese historians generally know the period following the collapse of the Tang dynasty as the period of the Five Dynasties 五代 and the Ten Kingdoms 十國. With so many changes of rule in a period of only fifty years, it can be appreciated that this was a time of considerable disintegration. During the five decades after the collapse of the Tang in 907, civil strife divided the empire into small states. Some of which, particularly in the north, were dominated by rulers of alien extraction. Amidst general administrative breakdown and internecine wars, Chinese historians today consider five successive Chinese states appearing in the north as legitimate. Concurrently, ten other kingdoms competed in the struggle to reunite the country. Meyer put this disarray into perspective:

> Extensive fighting and hard times characterized the Five Dynasties, but China was reunified after only some fifty years, in contrast to the three and a half centuries of political division that followed the Han disintegration. Never again was mainland China rent into competing regional political units for so long as half a century. Although the Middle Kingdom subsequently experienced chronic warlordism, military regionalism, and foreign domination after the Tang, China coalesced into an indestructible political entity. In peace or war, under native or foreign rule, the vision of unity, Zhongguo, was never lost. (1994)

The Song Dynasty 宋

These decades of discord came to a close in 960, when, by means of the Chenqiao 陳橋 Mutiny, Zhao Kuangyin 趙匡胤 first donned the yellow robes of imperial rule and founded the Song dynasty (960–1279). Zhao was the fourth example since the beginning of the Five Dynasties period of a general seizing power on the strength of his own forces. Ever since the closing years of the Tang dynasty, weak monarchs had been unable to prevent their own generals from breaking away and founding independent states. Aware of this threat, Zhao, in his new robes as the Emperor Taizu 太祖, orchestrated an arrangement by which his commanders agreed to relinquish authority over their armies and retire peacefully to the countryside. As a result, the Song system was more autocratic than the Tang system, placing more power into the hands of the emperor and persons acting on his behalf. For instance, centrally appointed civilian officials replaced regional military governors and their supporters. At the same time, China progressively weakened militarily and shrank territorially during the Song dynasty because of the continued and expanding pressures from nomads to the north.

The Song was divided into two consecutive periods: the Northern Song of 960–1127 with its series of nine emperors ruling from Kaifeng and the Southern Song of 1127–1279 with its nine monarchs located in Hangzhou. After the Song lost control of northern China in 1127 to the Khitan Liao dynasty, which the Jurchen Jin dynasty later conquered, they retreated to the South and became known as the Southern Song.

With the exception of its founder, almost all emperors of the Southern Song were mediocre, but the bureaucracy had matured to the point where political life nevertheless continued as usual. Consequently, this period in China is rather unique in world history. It witnessed a state that was weak militarily, but, at the same time, strong economically, morally and, culturally. From the moment it was founded, the Song dynasty was helpless against foreign aggression. Its only choice was to placate invaders by paying them off. Among the many explanations that can be offered for the Southern Song's failure to better handle the threat of the nomads, the simplest may be that the Chinese were simply losing the will to fight. Ultimately, Mongols overran the Song dynasty, but the consensus among modern scholars is that, by paying off their opponents with an annual tribute, the Song coped as best they could rather than going to war.

During the Song dynasty, China experienced a commercial revolution fostered by growing urbanization and a cultural renaissance. One of the most significant cultural influences was the large influx of well-educated commoners into the ranks of officialdom by means of the national examination system. The emperor himself presided over the final tier of this system, the palace examination. Successful candidates became known as the "disciples of the son of heaven." During the Tang, only a few dozen candidates had assumed this title each time the examinations were held. However, during the Song, this honor roll ran to several hundred annually. In the twenty years of Taizu's reign, there were nearly ten thousand new titles. This expansion was partially due to the fact that printing had developed rapidly in the Five Dynasties period, promoting literacy and education to the point that, for the first time in Chinese history, common people had realistic hopes that their sons might achieve status in the elite official class. The court of Emperor Taizu, where civil accomplishments took precedence over martial exploits, was composed of writers and scholars drawn from ordinary families rather than members of the ruling aristocracy, as had been the case under the Tang dynasty.

This strong emphasis on civil accomplishment and a government operating in the interests of the common people set the tone for the Song. With cultivated people running the country, cultured thinking permeated society. There was a spontaneous flourishing of philosophy and new ideas. The Song refined many of the developments of the previous centuries. Included among these refinements were not only the Tang ideal of the universal man, who combined the qualities of scholar, poet, painter, and statesman, but also historical writings, painting, calligraphy, and hard-glazed porcelain. Song intellectuals sought their answers to philosophical and political questions in the Confucian classics, now called Neo-Confucianism. This process renewed interest in the Confucian ideals and society of ancient times and coincided with the decline of Buddhism in China as the Chinese came to regard Buddhism as foreign and offering few practical guidelines for the solution of political and mundane problems.

In art, the bright color combinations of ink-and-wash painting gave way to mixed hues of gray with large areas of the surface left blank. Porcelain forms simplified and became more plain and pure in coloration. Deeply introspective literary practitioners, with their lofty moral standards, produced artistic achievements of the highest order, but they also seemed overcivilized, devoid of any streak of wildness, as if they were lacking part of what makes us human. This can be sensed in the contrast between the refined elegance of Song porcelain and the brash tricolor glaze pottery of the Tang dynasty. By Song times, the technique of high-fired, hard-glazed porcelain was fully developed. Porcelain was produced in abundance for use in the imperial palace and commoners' homes alike and increasingly for export throughout Asia and across the Indian Ocean to Africa and the Mediterranean world. Near the end of the Song dynasty, the now-famous blue-and-white porcelain of China emerged. The most common porcelain was the type known as celadon. In keeping with the simplicity of its designs, Song porcelain is characterized by a faint, incised motif and often has no decoration at all.

Poetry and painting gained importance in the Song. Evidence of a new familiarity with poetry can be seen in the fact that some poets began using the vernacular in their writings. In the past, it had been very unusual to use phrases from everyday life. The most popular poetic style of the Song is called *tzu* 詞. Tzu is characterized by lines and stanzas of irregular length, but it also has prosodic prescriptions that are rather rigid and in song form. The shi 詩 of the Tang period and the tzu of the Song are actually Chinese poetic styles that prevail up to the present.

Painting also reached new heights during the Song, which two main schools of painters represent. The first created decorative, yet realistic, paintings that showed great attention to detail. The second tried to depict inner realities and viewed painting to be an intimate personal expression. It has been said of Song painting, particularly bird and flower and bamboo portraits, that it reflects the profound and subtle Neo-Confucian philosophy of the world at the time. Zen Buddhist painting also flourished. It was characterized by a concentration on certain details of the subject with the remainder of the frame left undefined.

In addition to its cultural attainments, the Song dynasty is noteworthy for a commercial revolution and increased urbanization. Not only did cities develop as administrative centers, they also served the purposes of trade, industry, and maritime commerce. The roots of this vitality are to be found in a marked increase in the productivity of China's economy. Steady technological improvements raised the output of traditional industries. The introduction of a quickly maturing strain of rice that allowed two crops to be grown each season stimulated agriculture. Previously, only one had been possible. In addition, new water control projects that the Song undertook greatly expanded the acreage of irrigated paddy fields. As a result of these two innovations, it is estimated that rice harvests doubled between the eleventh and twelfth centuries. Increasing productivity made possible a corresponding increase in population, which, in circular fashion, further stimulated production.

The volume of trade rose in concert with the quickening tempo of domestic economic activity. For the first time, large cities appeared in China that were primarily commercial rather than administrative centers. The circulation of money became more widespread. In addition, there was a marked increase in foreign trade. Considerable overseas commerce had been carried on since Han times, but, during the Tang and especially the Song, the volume of foreign trade far surpassed all previous records. With improvements in maritime technology, including the use of the compass, an adjustable centerboard keel, and cotton sails in place of bamboo slats, China came to dominate trade in the South China Sea and beyond. The end result was that the seaports, rather than the old overland routes, became China's principal contact with the outside world. Indicative of China's economic leadership at this time is the fact that its exports were mostly manufactured goods such as silk, porcelains, books, and paintings while the imports were mostly raw materials such as spices, minerals, and horses. Hucker wrote:

> In the eleventh and twelfth centuries, China was not only the most populous and urbanized country in the world; it was also the most advanced and sophisticated country in the world in its agriculture, industry, marketing, and trade. In retrospect, Song China seems to have been on the verge of developing a genuine "modern" economy—commercialized, industrialized, monetized, and to some extent even mechanized. In most respects, eleventh-century China was at a level of economic development not achieved by any European state until the eighteenth century at the earliest. These achievements set the stage for the later empire's explosive population growth. But the pace of economic development then slowed. The complexities of the economic system seem eventually to have outgrown China's managerial competence. (1975)

Hucker's perceptive words foreshadow what was to follow in modern-day China. If economic success is not followed with appropriate political reform, all gains are eventually headed for failure.

CHAPTER ELEVEN

On the Road to Modern Times

The divergent paths of Europe and China took a reversal in the thirteenth century. Europe continued to accelerate through further cultural, economic, and political development of modernization. This time, Europe was open to new ideas. The Western thought preferences made scientific and industrial revolution attainable. On the other hand, China, after suffering much from the Mongolian military occupation, turned introvert in the Ming dynasty and closed to new ideas. Traditional Chinese philosophy and thought preferences were weak against mighty military powers. The Yuan dynasty unsettled the dynamic balance of yin and yang and clearly signaled the beginning of China's long decline.

Section One:
The Renaissance, Reformation, and Age of Discovery

From roughly AD 1000 onward, stability increased in the lands of Western Europe. With the exception of brief Mongol incursions, major barbarian invasions had ceased by this time. As described earlier, the people of Western Europe showed tremendous energy and persistence in all their activities, including religious, political, economic, and cultural. The advance of Christian kingdoms and military orders into previously pagan regions in the Baltic and Finnic northeast forced the assimilation of numerous native people into the European entity. In Spain, a slow reconquest of the captured Muslim-ruled territories began. Trade grew throughout Europe as the dangers of travel were reduced, and steady economic growth resumed.

Politically, the late Middle Ages were typified by the decline of feudal power, slowly increasing disorder, and, partly as an outcome of these two trends, the development of strong, royalty-based nation-states. Wars between kingdoms,

243

such as the Hundred Years' War between Great Britain and France, weakened the Christian nations in their confrontation with Islam. Black Death, the plague of 1346–1352, and the schism of the Christian church were disastrous for the old medieval order, laying the groundwork for great changes in the fifteenth and sixteenth centuries. In the east, the Byzantine Empire survived until 1453, but it was in a diminished and weakened form.

The Church promotes the notion that it pulled Europe through the Dark Ages. However, this ignores an important truth. The Church was actually largely responsible for the years of darkness. One of the ironies particularly acute for Christians is that the barbarian invasions and the Dark Ages coincided with the application to Europe of human interpretations of God's plan. The eleventh to thirteenth centuries saw the occurrence of seven major Crusades in Europe. As a result, the seaports of northern Italy and the cities of southern France benefited from a flourishing trade with the East. The economy quickened, a wealthy middle class developed, and the standard of living rose. By the fourteenth century, Venice had become the largest and richest city in Europe with a population of more than one hundred thousand and revenue greater than that of many kingdoms. But, from the fourteenth to fifteenth centuries, secularization of religion and the decay of the Church set in. By the sixteenth century, the Catholic Reformation shattered the universal medieval Roman church into a large number of local territorial churches, which secular rulers controlled. Regardless of whether the church remained Catholic in doctrine or adhered to one of the Protestant faiths, the secular authority controlled ecclesiastical appointments and church finances. Consequently, the immediate and decisive legacy of the Reformation was the transfer of power from church to state. The second half of the sixteenth century gave birth to the Scientific Revolution, clearly one of the most important developments in the Western intellectual tradition.

All of these advancements exacted an eventual sacrifice, however. According to Strayer (1991), the sixteenth century was not an easy period for the people of Western Europe. War, rebellion, and religious persecution occasionally seemed to be destroying the structure of society. Unlike the fourteenth century, a period of reconstruction followed every outbreak of violence. By the end of the century, men were working together more effectively than they had for generations. There was greater political security and wider economic opportunity. On these solid foundations, a new and larger structure of European civilization could be built. But, for the most part, the new structure had to be built out of old materials. The modern state, which furnished the central framework for the new civilization, was actually a patchwork of medieval institutions and medieval concepts of law and legitimacy, which religion buttressed. The new economic system, beginning to develop in the direction of capitalism, owed much to Italian bankers and merchants and even more to "the unknown men who had first instituted wind and water power for human muscle," so they had begun to make Europe a land of machinery instead of serfs. The new learning, in its most spectacular achievements, solved problems of medieval science rather than problems of classical textual criticism.

From materials adapted from Needham and quoted in chapter nine, we now know that the unknown men who first instituted wind and waterpower were actually the Chinese with their edge-runner mills.

The Renaissance

"Renaissance" derives from French and translates as "rebirth." Modern historians now recognize that this period was not a sharp break. Rather, it was an age of transition from medieval to modern civilization, taking place roughly from 1350–1600. The Renaissance got under way first in Italy and hence reflected the conditions and values of contemporary Italian society, a bustling urban society based on flourishing industries and the profitable commerce between Western Europe and the wealthy Byzantine and Islamic Empires. The great merchant families who controlled politics as well as trade and crafts dominated prosperous cities such as Venice, Genoa, Florence, Milan, and Pisa. These families patronized Renaissance artists and writers, whose thinking had, in turn, been strongly influenced by the rediscovery of ancient classics from Greece.

At the center of most Renaissance art and literature was the human being, the new Renaissance being, who was empowered to shape his own destiny rather than submit to being the plaything of supernatural forces. The belief emerged that a person need not be preoccupied with forebodings of supernatural forces. Rather, the purpose of life was to develop one's innate potential. This approach to life was very similar to pre-Yuan dynasty Chinese thought. Again, like the ancient Chinese, the humanism, secularism, and individualism of the Renaissance was reflected in its scholarship and education, which stressed the value of the classics as a means for self-improvement and a guide to social action. It emphasized that the cultivation of a student had a goal of living well and happily and functioning as responsible citizens. Another similarity between the Renaissance and ancient Chinese culture was found in the aesthetic and philosophical rather than scientific, leading figures who emphasized human beings and what they could accomplish.

Nor were these aspects of the Renaissance confined exclusively to Italy. Its innovations spread to Northern Europe in the sixteenth century. Stavrianos wrote:

Two factors that were responsible for the spread[:] … the Italian diplomats and generals who were employed by northern monarchs and the printing press which speeded up the circulation of books and ideas. Printing was particularly influential in Northern Europe because literacy was more widespread there than in the southern and eastern regions of Europe. The flood of printed matter fomented popular agitation concerning political and religious issues and so contributed substantially to the Reformation and ensuing religious and dynastic wars. (1983)

These emphases and unique conditions, in combination with the dynamism and revolutionary spirit of the Europeans, subsequently culminated in what would later come to be known as the Age of Discovery.

The rediscovery of ancient Greek learning, the printing press, and all the other forces that came together to create the Renaissance also impacted the Church. At the end of the fifteenth and beginning of the sixteenth centuries, Christian humanists sought to apply the new style of scholarship to the study of scriptures in their original languages and return to the first principles of their religion. The Renaissance belief in the perfectibility of man made people less content with things as they were. They were more interested in improving them, here and now. It is widely known that, at that time, the Church was corrupt. It held vast wealth, exercised enormous political power, waged war, and operated under the administration of corrupt clergy. The Christian humanists criticized these all-too-human failings while striving for a purer church. This precipitated a movement called the Reformation, which subsequently led to religious wars that spread across Europe.

The Reformation

The Reformation started in 1517 when the Augustinian monk, Martin Luther, challenged the validity of the sale of indulgences by the papacy in Rome. Luther articulated this and other ideas in ninety-five theses he posted on a church door in Wittenberg, Germany. His views spread like wildfire throughout Germany. Subsequently, controversy developed regarding numerous differences in doctrinal formulation between Catholics, Lutherans, and other Protestant denominations. At the center of this theological rift was the question of the source of religious authority. Luther argued that the Bible was the source of authority and denied the clergy had any necessary mediating role between the individual sinner and God. Based on his own personal experience of receiving the freely given grace of God, he boldly proclaimed the priesthood of all believers. Infused with his radical theology, the Protestant movement grew throughout Europe. It was significantly bolstered after John Calvin established headquarters in Geneva, making it the center of a vigorous propaganda campaign in 1541. Local nationalisms, which were beginning to emerge all over Europe, also played an important role in the spread of this movement. Technology as well had a role. The printing press spread Luther's views rapidly and widely through countries in central Europe, Scandinavia, and Great Britain.

The medieval Church was forced to respond to the challenge of Luther and Calvin and met them with the Catholic Reformation. With education, preaching, and emotional appeals, the Jesuits combated what they branded Protestant heresy. The Inquisition expanded its activities, and heretical books were confiscated and burned.

In the end, the Reformation smashed the medieval synthesis and destroyed the unity of the Christian matrix. The Church was shattered, witchcraft flourished, and Protestantism itself fragmented into numerous sects. Meanwhile, the power of monarchs increased and, according to Max Weber, the Reformation justified the spirit of capitalism. The intellectual developments of the sixteenth and seventeenth centuries produced an atmosphere that implied that human reason was capable of understanding the world and our place in it. These ideas were the precursor to the later Age of Enlightenment that eventually followed in the eighteenth century.

The period between 1543 and 1600, the time of the Renaissance and Reformation, has also been termed the Scientific Revolution. These years witnessed nothing less than an epistemological revolution in the way that individuals perceived the world and in which the era changed the human thought process. This was an intellectual revolution, specifically a revolution in human knowledge. Thinkers such as the Polish astronomer Nicolaus Copernicus (1473–1543), the French philosopher René Descartes (1596–1650), and the British physicist Sir Isaac Newton (1642–1727) overturned the authority of the Middle Ages and the classical world and escaped the fetters of their intellectual heritage. Even more than Renaissance scholars who discovered humanity and nature, the scientific revolutionaries attempted to understand and explain humans and the natural world.

The Ottoman Empire

The fifteenth and sixteenth centuries also saw the establishment of a series of great Islamic empires. The Ottoman Empire, a Turkish state with capitals first at Bursa, then Edirne, and finally in a captured Constantinople (modern Istanbul) began as a frontier warrior state and evolved into a powerful empire that lasted for six hundred years until 1923. By the middle of the sixteenth century, the empire covered

Anatolia, Egypt, the Levant, and much of southeast Europe, including Hungary. Its military success was due partly to the widespread use of firearms, especially huge siege cannons capable of destroying the protective walls of fortresses and cities. The Ottoman Turks had an unusually high tolerance for alien cultures and religions, especially when compared to the Christian West. This can be seen in their absorption of some of the Greek and Balkan cultures in the process of creating the Ottoman culture.

Arab and Indian merchants also carried Islam to Southeast Asia. Here, as in Africa and other regions, conversion was relatively easy because of the simplicity and adaptability of the new faith. Local practices and traditions were generally accepted and endorsed as holy through the simple addition of Islamic ritual. By the end of the fifteenth century, Islam had spread as far as Mindanao in the Philippines with its centers in areas of active trade contacts, such as on the Malayan peninsula and Indonesian archipelago. The continued expansion of the Muslim faith served to make Islam a world force by 1500 rather than simply a Middle Eastern power. This development has profoundly impacted the course of world affairs to the present day.

Given the formidability of the Ottoman Empire, the fall of Constantinople in 1453 shocked Europe. Because the Arabs and Islamic empires dominated both the land and sea routes to Asia, the Western Europeans were eager to break such trade monopolies by exploring new and direct routes to India in the hope of profiting from more than 250 varieties of spices native to the East.

The Age of Discovery

Few eras have gotten off to such a dramatic start or so fully captured people's imagination as the Age of Exploration and Discovery in Europe. To this day, we marvel at the voyages of Christopher Columbus, Vasco da Gama, and Ferdinand Magellan. The Renaissance spirit of the time motivated these and many other explorers. It was a willingness as well as a curiosity to experience and observe the world. There was the potential economic benefits from trade with India and Cathay beyond it. There was the simple desire for gold and silver and the political ambition of further colonization and conquest harking back to the ancient Greeks and Romans. Additionally, there was the religious fervor for saving souls and searching for a mythical Christian kingdom.

The Age of Exploration began in the mid- to late fifteenth century when the first Portuguese left the coastal waters of the Old World. The Spanish followed them. Finally, in the late fifteenth and early sixteenth centuries, the British, French, and Dutch set sail. The Portuguese sailor Vasco da Gama (1460–1524) made the first successful journey to India via the Cape of Good Hope in the 1490s, approximately eighty years after Admiral Zhenghe's voyage from China to East Africa. Portugal then built an empire based on its sea power and set up trading depots from West Africa to China with attendant military outposts to protect its investments. By the sixteenth century, Portuguese wealth had greatly increased, and Portugal became the primary importer of luxuries and spices from the East. The political and economic revival, a hallmark of Europe at the time, sustained this expansion. The Portuguese later realized even greater gains from their discovery of Brazil in 1500. Their widespread trading activity, together with a dominant presence in Africa, constituted the first wave of the age of exploration.

The Spanish rode the second wave of exploration. Unlike the Portuguese, who were motivated by trade, the Spanish founded their empire on conquest and colonization. The most renowned Spaniard was Christopher Columbus (1451–1506), who first set sail in 1492 with a tiny flotilla of three ships led by the *Santa Maria* and then subsequently sailed again in 1493, 1498, and in 1502. During his second voyage, on November 3, 1493, he sighted Dominica in the West Indies and then discovered the Virgin Islands and Puerto Rico, discoveries that represent the beginning of the European colonization and conquest of the Americas.

Europeans were usually warmly received in the New World. Witnessing the incredible wealth of their American hosts, the Europeans spent the next four hundred years taking it. Entire cultures vanished, and hundreds of millions of Native Americans were enslaved. Literate and stable societies were colonized and rendered illiterate, bereft of any basis for development. Thousands of tons of gold were shipped to Europe, providing the continent with the resources, surplus wealth, land, and manpower to undertake the most rapid development in history. Greed and a love of gold powered the Europeans. Exploration quickly turned into exploitation. For nearly four hundred years, the slave trade powered much of the European and then the North American economies. Although, at the time approximately fifteen million slaves reportedly entered America, conservative estimates today suggest that Africa alone lost fifty million of its strongest young men to the European and American slave trade. An obscenely profitable triangular trade system brought slaves from Africa to America and minerals and natural wealth from America to Europe. This triangle fueled Europe's Industrial Revolution.

Shortly after its discovery, Pope Alexander gave Central America to Spain. The ensuing destruction of Mexico from 1519 to 1521, led by Cortez and his handful of mercenaries, is a fascinating story of greed and power, which we refrain from telling only because of our limited space here. Under the Spaniard Francisco Pizarro, Europe then moved into South America, where a hundred years of looting satisfied European lust for gold before mining for the gold even became necessary. A century of war and introduced diseases cut Mexico's population by 50 percent. As local populations shrank, Africans were imported to supplement the labor force. By 1800, about half of the populations of Venezuela and Brazil were Africans imported by European businessmen.

Gold was not the only thing that drew Europe to South America. According to Stavrianos, the expansionism of European Christianity can partially explain the outward expansion of Europe:

> From the beginning, Christianity, by its emphasis on the brotherhood of man, asserted itself as a universal religion, and missionary activity has characterized the Christian church from the days of the apostles to the present. Furthermore, there has been no hesitancy to employ force in securing conversion ... The militancy of Christendom was also a reaction to repeated invasion from the East in earlier periods ... Thus Europe had a long-established crusading tradition, and the expansion overseas represented, in one sense, a continuation of this tradition. The early explorers and their backers were motivated partly by religious considerations. (1966)

Thus, it was not just gold, but God, that may have been the most compelling of the many motives that led Europeans to begin their overseas enterprises. As a result of this expansion, Europe's economy became more geared to international trade as both the consumers and producers in Europe became accustomed to and dependent upon foreign commodities and foreign markets. As populations increased, the scale of operations similarly expanded. This demographic pressure, together with the spur of competition between nations and city-states, drove merchants even further into the field in their quest for new sources, routes, and markets. Their competitive attitude was very different from that of their contemporaries in China, who had voyaged several thousand miles to eastern Africa for noneconomic reasons.

The Growth of Capitalism

In addition to expansion overseas, domestic European institutions were changing drastically as well, leading to an economy that historian Ray Huang called "mathematically manageable" (1988). Huang stated that capitalism is an example of mathematical manageability, a model that predicts the efficacy of an economic system. Socialism such as that found in certain northern European countries could also be mathematically manageable, as determined by the following definition. What makes capitalism (or socialism) work is a system of monetary management distinguished by three conditions: wide extension of credit, impersonal management, and mutual sharing of service facilities. Huang further qualified that in capitalism:

> ... the monetary management must extend to embrace the entire national economy including the agrarian sector no less than industry and commerce. A competent judiciary system is necessary to back it up, so that the interchangeability of value can be clarified and enforced and the accumulated wealth can be piled steadily higher. Implementing those conditions, a capitalist country permits private enterprise to play a dominant role; private capital therefore exercises a disproportionately wider influence over public life. With this price paid, the public frees itself from unnecessary government regulation and gives free rein to economic forces so that competition can achieve the greatest efficiency. (1988)

Renaissance Italy could be said to be the birthplace of capitalism, and Venice was its pacesetter. During the Italian Renaissance, Venice was not constrained by struggles with ecclesiastic courts, a divine monarchy, the interests of monasteries, seigniorial rights, trade guilds, labor unions, or the complexities of common law. The entire state functioned like a large trading company. In fact, it got to the point where commercial laws became civil laws. With this economic advantage, the city-state saw its prestige and influence reach its high point in the fourteenth and early fifteenth centuries. Venice consequently became a major contributor to European history.

When the Northern Renaissance later overtook the Italian Renaissance, the Dutch republic became the next banner-bearer of capitalism. Amsterdam, which the Reformation and Calvinism influenced, had been encouraged to develop its carrying trade to counterbalance the influence of the other Hanseatic cities. For a century and more, Amsterdam remained the foremost center in the Western world for the carrying trade, maritime insurance, commodity exchange, and money markets. Adam Smith devoted a whole section of *The Wealth of Nations* to a discussion of the operation of the Bank of Amsterdam, which was indeed a capitalist instrument par excellence.

Huang contended that, in the seventeenth century, the Dutch republic was both a major rival of, and inspiration to, Great Britain. In the early part of the century, Great Britain had not been mathematically manageable. However, this situation improved enormously toward the end of the century. By 1689, the restructuring of the English nation had been accomplished overall. In 1689, John Holt became chief justice of the King's Bench. Holt directed the common law courts to treat litigations involving merchants in accordance with mercantile practice. This directive had a profound influence on the life of the citizenry, especially in the areas of inheritance, mortgages, legal disposition of chattels, and damage settlements for nonfulfillment of contracts. Under this reorganization, parliamentary supremacy became the rule. Property rights were confirmed as the logic of a new mode of governance. In 1694, the Bank of England was born. It was a permanent institution with a role of lending money to the state to cover the national debt, thereby relieving the king of personal responsibility for this debt. Undoubtedly, state affairs were now being handled according to commercial principles.

At the opening of the eighteenth century, Great Britain had in place the three conditions by which Huang characterized the monetary management of capitalism: the extension of credit, impersonal management, and pooling of service facilities. Having achieved mathematical manageability, Britain began to overtake the Dutch republic as the center of international finance. It seemed that what the Dutch could do, the English could do better. Huang wrote:

> The secret was that once the infrastructure of the national economy was set up and its interlinks with the superstructure were realized through the merger of the common law with equity, the agrarian wealth and mercantile interests found a channel of interflow ... Looking back, the British could always see 1689 as a major milestone in their history. Other acts were modified and reversed, but the effect of the Glorious Revolution was permanent. (1999)

Regarding early capitalism, Huang further pointed out that "capitalism only triumphs when it becomes identified with the state when it is the state." This lesson needs to be learned by all latecomers to capitalism.

According to Joseph Needham (Huang 1999), the Renaissance and Reformation, the development of capitalism, and breakthroughs in modern science and technology in the Western Europe of the sixteenth to eighteenth centuries came as a package, mutually influencing with one thing leading to another. Great Britain had now achieved stability, and several other Western nations were in good order. Europe was again posed for further expansion.

Section Two:
The Mongolian Empire and Yuan Dynasty

During the thirteenth century, an impressive leader, Temujin 鐵木真, was to emerge from among the nomadic tribes that occupied the Mongolian steppes between the northern Daxing'an Mountains and the eastern bank of the Argun River. The skilled horsemen of this area became a formidable fighting force once united under Temujin's leadership. In 1206, Temujin was formally elected as ruler over Greater Mongolia, which encompassed the Mongolian Plateau and the Gobi Desert. He adopted the name and title of Genghis Khan, or universal ruler.

Genghis Khan 成吉思汗

Genghis Khan reorganized the Mongolian tribal structure into a military organization. He divided the entire population into military units of tens, hundreds, and thousands with accompanying households and cattle to supply provisions for them. He introduced strong discipline, law, and order; promoted education and knowledge; and encouraged economic prosperity for his citizens. Genghis Khan also introduced liberal reforms. After devoting five years (1204–1209) to the internal organization of the newly unified state, he began his expansive military campaigns against neighboring groups and then more distant empires. At the time of his death in 1227, Genghis Khan had conquered the territory from China to the Caspian Sea. His son, Ogodei, succeeded him in 1229, and he and other descendants extended the empire until it stretched from the Black Sea to the Korean Peninsula, the Russian princedoms to the Bulgar principalities, Central Asian territories, and all of East Asia. Genghis Khan's grandson, Kubilai Khan 忽必烈, established the Yuan Dynasty in China, moving the Mongolian capital from Harborin (Karakorum) in Mongolia to Dadu 大都, later called Beijing. From there, he ruled over Mongolia and China. Batu Khan, another warlord and grandson of Genghis Khan, led the Golden Horde in the conquest of Hungary, Bulgaria, and western and Central Asia during the thirteenth to fifteenth centuries. The Ilkhanates of the Middle East, which Ogodei originally ruled, established rule over the highly civilized nations of Iran, Iraq, Mesopotamia, India, and Persia. The resulting Mongolian empire was the largest our world has ever seen. The Mongol conquest of China occurred in a series of stages. Stephen Haw wrote:

The conquest of southern China was possible because the Mongols adapted to different methods of warfare. The extraordinary prowess of Mongolian cavalry had gained them enormous successes on the steppes and plains of Asia and eastern Europe, but was of much more limited usefulness in the wet and mountainous southern China. Cavalry charges could not be mounted across rivers, marshes and paddy-fields. Only after the Mongols had absorbed Chinese naval techniques, employing many Chinese sailors to handle vessels they had captured or which had voluntarily submitted, were their armies successful in the south. They had also taken over the use of gunpowder from the Chinese, which was of great assistance not only within China but also in the Mongol campaigns in western Asia. It was to a large extent due to Chinese influences on the Mongols that they were able to conquer and hold their huge empire. (2002)

This indeed was the painful irony of the time. China paid a staggering price for her resistance to the Mongol conquest. As Nolan (2004) pointed out, the country, as a whole, lost perhaps one-third or more of its population, estimated around thirty-five million, by the time the war was over. Not only were large numbers of people put to the sword, but crops and grain stores were systematically destroyed with the result of vast additional numbers starving to death.

The Yuan Dynasty 元

Genghis Khan's grandson, Kubilai Khan 忽 必 烈, established the Yuan dynasty in 1264. It lasted a little more than one hundred years until 1368. Although the entire period of the Yuan dynasty was actually a military occupation of China rather than an actual civil government, able rulers like Kubilai Khan understood that China would only be governable through the use of preexisting structures. Thus, the emperor retained many superficial features of Song government, for example, the secretariat, the six ministries, and the traditional division between the civil, military, and censorial branches of government. Kubilai adopted Chinese ceremonial and Confucian rites and even set up an office to collect materials for a history of the preceding dynasties. However, he declined to restore the government office examination system on the grounds that it might restrict his choice of officials to those who had knowledge of the Confucian classics. The Mongols installed translation offices. Although they relied on Chinese staff for administrative purposes, their deep distrust of their new subjects led to the decision that only

Mongols could be appointed to high office and tax administration could only be laid in the hands of Muslims, who were allies of the Mongols.

Mongol rule, despite its many unifying traits, exacerbated a deep discrimination among different ethnic groups of the empire. The population was classified in occupational classes based on a combination of ethnic and political considerations. The highest class was the Mongols. Next was their allies and non-Chinese people from Inner Asia (called Semuren 色目人). The third class was the inhabitants of northern China (the Han people), including the Qidans. The lowest class was the southern Chinese (called Manzi 蠻子, or barbarians). This discrimination formed the basis for taxation and penal law. Mixed marriages were forbidden. Promotion outside one's class was impossible. Because Chinese intellectuals were prohibited from climbing to higher positions within the ladder of bureaucracy, they withdrew to more personal pursuits and engaged in arts and literature. Novels, vernacular literature, and the popular theatre gained acceptance among the highly educated.

The period of Mongol rule was also one of damage to the economy and a decline in Chinese living standards. According to taxation figures, the combined population of Song and Jin China amounted to well more than one hundred million. However, according to a census carried out in 1290, which admittedly excluded Yunnan and other areas and did not enumerate several categories of people, the population had dwindled to less than sixty million. This population decline has been attributed to the Mongol invasion of the north, the confiscation of land for distribution to the invaders, and the application of heavy taxation to those Chinese who retained the land. This precipitated a wave of southward migration. In addition, the Mongols were responsible for the spread of diseases across Eurasia, such as the bubonic plague, resulting in the deaths of an estimated twelve million Chinese.

The Yuan dynasty also stands accused of both sins of omission and commission in its subsequent management of the economy. The consequence of its failure to maintain river defenses finally became evident with the massive flooding of the Yellow River in 1344. Yet Roberts (1999) maintained that the Mongol handling of economic affairs was not entirely one-sided. Kubilai put economic measures in place to alleviate the grave situation. His administration encouraged agriculture and commerce. The Grand Canal, inoperative since the Northern Song, was rebuilt and extended anew to Beijing. Cotton production increased beyond the level of its Song beginnings. Sorghum was introduced and quickly became an important supplemental food crop in northern China. Much of the resulting prosperity was superficial as the economy suffered from corrupt, inept government, and, especially, runaway inflation brought on by monetary manipulations.

Landlordism was more rampant than ever, and more Chinese were reduced to outright slave status than at any other time in history (Hucker 1975). However, after the prosperity of the Song dynasty, China never regained such a high level of economic prosperity. Still, China was the richest part of the domains of the Grand Khan, supplying the Mongolian court with all or most of the major commodities it required, especially grain, silks, and porcelain. Because of China's rich resources, the Mongols were able to live in a luxurious style that their old steppe homeland could never have afforded them.

The Mongol emperors, beginning with Kubilai, sought to preserve their Mongol cultural inheritance. One example was the Mongol religion, a form of shamanism. Nevertheless, no attempt was made to impose Mongol religious beliefs on the Chinese, and the Yuan period was notable for its religious freedom. The Mongols' reliance on divination in deciding upon a course of action led to the use of Daoist adepts. The Daoist leader, Qiu Chu Ji 丘處機, had attended a famous meeting with Genghis Khan in 1219 and gained privileges for his followers that were not made available to Buddhists. Yet a series of public debates between the Buddhists and the Daoists was encouraged between 1255–1258. Following these debates, Kubilai decided in favor of the Buddhists and ruled that Daoist excesses should be curbed. The Tibetan lama, Phags-pa, played a leading role in these debates. Because his form of Buddhism with its colorful pageantry and emphasis on magic had more appeal to the Mongols, he was appointed state preceptor in 1260. Tibetan Buddhism subsequently took a firm hold in China. The Buddhists eventually made the Mongol emperors legitimate.

The Mongol attitude toward Confucianism was more circumspect. Kubilai's ignorance of written Chinese debarred him from a proper understanding of the Confucian texts. Not until Ayurbarwada 仁宗 later came to the throne did a Mongol emperor have a working knowledge of written Chinese. Nevertheless, Kubilai recognized the importance of Confucianism, employing some Confucian officials and promoting the translation of the Confucian classics into the Mongol language. In the Yuan period, therefore, Confucian scholars were placed in a dilemma. Some reasoned that their Confucian duty required them to serve the Mongols in the hope of civilizing them; others refused to condone the Mongol presence and would not compromise and accept office. The protest efforts of this group have been identified in Yuan literature. In 1313, the civil service examination was reintroduced. Although the inheritance of office continued in parallel with the examinations and preferential treatment was still accorded to Mongols and other foreigners, the resumption of the exams marked the end of Mongol resistance to the sinicization process. Mongol emperors now became proficient in traditional Chinese arts and literature. Unfortunately, this did not make them any more acceptable to their Chinese subjects. As the dynasty began to decline in power, revolts became increasingly common.

The conquered populations endured many hardships under their Mongolian conquerors, such as burned and destroyed cities, heavy taxation, forced labor, and the necessity of paying tribute. But the Mongolian empire brought about positive effects as well. The Yuan dynasty fostered the arts. Drama became a firmly established art form during the Yuan dynasty. Some 700 plays, which included singing and dancing, were written under the Yuan. About 150 of these have survived and form what has come to be known as the "Yuan northern drama" 元 北 劇 because many were written for performance in Beijing. The modern Beijing opera descends from these plays, and many of the scripts have been translated into Western languages, such is their popularity. On the whole, the Yuan period saw a proliferation of literary activity in both drama and fiction. A common element was that both were written in the vernacular, which gave them access to a wider audience and readership. The popularity of theater in the Yuan period also owed a great deal to Mongol patronage because the Mongols could understand the colloquial dialogue. This is significant because, in later years and actually continuing to the present day, Confucian values and morality have been propagated and disseminated among the general populace of China through the rich tradition of folk drama and plays. This is especially true among the illiterate peasants of the countryside. Chinese people love these folk stories and dramas, which remain well preserved and popular today.

Another positive effect was that the great expanse of the empire allowed trade and travel to flourish between different countries, encouraging continued trade along the famous Silk Road and forming additional trade routes throughout the vast Eurasian continent. The Mongolian empire brought together Western and Eastern cultures, allowing them to intertwine. The capital at Harhorin, built during Ogedei's rule around 1235, had a metropolitan culture and served as a center of trade of the multicultural exchange of arts and sciences and religious haven.

Stephen Haw summarized the effect of the Mongolian military occupation in China:

> The Mongol conquest was a turning point in Chinese history. There had been a more or less continuous development of Chinese civilization up to the Song dynasty, and there is no doubt that many of the achievements of the Chinese, particularly in science and technology, reached a high point under the Song. The Mongols caused a distinct shift of direction, destroying a great deal and bringing little to compensate. Chinese culture was by no means annihilated, but it became more introverted. The earlier Mongol emperors had withdrawn all imperial

patronage from Chinese cultural activities, leaving the Chinese literati to paint and write mainly for private enjoyment only. Non-traditional forms such as the novel and drama increased greatly in importance. The Mongols also left a legacy of a more strongly centralized and autocratic system of government, restrictive of individuality and innovation. As a result, Chinese culture lost much of its vitality and vigor. The shock to Chinese pride of being subjected to foreign rule also greatly increased Chinese suspicion of outside influences. (2002)

Despite the many advances of the Yuan period, this era of subjugation was actually the beginning of a downward spiral for Chinese civilization.

The Flow of Trade and Technology

Not only did the Mongolian empire quicken the flow of trade within Eurasia, it also accelerated the diffusion of technology. During the medieval period, the technology of China was far more advanced than that of Europe, so the Chinese were usually the exporters rather than the recipients in the Eurasian interchange. L. S. Stavrianos described the broadening of the European perspective at the time:

> The great breakthrough came with the Mongol Empire. Its existence brought about the transition from a Mediterranean to a Eurasian perspective, just as the voyages of Columbus and da Gama later brought about a transition from a Eurasian to a global perspective. The travels of merchants, missionaries, and prisoners of war revealed the existence of a great empire in the Far East that not only equaled but also surpassed Europe in population, wealth, and level of civilization. Nor was this a one-way process, for the East now became aware of the West, and vice versa. Marco Polo, who opened the eyes of the West to Cathay, had his counterparts in China and the Middle East. (1983)

Marco Polo is well known to many educated in the Western world as one of the first travelers to visit China. Not many realize he was in fact an official in the Mongolian court. His memoir, *The Description of the World*, made a definite impact on the world's perceptions of China.

During the first fourteen centuries of the Christian era, China was the great center of technological innovation and transmitted a multitude of inventions to the rest of Eurasia (Stavrianos 1983). These included such important breakthroughs as gunpowder, the magnet, printing, paper, the sternpost rudder, the foot stirrup, and the breast strap harness. In particular, this harness tripled the weight a horse could pull. Without which, the northern European heavy plough would not been possible. Without which, we would not have witnessed the crucial transformation of old Roman farming practices. The British philosopher-scientist Francis Bacon (1561–1626) provided a revealing perspective:

> We should note the force, effect, and consequences of inventions which are nowhere more conspicuous than in those three which were unknown to the ancients, namely, printing, gunpowder, and the compass. For these three have changed the appearance and state of the whole world. (Stavrianos 1983)

Indeed, these three inventions alone were essential for the subsequent advancement in the Western world. Printing advanced the education that became key to the Renaissance. The use of gunpowder led to European military superiority and imperialism. The use of the compass and the sternpost rudder made the dawn of the Age of Exploration possible, leading to European dominance at sea and the discovery of the New World. As Joseph Needham noted in his publication, *Science in Traditional China*, the number of technologies transferred from China to the West vastly outnumber those from the West to the East.

In addition, the Chinese also domesticated numerous fruits and plants that later spread throughout Eurasia. These included the chrysanthemum, camellia, azalea, tea rose, Chinese aster, lemon, and orange.

CHAPTER TWELVE

Rebirth and Decay

The rebirth of Europe quickened as advanced ideas and knowledge were absorbed, digested, applied, and reinvented. The scientific revolution, Reformation, and Enlightenment have changed traditional cultural, philosophical, and religious outlook of Europeans toward more practical and utilitarian. In the meantime, Chinese decay continued through the introvert Ming dynasty when China was closed to new ideas and the establishment of another nomad dynasty, the Qing, worsened the situation. These are the topics of this chapter's investigation.

Section One:
The Age of Enlightenment, Revolutions, and Modern Europe

As the nomadic Manchu tribes were overrunning China proper and establishing the Qing dynasty, far to the west, the Europeans were finally putting their house in order and were ready to expand culturally, economically and politically.

The Enlightenment

Culturally, the European period between 1680 and 1789 is termed the Enlightenment, a time with its origins in the scientific and intellectual revolutions of the seventeenth century as well as the fertile economic and political environment of the era. Enlightenment thinkers felt that both change and reason were not only possible, but eminently desirable for the sake of human liberty. Enlightenment philosophers, notably Descartes, Pascal, Bayle, Montesquieu, Voltaire, Leibniz, Diderot, and Rousseau, originated concepts that undermined existing social and political structures, providing impetus to further changes. Some of these thinkers, including Voltaire, Leibniz, and Rousseau, admired Chinese culture and sought to apply reason and common sense to nearly all the major institutions and mores of the day. China, as described in the writings of the Jesuits, provided the philosophers with an interesting reference model and inspiration in secular ethics and meritocratic bureaucracy.

The Enlightenment introduced natural rights into practical politics, catalyzing the explosive energy witnessed in the French Revolution. Thinkers of the period attacked Christianity for its rejection of science, focus on otherworldliness, and belief in humanity's depravity. The major themes of the era were a rationalism based on facts; cosmology based on Newtonian physics; secularism characterized by the application of scientific theories to religion and society; the adoption of a scientific method based on observation and experimentation; utilitarianism founded on laws created for the common good rather than special interests; freedom from prejudice; constitutionalism with legal and penal reforms; and cosmopolitanism. The Enlightenment was an era of optimism and self-confidence, a reversal of medieval thinking, whereby people believed anything was possible. Tolerance flourished, and there was a greater acceptance of different societies and cultures. Although the primary impetus for this movement was essentially middle class and centered in France, the Enlightenment labored for all humanity.

In economics, the key Enlightenment concept was that of *laissez-faire*, the French equivalent of wuwei. In other words, let the people do what they will, and let nature take its course. This concept's opposition to governmental intervention was a reaction to mercantilism, the rigid regulation of economic life. In the seventeenth century, mercantilism had been accepted as a necessary condition for national security. By the early eighteenth century, it seemed not only superfluous, but damaging as well. Adam Smith argued for the *laissez-faire* notion that individuals are motivated by self-interest so far as their economic activities are concerned, national welfare is simply the sum of the individual interests operating within a nation, and each person knows his or her own interest better than any statesman.

Industrial Revolution

Having achieved mathematical manageability, Great Britain and other European powers were at the threshold of commercial, scientific, and industrial revolutions. A change in internationally traded goods characterized the commercial revolution. Novel overseas products, such as new beverages (cocoa, tea, and coffee); the latest dyes (indigo, cochineal, and brazilwood); new flavors (allspice and vanilla); and unique new foodstuffs (guinea fowl and turkeys, Newfoundland cod) became

staples of consumption in Europe and experienced growth in commercial importance. As a result, the volume of overseas trade increased dramatically. The commercial revolution, in turn, contributed to the industrial revolution in several
important respects. It provided large and expanding markets for European industries. It met the demands of new markets by catalyzing improvement in the organization and technology of various industries. It contributed to the large capital
reserves needed for industrial developments. Profitable commercial enterprise,
together with the accompanying technological growth and institutional change,
set the stage for the Industrial Revolution to take off around 1800.

Due to its early lead in basic coal and iron industries and the availability of
fluid capital for the financing of the Industrial Revolution, Great Britain was the
first to achieve this takeoff. Noteworthy also is the impressive concentration of
managerial talent in Great Britain. Stavrianos noted, "Freedom from convention
and stress on personal responsibility produced a disproportionate quota of experiments and inventors among Nonconformists, while their frugality led them to
plow profits back into business rather than to squander them in luxurious living"
(1983).

In addition to these advantages, Great Britain also had the benefit of a mobile
and plentiful supply of labor, made available by the earlier disintegration of the
guilds and the enclosing of traditional tracts of farmland. Between 1714 and
1820, more than six million acres of British land were enclosed to facilitate more
efficient mechanized agriculture.

As the commercial revolution of the nineteenth century proceeded, science
also became an increasingly important part of Western society. At the beginning
of the century, science still existed on the periphery of economic and social life.
By the century's end, it was creating entirely new industries as well as contributing
to established older ones. James Watt invented and patented the steam engine in
Great Britain in 1769. New fuels, such as coal and petroleum, were later incorporated into the evolving designs of these steam engines. This engine revolutionized
many industries, including textiles and manufacturing. Indeed, the historical significance of the steam engine cannot be exaggerated because it ended the age-old
human dependence on animal, wind, and waterpower. By the end of the eighteenth century, the manufacturing of thread and cloth was slowly moving out of
the family cottage economy and into large factory mills, but this transition would
not be fully realized until the middle of the nineteenth century. By then, the
steam engine had become the major source of motive power in Great Britain and
Europe, causing an explosion of factory-based, technology-driven manufacturing.
Great Britain proudly proclaimed itself the "workshop of the world," a position

it retained until the end of the nineteenth century when Germany, Japan, and United States overtook it.

The Industrial Revolution heralded a revolution in communication and transportation as well. The expansion of textile, mining, and metallurgical industries created a need for improved transportation facilities. The result was a canal and road building boom in Great Britain. After 1830, the railroad challenged the efficacy of both roads and waterways. Just eight years later, in 1838, Britain had 500 miles of railroad. By 1870, there was 15,500 miles. By the middle of the nineteenth century, the electric telegraph had been invented. In 1866, a transatlantic cable was laid, establishing instant communication between the Old and New World. Each of these improvements in communication and transportation further increased trade, forcing competing industries in Europe and America to improve their organization and technology in a dynamic spiral of demand, invention, productivity, and capital accumulation.

In the late nineteenth and early twentieth centuries, the core of industrial development shifted to the automotive, electrical, communication, and petroleum industries. In the period before and during World War II, a qualitative change occurred in the relationship between the military, technology, and society at large, a change that ultimately favored the military. The military industrial complex made its first appearance in the late nineteenth century. At the time, military technology was evolving rapidly, climaxing in the production of the atomic bomb at the conclusion of World War II. Much of our modern technology has its roots in the military efforts of this era. In addition, cheap oil strengthened the boom in technology. This cheap oil literally fueled the industrialized economies of the First World at negligible cost. The net result was that, between 1955 and 1980, global output in dollars, the sum total of all countries' GNP, tripled in real terms, measured in constant dollars. During that same period, global GNP per capita doubled even though the world's population rose from 2.8 to 4.4 billion people (Stravrianos 1997).

Multinational corporations spearheaded this global economic expansion. Whereas Germany led the nineteenth-century world in applying science to industry, the United States pioneered mass production techniques through assembly-line manufacturing. The classic example of this is Henry Ford's endless conveyor belt. Futurist Alvin Toffler characterized this late stage of the Industrial Revolution in the twentieth century as massification, standardization, specialization, synchronization, concentration, maximization, and centralization (1980). All of which are necessary for industries to efficiently produce goods, particularly in assembly-line mass production ventures like textiles or the automotive industry.

Modernity

The Industrial Revolution forever altered the production capacity of Great Britain, Europe, and the United States. But the revolution was more than the sum of its new machines, factories, increased productivity, and improved standard of living. Like other revolutions, it also transformed society. A new working class and middle class emerged. New social relationships formed. Ben Franklin famously said that "time is money." Nowhere was this more true than in the society of the Industrial Revolution. People were no longer treated as individuals. They were commodities to be bought and sold on the open market. Charles Dickens's descriptions of eighteenth-century Britain are a testament to the involuntary human sacrifice of early industrial capitalism. With their new machines, proponents of the Industrial Revolution contended that humans now had, in addition to the opportunity and knowledge, the physical means to completely subdue nature. This vision was all-important, optimistic, and progressive. Humankind was going somewhere. Life had direction, and progress was paramount. The history of human society was idealized as a history of progress, forever forward and forever upward.

This attitude was implicit throughout the Enlightenment and made reality during the French and Industrial Revolutions. With relatively few exceptions, eighteenth-century philosophies embraced the idea of human progress with an intensity no longer matched in our own century. Human happiness, improved morality, and an increase in knowledge all seemed within reach. "Modernity" is the term that historians use to describe the resulting individualist and rationalist culture. Modernity accompanied the growth of science, the Industrial Revolution, the rise of capitalism and constitutional democracy, and, at the same time, the rise of socialism as an ideology and a political system. In day-to-day culture, modernity was an intellectual, not a material or political phenomenon. It formed the underlying constellation of beliefs, values, aspirations, and demands that led people in the West to profoundly alter their way of life.

Political expansion also accompanied the cultural and economic expansion of this era in the West. In government, the key Enlightenment phrase was the "social contract." John Locke first formulated the contract theory of government in 1690, but Rousseau subsequently transformed this theory from a political contract into a social one, which involved an agreement among the people themselves. Rousseau viewed government as simply a "commission," and he justified revolution as a restoration to the sovereign people of its rightful power (Stavrianos 1983). The immediate success of the Enlightenment was persuading a number of European monarchs to accept at least some of their doctrines. Some of these monarchs, while they still held to the belief that they ruled by divine right, were now ready to accept that governmental authority should benefit the people. From this notion arose the term "benevolent despot." Nevertheless, Stavrianos cautioned against overrating the role of benevolent despots in putting the doctrines of the Enlightenment to work because there was little practical impact of the era upon the masses of Europe prior to the outbreak of the French Revolution in 1789.

The eighteenth century saw the maturation of the modern state. For some eighty years, between the Treaties of Utrecht and Napoleon, no single state threatened domination of Europe. A balance of power, rather than a hegemony, existed. Yet, there were three major zones of conflict during the eighteenth century: Central Europe, Eastern Europe, and the colonies. Central Europe experienced dynastic rivalries, particularly between the Hapsburgs and Hohenzollerns. Under Maria Theresa, Austria created an alliance with France and Russia against Prussia. In Eastern Europe, Russia grew at the expense of Poland and Turkey with Poland eventually disappearing as Russia and Prussia became stronger. Frederick the Great of Prussia built a large army and invaded foreign territories in a quest for expansion. The Peace of Hubertusberg in 1763 finally settled the European continental phase of the Seven Years' War (1756–1763). The rise of Paris and Vienna as cultural centers boasted the national powers of France and Austria. From the perspective of expansionism from 1689 to 1763, France and Great Britain had been the two greatest colonizing nations, battling for empires in North America and India. However, the balance of power in colonization had slowly shifted away from France and Spain to England. With their victory over the French in the Seven Years' War, also known as the French and Indian War in America, Great Britain acquired Canada and all of France's possessions east of the Mississippi. France also ceded New Orleans and the Louisiana Territory to Spain. The removal of the French threat in Canada was a major impetus in the American colonies' break with Great Britain. The Seven Years' War was also fought between France and Great Britain in India, where the French were also decisively defeated at the Battle of Plassey in 1757. With the Treaty of Paris in 1763, Great Britain became the greatest commercial and colonial power in the world.

The American and French Revolution

The British victory created new problems for Great Britain at the same time it settled old ones. A significant new problem was the growing spirit of defiance in America now that the danger of a French attack had been removed. Another was the decision of the British government, following its acquisition of vast new colonial territories, to tighten its imperial organization. The American Revolution arose in large part due to the conflicting claims of British imperial authority and

American colonial self-government. The resulting sequence of dramatic events is familiar—the East India Company's tea monopoly, the Boston Tea Party, the Intolerable Acts intended as punishment for the vandalism in Boston harbor, and the Quebec Act of 1774—contributed to eventual revolution.

The First Continental Congress met in Philadelphia in September 1774 and organized a boycott against British goods. Fighting began the next year. When the Second Continental Congress met in May 1775, it had a full-fledged war on its hands and proceeded to raise an American army. On July 4, 1776, Congress adopted the Declaration of Independence, signaling the birth of the American Republic. Stavrianos wrote:

> From the viewpoint of world history the American Revolution is signif-
> icant not because it created an independent state but because it created
> a new and different type of state. The Declaration of Independence
> proclaimed, "we hold these truths to be self-evident: that all men are
> created equal." Now the American people, both during and after the
> Revolution, passed laws to make this declaration true in real life as well
> as on paper. They seized and distributed the large estates owned by the
> Tories. They extended the franchise until all men (but not women) had
> the right to vote. Many state governments passed laws forbidding the
> importation of slaves. Established churches were abolished, and free-
> dom of religion became the law of the land. All Thirteen States adopted
> constitutions which included Bills of Rights that guaranteed the natural
> rights of citizens. (1983)

The establishment of this independent republic in the New World was widely interpreted in Europe as a sign that the ideas of the Enlightenment were practicable. It was possible for people to establish a state and a workable system of government based on the rights of the individual. Thus, America became a symbol of freedom and opportunity, envied as a new land that was free from the burdens and chains of the past.

The French Revolution from 1789 to 1799 witnessed the overthrow of the absolute monarchy by democrats and republicans and the consequent radical restructuring of the Roman Catholic Church. While France would oscillate between republic, empire, and monarchy for seventy-five years after the fall of the First Republic in a coup by Napoleon Bonaparte, the revolution spelled a definitive end to the *ancien régime*. In the popular imagination of France, it eclipses all subsequent revolutions to this day. The French Revolution is clearly one of the central events in Western civilization, even more so than the English or American revolutions. The more moderate American Revolution, in comparison, was much less influential upon the world of its time, even if it was eventually more successful and less bloody. The French Revolution met less enduring success. Since 1793, France has had no less than eleven subsequent constitutions while the United States still uses their first. The chaos and violence of the French Revolution and Napoleon's ascendancy continued to plague Europe until the last fifty years. For example, during the Reign of Terror from 1793 to 1794, some eleven thousand individuals died as enemies of the state by a horrendous new development of modern Western civilization, institutionalized violence, or the lethal elimination by the state of its political opposition. Later, Stalinist Russia and Nazi Germany would overshadow the despotic figures of the French Revolution. Nevertheless, not only did the French Revolution mark the triumph of the bourgeoisie, it contributed to the full awakening of the masses. Middle-class liberalism came to the forefront, but so did nationalism with its appeal to people in all segments of society. In addition, the French Revolution was a legal debate between the monarchy and the aristocracy over the financing of the state and the political authority that each claimed to enjoy and exercise.

The World War and Peace

Napoleon, who conquered much of Europe, was ultimately defeated in 1815. Some of the old European regimes were restored at that point, but others were not. Then, a great many events filled the pages of Europe's history over the following decades. The next chapter of European history was the revolutions of 1848, which responded to problems resulting from social changes in many European countries. The Spring of Nations involved France, the German states, the Habsburg Monarchy, and the Italian states. Then the dual monarchy of Austria-Hungary was formed in 1867. The disintegration of the Ottoman Empire continued with numerous internal rebellions as well as wars with liberated countries in the Balkans and four more Russo-Turkish Wars. The Great Powers—Great Britain, France, Austria, and Prussia—were also involved in the Crimean War (1854–1856) in which Great Britain and France aided the Ottomans against the Russians as well as in the Congress of Berlin that produced the Treaty of Berlin in 1878.

Mass migration took place from Europe to the United States. The period between 1861 and 1865 gave rise to the American Civil War and the end of the global slave trade. During the reign of Queen Victoria, Great Britain was the leading economic power in the world, giving the title of the Victorian Age to much of the century. Europeans conquered and colonized most of Africa and parts of Asia. The Meiji Restoration of 1868 opened Japan to modern influences and returned the emperor to power. The nineteenth century was indeed an age of European expansion and war, nationalism, imperialism, and colonialism.

A contributing cause for the climate of war during the nineteenth century was the intellectual current of the day, that is, social Darwinism, or the survival of the fittest. This was a concept that Darwin neither actually proposed nor endorsed. Social Darwinism viewed human culture, politics, economics, and ethics as biological organisms subject to the law of the survival of the fittest. Capitalism of the *laissez-faire* variety, could be justified as dog eat dog. Excessive nationalism could be justified because only the fittest nations would survive and military force was a means of proving one's right to do so. Friedrich Nietzsche maintained that certain ethnic groups were comprised of superior people and only they were fit to exist. His superman was above right and wrong, so he did not have to justify his behavior. English citizens viewed themselves as the most evolved humans, saddled with a white man's burden of civilizing the somehow deficient Africans, Chinese, and Indians. Germans began to preach the doctrine of Pan-Germanism while the Russians advocated Pan-Slavism. This way of thinking ultimately set the stage for the two world wars of the twentieth century, unleashing a bloodbath of war and destruction that dwarfed the conflicts of earlier periods and resulted in the violent deaths of approximately 160 million human beings. The early twentieth century also witnessed the Russian Revolutions of 1905 and 1917 and the rise of socialism and communism as ideologies, even though their actual practices were incongruent with the ideology, in Russia, Eastern Europe, and East Asia, resulting in ideological and international conflicts such as the Korean War, Vietnam War, and Cold War. The modern day journalist and editor Dr. Josef Joffe characterized the twentieth century as the century of the three Ts: total war, totalitarianism, and terror. The ultimate result was unprecedented human suffering, the aftermath of which we still feel today.

The twentieth century was also remarkable in the shifts that technological, medical, social, ideological, and international innovations induced. The trends of mechanization in goods and services and networks of global communication, which began in the nineteenth century, continued at an even more rapid pace in the twentieth century. This was an era of innovation, including the automobile, airplane, space flight, satellite communication, radio, television, telephone, washing machine, air-conditioning, computer, Internet, pesticides and herbicides, and atomic and nuclear weapons and energy. It was also a century of war and peace, ideological struggle, consumerism, globalization, and national aspirations for self sufficiency and independence. The ethical, social, and political implications of the twentieth century are still too recent to be assessed. Even though the century may have concluded, its page in history has not yet been fully written. But we do already know that, in both its positive and negative influences, the twentieth century was profound and perhaps unmatched by any era of history.

Section Two:
The Late Dynasties of Ming and Qing

In the latter half of the fourteenth century, at the opposite end of Eurasia from Western Europe, the stage was not yet set for the emergence of the modern nation-state. Change was far from absent, however, as the Chinese people of the time were driving out their Mongol overlords to form a new native dynasty, the Ming (1368–1644). In fact, their success was so great that Mongol power across all of East Asia collapsed. Chinese armies were able to drive north well beyond the Great Wall. Charles Hucker described this dramatic era of change, the full significance of which can only be perceived retrospectively:

> The conquest by the Mongols and their century-long military occupation had been an unprecedented shock for the Chinese, despite their long experience of fighting off or, alternatively, accommodating northern invaders. Never before had all Chinese been subjugated by aliens, and never before had leadership roles in China been so thoroughly preempted by outsiders as was the case with the Mongols and their non-Chinese hangers-on. The natural leaders of China's traditional society, the educated landowners, had been partly killed off in the conquest. Survivors and would be successors had been either drawn into collaboration with the conquerors for profit, or from confused conceptions of loyalty, or driven into apolitical eremitism and dilettantism. In either case, their potentiality as leaders of rebellion withered. The consequence was that China's recovery, when it came, was equally unprecedented, in that it was led, as it were by default, by men of the lowest social classes devoid of roots in the traditional high culture. (1978)

The Ming Dynasty 明

The Ming dynasty was the perfect example of a dynasty born from the lowest social classes of society. Of all the dynastic founders in Chinese history, Zhu Yuanzhang 朱元璋, founder of the Ming, came from the humblest origins. Understandably, this determined the outlook of the new dynasty. Before he became emperor, Zhu Yuanzhang was a Buddhist monk performing menial work and a mendicant. He was so poor that he was unable to afford coffins for the burial of his parents when they died in a famine in 1344. A self-taught and skillful manipulator, he was able to use his organizational talents to pick up the pieces that the Mongols left. He situated his imperial capital at Nanjing, and the Ming dynasty was the first peasant-dominated reign in China, leaving a permanent imprint on Chinese political, economic and social history.

Many of the domestic problems of the Ming dynasty were structural in nature and existed almost from the beginning as a result of the way the dynasty was formed. Centralization of power was the most striking feature of Zhu Yuanzhang's style of management. In Huang's words, "If this system were ever activated in the United States, Washington would not only be empowered to appoint the governors of California and Texas, but also the mayor of Sacramento and the sheriff of Austin, and beyond that to regulate their salaries and scrutinize their office budgets" (1998).

In 1380, the first Ming emperor made the most substantial change yet in the structure of the central government. Suspecting a chief councilor of treason, Zhu Yuanzhang abolished the secretariat's executive posts, leaving general administration fragmented among the six ministries, and made himself their sole coordinator. In effect, he made himself his own prime minister.

The secretariat had been the main central administrative body under past dynasties. Then, when the emperorship became hereditary, the Chinese established the office of the prime or chief minister who was responsible for the effective operation of the bureaucracy. They reasoned that incompetent emperors could come and go, but instituting the office of prime minister guaranteed a level of continuity and competence in the government. But the founder of the Ming dynasty wished to concentrate absolute authority in his own hands. In doing so, he effectively removed the only insurance against incompetent emperors. Unfortunately for the Chinese people, most of the emperors of the Ming dynasty were incompetent and weak, denying China of effective leadership for a long time. The authority of the court as well declined during these years under the influence of powerful eunuchs and officers of the inner court.

In addition, Zhu Yuanzhang fragmented the chief military commission into five agencies all with the same name. He divided among them, via confusing geographic jurisdictions, control over the empire's military garrisons. Thus, he made himself, in effect, his own military chief of staff. To achieve this unprecedented centralization, Zhu Yuanzhang is known to have conducted four waves of political purges from 1376 to 1393. The victims of this reign of terror were high officials, ranking army officers, ordinary bureaucrats, students of government, local landowners, and clan leaders. Historians have estimated that no less than one hundred thousand people lost their lives in these trials.

The first Ming emperor also erred by apportioning excessive power to his own family by creating principalities for each of his twenty-six sons. Though their administration was placed under central government control, the princes had authority over considerable military forces, giving them a great deal of power. Following his term of centralized control, Zhu Yuanzhang was succeeded briefly by his grandson, Zhu Jianwen 朱 允 汶, who was then deposed by his fourth uncle, Zhu Di 朱 棣, also known as the Yongle emperor. Yongle 永 樂 (1403–1424) was a powerful emperor, transferring the capital from Nanjing to Beijing, thus permitting closer control over the military forces of the north. He was actually the last capable emperor of the Ming dynasty with the exception, perhaps, of its last emperor.

Unlike other dynastic transitions, upon coming to power, the Ming dynasty did not inherit a pool of experienced and reputable officials from the Yuan. It had to recruit many officials. While some were obtained through the revival of the traditional state examination system in 1382, others were from local recommendation. The first Ming emperor took a particular interest in education and ordered the establishment of schools in every prefecture, subprefecture, and district with public funds supporting both staff and students. This has been described as the beginning of an empire-wide, state-supported educational system. Unfortunately, many factors reduced the intellectual quality of examination graduates in the late Ming dynasty and even more so in the following Qing dynasty. Hucker explained:

> For one thing, free thought was inhibited by a requirement initiated in Yuan times that candidates must utilize only classical interpretations approved by the Chu Hsi [Zhu Xi] school of Neo-Confucianism; deviant interpretations of the classics were considered heretical. In addition, from mid-Ming times there developed a standard rhetorical form in which examination essays were to be written—an eight-part structure of presentation popularly called the "eight-legged essay" (pa-ku wen) [or ba-gu wen 八 股 文]. Form (something that is plainly easier to grade objectively than content) became an increasingly important consideration, until by the mid-Ch'ing [Qing], examiners—and consequently students throughout the country—were more interested in the rhetorical structure of an essay than in any ideas it contained. Handbooks on the writing of eight-legged essays were produced, and by the nineteenth century the range of likely examination questions was so predictable that mass-produced answer books were available for prospective candidates to memorize. The quality of the examinations even degenerated

to the point where examiners graded answers primarily on the basis of calligraphy, ignoring not only intellectual content, but even rhetorical form. (1975)

This is a good example of how the elements essential to the functioning of the Chinese bureaucracy were gradually dismantled by its despotic and dogmatic replacements during the Ming and Qing dynasties. As emperors lacking in capability and legitimacy, which characterized most of the Ming emperors, assumed power, reliance on the social values and morality of the people became a basis of governance. Neo-Confucianism was indoctrinated into a rigid ideological dogma and became a series of simplified rules to be followed unquestioningly. Citizens of all descriptions became hypocritical, using high-sounding words as justification for less than honorable actions:

> That man was superior to woman, the aged superior to the young, and educated elite superior to the illiterate was more than ever held as self-evident as part of the Natural Law. Since these principles carried neither the weight of economy nor the variance between and among the several geographical sections, their universality strengthened the empire's solidarity. But the reliance on cultural cohesion made the Ming Empire static. Its timeless and changeless outlook forbade development in any new direction. Toward the end of the dynasty, genuine clashes of interest could not be stated in explicit terms. Power struggles, even arising from disputes that were technical in nature, had to be disguised as moral issues. (Huang 1998)

Because the bureaucrats were preoccupied with the concept of governance through cultural cohesion and maintained a fixed vision, they managed to make all districts appear artificially identical. In contrast to an international trend of the time toward pluralism and diversity, the Ming bureaucracy turned inward and acted in a way contradictory to the open societies of the Song and Tang dynasty reformers. The introverted Ming dynasty that followed the Yuan occupation signaled the beginning of economic and moral decline in the ancient Chinese nation.

There was only one exception to the self-imposed isolation of the Ming dynasty, the voyages of General Zhenghe 鄭 和. Between 1405 and 1433, he made a total of seven maritime expeditions that rounded Southeast Asia and Indian Ocean. He pressed on as far as the Red Sea and the coast of East Africa. This was eighty years before Portugal's Vasco da Gama discovered the same region via the Cape of Good Hope.

The first expedition of Zhenghe was the largest, comprising 317 ships and 27,870 men. His nine-masted, 400-foot flagship carried up to 500 troops. Then, that armada was the largest naval expedition in history. The objective of this expedition, commissioned under the reign of Yongle, was not to expand the boundaries of China through conquest or colonization. Rather, it was to explore cultural, political, and trade opportunities. Despite the merits of General Zhenghe's voyage, Chinese imperial subjects were once again forbidden to either build oceangoing ships or leave the country by the end of the fifteenth century. These restrictions on emigration and shipbuilding were largely lifted only in the mid-seventeenth century.

Postmodern historians, including Jonathan Spence, Kenneth Pomeranz, and Joanna Waley-Cohen, deny that China turned inward at all and point out that this view of the Ming dynasty is inconsistent with the growing volume of trade and commerce between China and Southeast Asia at the time. For example, when the Portuguese reached India, they found a booming trade network, which they followed to China. In the sixteenth century, Europeans started to appear on the eastern shores of China, where they founded China's first European settlement at Macao (Macau today). While the views of historians in this camp may be true from a European perspective, they are not consistent within the framework of China's past experiences.

Demonstrating a Confucian aversion to trade, the Ming encouraged the creation of self-supporting agricultural communities. The Ming dynasty expropriated land tenure developments of the late Song and Yuan times. Great landed estates were confiscated, fragmented, and rented out. Consequently, following the death of Emperor Yongle, independent peasant landholders dominated Chinese agriculture. The resulting Ming agricultural community had a certain utopian character, as previously described. According to Huang (1988), China seemed more like a huge village community rather than a nation.

By rendering a country of millions of square miles into a compact and homogenous whole, the Ming government was then able to substitute certain administrative controls for a complex division of labor and interchangeability of service and goods, as the national economy would have normally worked out. However, in the late Ming, following contact with the Europeans, a silver-based money economy emerged as a response to the development of relatively large-scale mercantile and industrial enterprises under private as well as state ownership. Most notable was the great textile centers of the southeast. Some historians view this premature development of European-style mercantilism and industrialization as a further factor in the decline of the Ming dynasty. Although the flow of silver from the New World, payment for Chinese exports of tea, silk and ceramics, stimulated commerce and Chinese businessmen devised a way of mass producing cheaper types of porcelain to satisfy European markets, a comparison of Chinese economic patterns to those in Europe during the genesis of capitalism illustrate why state backing of capitalism was crucial.

In Europe, governmental controls, subsidies and monopolies encouraged and protected the early capitalists, who generated most of their profits from the buying and selling of goods. The bourgeoisie were a viable new tax base for the crown in Europe. The same was not true in China. To the contrary, the taxation system of the Ming dynasty proved a handicap. According to Huang (1988), it could be said that the first Ming emperor had created a fiscal framework that was too crude and simple for its time. After the third emperor overburdened the system to serve a purpose for which it had not been designed, the fifth emperor of the dynasty rescued the system from a total collapse. By then, any possibility for a restructuring had already slipped away. A more integrated system would have required the introduction of new accounting methods, which would have called for a reorientation and reorganization of the bureaucracy as well as the creation of banking and other service facilities. However, the court in Beijing did not even have the monetary means to maintain the old system in a generally satisfactory manner. The paper currency, despite the efforts of Zhu Zhanji 朱瞻基, the fifth emperor, and his minister of revenue Xia Yuanji 夏元吉 to give it a new lease on life, fell into disuse. Past irresponsibility in overissuing the note had pushed them beyond the point of no return. Moreover, relying on paper money as the legal tender, the foregoing Yuan dynasty had neglected to mint bronze coins, the traditional medium of exchange. As Huang maintained, with the inflow of silver from overseas, the population embraced the unminted metal. Its circulation was spontaneous and widespread. In the end, not only did the Ming dynasty have to ignore its own order prohibiting its use in private transactions, it also accepted it as a standard in public finance. By then, the lack of governmental control was complete. It had no knowledge of the amount of money in circulation. It also did not have much power to manipulate it. Its separation from the natural power of the national economy was a characteristic of Ming administration. As the government had little functional maneuverability, its reliance on Confucian ideology intensified. Its exercise of political power became excessive. In many respects, it turned into a negative influence. Despite all these negatives, the Ming dynasty survived sixteen emperors and almost three centuries until 1644 when it fell to another nomadic culture from the north, the Manchu.

During these centuries of Ming rule, technological advances, after reaching a highpoint during the Song, did not continue quite so vigorously. Nevertheless, hydraulic engineering and pharmacology were two areas in which the Ming people did make significant progress. In agriculture, major events included the introduction of tobacco, maize, sweet potato, and peanut from the New World. The last two food plants were of particular value because they could grow on hilly land that had previously been uncultivable. It is estimated that, during the Ming period, the population of China rose from about 65 million to about 150 million people and the acreage of land under cultivation increased from less than 400 million *mu* (one-seventh of an acre) to approximately 500 million *mu*. (Huang, 1988) This was partly due to internal migration, most noticeably to Yunnan and Guizhou.

In the early seventeenth century, internal revolts tore apart the Ming empire. The most serious of these broke out in 1629, and it soon ravaged most of the area between the Yangtze and the Huai Rivers, from Sichuan and Shaanxi in the west, and to the Nanjing area in the east. The problems this revolt caused in the major economic zone along the Yangtze Valley increased government difficulties. In 1644, the most powerful of the rebel leaders, Li Zicheng, marched on Beijing. The Ming emperor was unable to raise sufficient forces to resist and hanged himself from a tree on Coal Hill that stood on the northern side of Beijing's Forbidden City. Thus, the Ming dynasty ended.

The Qing Dynasty 清

The Aisin-Gioro 愛新覺羅 family of the Manchus, who lived in the vicinity of the Changbai mountains to the east of the present-day city of Jilin, founded the subsequent Qing dynasty (1644–1911). The Manchus originated from the Jurchen tribes, which had plagued the Northern Song. By the early seventeenth century, they had perfected an efficient military organization and possessed a script derived from Mongolia. In 1616, Emperor Nurhachi 努爾哈赤 founded the Manchu state through consolidation of various clans and tribes. A line of capable men succeeded him, including Abahai (1592–1643), his eighth son who assumed the throne upon his father's death in 1626. In 1636, at the capital Shenyang, he proclaimed the Qing dynasty. Under his guidance, the Manchus conquered Inner Mongolia and temporarily subjugated Korea. As regent, Abahai ruled the Manchu kingdom until his death in 1651. By which time, the Manchus were securely ensconced in Beijing, and the throne had been transferred to Emperor Shunzhi 順治. His rule encompassed all of China, but it was brief (1644–1661) and then succeeded by Kangxi 康熙 (1661–1722), Yongzheng 雍正 (1723–1735), and Qianlong 乾隆 (1736–1796). These were three of the most capable emperors in Chinese history. Between them, these four emperors rounded out the boundaries of the China that we see today, effectively doubling the size of the Ming territory and extending military campaigns into Central Asia, Nepal, and Burma. Domestically, they introduced a policy of censorship through which they attempted to eliminate antidynastic literature while simultaneously promoting Chinese culture. The latter three emperors, who historians considered to be benevolent despots, brought a temporary prosperity to China from the second half of the seventeenth century to the close of the eighteenth, but they ultimately failed to solve structural problems that they inherited from the Ming.

Although the Manchus of the Qing dynasty were not Han Chinese and therefore faced strong resistance, especially in the south, they had actually assimilated a great deal of Chinese culture before conquering China proper. Unlike the Mongols, they realized that, to dominate the empire, they would have to do things the Chinese way. Accordingly, the Manchus retained many institutions of Ming and even earlier Chinese derivation. However, this strategy proved unfortunate, considering the despotic nature of Ming institutions and bureaucracy. While the despotism of Ming emperors was merely ineffective at the level of the ordinary people, this was not the case with the Qing rule. An infamous literary inquisition provides a good example of the controlling and repressive nature of the Qing government. Members of official circles investigated at length any published item suspected of being seditious. As a rule, it was brought to the attention of the emperor. When imperial vengeance raged most violently, an inquiry could involve several hundred persons. Superficially, the Manchu leaders of the Qing dynasty continued Confucian court practices, temple rituals, and the Confucian civil service system. But Han Chinese were barred from the highest offices and the military, except in the case of civil services located outside the capital where Chinese officials predominated over Manchu. The resulting Ming Neo-Confucian philosophy, emphasizing the obedience of subject to ruler, was enforced as the state creed. Manchu influence was so pervasive that their custom of braiding men's hair into pigtails was enforced on the Han population. Any male seen outdoors without a pigtail was subject to beheading.

Ever suspicious of the Han Chinese, the Qing rulers implemented measures aimed at preventing the absorption of the Manchus into the dominant Han Chinese population. Han Chinese were prohibited from migrating into the Manchu homeland; Manchus were forbidden to engage in trade or manual labor. Intermarriage between the two groups was forbidden. In many governmental positions, a system of dual appointments was used. The Chinese appointee was required to do the substantive work, and the Manchu ensured Han loyalty to Qing rule. Yet all the atrocities and provocations did not lead to racial tension in the modern sense. Huang explained:

The absence of a permanent grudge helps us to understand that nation-alism in its present form and as we experience it today is a product of modern society, where cultural influence and economic interest make the individual feel so conscious of the corporate uniqueness of which he is a part that a drastic alteration of those values by foreign intervention inevitably incites massive and intense reactions. In the seventeenth and eighteenth centuries neither did the Manchus make a serious effort at alteration nor did the Chinese feel that their cultural tradition was in fact threatened. Only a small segment of the population was incited. (1988)

After an initial wave of resistance, Manchu relations with the Chinese improved. Intermarriage, forbidden by law, actually occurred with regularity. As time went on, more Chinese bureaucrats served in high governmental positions, such as those of governor and governor-general. Unsurprisingly, when modern-minded historians search through Qing records for the causes of Chinese nation-alism, they find none. Indeed, imperial subjects born after the Manchu conquest had no perception of collaborating with an alien dynasty. They were serving their own empire, which was a duty to them. By the end of the Qing dynasty, almost all Manchus had been assimilated into the single, great Chinese family we witness today, even in Manchuria itself.

The Qing also succeeded where the Ming had failed in governmental finance. Huang explained that the direction of expenditures was reversed (1988). During the time of fiscal expansion, the Qing emperors exercised more authority than the ritualistic figureheads of the late Ming. Instead of extending the influence of silver into peripheral areas, the new dynasty compressed the circulation of the precious metal within its own familiar ground. Furthermore, the disentitlement of Ming rank-holders cleared a major obstacle to local administration while opening the door for new forced contributions and a renewed sale of ranks. In the meantime, the Manchus enforced tax laws, and minted bronze coins in earnest, a state func-tion that the Ming had persistently neglected. During the first decade of the new dynasty, China produced more of these coins than the previous dynasty had in its entire 276-year reign. Thus, cheap money was made available to the populace.

In the eighteenth century, according to J. A. G. Roberts (1999), the popula-tion of the Qing doubled to an estimated 300 million people, but little new land had been added, and agricultural yields per acre were nearly as high as could be achieved using the available technology. Eventually, at some point between 1750 and 1775, the amount of food available per capita began to decline, leading to a reduction in demand for goods other than basic necessities and a fall in the cost of labor. Under these circumstances, there was no case for investing in technological improvement. Combined with the population increase, this disincentive could partially explain the stagnation of the late Qing economy. According to Paul Bairoch's research comparing historical national output in different areas of the world (Nolan 2004), China's estimated share of global manufacturing output stood at 33 percent in 1750, compared with 25 percent for India/Pakistan and just 18 percent for the West. China's per capita GNP was $228 (US$) in 1800 (at 1960 prices), compared with $150–$200 (US$) for Great Britain and France combined. This contrast would have been even more dramatic if statistics were available for the period prior to the Chinese decline. Nolan pointed out that, until the nineteenth century, the dominant view of European intellectuals was that China was materially superior to Europe.

Today, more than two hundred years later and with the benefit of hindsight, we might appraise the so-called prosperity of the early Qing dynasty somewhat differently than the historians of that time. Huang pointed out:

> The combined reigns of the four early Qing emperors, splendidly successful as they seemed to be, were in the vision of macrohistory anachronistic. With all the fiscal surpluses passing through their hands, those rulers did little to revamp the superstructure of the empire or to strengthen the middle echelon of the government. A central treasury was still missing. The empire's financial resources were still handled by lateral transactions, thus yielding vital statistics always of doubtful quality. Civil laws that could have linked government operation with the rising economic trends were still not in place. China remained a conglomeration of village communities. (1988)

It could be argued that this perspective on the Qing is too harsh because we are all products of history and the perspectives of our own culture limits our vision. Nonetheless, toward the end of the reign of the Qianlong emperor, there were signs of dynastic decline. Roberts (1999) explored this period and uncovered three issues he deemed early signs of the subsequent decline: changes in literary and intellectual life, popular religion and the rise of rebellion, and bureaucratic corruption.

One contemporary view holds that the nineteenth century was the era in which Qing control weakened and prosperity diminished. During this century, China suffered massive social strife, economic stagnation, and explosive population growth. All of which, incidentally, coincided with Western access to and influence of China. The late Qing dynasty became even more arrogant in its parochialism and blindly opposed ideas that departed from its own. Corruption, incompetent officialdom, weak armament, financial deficits, polarization of rich and poor, and rebellion marked this era. Despite these many events, all of which are fascinating to historians, it is not our intention to cover the modern history of China in this volume. We will, however, describe specific events in modern China in order to draw comparisons to the Western experience, predominantly in our concluding chapters.

During the nineteenth century, Britain briefly desired to continue its illegal opium trade with China via its colonial base in India. This collided with Qing imperial edicts prohibiting the addictive drug. As a result, the First Opium War erupted in 1840, eventually concluding with China's defeat. Subsequently, Britain and other Western powers, including the United States, forcibly occupied concessions within China and created special commercial privileges for themselves. Then Hong Kong was ceded to Britain in 1842 under the Treaty of Nanjing. Additional factors, notably the Taiping 太 平 天 國 and other rebellions, a Russian-supported Muslim independence movement in Xinjiang, and indemnity payments to the Western powers following the Opium Wars, drained Chinese resources and helped to topple the Qing dynasty in 1911, ultimately putting an end to Imperial China.

As Europe entered the Industrial Revolution, China's role in the global economy changed drastically. By 1913, its share of world manufacturing output had fallen from 33 to under 4 percent. The West had risen from 18 to 82 percent (Bairoch 1982, Nolan 2004). With this dramatic change of fortune, the predominant image of China shifted to one of stagnant, impoverished despotism. Very few Chinese deny this reality of the past two hundred years. The establishment of the Chinese Republic in 1911 and, subsequently, the People's Republic in 1949 formally declared Chinese membership in the modern world. Sadly, the suffering of the Chinese people continued.

Part Four

Past, Present, and Future

The six preceding chapters have outlined and compared periods of Chinese and Western history. We have found that differences in thinking, philosophy, and perspectives on human relationships strongly influenced the historical development of both civilizations. Yet questions remain. Are there regularities in the history of the world? What are the lessons of history that can serve us in the present? Where are we going from here? What can we learn from each other?

CHAPTER THIRTEEN

The Lessons of History

Are there regularities in the history of the world? Any attempt to address this question must first acknowledge and grapple with the nature of historical inquiry itself. Very few historians attempt to deal with the great sweep of human history. Thus, in section one, we have created a short list of previous efforts to organize and interpret history with trends and patterns for those readers who wish to explore this subject further. In section two, we put forth lessons that can be learned from the patterns seen thus far.

Section One:
Past, Present, and Future Trends

Early Works

The first notable attempt at identifying trends in history was Oswald Spengler's classic two-volume set, *The Decline of the West* (1926 and 1932). Arnold Toynbee then took the fundamental thesis of Spengler that civilizations have a predictable cycle of overall direction. Between 1934 and 1961, he wrote the twelve volumes of *The Study of History*. This vast work ranged across twenty-one human civilizations and six thousand years of human history, drawing from them a series of general laws according to which civilizations rise, develop, and eventually collapse. In Toynbee's volumes, the problems of history are considered in terms of cultural groups rather than nationalities. The main thesis of the work is that the well-being of a civilization depends on its ability to respond successfully to challenges, especially moral and religious challenges, rather than physical or environmental ones. Toynbee's laws are detailed and exact. For example, he suggested four methods by which great individuals appear in history to save civilizations in

283

danger of imminent collapse and then presented the stages in which new institutions emerge from the body of a disintegrating civilization. The press hailed his work as an immortal masterpiece. However, Toynbee has also been criticized for arbitrary generalizations, factual errors, and overemphasizing the regenerative force of religion. Both Toynbee and his predecessor Spengler broke with the tradition of a unitary and progressive history of humankind, a tradition that began with the Christian historians and culminated in Hegel and Marx. Both Toynbee and Spengler return to the cyclical histories of individual people that characterized Greek and Roman historiography.

In 1963, Patrick Gardiner published *Theories of History*, which looked at historical regularities and studied questions concerning the nature of historical knowledge itself, the relations between history and science, and the theoretical and practical possibility of providing comprehensive schemes within which the material of history can be systematically arranged. According to Gardiner, by the opening of the twentieth century, the philosophy of history had split into two distinct halves. Speculation and systematization continued to be found in the work of writers such as Spengler and Toynbee, but, side by side with this, a quite separate form of inquiry had grown up, directed toward the analysis of historical procedures, categories, and terms. The first attempt was to depict the world as a unitary, connected system, the ultimate character of that could be arrived at by using purely *a priori* reasoning. The latter philosophy, as Gardiner espoused, contended that metaphysical statements and theories, while not devoid of sense, as argued in the early days of logical positivism, could not be considered reliable sources of information about the world in the way that empirical statements and theories are. Such metaphysics thus require careful analysis and interpretation. Gardiner's work is an impressive concentration of materials with sections covering the interpretation of historical process, the nature of historical knowledge, critiques of classical theories of history, explanation of laws, and the relationship of history and the social sciences. Writings from more than thirty-five historians and philosophers are presented with commentaries.

The Durants

In 1968, a year after completing the tenth volume of their now eleven-volume set, *The Story of Civilization*, Will and Ariel Durant wrote the classic short work, *The Lessons of History*, a full exposition of the successful values common to various civilizations throughout history. They consider each of several factors, including environment, race, character, morals, religion, economics, government, and war, to be important for the growth and decay of civilizations. For example, according to Karl Marx, history is economics in action, that is, the contest among individuals, groups, classes, and states for food, fuel, materials, and economic power. Marx believed political forms, religious institutions, and cultural creations were rooted in economic realities. The Durants, however, contended that Marx underestimated the role played by noneconomic incentives in the behavior of the masses, specifically religious fervor in the case of the Muslim or Spanish armies, nationalistic ardor as the world witnessed with Hitler's troops and Japan's kamikazes, or the self-fertilizing fury of the mobs of the French Revolution. In these and other such cases, the motives of the leaders may be economic, but the passions of the masses largely determined the result. In many other instances, political or military power was apparently the cause rather than the result of economic operations. In terms of economic activities, the Durants observed:

> Normally and generally men are judged by their ability to produce—except in war, when they are ranked according to their ability to destroy. Since practical ability differs from person to person, the majority of such abilities, in nearly all societies, is gathered in a minority of men. The concentration of wealth is a natural result of this concentration of ability, and regularly recurs in history. The rate of concentration varies (other factors being equal) with economic freedom permitted by morals and the laws. Despotism may for a time retard the concentration; democracy, allowing the most liberty, accelerates it. In progressive societies the concentration may reach a point where the strength of number in the many poor rivals the strength of ability in the few rich; then the unstable equilibrium generates a critical situation, which history has diversely met by legislation redistributing wealth or by revolution distributing poverty. The concentration of wealth is natural and inevitable, and is periodically alleviated by violent or peaceable partial redistribution. In this view all economic history is the slow heartbeat of social organism, a vast systole and diastole of concentrating wealth and compulsive recirculation. (1968)

Indeed, in our own era of technological revolution, free markets, and economic globalization, we can see the disparity between rich and poor widening. But can we learn from the lessons of history that the Durants articulated?

Religion is another factor central to the Durants' cyclical model of culture:

> One lesson of history is that religion has many lives, and a habit of resurrection. Puritanism and paganism—the repression and expression of the senses and desires—alternate in mutual reaction in history.

Generally religion and Puritanism prevail in periods when the laws are feeble and morals must bear the burden of maintaining social order; skepticism and paganism (other factors being equal) progress as the rising power of law and government permits the decline of the church, the family, and morality without basically endangering the stability of the state. In our time the strength of the state has united with the several forces to relax faith and morals, and to allow paganism to resume its natural sway. Probably our excesses will bring another reaction; moral disorder may generate a religious revival; atheists may again send their children to Catholic schools to give them the disciplines of religious belief. (1968)

With the second presidential inauguration of George Bush on January 20, 2005, and the increasing signs of fundamentalist religious revival in the United States, the words of the prophets resonate in our ears.

Modern Works

Through the lens of economics, Karl Marx also attempted to chronicle the regularities of history. But while Marx is known to have divided history into five stages, specifically primitive communism, slavery, feudalism, capitalism, and communism, contemporary historian L. S. Stavrianos, in *Lifelines from the Past*, conceptualized human history in three categories, including kinship societies, tributary societies, and capitalist societies. In each category, he studied four lifeline issues of ecology, gender relations, social relations, and war that encompassed the broadest areas of human experience. Stavrianos contended that the transition from kinship society to tributary society was a fateful turning point in human history. Compared to kinship societies with their shared egalitarianism and warm communal bonds, tributary societies were impersonal and exploitative. Based on tribute in the form of goods and services or money collected forcibly from a mass of cultivators and artisans, tributary societies operated for the benefit of a small ruling elite. Thus, just as population pressure forced the hunter-gatherers to exploit their local resources more intensively and develop agriculture in the process, so population pressure forced the early agriculturists to exploit their local resources more intensively, thereby creating tributary social organizations. Yet, the actual shift from kinship to tributary society was gradual and prolonged. In this process, humans began to make their transition from food gathering to food producing, a transition repeatedly and independently experienced all over the globe. The increase in productivity seen in tributary societies, through the invention of agriculture, did solve the most critical problem facing kinship societies, that is, overpopulation. But tributary societies lacked incentives and the necessary desire for further technological change. These deficits fostered the subsequent transition to capitalism.

According to Stavrianos, capitalism's ruling principle of profit or perish furnished it with an intrinsic dynamism that persists to the present. From its origins in northwestern Europe in early modern times, capitalism has evolved through three stages from commercial to industrial to our current high-tech capitalism. Each stage was characterized by a combination of unrelenting and ever-increasing productivity with unrelenting and ever-increasing consumerism, the inescapable corollary of such productivity. Capitalism's basic competitive drive impels bursts of technological and institutional innovation. With these, there is increased productivity. Its creative impulse is so compelling that capitalism has enveloped the entire globe, overwhelming traditional cultures and economies and transforming people on every continent. Capitalism is now so globally pervasive and so taken for granted that it seems inevitable we would consider it an unavoidable manifestation of human nature. This seemingly irresistible process also occasions destruction because destruction is the inevitable concomitant of relentless creativity. Self-generating technological exuberance and economic expansionism has shown its ability to overrun any institution and object, animate or inanimate, standing in the way. The particular combination of creativity and destruction that capitalism has generated provides the foundation both for the extraordinary achievements and the appalling setbacks of recent centuries and the unprecedented promise and peril of our own time.

Toffler's Waves

Renowned futurist Alvin Toffler has written three books over the past three decades, starting with *The Future Shock* (1970), followed by *The Third Wave* (1980), and *The Power Shift* (1990). Each of these three best sellers has contributed significantly to our understanding of the nature of social and political development. In short, Toffler organized the profound changes of history into three waves. The first wave was the invention of agriculture ten thousand years ago and its subsequent adoption throughout the succeeding thousands of years. The Industrial Revolution touched off the second wave, and it took a mere three hundred years to culminate in the industrial civilization of the twentieth century. We are currently on the verge of the third wave, or the information age, electronic era, space age, or global village. Toffler predicted that this wave will sweep across history and spend itself in a few short decades.

Before the first wave of change, most humans lived in small, often migratory, groups and fed themselves by foraging, fishing, hunting, or herding. As the agricultural revolution began to creep slowly across the planet, it created villages, settlements, cultivated land, and a new way of life. In the agricultural societies that followed this revolution, land was the basis of the economy. Life, culture, family structure, and politics were organized around the village. In each of these societies, a simple division of labor prevailed. A few clearly defined castes and classes arose, including a nobility, priesthood, warriors, helots, and slaves or serfs. A rigidly authoritarian power distribution governed all. Birth usually determined one's position in life. The economy was decentralized so that each community produced most of its own necessities. First wave societies drew their energy from living batteries, human and animal muscle power, or sun, wind, and water, exploiting only renewable energy sources.

As the second wave of industrialization moved across various societies, drastic changes took place in many different ways. Instead of the essentially self-sufficient people and communities of the first wave, industrialization created a civilization in which virtually no one was self-sufficient. Even farmers depended on food, goods, and services produced by someone else. Wherever the second wave struck, the purpose of production shifted from personal use to exchange. Commercial values, the market economy, and money system became the primary goal of government. The explosive expansion of markets contributed to the fastest rise in living standards that the world had ever experienced. The foundation of the second wave society was money, not land. The energy base was nonrenewable fossil fuels such as coal, oil, and gas.

The divorce of production from consumption, which became a defining feature of all industrial or second wave societies, even impacted our psyches and assumptions about personality. Behavior came to be seen as a set of transactions. Instead of a society based on friendship, kinship, or tribal and feudal allegiances, a civilization arose that was based on the actual or implied ties of contracts. Even husbands and wives today speak of marital contracts. In addition, the dichotomy between these two roles, producer and consumer, created a dual personality. Two opposing sets of values informed the same person. As a producer, he or she was taught by family, school and employer to defer gratification and be disciplined, controlled, restrained, obedient, and a team player. As a consumer, he or she was simultaneously taught to seek instant gratification, be hedonistic rather than calculating, abandon discipline and pursue individualistic pleasure. In short, he or she was to be a totally different kind of person.

Toffler also enunciated a set of rules or principles necessary for the functioning of a second wave society. Whereas the first wave society lacked the technology to connect people across large distances, the second wave was characterized by high-way systems, cars, airplanes, telephones, and mainframe computers that linked remote outposts to central controls. The result was massification. Other characteristics of the second wave were standardization, specialization, synchronization, concentration, maximization, and centralization. All of which were necessary for efficient production, particularly for assembly-line mass production such as that common in the textile or automotive industries. Ironically, while these many forces of centralization were at work, fragmentation occurred as well. Toffler wrote:

> Industrialism, as we have seen, broke society into thousands of inter-locking parts—factories, churches, schools, trade unions, prisons, hospitals, and the like. It broke the line of command between church, states, and individual. It broke knowledge into specialized disciplines. It broke jobs into fragments. It broke families into smaller units. In doing so, it shattered community life and culture. Somebody had to put things back together in a different form. This need gave rise to many new kinds of specialists whose basic task was integration. Calling themselves administrators, commissars, coordinators, presidents, vice-presidents, bureaucrats, or managers, they cropped up in every business, in every government, and at every level of society. And they proved indispensable. They were the integrators. (1990)

All these changes drastically revolutionized human relationships, psychologically, socially, and politically. Toffler continued his description of the successive waves:

> Before we know it the triumph of the second wave civilization has already imposed its will on millions, and ultimately billions, of human beings. It pushed its tentacles across the planet, transforming everything with which it came in contact, and it carried with it more than technology or trade. Colliding with First Wave civilization, the Second Wave created not only a new reality but also a new way of thinking about reality. Clashing at a thousand points with the values, concepts, myths and morals of agricultural society, the Second Wave brought with it a redefinition of God, of justice, of love, of power, of beauty. It stirred up new ideas, attitudes, and analogies. It subverted and superseded ancient assumptions about time, space, matter, and causality. A powerful, coherent worldview emerged that not only explained but justified Second Wave reality. On the surface, it seemed, there was no mainstream at all. Rather, it appeared that there were two powerful ideological currents in

conflict. By the middle of the nineteenth century every industrializing nation had its sharply defined left wing and its right, its advocates of individualism and free enterprise, and its advocates of collectivism and socialism ... On one side were totalitarian regimes, on the other the so-called liberal democracies. Guns and bombs stood ready to take up where logical arguments ended. (1990)

Toffler depicted the end of the second wave, which culminates in our familiar world at the end of the twentieth century. He was ready to forecast the future through the changes we are beginning to witness today.

With the dawn of the information age, the third wave, we again expect to see drastic revolutionary changes. The primary resource in the third wave is knowledge. The supply of knowledge is anything but scarce. Unlike commodities like money, knowledge is inexhaustible. Information technology is also different from the manufacturing industries of the second wave because the energy requirements for microelectronics and information-based industries are low. The fundamental characteristics of the second wave, such as massification, standardization, specialization, and so forth, are no longer the keys for success in the knowledge economy. We are living at a moment when the entire structure of power that previously held the world together is beginning to disintegrate. These changes will once again revolutionize human relationships, globalize our economy, and impact every level of human society, including our thought processes. We will turn to the consequence of this in the final chapter.

Robertson's Waves

Instead of using the development of technologies as a defining criterion, historian Robbie Robertson's *The Three Waves of Globalization* posited globalization as the primary social dynamic force. Robertson's focus is on the past five hundred years. Within each period, he identified three distinct global waves of interconnectedness. The first, after 1500, centered on the globalization of regional trade. The second, after 1800, gained its impetus from industrialization. Finally, the third derived from the architecture of the new world order after 1945. Each of these waves began with an event, sometimes a war, that created an opportunity for its burgeoning as a global force for change. Each wave produced new interconnections and generated new synergies that eventually led to its own transformation. No wave has ever been the creation of one country or culture, even though hegemons and would-be hegemons have occasionally attempted to monopolize them for their own advantage. Waves encompass many cultures. They enable cultures to interact. Although not all cultures are necessarily judged as equals, they enable cross-fertilization. As social animals, humans have always pursued a range of collective strategies to ensure their survival and well-being. They have migrated, conquered, traded, and innovated. As societies grew larger and more interconnected, a broadening range of strategies was adopted. Human environments, population sizes and movements, technologies and economies, and cultures influenced social transformation and interconnectiveness. The vast number of potential differences between these various factors has always ensured that no one society was identical to another.

Before 1500, societies generally gained historical significance only because they connected with other people and created something greater than themselves. During this time, humans possessed no innate global consciousness. They generally lived extremely local and parochial lives. Yet their lives became increasingly interconnected and, consequently, gained new significance. The new technology of agriculture represented an opportunity to exploit the resources at hand, enabling larger populations and communities to coalesce as villages, towns, cities, and states. Around the world, the dynamics of human societies were similar. Communities differed in their ability to transform those dynamics.

According to Robertson's theories, the larger a community, the greater its potential for specialization and stratification. In many respects, populous China was the most successful agricultural society in the world before 1500. It was an engine of world growth, buoyed by trade surpluses that rippled through its large economy, especially during the Song dynasty of 960 to 1279. It was a country that did not rely on conquest to sustain itself. Instead, it focused on internal migration, commerce, and technological change to generate the surpluses required to sustain its large bureaucracy and armies. By the start of the second millennium, China's presence in the markets of West Asia was already keenly felt, a result of both land and sea Silk Roads. Under the Song dynasty, centuries before the Portuguese discovery of eastern Africa, maritime trade was already flourishing between China, southeastern Asia, and nations around the Indian Ocean, extending to West Asia and East Africa. Trade created the linkages for this embryonic world economy, but China's technology made it possible, as signaled by the seven voyages of Admiral Zheng He of the early Ming dynasty.

During the sixteenth century, human societies experienced a fundamental change in the nature of their interconnections. Previously isolated communities suddenly found themselves dangerously exposed to new global forces. The experience positively transformed many societies; others were enslaved. The discovery of silver and gold in the Americas provided Europe with the means to participate directly in the huge Asian economy, thus transforming intersecting regional trade networks into global relationships. Robertson's first wave of globalization was driven by more than local European dynamics, even though one of its consequences was to reconstruct Europe as "the epicenter of a revolution that transformed global relations" (2003). Europe helped to connect the world in a way that had not previously been possible, and the effects of this first wave were tremendous. For the first time, foods were exchanged globally with new supplies from the Americas helping populations to expand rapidly and enabling Europe to utilize scarce land for nonagricultural purposes. As a result, the pace of urbanization in Europe quickened. The spice trade also helped the South and Southeast Asian population increase while these regions' economies were monetized and globally integrated. All of Asia's fiscal systems soon reacted to the huge influx of silver and gold. Chinese tea plantations expanded. Spice production increased, and textile workshops expanded in India. On the other hand, European nations such as Great Britain were clearly worried about the continuous depletion of their silver stock, causing anxiety and greed that led to the opium trade and the Opium War. Thus, the first wave of globalization ultimately had a destabilizing effect in both Asia and Europe.

Robertson's second wave of globalization, driven by technology instead of the trade and commerce that initiated the first wave, began in 1800. It was the age of imperialism and colonialism in the wake of the successful Industrial Revolution in Europe. The global impact of the second wave was much deeper and more rapid because it inherited the preexisting networks of the first wave. Improved communications and transportation systems reduced distances and enabled the movement of goods and people on a scale never before possible. The Europeans benefited most from this mobility. According to Robertson, more than sixty million left Europe for the Americas, Australasia, and southern and east Africa between 1815 and 1914. One million went to north Africa alone. But Europeans were not the only immigrants during this century. Nearly twenty million Chinese and Japanese migrated, as did some two million Indian citizens. The second wave also inherited industrial systems of production that connected new sources of raw materials, again on a scale that seemed to constantly escalate. Production on this scale generated wealth that surged through industrial economies much more impressively than even the Spanish bullion. Indeed, there seemed no end to the production and reproduction.

From these technological effects of transportation, communication, and production came the second wave's most significant influence. It completely transformed societies in various ways. First, it took an industrial form in societies whose proximity, interconnections, market value, or autonomy enabled them to respond to Great Britain's industrialization. Over the course of the nineteenth century, the populations of such societies increased while becoming more urbanized and less dependent on agriculture. Between 1800 and 1914, Europe's population more than doubled, and income per capita increased 300 percent. Secondly, societies that were unable, unwilling, or unaware of the need to respond urgently to the industrial era very quickly found themselves captive to a new international division of labor. They became colonies. During the early eighteenth century, the ratio of wealth between Europeans and their future colonies was often no more than two to one. By 1900, the ratio stood at five to one. By the time colonialism ended in the 1960s, it was fifteen to one (Robertson 2003). Other societies that remained uninfluenced by colonialism, such as China, managed to retain a semblance of autonomy, but they increasingly lost control of their economies. Thus, not only did colonialism weaken globalization, it created handicaps that would prove difficult for the next wave to overcome. Finally, at the end of the second wave, imperialism thrust Europe into the two world wars.

Robertson's third wave of globalization, our present era, began in 1945 with the end of World War II. Robertson contended:

> The collapse of the second wave of globalization demonstrated the necessity for specifically global strategies to enhance international cooperation and deepen prosperity. Indeed, the architects of the post-war third wave of globalization knew that they had been awarded a rare opportunity to provide for a future vastly different from the disastrous past from which they had just emerged. Much of the initiative for change came from the United States of America, which, alone of all the industrialized nations, emerged from war confident and economically rejuvenated. Its consumer economy had been protected by a deliberate government decision in 1942 to slow its rate of mobilization. This delayed the Allied invasion of Western Europe, but it enabled the US standard of living to rise 15 per cent during the war. Its British and Soviet allies enjoyed no such advantage. Their living standard fell by one third ... But most importantly, the United States emerged from war with its industrial stock undamaged and its economy booming. Its gross national product (GNP) had more than doubled between 1939 and 1945, and within another four years its per capita income would be twice that of Britain, three times France's, five times Germany's and seven times the Soviet Union's. (2003)

The resulting economic superiority bestowed an unprecedented opportunity on the United States to establish a new international order.

Consequently, the third wave of globalization began with a sense of globalism, that is, a global perspective and consciousness that earlier waves had lacked. Robertson claimed that democratization, in addition to the presence of technology, is a fundamental dynamic of globalization. Simultaneously, democratization is also a by-product of globalization. Just like industrialization, it is its child. Robertson argued:

> Democracy did not originate in Classical Greece. Whatever similarities exist between Greek forms of democracy and our own derive from a common reliance on commerce. Commerce- (and technology-) based societies depend for their success on a wider ownership of resources and wider political franchises than conquest societies require; in other words they necessitate democratized political and economic systems. Contemporary societies share these features, but not because of any cultural or historical connection with Ancient Greece. Rather their contemporary origins lie in the social and economic changes wrought by globalization. (2003)

The force and impact of globalization is integral to who we are and where we are headed. It will be explained further.

Section Two:
The Lessons of History

Will and Ariel Durant's celebrated study, *The Lessons of History*, was originally written as part of the eleven volumes of *The Story of Civilization* (1935–1975), a comprehensive survey of human history filled with dazzling insights into the nature of human experience, the evolution of civilization, and the cultures of humankind. Yet, in another context, the idea that history contains lessons is very controversial, basing enjoinders of action upon a misunderstanding of what history is and what it can achieve. For example, in the aftermath of the horrific events of September 11, 2001, we have heard words to the effect that history teaches us that we must act with overwhelming force against a terrorist threat or history teaches us that we must stop dictators while they are weak and unprepared for full-scale war. These exhortations fail to recognize that what we call history is simply one historian's effort to construct a coherent world of the past, based on the evidence available to him or her in the present. In order to construct such a past, the historian strives to place each detail of the past into a plausible and comprehensible course of events.

The actions of particular historical figures are seen as the intelligible outcome of the situation in which they found themselves, based on their understanding of that situation in the moment at which it occurred. Yet, because history draws from an entire world of detailed, specific events, the idea of general laws of history is self-contradictory. Of course, historical actors should be understood as obeying the general laws independently derived by other disciplines, such as the laws of economics, psychology, or sociology. But history itself can generate no such laws because, in the process of doing so, it would abstract away the details of events, the very subject matter of history.

While many people, politicians perhaps chief among them, attempt to learn from history, history itself shows that very few so-called lessons have been appropriate to contemporary application. History has repeatedly been proven a very bad predictor of future events. History never repeats itself exactly. Nothing in human society ever happens twice under exactly the same conditions or in exactly the same way. Historian E. H. Carr repeatedly argued that the historian's role is to employ an understanding of the past in order to gain control of the present and for the benefit of the future. Yet, very few historians look to the past as a basis for concrete predictions. Yes, history can produce generalizations. However, the broader these are, the more exceptions there are likely to be, and the farther they will become removed from any hard evidence that can be cited in their support. History cannot create any laws or rules with predictive power.

History deals with the actions of both individual humans and groups of individuals. It describes the conditions, that is, the state of the natural and social environments, under which people live and the way people's consciousness reacts to those conditions. History assumes that every individual is born into a defined social and natural milieu and his or her behavior is determined by cumulative exposure to actions, experiences, and knowledge of the self, both through direct experience and vicariously through experiences of preceding generations or contemporaries. An actual person lives as a member of a family, a race, and age; citizen of a country; member of a definite social group; and practitioner of a certain vocation. Yet history documents only the ideas and the ends that were motivated by or pursued as a result of these formative circumstances. In the course of events that make up a historical subject's life, history does not recognize any other meaning and sense than that attributed to the subject by historians judging from the point of view of their own human concerns. In other words, there are no foundational givens, that is, no immanent truths to social existence. On the contrary, the social and cultural world is apprehended only via our understanding of it, an understanding that is a product of the complex intersection of specific histories, discursive formations and political articulations, and reflexive ordering of human life. All of which combine to provide an overall web of meanings.

Recognizing these limitations, it is nevertheless true that history can identify and generalize patterns, trends, and structures in our past with a high degree of plausibility. This is because the forces behind the occurrence of historical events, for example, economic, social, ethical, political, and forth, belong to the better-understood social scientific disciplines. The same human psychology, the same passions of human nature that influence our own daily existence, guide actors in history. Therefore, such figures are comprehensible in human terms.

Within this understanding of the subjective nature of history, we venture to use history as a reference in examining some of our current problems. The following so-called lessons represent our personal observations and generalizations, based on our understanding of the past and perception of its relevance to the contemporary situation. We hope these lessons, founded on our own historical perspectives, will help our readers to better interpret some of the current and future events. We do not claim any greater significance for these lessons, nor should the reader infer any.

- **Lesson One:** Values and value judgments are often culturally dependent. Therefore, the use of force is never effective in achieving a permanent resolution of conflicts. Before going to war, we should reconsider our justifications by placing ourselves in our rival's situation, within their cultural and historical context. By doing so, we may find a way to achieve our objectives without unnecessary sacrifice and while avoiding compromising our own values and principles. We should empathize with our antagonist!

Misconceptions, misunderstandings, misjudgments, and miscalculations often cause wars between states or animosity between peoples. To prevent the unnecessary tragedy of war, empathy is required. Ralph K. White, political scientist and an advocate of realistic empathy, explained:

> Empathy is the great corrective for all forms of war-promoting misperception. It means simply understanding the thoughts and feelings of others. It is distinguished from sympathy, which is defined as feeling with others—as being in agreement with them. Empathy with opponents is therefore psychologically possible even when a conflict is so intense that sympathy is out of the question. We are not talking about warmth or approval, and certainly not about agreeing with, or siding with, but only about realistic understanding. (1984)

On the implementation of empathy, White continued:

How can empathy be achieved? It means jumping in imagination into another person's skin, imagining what it might be like to look out at his world through his eyes, and imagining how you might feel about what you saw. It means being the other person, at least for a while, and postponing skeptical analysis until later ... Most of all it means trying to look at one's own group's behavior honestly, as it might appear when seen through the other's eyes, recognizing that his eyes are almost certainly jaundiced, but recognizing also that he has the advantage of not seeing our group's behavior through the rose-colored glasses that we ourselves normally wear. We may have grounds for distrust, fear, and anger that we have not permitted ourselves to see. That is the point where honesty comes in. An honest look at the other implies an honest look at oneself. (1984)

A variety of possible historical cases illustrate this lesson. An example that may actually be the most appropriate occurred not too long ago. More than three million people were killed in the Vietnam War, and millions of others remain deeply haunted by what happened during those years. As far as we know, this is the only case in history where both adversaries met after the war to document what actually happened and determine what could be learned from the tragedy. In six sets of unprecedented meetings held in Hanoi, Vietnam, between November 1995 and February 1998, and a seventh meeting held in Italy in July 1998, scholars, former civilians, and military officials from both Vietnam and the United States met to engage in a sincere dialogue about the war. They moved beyond blame, that is, beyond us and them. Instead, for the first time, they examined the complex interplay between two opposing sides and the unspeakable tragedy to which this interplay led. Robert McNamara, secretary of defense in the Kennedy and Johnson administrations, documented these frank, revealing, and sometimes astonishing dialogues in which the two groups walked step-by-step through the war, analyzing each decision and action from both sides, and ultimately producing the document, *Argument Without End: In Search of Answers to the Vietnam Tragedy*. In the document, McNamara and his colleagues described precisely where the Americans and North Vietnamese made crucial mistakes that first resulted in the war and later led to a prolonging of the war. We also see irrefutably why the war could not have been won militarily by the United States unless it had either resorted to genocide or triggered a devastating war with China or Soviet Union.

McNamara and his colleagues wrote an inspiring chapter, "Learning from Tragedy: Lessons of Vietnam for the Twenty-First Century," wherein they singled out the central failure of empathy and communication. Each side fundamentally misread the mind-set of its enemy and there was an absence of high-level contact between the two sides even when the war began escalating. One of the most striking features of these dialogues is the profundity of mutual ignorance and its dangerous consequences. McNamara recounted:

> As Chester Cooper commented on the first day of the June 1997 conference, American ignorance of Asia was such that "we did not know what we did not know. And that was one of our problems when we got involved here in Vietnam." Later in the same session, focusing on the mindsets of both sides during the early 1960s, Nicholas Katzenbach suggested that the ignorance was mutual and that "one of the reasons for the misconceptions in these various mindsets comes from the fact that ... each country is focused on its own problem." There is a natural tendency for a party to a conflict to focus disproportionately on its own problems and, therefore, to mistakenly attribute the actions and motivations of others to factors affecting one's own situation—but not the adversary's. (1999)

This is indeed a valuable lesson, one which McNamara is well qualified to review because of his personal involvement in the war. He contended:

> In every way, American ignorance of the history, language, and culture of Vietnam was immense. Vietnamese ignorance of the United States and U.S. decision-making was at least as great. This profound mutual ignorance encouraged each side to project onto the other motivations and objectives that had little, if any, semblance to reality. Indeed, each projected onto the other motivations and intentions that ultimately proved to be tragically wrong. The U.S. leadership after World War II greatly feared the hegemonic impulses of the Soviet Union in Eastern Europe, even in Western Europe. Since it assumed that all communist countries operated according to the same logic (and perhaps even received orders from Moscow), the U.S. proceeded to project those presumed impulses onto Vietnam, assuming that Hanoi must be acting as a pawn of a global communist movement. Yet as Vietnamese scholar Luu Doan Huynh said pointedly to the Americans during one of the dialogues: "If I may say so, you were not only wrong, but you had, so to speak, lost your minds. Vietnam, a part of the Chinese expansionist game in Asia? For anyone who knows the history of Indochina, this is incomprehensible." The American obsession with the global chessboard of the Cold War blinded leaders in Washington to the decisive impor-

tance of Vietnamese nationalism and the desire of the Vietnamese people for reunification. (1999)

Mutual ignorance of the situation, culture, and history of their adversaries resulted in tragedy for both the Americans and the Vietnamese. Unthinkably, the situation could have been even worse. Humankind was threatened with a nuclear holocaust on several occasions during the Cold War.

A few short decades later, with daily news of the mounting casualties in Iraq and the continuing possibility of a clash between nuclear powers, would this not be a good time for all of us, especially world leaders, to revisit this lesson?

• **Lesson Two:** The worst crimes and the greatest evils against humanity are often based in self-righteousness and committed in the name of the highest virtues. Fanaticism, especially of a political or religious nature, has been one of the major causes of mass human suffering. To avoid such suffering, we must first disallow our political and religious leaders the use of ideology as a cause for discrimination. Secondly, we must learn mutual tolerance and respect for other races, religions, customs, and traditions.

References to the worst crime of self-righteousness have existed throughout history. Obviously, the evidence of history and of our own time shows that humankind often falls victim to a sort of disease of the mind that has the power to devastate cities and destroy civilizations, killing millions of people. Al Qaeda carries out its actions in the name of Islam, which is a gross perversion. Religious wars are the cruelest because human beings are maimed and killed in the name of the divine. The Crusaders, the Conquest and the Reconquest, the Irish war between the Catholics and Protestants, and the religious war between India and Pakistan are all good examples of this horrible irony. Social and economic woes can be corrected, but religious faith is confounding to change. Religious, ethical, and ideological conflicts can turn genocidal when one disputant believes that rightness is completely on his side. For example, the savagery of the oppressive Stalinist era was committed in the name of communism, an ideology that, ironically, embodies the realization of the socialist dream to liberate the poor and oppressed masses. Far too many times in human history, political and ideological propaganda has deceived masses of people.

This second lesson clearly echoes the atrocities committed by the Nazis and Japanese armies during World War II. The Nazis provide one of the most vivid examples of self-righteousness in their development of nationalist and racist myths promoting the superiority of the Aryan race, an ancient northern European people, and the inferiority of the Jewish people. The resulting millions of deaths remain a permanent scar on our century. Historians, archaeologists, anthropologists, and other academics were used to advance the Nazi's scientific research. But Robert Proctor, in *Racial Hygiene* (1988), demonstrated that the widespread perception of a passive scientific community coerced into cooperation with the Nazis fails to grasp the reality of what actually happened, that is, many of the political initiatives of the Nazis arose from within the scientific community itself and medical scientists actively designed and administered key elements of the National socialist policy. Proctor also presented a comprehensive account of German medical involvement in the development of sterilization and castration laws, the laws banning marriage between Jews and non-Jews, and the massive program to destroy lives not worth living. His study traced attempts on the part of doctors to conceive of the Jewish problem as a medical problem and revealed how medical journals openly discussed the need to find a final solution to Germany's Jewish and Gypsy problems. Proctor is careful to make us aware that such thinking was not unique to Germany. We find its counterpart in Japanese militarism in Asia around the same time. For instance, the involvement of the Japanese armies at the Nanjing Massacre. Most Americans, with their Cold War mentality, are not aware of this chilling echo of Nazism. The uncomfortable truth is that the Social Darwinism of the late nineteenth century in America and Europe gave rise to theories of racial hygiene that enthusiasts of various nationalities embraced in the hope of breeding an ostensibly better, healthier, stronger race of people.

In discussing political or religious fanaticism, we are reminded that Chinese are mostly practical, not ideological. Despite reprehensible crimes that certain Chinese emperors committed in the name of their heavenly power, such rulers were neither ideologically nor religiously oriented. Even though those imperial days are gone forever, we have learned from Chinese history that catastrophe often accompanied the involvement of ideology in national affairs. For instance, early Confucianism was very practical in nature, and its virtues were allied with human spontaneity and education. As Confucianism became more ideological and political during the Han dynasty, its doctrines grew increasingly dogmatic, and proponents sank more into hypocrisy. Then in the name of Neo-Confucianism, the Ming and Qing dynasties became despotic. Society stagnated, and the people suffered. When the People's Republic adopted Marxist/Leninist Communism as its ideology in 1949, social and political experimentations, such as the Great Leap Forward and the Cultural Revolution, resulted in instability, untold suffering, and death for millions of Chinese people. It was not until Deng Xiaoping boldly put aside all ideologies that China was able to return to the path of economic reconstruction, initiating the growing national prosperity we witness today. This is a lesson that all countries of the world should learn, particularly those experiencing significant development. Peace-loving citizens of the world should always be on guard against political and religious leaders who discriminate between people or wage war against others in the name of ideology or religion.

• **Lesson Three:** Human creativity is the basis for technological, social, economic, and political advancement as well as fulfillment and happiness. Because cultural, social, and political diversity, built on a foundation of harmonious human values, is a prerequisite for such creativity, plurality is therefore a basic foundational requirement for human existence and a way to maintain creativity and spontaneity, which opens the path to fulfillment and happiness for all people.

The Chinese precept of diversity in harmony is particularly relevant in understanding the application of this third lesson to our ever-contracting global village. The most creative period in human history is what Karl Jasper has called the Axial Age. In about the same span of several centuries, intellectual systems around the world generated various classical systems of ideas and values. For example, the One Hundred School period of China's Warring States, Greece's Classical Golden Age, and the Upanishads and Buddhism in India. Although some critics disagree with the term of "Axial Age," it was indeed a period of immense creativity coincident with a broad diversity of technological, cultural, social, economic, and political advancements. The creativity of this era has remained unmatched by any other time with only the industrial and contemporary information revolutions perhaps approaching similar significance. Indeed, the dynamism unleashed during the Axial Age continues to this day.

Yet, diversity does not preclude commonality and shared values. Between friends and among families, societies, and states, it is an innate characteristic that we enjoy human commonality and shared values, such as mutual affection for each other, love, loyalty, happiness, and a dislike of alienation, hatred, betrayal, and misery. Thus, pluralism refers both to the infinite variety of individual values, personalities, and goals and the complexities and fellowship of social belonging, which is essential for fulfillment and happiness for all humankind, not just a few.

In an age of increasing specialization, there is a growing need for integration to supplement specialization. No complex, nonlinear system can be adequately described by dividing it into subsystems or various predefined aspects. If those subsystems, all existing in strong interaction with one another, are studied separately, even with great care, the results, when put together, do not give a useful picture of the whole. That is why human interconnectedness is so important.

Diversity, however, is a double-edged sword because it manifests potentially volatile human emotions and values. On one hand, diversity empowers innovation and creativity. Cultural and political diversity, built on a foundation of common values, are essential for human progress, just as biodiversity is important to bioevolution. On the other hand, diversity can generate conflicts, which can lead to destruction if not handled properly. This is why the Chinese model of diversity in harmony provides such an important social value and political ideal.

To grasp this precept, we need to understand and apply the concept of interdependence as a foundation for positive relationship building. It must first occur in the context of two individuals. It must then occur within societies and nations and finally among diverse global states. Harmony implies dignity, trust, respect, and community. It also demands the development of clear rules determined by common consensus and derived from shared values and a rigorous policing of those rules in order to control emotions and greed, thus binding the participants together. We need rules and institutions to enable us to make decisions, express our collective judgment of right and wrong, and protect diversity in harmony. Once set in place, these rules and institutions must then be allowed to evolve according to our collective moral sense. If any single party begins to believe it has a monopoly on truth or wisdom, evil will germinate (Lesson Two).

- **Lesson Four:** Every person, culture, society, and state is unique, yet each shares some essential attributes with others. In order for a person, culture, society, or state to survive and flourish, it must absorb nutrients both from its own tradition and the traditions of others. But it cannot simply copy. Traditional and external political, religious, and economic ideas and concepts are applicable to current situations only after they are properly digested, synthesized, internalized, and integrated under local conditions and contexts. The record of human existence is a narrative of understanding, overcoming, and recreating our own assumptions, traditions, received wisdom, and culturally conditioned viewpoints in order to appreciate and accommodate the viewpoints and the resulting actions of others, past or present. In the face of the ever-changing conditions and problems that humankind faces, ideals, traditions, and established institutions must be dynamically transformed and renewed.

In the course of our daily lives and scientific endeavors, we build on our knowledge, a mass of theories that have held up to testing over extended periods of time. Because these theories have not been falsified by such repeated testing, they become part of our store of human knowledge. Certain knowledge accumulates through time and becomes the basis of custom or tradition. Most traditions, past or present, are forged in association with the activities by which human beings meet their needs for existence. Through which, they aspire for fulfillment.

Accordingly, tradition is not an abstract contrivance that eschews change and development. Its vitality actually lies in its development.

At the personal level, continuous learning and self-cultivation from our own and other people's traditions are of utmost importance for our success and fulfillment under any conditions. More broadly, according to historian Robbie Robertson, the history of humanity, especially over the past five hundred years, is marked by a similar process of ever-developing interconnectedness. This interdependence has extended opportunities for human empowerment and promoted social transformation via the influence of varying human environments, population sizes and movements, technologies, economies, and cultures. Differences between these factors have always ensured that no one society or state became identical to another. The uniqueness of individuals, societies, and states is therefore presupposed.

Tu Wei-ming contended, "Just as the self must overcome egoism to become authentically human, the family must overcome parochialism, the state must overcome ethnocentrism, the world must overcome anthropocentrism to become authentically human" (1989).

Indeed, the advancement of humankind's cultural, social, and political states can be measured by degrees of self-transcendence. The Renaissance and the Industrial Revolution with its accompanying modernization furnish the best examples of how traditions are transformed and renewed when new conditions are introduced into the sphere of human existence. We have gleaned from Chinese history that, at the personal level, the individual achievements of historical figures have always been measured by the degree to which he or she was self-cultivated and able to self-transcend with the ultimate goal of serving the family, society, and state. Similarly, at the state level, the most prosperous times in Chinese history have always been those periods when China was open to foreign influence and emperors listened to the advice of their officials, for example, the early Tang dynasty. The worst times occurred when China was closed to foreign influence and emperors and their officials were unreceptive to advice, for example, the Ming dynasty. One of the best examples for successful cross-cultural synthesis, the fruit of the former more open stance, was the sinicization of Buddhism from India during the Sui and Tang dynasties.

At the global level, the world today is enjoying an unprecedented prosperity, evident since the latter part of the twentieth century, when information technology began to transform the way we communicate and learn from each other with the result that we have overcome some of our traditions and prejudices.

Respecting diversity and learning from others does not mean that we cease to recognize and acknowledge strengths and weaknesses. Some cultural values are more suited to our present human needs than others. Some economic systems are more productive. Some political structures are better able to mobilize the creative energies of their people. We must be honest and courageous enough to concede that others may be superior to us in a particular arena and it is in our interest to learn from them. Still, no individual or collective should force its views on another. We cannot impose ideological, religious, political, or economic systems on societies whose histories and traditions differ from our own. We need to create an open environment that encourages mutual learning and healthy competition. Human connectedness, productivity, prosperity, and fulfillment are inextricably related.

CHAPTER FOURTEEN

Learning from Each Other

The previous seven chapters were concerned with the history of China and Europe and the philosophy of history itself. These chapters show where we have been by comparing the forces, specifically cultural, social, political, and religious at work in various stages of Chinese and Western history and examining the outcomes of diverse value systems, beliefs, philosophies, and thinking preferences. Before we can answer how we can learn from each other, let us first look at the past, present, and future trends in order to see where we are going from here.

Section One: Where Are We Going from Here?

History deals with individual and group responses to the state of their natural and social environment. These responses are influenced by all the experiences to which the individuals' ancestors were exposed in combination with those to which they themselves have been exposed so far. In addition, historical action is a dynamic process of creating, diffusing, and manifesting values, which retain the character of their respective era.

Each historical era is characterized by its vision, ideas, principles, value systems, general methods, actions of its people, and decisions of its inhabitants to either select from their own traditions or emulate the traditions of others, depending on what is considered best suited to the environmental conditions and cultural contexts of the day. This process is sporadic and nonlinear. Its outcome, while unpredictable, is seldom something to be judged right or wrong in itself. Ultimately, history must judge these processes based on their potential for and achievements in the improvement of the welfare of their own people and their contribution to other people. Many thinkers of our time are engaged in examining our world, traditions, and relationship to cultures throughout human history, searching for the ideas, dynamics, and characteristics of our own era and the meanings we carry with us into a new millennium.

Indeed, we are here at the dawn of the twenty-first century, a new millennium. From every indication, we are in the midst of changes of immense proportions with profound significance. This is what we have called the third wave, information revolution, space age, or global village. The major theme of the new millennium is clearly technology, globalization, and post-postmodern reconstruction. These elements impact us drastically, having already reached virtually every home in every corner of our world with a speed unmatched at any other time in history.

Challenges of the Twenty-first Century

China and the West face different challenges in the new millennium. Each of these cultures exists as it does today because of the products or by-products of distinct cultures, histories, and traditions. Each civilization is progressing through its own stages, pursuing diverging paths of cultural, economic, social, and political development.

The United States and Europe are highly industrialized, militarily strong, and culturally and politically influential, and they contain a mass of powerful, globally competitive firms. In addition, the United States and Europe can assert strong controls over international capital movements when they deem such controls are needed. However, the West's traditional social, religious, and political institutions are showing signs of decline and await a renewal. In the post-postmodern Western world, there exists a need for reconstruction, a searching for new meaning and redefinition with regard to many of its cultural, social, and political values and traditions. Among them are capitalism, democracy, individualism, communitarianism, neo-liberalism, the rule of law, and other ideals. Hopefully, these renewed visions lead to future directions and new traditions will evolve. Further, through this renewal, some of the challenges of the new millennium, specifically globalization, sustainability of industrial development, limited resources, wealth imbalance, terrorism, social degradation, and so forth, can begin to be addressed. Yet, many of the challenges we face in the new millennium cannot be solved without a critical breakthrough in our own thinking, attitude, philosophy, and established traditions. Other cultures and spiritual resources, those of the Chinese and others from the non-Western world, cannot provide answers. But they can help by offering what they have learned from their own tradition, thought, philosophy, and experience in meeting similar problems in their own history. Through the eyes of others, perhaps we in the West can see our own situation in a revealing light.

China, in contrast to the United States and Europe and despite its great economic achievements over the last two decades, is comparatively weak technologically, economically, politically, and militarily. It faces many social and ethical problems typically encountered in the development of Third World countries. In addition, China has problems of an historical nature, such as the threat of segregation across the Taiwanese Strait. Thus, China also needs a cultural and spiritual renewal. Although China is now taking only small, single steps, it is bestowed with one of the most unique opportunities of our time. It has a chance to build new social, legal, and political institutions as well as new ideals and traditions that will have profound and lasting consequence for the entire world, not just the Chinese people. China can benefit greatly from the experience of advanced developed countries as multiple forces converge on a China in the process of transforming itself.

More importantly, from our perspective, China must guard against repeating the mistakes that some advanced countries have made in their own development, such as overdependence on privately owned automobiles and disregard for damage to our ecological systems. Given the immense Chinese population and the country's limited natural resources, neither China nor Mother Earth can survive the same model that the United States, Europe, and Japan have adopted in their road to industrialization. Sustainability is the key word, and China must be creative and innovative in its development. The rest of the world should offer its help wherever it can because we are all in this situation together. There is only one global village. The destiny of China is no longer an individual, local, or national issue. It is a regional and global one. Its successes and failures are now and will always be of global proportion and significance.

In this section, we will concentrate on the major themes of technology and globalization, attempting to understand them from an historical perspective and conducting a search for its trends and future implications. Some of the evident trends are not entirely optimistic. Astronomer Martin Rees (2003) pointed out that humanity is more at risk in the twenty-first century than ever before, for example, the misapplication of science, acts of mega terror and open warfare between nuclear powers, human-induced pressures on the global environment, and natural calamities, and the new diseases that occupy so much media attention today. However, in this book, we will concentrate on human aspirations, that is, the positive and some of the negative, aspects of our human endeavors under both favorable and unfavorable conditions. Within this focus, we will assume the best human ingenuity and creativity are available because we have already witnessed these qualities during the end of the last century. We will then present some thoughts on the social, cultural, and political consequences of globalization and technological advancement and the need for post-postmodern reconstruction. Our goal is to cultivate an understanding of the aspirations of our own time and discern trends, especially in Chinese and Western civilizations. From which, we can effectively address the important questions of why must we learn from each other and how.

Knowledge-based Society

The so-called third wave civilization, according to the progenitor of the term, Alvin Toffler, is an information and knowledge-based society that emerged from the industrial society of the second wave. It is responsible for many changes that we see in today's world, including new family and social relationships; ways of working, loving, and living; a new economy; new political conflicts and regional wars; and an altered consciousness beyond all of this. These outcomes are the result of powerful new technologies reshaping our world, including computers, electronic communications, jet and space travel, high-tech weaponry, applied biotechnology, nuclear and natural power, and the capacity of the Internet to link literate individuals and businesses into a global network of communication, commerce, and learning. The third wave, as Toffler described, brings a genuinely new way of life based on diversified, renewable, energy sources; methods of production that make most factory-assembly lines obsolete; new, non-nuclear families; novel institutions; and radically changed schools and corporations of the future. The emergent civilization continues to write a new code of behavior, carrying us beyond the standardization, massification, synchronization, and centralization of the industrial era and beyond the previously witnessed concentration of energy, money, and power. It asserts the current technological, economic, political, and cultural upheavals are not random or chaotic occurrences. Rather, they are steps in the formation of a new era. Toffler argued that, in this new era, the control of knowledge has become the principal means to create wealth and power.

Toffler's major forecasts for the twenty-first century include the disappearance of anything resembling a factory-based production system, mass customized products with consumers integrated into the production process, empowerment of the home rather than the society, decentralization of ideas and duties, and attainment of the ideal of congruence between private and public sectors. Aided by the widespread use of computers and other communications technologies, this power shift to knowledge-based structures will dramatically alter the world's institutions and social and political balance. Michael Mazarr (1999) echoed Toffler on the issues of technological, social, and economic changes by taking insights from a host of disciplines, for example, economics, sociology, political science, and others, and molding them into a comprehensive view of the forces he predicted will shape the future, forces that will be empowering, democratizing, egalitarian, and environmentally healthy. Mazarr contended that the knowledge era tends to break down boundaries between disciplines, industries, and countries. As boundaries between disciplines fade, the lines connecting many diverse fields, like threads of an interdisciplinary reality, become crucial. We recognize many of those threads already and call them networks and systems. Mazarr also outlined three of the most important factors in the transition to the new society: the decisive role of education, the primacy of moral values, and the need for a renewed capitalism, which, unlike the capitalism Marx described, is a system responsive to human values that is built on the foundation of a healthy society and demonstrates respect for human beings and natural ecology. The goal of such capitalism, according to Mazarr, is fulfillment of the inherent capacities of the individual and new possibilities of the society, nation, and race; the satisfaction of human needs, spiritual as well as material; the emergence of new qualities of experience to be enjoyed; and the building of personalities.

This interpretation of imminent social changes is similar to that of Harry Dent (1998), whose new paradigm, the network organization, argued that we are moving from a standardized top-down assembly line organization to a customized bottom-up network organization model, capable of handling all routine left brain thinking work. The result is a return to a customer focus, that is, the resurgence of small, dynamic working teams and placing more value on creative, right brain, entrepreneurial skills. In our lifetimes, we will see a return to small-town living, albeit with a high-tech emphasis, with increased political participation and decision-making in our local communities, more diverse lifestyles, and a lower-cost, higher-quality standard of living due to less congestion and pollution. The sophisticated communication technologies driving the current information revolution will ironically make our world more human, specifically creative, interactive, and intimate. According to these optimistic views, human interactivity and creativity will come to the fore while bureaucracy and technocracy will recede into the background.

The so-called network or right brain revolution, the real information revolution, will have two components: the increasing automation of repetitive, left brain tasks and the linking of all customers, workers, and organizations into one real-time communication system via network and Internet technologies. In this context, the browser-server model of networked systems works well for both management of information and human organizations.

The fundamental idea behind the browser-server model is to push as much information as possible to the frontline browser so users have the information they need at their fingertips to make rapid and creative decisions. More specialized information, which is consequently used less often, is stored on servers, where it acts as support upon demand. Employees in the back line, who specialize in particular kinds of products or knowledge, help those on the front line. This model is exactly what we see on the Internet today. We can anticipate companies and other institutions beginning to function as networks of human front-line browsers and back-line/servers, a system that would eliminate the bureaucracy that so frequently interferes with the efficient interaction between the two. Entire industries, governments, and nations could reorganize themselves via this model, rapidly meeting their users' particular needs. Many new and novel forms of social, political, and cultural institution will be developed based on this model.

Globalization

Accompanying the rapid technological advancement of the twenty-first century are the dynamics of globalization. Globalization means many things to many people. How one defines it often reflects as much about one's worldview as it says about the phenomenon itself. The diverse drivers for globalization are technological, economic, historical, cultural, and political, and they have resulted in a world that is now more interdependent, connected, smaller, and faster-paced. Globalization, in turn, is the underlying structural dynamic that drives social, political, economic, and cultural-ideological processes around the world. The spatial reach and density of global and transnational interconnectedness weaves complex webs and networks of relations between communities, states, international institutions, nongovernmental organizations, and multinational corporations, networks that comprise the emergent global order. Borders have become more permeable; nations appear to have less power relative to corporations and civil society than in the past. Under the conditions of globalization, local, national, and even continental notions of political, social and economic space are reformed, such that they are no longer necessarily coterminous with established legal and territorial boundaries. Some examples of this change can be seen in new regional economic zones, such as the EU (European Union), NAFTA (North America Free Trade Association), APEC (Asia-Pacific Economic Cooperation) and ASEAN (Association of Southeast Asian Nations); new mechanisms of governance, for example, WTO (World Trade Organization), the World Bank, and IMF (International Monetary Fund); new cultural complexes, such as the Asian

Diaspora; and an increase in the number of standards applied globally, such as intellectual property and copyright laws.

Corporate globalization usually begins with international trade. After selling products across national borders, corporations move to foreign investment. Such investment then frequently results in the production of products and services in a foreign country as a means of avoiding transportation costs or import restrictions or take advantage of less expensive labor, capital, or materials. The resulting integration of local, national, and regional economies, partially because of advances in transportation and communication technologies, creates new global pools of labor, financing, and other resources in addition to a common technology base and marketplace. Above all, it has begun transforming the world into one single economy.

Indeed, globalization has created a niche that multinational corporations has rapidly filled. From a corporation's point of view, globalization can be defined more narrowly as a process of corporate structuring that focuses a company's core competency on the worldwide market and creates growth and profits through larger sales, economies of scale, more cost-effective production and distribution, access to less expensive capital, lower labor costs, and an increasing number of common elements of design and production. Joint ventures, acquisitions, co-production, and licensing are some of the legal structures that can further a corporation's globalization efforts.

However, the resources and power gained through many corporations' rapid expansion into this niche has undermined some of the prerogatives of the nation-state. Sovereign nations have been crisscrossed and undermined by multinational actors, notably corporations that export jobs to parts of the world where labor costs are lowest and those that induce competition between countries and locations that are competing to provide the cheapest fiscal conditions for potential investors. Nevertheless, economic globalization has become identified with a number of positive trends, including freer trade; greater international movement of commodities, money, information, and people; and the general development of globe-spanning markets and economic relationships. Most economists applaud economic globalization because it promotes efficiency and specialization.

Critics of globalization, however, have associated globalization with widening economic and social disparities, both nationally and globally; the growing exhaustion of natural resources; and damage to the natural environment and the ecological system. A closer examination by David Korten (2001) revealed that the globalization process has created "expanding islands of wealth in poor countries and swelling seas of poverty in wealthy countries." Consider a single statistic that Korten quoted:

There are now [in 1998] 477 billionaires in the world, up from only 274 in 1991. Their combined assets are roughly equal to the combined annual incomes of the poorest half of humanity—2.8 billion people.

This is a direct consequence of an unregulated global economy. In a lecture to the twenty-second World Conference of the Society for International Development, Korten expressed his doubt about some of the beneficial effects of the global economy. He stated that there is:

> ... an epic struggle of power and values between people most everywhere and the institutions of the global economy. The outcome of this struggle will likely determine whether the twenty-first century marks the descent of our species into an anarchy of greed, violence, deprivation, and environmental destruction that could well lead to our own extinction. Or the emergence of prosperous life-centered civil societies in which all people are able to live without want in peace with one another and in balance with the planet. (1997)

Robertson's third wave of globalization is understood as the outcome of increasing democratization and human connectedness. In addition to the economic effects of these changes, this connectivity is a process of developing a new global consciousness, a nascent consciousness that focuses on the importance of understanding our place in the universe, the nature of that universe, and the evolution of humans as a species. Robertson's proposal for developing global consciousness suggests that we:

> first ... direct our basic desires into forms that can be achieved without war, and in cooperative ways. It is in this respect that ideologies, institutions and education come into their own. But second, we need to remember that our very basic material desires require equally basic material solutions. Human history ... has demonstrated that of all the strategies experienced by the people, democratization has the greatest chance of success. And quite explicitly, democratization means more than just the right to vote and hold opinions independent of church and state. It means, as postwar strategists have argued, economic democratization, the deepening of markets, and individual empowerment. It is these that the third wave or its successor must now consciously address on a global scale. (2003)

Similarly, the Swiss theologian Hans Kung formulated a global ethic that contains four commitments: a culture of nonviolence and respect of life; a culture of solidarity and a just economic order; a culture of tolerance and a life of truthfulness; and a culture of equal rights, particularly with respect to racial and gender equality (1998). Indeed, where globalization takes us from here strongly depends on how well we can implement these social and ethical commitments, strategies, and actions.

Globalization also raises another important social issue, that is, the polarization of skills and knowledge. Globalization is progressively exposing social fissures between those with the education, skills, and mobility to flourish in an unfettered world market, that is, the apparent winners, and those without such resources. These apparent losers are increasingly anxious about their standards of living and future security. The result is severe tension between the market and broad sectors of society with government caught in the middle. Dani Rodrik (1997) asked if globalization has gone too far. He argued forcefully that the world economy faces a serious challenge in ensuring that international economic integration does not contribute to domestic social disintegration. He focused on three major sources of tension between globalization and social stability: the transformation of the employment relationship, conflict between international trade and social norms, and the pressures brought to bear on national governments in maintaining domestic cohesion and social welfare systems. Rodrik made a unique and persuasive case that the winners have as much at stake from the possible consequences of social instability as do the losers. He pointed out that "social disintegration is not a spectator sport; those on the sidelines also get splashed with mud from the field. Ultimately, the deepening of social fissures can harm all" (1997). Thus, the problems of unequal wealth distribution must be solved fairly, nationally, and internationally, if we are to proceed responsibly.

According to Robertson, the first two waves of globalization failed because the goals of its hegemons, namely Spain, Holland, Great Britain, and other European powers, were always nationally or imperially focused. Globalization became the exclusive tool for their own national aggrandizement, often achieved by institutionalized coercive power. But exclusion as the basis for sustainable global interactions is paradoxical. The same might be said of the hegemon of the third wave, the United States. Its globalism did at least set in place institutions capable of, in theory if not in practice, independently developing global policies. The difference partially lies in the United States' desire to avoid the mistakes of the second wave, but it also lies in the fact that American hegemony coincided with a remarkable process of democratization that radically transformed their society and enabled the emergence of dynamic structures for global cooperation. Unfortunately, American foreign policies are often double standards. The domestic ideal of democracy, liberty, and equality is inconsistent with many of its foreign actions. Nevertheless, the trend toward political globalization, or global governance, is slowly evolving. If it continues to do so, it will eventuate in a single global state that could effectively outlaw warfare and enforce its illegality, such as is gradually happening through the United Nations, NATO, and other regional organizations.

Citizens of our world should not allow globalization to be privatized for any special interest or become the privileged agenda of national and transnational entities. Robertson emphasized that "people need to reclaim ownership of globalization and democratize the process." David Loy (2003), an authority on Western Buddhism, preached that people should transform the three causes of human suffering, that is, greed, ill will, and delusion, into their positive counterparts of generosity, loving kindness, and wisdom. The need for this transformation is equally applicable to global institutions.

Combining the opportunities for technological advancement with the dynamic trends of globalization and assuming that negative effects can be overcome, there is a case for guarded optimism for the twenty-first century. This view is grounded in the belief that human ingenuity and willpower can overcome many of the problems facing us, as our past history has demonstrated. A study by researchers of the Hudson Institute, published in *Riding the Next Wave* (ed. Duesterberg and London 2001), emphasized the importance of new technology in solving some of our current problems and presented an overview of the possible contours of the twenty-first century by exploring the probability and scope of change in demographics, national defense, biotechnology, urban development, space exploration, and much more. The authors predicted that many economic, demographic, and technological forces, such as demassification, improved efficiency, invention of new technologies, decentralization of economies, recycling, alternative materials, and new resources, will contribute to an easing of pressure on twenty-first century resources and the natural environment. They projected a century of success and tremendous growth spreading throughout the globe, benefiting workers and developing countries in ways previously thought unattainable outside the industrialized world. According to their projections, the world of the twenty-first century will offer more wealth, longer life expectancy, improved security, and greater opportunity for the exercise of free will than people have ever known before. However, we contend that an understanding of many critical provisions and conditions should appropriately temper this optimism. One of these provisions is the successful reconstruction of post-postmodern ethics.

Ethical Reconstruction

Modernity is characterized by its underlying Enlightenment mentality of rationalism, individualism, universality, progress, fraternity, liberty, equality, democracy, and capitalism. This Enlightenment mentality is still the most influential moral discourse in the political culture of the modern age. It manifests itself as human awakening, the discovery of the human potential for global transformation, and the realization of human desire to become the measure and master of all things.

This mentality, however, met with critical review after World War II and especially during the Vietnam War in the mid-1960s. The story of postwar ethics is one of accelerated disillusion, cynicism, and uncertainty. The efficient and rational industrialized slaughter of millions of innocent civilians by a civilized Western nation hastened an erosion of belief in human potential and its ideological and ethical progress. These wars clearly made the central role of reason in planning and discharging so much human suffering. As a result, a comprehensive understanding of the Enlightenment mentality requires a frank discussion of the dark side of the modern West as well.

The paradox in the West of our Enlightenment heritage nudged us to the edge of the new abyss of postmodernism. Postmodern thinkers began to question all traditional values. They reminded us how self-contained and liquid language and meanings are and how dangerous this liquidity can be. Postmodern ethical skepticism then turned into relativism. Postmodernism, globalization, and rapid technological changes have continued to create uncertainty, variety, insecurity, and social alienation while eroding communality. Our present society is characterized by multinational corporations, information superhighways, technology-driven sciences, mass communications media, and conspicuous consumption. We are frequent conversation partners with associates thousands of miles away, but we are just as frequently strangers to our neighbors, colleagues, and relatives. The global village exhibits "sharp difference, severe differentiation, drastic demarcation, thunderous dissonance, and outright discrimination. The world, compressed into an interconnected ecological, financial, commercial, trading, and electronic system, has never been so divided in wealth, influence, and power" (Tu 1998).

Even in the most economically advanced nations, the pervasive mood is one of discontent, anxiety, and frustration. It is a dangerous truth that, if people feel helpless, politically alienated, and isolated from the decision-making process, they will not fulfill their roles as informed participants in a democratic process. For many, life generally loses its purpose. On the other hand, religious extremism, such as the Islamic and Christian fundamentalist movements, grows at a rapid pace, threatening world peace. Thus, it is the greatest challenge of the new millennium to redefine our own identity and relationship with others, seek new social and political meaning in our institutions, and reconstruct common ideals and traditions. The best first step in meeting such challenges may be to understand and learn from our own past and benefit from the thinking preferences, local conditions, customs, cultures, and traditions of other societies across the globe and throughout history.

According to John Dewey, a chief task of those who call themselves philosophers is to help rid us of the useless lumber that blocks our highways of thought and make clear our path to the future. According to Hall and Ames (Bell and Chaibong 2003), some of the lumber blocking the highways of thought between China and the West includes a legal formalism that mitigates the role of rituals as socializing processes; a concept of the autonomous individual that would negate the Confucian sense of the socially constituted self; a quantitative concept of equality that fails to note the qualitative distinctiveness of persons; an economic system that further exacerbates the pervasiveness of merely quantitative considerations of merit; a preoccupation with formal institutions as the determinative criteria for adjudicating social progress; and an insistence upon individual rights to the detriment of social responsibilities. The authors asserted that the American pragmatic tradition offers an attractive resource for the engagement of Confucian and Western sensibilities on the subject of democratic ideals and institutions precisely because its intellectual goals and practices are not developments of the European Enlightenment and do not, therefore, share the features of modernity that would disqualify it as a possible connector, or mediator, with Asian sensibilities. Nevertheless, before we are all able to clear our highways of thought, we shall return to the reality of the present world.

Section Two:
Challenges Facing the West

At the beginning of the third millennium, the immediate challenges facing developed Western nations in the global arena are clear, specifically international terrorism, communal violence, and sectarian conflicts. Most are rooted in religion and history. In addition, nuclear proliferation and the threat of a nuclear war, a dark cloud that still hangs over humanity, escalates the danger anytime there is tension or conflict between the world's nuclear powers.

The War on Terrorism

In the first lesson in the last chapter, McNamara and the experience of the Vietnam War impart the lessons of a tragedy caused and prolonged by misconceptions, misunderstanding, misjudgment, miscalculation, miscommunication, and mutual ignorance of each other's thinking, intentions, history, and cultural traditions. The current leadership of the United States has obviously not learned from this lesson in Vietnam.

More than five years after the horrendous events of September 11, 2001, the decision-makers of the United States remain committed to the same mistakes in their war against international terrorism, communal violence, and sectarian conflicts. They still essentially ignore the thinking, culture, tradition, history, and social and political conditions of their adversaries. For example, American ignorance of the difference between fundamentalist Islamic terrorism, such as that espoused by *Al Qaeda*, and the secular despotic regime of Saddam Hussein, which is similar only in that both are products of culture and history, has led the United States into the second war in Iraq, a diversion to and expansion of the war on terrorism. By invading and occupying Iraq, the United States extended rather than confined the battle. This extension of the battlefield has spread available resources thin, increased casualties, provoked fear in most Muslim countries, alienated allies, and dishonored the United Nations. The situation is further aggravated by the absence of a comprehensive American postwar strategy, which also would need to be built on an understanding of Iraqi culture, religion, and tradition.

It is true that Islamic fundamentalism is a serious threat to humanity, but Bush's doctrine is just as deadly. President Bush's national security strategy delivered in a speech at West Point, New York on June 1, 2002 commits the United States to "defend[ing] liberty and justice because these principles are right and true for all people everywhere." It also promises to:

> [S]tand firmly for the non-negotiable demands of human dignity: the rule of law; limits on the absolute power of state; free speech; freedom of worship; equal justice; respect for women; religious and ethnic tolerance; and respect of private property.

While these values are defensible in their own right, the self-righteous attitude, unilateralism, and strategy of preemptive war is irrational, ineffective, unconvincing, and dangerous to their foes and allies alike and most other countries as well, as espoused in the second lesson.

Despite the overwhelming superiority of the American military and its allies, killing and suffering persists in the Middle East with no end in sight. Neither

Americans nor most other people of the world feel any safer from terrorism, and the danger of prolonged and expanded regional war mounts ever higher. It could easily involve Lebanon, Syria, and Iran. If we are not careful, our current barely tenable situation threatens to develop into a clash between civilizations, placing world peace further in jeopardy.

This ruinous development does not result from lack of resolution on the part of the United States and its allies. Billions of dollars have been spent already, large amounts of American money still pour in, and the mighty force of America is fully committed. We are certain that the American government is sparing nothing in the effort to win this war, but its critics argue that it is not winnable with the present strategy. With the possible development of weapons of mass destruction, whether nuclear, chemical, or biological, and the possibility of conflict between nuclear powers, the very existence of civilization as we know it today could easily be threatened. Our world simply cannot afford another arms race that could lead to a full-scale war, unleashing such potential destructive power that the world might not be able to recover from its catastrophic effects. Obviously, at this point, innovative ideas are needed if world peace is to be maintained. Creative thinking, workable strategies, and maybe a brand-new approach or paradigm are required.

In chapter three, we illustrated that Western thinking preferences are causal, absolute, rational, static, and substantial, characteristics which subsequently led to ontological and religious dualism. This dualism is clearly demonstrated by President Bush's frequent characterization of the war on terrorism as a war between the "civilized" people and "an ungodly civilization lacking any core spiritual values" or between "freedom and democracy" and "evil," "coward[liness]," and "irrational[ity]." In successive statements, American leaders assume that God is allied exclusively with the American people and the right-minded of the world in their response to the evil nature of the terrorists. The same dualistic thinking is also apparent on the other side of the conflict. Cultures with some sympathy for the terrorists assume that Allah is on their side in opposing the evil impact on their communities of American policy and Western civilization. They label the United States and Israel as big Satan and little Satan, respectively.

As described in chapter thirteen, this self-righteous attitude and dualistic thinking is perilous, providing little prospect that the war against terrorism will experience either conflict reconciliation or problem resolution. This is, after all, the same dualistic rationale that we saw during the Cold War, endangering world peace with the threat of a nuclear encounter that could produce no winner. If there is any hope for future rapprochement between adversaries or even just a simple compromise, the mind-set and attitude of both sides must be more accommodating. Ideas or mediation facilitated by a third party, an independently distinctive civilization experienced in conflict and religious resolution, such as the Chinese, might help to mollify such intricate situations.

In chapter thirteen, we also mentioned that religious extremism is responsible for much of the human suffering throughout Western history. Yet, religion, defined in a broad sense, is important in all societies and occupies a crucial place in all cultures. Here, an interesting observation comes to the fore. Throughout history, religious belief is the area wherein the Chinese diverge most conspicuously from Westerners. For most people in the West, a person's religious affiliation is a matter of total commitment. Choosing one religion implies exclusion from all other religions. In recent years, parallel to the multiculturalism movement, there have been debates among Western theologians about religious pluralism and religious diversity. Pope Benedict XVII actually condones these new initiatives. Yet this seemingly novel concept of multicitizenship in religion has always been a part of everyday life for the Chinese (Chenyang Li 1999).

In Chinese culture, there is a fairly harmonious interplay between the three major religions of Confucianism, Daoism, and Buddhism. Not only is this interplay evident in society as a whole, it is within individuals as well. A Chinese person can pay tribute to a Daoist temple today and participate in a Buddhist ceremony tomorrow, all the while claiming devotion to Confucianism. As described in chapters three and six, the Chinese have a tendency to strive for a balance by harmonizing the different aspects of objects found within their lives. The tendency is to let each aspect have its turn. Thus, instead of mixing together, they work together alternately. In Chinese thinking, different religions have different strengths and weaknesses. Therefore, they may play different roles in the same person's life. However, for Westerners to adopt such an attitude would require a very drastic change in religious thinking, necessitating a belief in certain human values, such as love, that transcends religion.

With regard to terrorism, the challenge we face in Western society lies in the fact that terrorism is a symptom, not a cause. According to Edward Woo (2002), there are eight causes of terrorism:

- Hatred, revenge, retaliation, the concept of an eye for an eye

- Deviant notions of justice

- Misguided interpretation of religious teachings

- Frustration created by oppression with no solution in sight

- Fanatical impulse

- Perverted senses of nationalism and patriotism

- The lack of a proper sense of righteousness

- Greed, specifically making use of patriotism or revenge as a justification for criminal conduct.

These eight causes apply equally as sources of motivation for individuals, groups, or state-sponsored terrorism. Whatever the real cause may be in the present case of terrorism, we can all agree that the perpetrators should receive due punishment. Beyond that, the way to solve the problem of terrorism is with prevention by finding a way to reduce and, if possible, eliminate the underlying grievances. Confucius teaches us in *The Analects*, "We must not impose on others what we don't want them to impose on us."

In chapter six, we described Chinese precepts of harmony in diversity, ritual, warfare, and the propensity of things. All can contribute to the amiable handling of the situation under discussion. The solution is to refrain from dualist thinking characterized by us against them. Instead, we must try to think in terms of complementarity, understanding, empathy, tolerance, generosity, and mutual respect. This is particularly true for a party in the position of dominance, such as the United States and Europe. If we could view terrorism as a terrible last act of desperation, engaged in by people who believed they had no other way to make themselves heard than to resort to violence and mayhem, even to the point of sacrificing their own lives, we could afford to extend the traditional Christian values of generosity, forgiveness, and empathy to our less-fortunate adversaries.

On the more practical side, justifiable grievances, for example, the plight of refugees, must be adequately addressed so some important sources of terrorist recruitment can be eliminated. Money is better spent in these camps and regions than in armaments. The United Nations and other international organizations, too, must play a key role for peace. It is time for the mending of fences and settling historical differences and animosities, a project we are sure the majority of the world's people would support, especially in this age of the shrinking global community. As citizens of the world and especially as citizens of developed countries, we have the responsibility to avail ourselves of our democratic rights and ensure our governments' policies are beneficial to humanity.

Spiritual Rejuvenation

This brings us to the next set of millennial challenges that the West faces, that is, our dated spirituality, ideals, and institutions. Toward the end of the preceding section, we outlined the condition of the post-postmodern Western world, whose institutions and ideals, specifically Enlightenment commitments such as capitalism, socialism, nationalism, democracy, liberalism, civil and military bureaucracies, equality, and distributive justice, need a thorough reexamination, renewal, or redefinition. Rapid advancements in communications technology and globalization have simply rendered many of these institutions obsolete. Tu Weiming has called us to think beyond the Enlightenment mentality and explore the spiritual resources that may help us to broaden the scope of the Enlightenment project, deepen its moral sensitivity, and, if necessary, creatively transform its genetic constraints in order to fully realize its potential as a worldview for the human condition as a whole. In the fourth lesson of the last chapter, we emphasized that there is a constant need for traditions and cultures to renew by learning both from others and their own past resources. In an age of globalization, humankind needs more than ever to find rootedness and localization (Tu 1998). A renewed culture and tradition are enabling forces, which are capable of shaping the contour of our future society and nationhood.

According to Tu, three kinds of spiritual resources are available to us, and a fourth is in the process of development. The first involves the ethico-religious traditions of the modern West, notably Greek philosophy, Judaism, and Christianity. Within these traditions, the exclusive dichotomies of matter/spirit, body/mind, sacred/profane, human/nature, and creator/creature must be transcended to allow supreme values, such as the sanctity of the earth, the continuity of being, the beneficial interaction between the human community and nature, and mutuality between humankind and heaven, to receive the saliency they deserve in philosophy, religion, and theology. The second kind of spiritual resource is derived from non-Western, Axial Age civilizations, which include Hinduism, Jainism, and Buddhism in South and Southeast Asia; Daoism and Confucianism in East Asia; and Islam. These traditions provide sophisticated and practicable resources in the form of worldviews, rituals, institutions, styles of education, and patterns of human relatedness. They can help to develop ways of life, both as a continuation of and alternative to the Western European and North American exemplification of the Enlightenment mentality. We have already highlighted some of the Chinese contributions to the spiritual resources of humankind, emphasizing the complementarity of Western and Chinese civilizations and the fact that Western culture is strongly yang and thus needs a yin component to achieve a dynamic balance. (See chapter three for notions on how Chinese culture can help in this matter.) The possibility of developing a better balanced, more humane, and sustainable environment, personality, communities, and nationhood based on these ideas and experiences should not be overly exaggerated, but neither should it be undermined.

Tu's third kind of spiritual resource involves the primal traditions, specifically Native American, Hawaiian, Maori, and numerous tribal indigenous religious traditions. These cultures have, with both physical strength and even aesthetic elegance, sustained human life since Neolithic times. The implications for practical living are far-reaching. For example, their deep experience of rootedness, rituals of bonding in ordinary daily human interaction, emphasis on participation rather than control in motivation, empathic understanding rather than empiricist apprehension in epistemology, worldviews based on respect for the transcendent rather than domination over nature, and fulfillment rather than alienation in human experience, all still have direct relevance in our reconstruction.

Finally, Tu suggested a fourth kind of spiritual resource that is emergent from the core of the Enlightenment project itself. Our disciplined reflection, a communal act rather than an isolated struggle, is a first step toward the creative zone that religious leaders and teachers of ethics envision. The feminist critique of tradition, the concern for the environment, and the persuasion of religious pluralism are examples of this new corporate critical self-awareness. The development of global civil societies could be a result of such reflection.

Renewal of Economic Institutions

Once we have transcended Enlightenment mentality, the embedded economic, social, and political orders and institutions of the Enlightenment, such as capitalism, liberalism, and democracy, require redefinition.

For instance, consider capitalism. In chapter twelve, we described incipient capitalism, its relationship to mathematical manageability, and its contribution to the commercial, scientific, and industrial revolutions as well as early globalization. Recently, in a collaborative publication involving researchers from the United States, Japan, Hong Kong, and China entitled *The Resurgence of East Asia, 500, 150 and 50 Year Perspectives* (2003), Arrighi and others argued that there were two paths of economic development: the industrial revolution path, which started in Western Europe, and the industrious revolution path, which developed in East Asia. The researchers proposed that the two paths illustrate the difference between the Braudelian capitalist dynamics and the Smithian market dynamics. The former tends to generate surpluses of means of payment, the accumulation of such surpluses being pursued as an end in itself with the organization of production vertically integrated and driven by manufacturing considerations. In the latter path, capital surpluses do not tend to accumulate in the same way, that is, money being simply a means of transforming one set of commodities into another of greater usable value, with the organization of production a system of informally integrated networks driven by distributing considerations. Braudelian capitalism is technology-, resource-, and capital-intensive. The Smithian market commercialism is labor-intensive and resource-conserving.

This two-path, three-phase model of economic development explains the divergence and convergence of Western and East Asian economies over the past five hundred years. Essentially, this model illustrates the differences between the technology-, resource-, and capital-intensive Braudelian capitalism of the West versus the labor-intensive and resource-saving Smithian market commercialism of East Asia. Braudelian capitalism has been renowned for its relentless pursuit of profit. Many commercial laws and much antitrust legislation was designed to regulate its growth within national boundaries. The East Asian Smithian model, on the other hand, managed to combine rapid economic development with relatively egalitarian distribution of income (Pasell 1996). This efficacious combination was a result of Confucian perspectives on wealth distribution and social justice (Bell and Chaibong 2003). The thinking differences between these two systems have been amplified under the light of globalization and rapid technological advancement. Capitalism itself, therefore, is in need of renewal and redefinition as the two systems converge.

With the present state of globalization, given advanced information and communications technology, very few international laws and regulations restrict free cross-border capital flows, the amount of which is so staggering, averaging on the order of one-and-a-half to two trillion American dollars per day in 1999, that no single nation can effectively control it (Friedman 1999). The negative effect of this uncontrollable free capital was demonstrated in the Mexican Tequila Crisis from 1994 to 1995, the Asian Financial Crisis of 1997 to 1998, the Russian crisis of 1998, and the Argentinean crisis of 2001 to 2002. In each of these cases, the bursting of the bubble created by these uncontrollable capital flows resulted in lasting social and economic consequences of global dimensions and caused immeasurable human suffering. The dynamics of rampaging capital, exclusively profit-oriented multinational corporations, and corrupt third-world governments and their officials in addition to the lack of moral authority and persuasion within the society and, of course, human greed all cry out for the establishment of a new global order, ethics, governance, and institutions that can protect individual citizens in both developed and developing countries.

Free-market fundamentalism has come to dominate the upper reaches of American political and corporate life since the rise of the New Right in the late twentieth century. Peter Nolan (2004) listed some of the shortcomings of free-market fundamentalism, which includes extreme inequality, failure to sustain a social cohesion capable of meeting people's fundamental needs for security and stability, unethical and solely profit-induced production and consumerism, political choices controlled by special interest groups and their lobbyists, financial scandals, and unethical business practices. These are the multifarious results of financial deregulation. Max Weber contended that American capitalism flourished on the strength of its puritan Protestant ethics, but it will be one of the great challenges of the third millennium for the United States to renew its capitalist institutions to incorporate a new ethical dimension. Western ethics have always been embedded in and associated with religious beliefs. However, in an age of globalization and pluralistic social and religious conditions, Western ethics are no longer universally acceptable. Western cultures now need to construct a new social ethic based on secular beliefs about shared human values in order to fit into the new millennium. Chinese ethics, which are mainly secular in nature, provide some provoking thoughts for this effort.

Renewal of Social Ideals and Ethics

Social and economic ethics are always intertwined. Jeremy Brecher and others (2000) offered a blueprint for a global new deal based on seven basic principles gleaned from a citizen's perspective. The first principle calls for an upward leveling of labor and environmental, social, and human rights conditions by enforcing minimum global standards for labor rights and environmental stewardship on corporations. The second suggests the democratization of social institutions at every level from the local to the global. This includes inviting all citizens of the world into the dialogue on the future of the global economy. The third principle demands that decision-making processes occur as close as possible to those who are impacted by the outcome of the decision. This means that corporations should be held accountable to local, community-controlled institutions. The fourth precept of the blueprint envisions a closing of the gap between the global rich and poor. In addition to endorsing global redistribution measures, the authors urge international financial institutions to cancel the remaining debts of the poorest countries. The fifth and sixth principles call for a strict enforcement of international environmental agreements and the creation of prosperity in accordance with human and environmental needs. The final principle demands a more effective system of protection against global recessions. Although some may consider these seven principles unrealistic, they nevertheless can serve as idealistic guidelines for institutions on the horizon of the twenty-first century.

The Swiss theologian Hans Kung (1998) also formulated a global ethic comprised of four commitments: a culture of nonviolence and respectfulness for life, a culture of solidarity possessed of a just economic order, a culture of tolerance and truthfulness, and a culture of equal rights, particularly racial and gender equality. According to his ethic, the essence of good governance is the creation of a society or environment wherein people have an equal opportunity to live in peace and harmony, have a reasonably good standard of living, and have the opportunity and freedom to develop the best of their human qualities.

The Chinese worldview and historical experience over the past thousands of years, as described in the preceding chapters, are rooted in the principle of governance based on peace and harmony at all levels, that is, self, community, nature, and the transcendent. This tradition has direct relevance in the present post-post-modern reconstruction project articulated previously. According to Tu, Confucian precepts of embeddedness and rootedness have much to contribute to our present aspirations. In addition, the Confucian commitment to ethical education, respect for life and nature, and values and traditions should provide added inspiration for Western educational planners. The challenge in the new millennium is to envision and work to realize a global economic and social system based on the principles of justice, equality, and fairness, whose operation is transparent, dependable, and accountable to all of its citizens. The successful designers of such a system will have to draw upon the salient features of all past systems as well as the intricately interacting ideas, values, and beliefs found in all four spiritual resources described previously.

Renewal of Democratic Institutions

In chapter six, the ideal Western democratic political order is described. While the desirability of the democratic ideal has never been in doubt, the institution of democracy is less than perfect in practice. Yet it is still arguably the best system we have, and we will not belabor the discussion of democracy itself any further. After three hundred years of development, however, democracy has become entrenched in a multiparty election system, which has many undesirable features. Sor-Hoon Tan (2003) observes, "Actually existing democracies are so dominated and controlled by a bewildering array of external and impersonal forces that some claim that government by the people can 'now hardly amount to more than empty verbiage.' Many who believe in the ideal of democracy nevertheless find too big a gap between ideal and existing democracies" (2003).

What passes for democracy today is "government by a few, approved by a large number (not always a majority), for one or another coalition of special interests" (Tan 2003). Critics who have been described as communitarian also reject the overemphasis on individual autonomy that dominates Western liberal democracy. They argue that democracy, both in theory and practice, needs to be rejuvenated with communitarian concerns. Others, such as Edward Woo (2002), argue that the multiparty election system of the democracies with which we are familiar is too confrontational. Woo explained that there is always a risk before the election of a conflict between the different factions within a country and there is the danger of a dictator emerging after the election, such as in the case of Hitler. As a result, with the exception of election time, the people effectively do not have any say most of the time. Woo also argued that multiparty election systems work best in societies of predominantly uniform culture, such as the melting pot of the United States, rather than territories where a strong mixed ethnic population with diverse religious beliefs exists.

One of the challenges of the new millennium will be to revitalize our democratic institutions, such that ethics become part of the political order and our politicians become more responsive to both individual and group concerns and needs as well as more transparent and accountable in their actions. Woo advocated a nonconfrontational democracy that separates the policymaking and administrative functions of government. In his model, the policymaking function can be achieved through direct Internet polling of all citizens on specific issues, thus making governance truly democratic. The administrative function can be achieved through the cooperation and mutual supervision of the two most popular parties of an election. Woo also advocated combining salient Chinese and Western virtues in the proper balance between rights and responsibilities.

In contrast, Sor-Han Tan proposed a cultivation and reconstruction of what she calls "Confucian democracy," which is different from Western liberal democracies by having a strong ethical component. By combining the Confucian concern with cultural and moral processes and the Deweyan pragmatic concern with political democracy, Tan was able to reconstruct a Confucianism that opposes authoritarianism and is more akin to Dewey's pragmatism, itself a form of participatory democracy. Deweyan pragmatism might be better understood as a way of organizing and meliorating experience rather than as a potted ideology. Tan synthesized the two philosophies through a comparative examination of individuals and community, democratic ideals of equality and freedom, and the nature of ethical and political order. The main argument for a Confucian democracy, according to Tan, is that it is ultimately the best way to ensure the government operates for the benefit of the people. If we understand government for the people, as we should, to not only consist of providing material welfare, but also contribute to personal fulfillment in a flourishing community, then government by the people is an indispensable, constitutive means of government for the people. The Confucian preoccupation with self-cultivation and education will enhance the functioning of such a democracy, a democracy we have not yet managed to attain.

Energy and Environmental Challenges

One of the most challenging problems facing humankind in the twenty-first century is in reconciling needs for economic development, energy security, and environmental conservation. An energy-inefficient and fossil fuel-intensive energy future presents a variety of problems for the world, including rapid global warming, high levels of investment in energy supply, increased local and regional air pollution, greater national and international security risks, rapid petroleum depletion, and continued inequity. Together, these amount to a serious threat to the environmental integrity of our planet, our standards of living, and the ability of the developing world to climb out of poverty. Howard Geller summarized this problem and provided partial solutions with three key points:

1. Current energy sources and patterns of energy use are unsustainable. Continuing to consume ever-greater amounts of fossil fuels will cause too much damage to the environment, risk unprecedented climate change, and rapidly deplete petroleum resources. Current trends in energy supply and demand will also exacerbate inequity and tensions among nations, tensions that fuel regional conflict and outbursts reminiscent of 9/11. In short, continuing on a business-as-usual path will put the well-being of future generations at risk.

2. An energy revolution is possible and desirable. By emphasizing much greater energy efficiency and growing reliance on renewable energy sources such as solar energy, wind power, and bioenergy, all the problems associated with current energy patterns and trends can be mitigated. However, a formidable set of barriers is limiting the rate of energy efficient improvement and the transition to renewable energy sources in most parts of the world.

3. It is possible to overcome these barriers through enlightened public policies. Experience with policies for increasing energy efficiency and renewable energy use is growing, providing many successful models and lessons that can guide further action. Expanding the adoption of successful policies as well as increasing and focusing international efforts could accelerate the energy revolution and result in a more sustainable energy future. (2003)

Fossil fuels are currently the primary source of the cheap energy that powers our modern industrial civilization. Industrial civilization, as we know it, cannot exist without petroleum. In addition to energy supply, our lifestyle also very much depends on petroleum consumption. More than seventy thousand products that are manufactured use petroleum as a raw feedstock. This includes plastics, acrylics, cosmetics, paints, varnishes, asphalts, fertilizers, medications, and so forth. Many scientists believe global production of petroleum will peak within the next ten years. It is forecast that, around 2030, the worldwide demand for oil will out-pace worldwide production by a significant margin. As a result, the price will sky-rocket, oil-dependent economies will crumble, and resource wars will explode.

To avoid such a disastrous event, we should definitely use the earth's remaining fossil fuel supply wisely, efficiently, and effectively. The key is to build a sustainable world based on ecological economics. Before then, we must first understand factors such as energy transformations, biophysical constraints, environmental deterioration, the human characteristics that drive production and consumption, and the assumptions of neoclassical economics. According to the 18th World Energy Congress in 2001, there are four key challenges to enhancing energy security and promoting greater harmony throughout the world:

- Achieving commercial energy access for the two billion people in the world who do not now have it

- Improving political and legal stability at the global and regional levels

- Keeping all energy options open, including the safe use of nuclear power and the promotion of renewable energy

- Increasing efficiency through competition and technology diffusion

These challenges are all closely related. Before the blueprint for the creation of a sustainable world is available to us, individuals, societies, and various levels of government all have their own part to play in promoting this cause. Before we run out of fossil fuels, however, we must make every effort to take care of the environment and avoid more damage from our human action.

It is now conclusive that green house gas emission, including methane, nitrous oxide, ozone, chlorofluorocarbons and their replacements, and carbon dioxide, is one of the key causes for global warming and human activity is the main driver. According to a report released by the IPCC, the United Nation's Intergovernmental Panel on Climate Change, on February 2, 2007, the world faces an average temperature rise of around three degrees Centigrade this century if greenhouse gas emissions continue to rise at their current pace and allowed to double from their preindustrial level. The new report says that warming during the last one hundred years was 0.74 degrees Centigrade with most of the warming occurring during the past fifty years. The warming per decade for the next twenty years is projected to be 0.2 degrees Centigrade per decade.

To date, this report is the most conclusive scientific evidence that the warming of the climate system is unequivocal and accelerating. As a result of their research, the IPCC won the 2007 Nobel Peace Prize. The Executive Secretary of the United Nations Framework Convention on Climate Change, Yvo de Boer, has called for speedy and decisive international action to combat the phenomenon.

According to the Stern review issued in 2006 by the United Kingdom government, an average temperature rise of three degrees Celsius would translate into severe water shortages and lower crop yields around the world with climate change already causing setbacks to economic and social progress in developing countries. The world should act now because the economic costs of inaction, for example, permanent displacement of millions of people, will be much higher than the cost of any action.

Specifically, the use of automobiles is the most wasteful of all fossil fuel usages, and it is one of the primary culprits in environmental damage, especially in developed countries. For example, the United States constitutes 5 percent of the world population, but it consumes eighteen billion barrels of oil equivalent (BBOE), seven billion barrels of oil, and eleven BBOE of coal, gas, uranium, and hydrogen in 2005. It was responsible for about 26 percent of global greenhouse gas emissions.(Huber and Mills 2006) The United States has the highest motorization rate in the world and perhaps the most mature automobile industry. But it also causes the most damage to the environment on a per capita basis. It will take decades of research and implementation before improved technology and efficiency, zero-emission fossil fuels, gas hydrate, renewable fuels such as solar, wind, biofuels, and alternate fuels such as nuclear fission and fusion, will significantly impact this picture. Increasing demand from developing countries, such as China and India, will even further jeopardize the situation.

However, there are already some signs of encouragement. Figures supplied by Amory Lovins in the September 1995 issue of *Scientific American* support this contention by advocating "winning the oil endgame" with technology and better efficiency:

> ... artificially combining lightweight materials with innovations in propulsion and aerodynamics could cut oil use by cars, trucks and planes by two thirds without compromising comfort, safety, performance or affordability.

The United States now uses 47 percent less energy per dollar of economic output than it did thirty years ago, lowering costs by $1 billion a day. The efficiency revolution continues. A practical team at the nonprofit Rocky Mountain Institute has recently developed new construction designs offering energy savings of 89 percent for a data center, about 75 percent for a chemical plant, and 70 to 90 percent for a supermarket. In the United States, some states and municipalities are providing leadership on energy efficiency and renewable energy implementation.

Other countries, such as Brazil, which already supplement its oil consumption in cars with 40 percent ethanol, are transforming their energy reliance more to renewable fuels. According to Geller (2003), wind power is the world's fastest-growing major energy source with cumulative installed wind capacity increasing by more than a factor of ten between 1992 and 2001. Wind power capacity is now increasing 30 to 35 percent per year. The European Union aims to double its renewable energy use by 2010, meaning that renewable sources would provide 12 percent of total energy supply and 22 percent of the electricity supply that year. Some European countries have adopted their own more ambitious goals. For example, the United Kingdom plans to increase the fraction of electricity generated by renewable energy from 2 percent in 2000 to about 10 percent in 2010. Spain plans to obtain 12 percent of its electricity in 2010 from wind power alone. Meanwhile, Denmark plans to increase the contribution of renewable energy sources from about 10 percent of total energy supply in 2000 to 18 percent by 2010 and 35 percent by 2030. This reminds us how mankind has faced many challenges through the ages, but it has always found an innovative solution to each of them once they have realized it is a problem.

Meanwhile, we urgently need energy conservation measures that include the protection, preservation, management, and restoration of energy resources and its usage. Governmental incentives and disincentives as well as rules and regulations are all effective means in achieving this objective. In addition, a holistic, comprehensive approach to energy, including its social and cultural dimensions, is needed. The most important lesson that can be drawn from past experience is that public policies that are well designed and implemented can overcome the barriers to greater energy efficiency, renewable energy use, and cleaner fossil fuel technologies. This conclusion was confirmed in the case studies by Geller (2003) of policy initiatives worldwide as well as in forward-looking policy assessments for the United States and Brazil.

Democratization of environmental issues is also making an impact. For example, Canadian people are increasingly environmentally conscious. As a result, both government and its opposition now have to construct political platforms that are ecologically sound and environmentally friendly. Environmentally conscious consumers, together with sound governmental incentives and policies, can most effectively influence producers, such as car manufacturers, to produce green products and invest more in research and development of such products. Clearly, the future of our Mother Earth and all humankind will depend on how well individuals, industries, and all levels of governments play their roles in these crucial ecological and environmental issues.

Section Three:
Challenges Facing China

It is debatable if postmodern conditions ever existed in China. Over the past couple of centuries, the Chinese people have been struggling to build a modern nation that could match the developed countries of Europe, Japan and the United States. Democracy and science were the slogans of modernity for the Chinese intellectuals during the May 4th Movement of 1919. Today, as China reinvigorates its society and nationhood with the establishment of new cultural, economic, technological, legal, social, and political institutions, whatever experiences, aspirations, and ideals have captured the imagination of Westerners will consequently be of keen interest to the Chinese people and their government. China has learned and is continuing to learn from the West. How Westerners face the challenges described in the preceding section will be a source of valuable information and guidance for present and future Chinese planners. But future conditions are unpredictable. China will need to meet its challenges in its own unique and innovative way.

Learning from the West does not mean that China will follow the same path to modernization. Rather, with both foresight and hindsight and based on the experiences of the West and Japan, China should define its own future in a global context that is better adapted to our present environment. After centuries of deconstruction, the Chinese people are free of the notion that tradition and ideology are immutable once established. Consequently, China is bestowed with a golden opportunity to build a new tradition, ideal, and institutions inspired by the best, regardless of where in the world the best is found. This is a challenge of profound consequences. We hope China can avoid repeating the mistakes made by the developed countries during their own process of industrialization. This hope actually represents one of the key motivations for the writing of this book.

Education and Spiritual Rejuvenation

Ironically, one of the greatest challenges facing the Chinese in the new millennium is the reconstruction of their own cultural values and social ethics. As explained in chapter four, China has historically taken pride in its identity as a society of virtue and high morality. Ethics, social and personal, are a genuine concern of every school of traditional Chinese philosophy. Yet, also described in chapter twelve is the decline of Chinese culture after the South Song dynasty when Neo-Confucianism was transformed into a rigid ideological dogma, becoming nothing more than simple rules that people followed unquestioningly. Chinese citizens, at both state and private levels, became hypocritical, using the high-sounding words of a tainted Confucianism as justification for their less-than-honorable actions. This declining moral trend continued in the Ming and Qing dynasties, was redefined through the May 4th Movement, a reaction to outside Western influences, and climaxed during the Cultural Revolution of the 1960s, when deconstruction peaked and the vicious denouncement of Chinese values and traditions was completed. Even the most foundational and deeply embedded traditional Chinese value of filial piety was challenged and condemned as feudal. Then the present era of economic reform arrived. Since the late 1980s, money, more than anything else, has become the major pursuit of Chinese life.

Thus, the lack of social and economic ethics of some Chinese individuals, government officials, and businesses as well as their resulting actions have sadly come to dominate the daily news in China. Ignorance, erosion of civility, lack of social responsibility, absence of civic values, hyperconsumerism, and neglect of spiritual values continue to afflict Chinese culture and concerned Chinese citizens today. Corruption is rampant. Social unrest is quickened and widespread, threatening social stability. Unethical business practices persist, threatening the confidence of consumers and reputation of Chinese products. The situation is pathetic, particularly for anyone who is genuinely concerned with the future of China, its culture, and its people.

To meet this challenge, the Chinese people and their government must first recognize the gravity of the situation and promptly follow this recognition with the implementation of a combined strategy of moral education and civil laws. Confucius taught Ran You how to manage the affairs of the Kingdom of Wei. His instruction came in three steps:

1. Augment the population.

2. Enrich the people.

3. Educate the people (*Analects* 13.9).

Today, the citizens of China are at the second and third steps of the remedy.

In every era, people write their own collective moral codes. Times change. China will never return to its ancient traditions and imperial ethics. Within this mutability, what is the meaning of moral education? In chapter six, moral, social, and educational issues were discussed in terms of the modern sciences of psychology and social theory. This discourse can be combined with traditional values to form the basis for a moral education. That is, within an individual, develop a social and global consciousness as well as a full personality. Become a free spirit with sound mind and a healthy body who is capable of giving and receiving love and affection. Cultivate a respect for labor with a proper balanced sense of rights and responsibilities and a committed belief in the humanitarian values of reciprocity, justice, fairness, equality, peace, and human brotherhood.

Other values are central to this open education, including an adoption of scientific methods and thinking, love and respect for nature, a caring for the environment and resource conservation, and an artistic appreciation. The individual, his or her family, school, society, and state should all be partners in this education. Furthermore, the goals of moral education cannot be attained by unnatural or artificial methods such as indoctrination. This would be internally incongruent and perhaps even paradoxical. Only morality learned in the natural setting of daily life can be retained with natural feeling. There should be no fundamental differences between the family and school in terms of education for moral development. The Chinese heritage of a harmonious family and community that is respectful of elders and teachers with a modern sense of individuality are the keys to resolving most of the educational and social problems of youth in a natural way with families and communities working in concert.

In the fourth lesson in chapter thirteen, the pluralistic and open nature of an effective education is stressed. This has particular relevance to Chinese education. Historically, when a leftist political ideology dominated the political arena in China, all non-Marxist cultural studies were considered harmful and, therefore, prohibited. China today needs new and open thinking, ideologies, and traditions rooted in the best human virtues and values drawn from both contemporary and traditional Chinese thinkers as well as anywhere else in the world at large. It is important to divorce education from short-term government politics, another painful lesson of Chinese history. Fortunately, Chinese families still retain education as a top priority in their children's growth and development, perhaps as part of the Confucian tradition. The Chinese government must recognize this heritage as a competitive advantage over many of the advanced developed countries of Europe and the United States and capitalize on this advantage by further committing resources to building the necessary infrastructure for culture and education with the goal of an educational institution truly fitting for the twenty-first century. The return on this investment in valuable social capital would be immeasurable.

Over the past decade, the Chinese government has devoted a mere 2.4 percent of GDP to public education, far lower than the average of 4.1 percent committed in other developing countries. The national educational budget in China is mainly spent on urban universities and colleges rather than on the more than two hundred million primary and secondary school students. In addition, since the mid-1990s, lower tiers of government have been expected to foot their education bills using local tax revenues. However, many local governments are crippled by debt and on the verge of bankruptcy, which hampers the local education system. This is a problem replicated throughout the country (Mar and Richter 2003). The Chinese government's emphasis on training more engineers and scientists for the sake of short-term economic development must not be sustained at the expense of general moral and cultural education, especially at the local level. Mar and Richter further revealed that the current Chinese educational system scores well on producing brilliant scientists and mathematicians, but it scores miserably on producing critical thinkers and questioners, the individuals who form the bedrock of continual innovation and renaissance. The elite universities set the trend, but the federal ministry and school administration must adopt a more proactive stance in freeing up thinking in order for the true intellectual prowess of Chinese students to be cultivated. China still has much to learn from American and Japanese experiences in this respect.

New Political Institutions

Traditional Chinese education stresses ethical self-cultivation and governance by setting an example. This pedagogy does indeed have modern relevance. Chinese leaders and the ruling party must establish a high ethical standard that others can emulate for themselves. Similar to the mandate of heaven of the imperial era, the one-party political system of China demands that the leaders and officials of the government be persons of high virtue and cultivated morality. They must be governed by integrity, fairness, and justice and have their performance judged on merit. In this case, merit is defined as benefits, both material and spiritual, conferred by leaders upon the people they serve, the environment under their care, and their contribution to the future development of individuals, society, and country. A system of checks and balances should be established. If the ruling party fails to discharge such a mandate, it is the right of the people to replace it by forming a new government. This traditional model of governance is complementary to modern Western ideals of equality, liberty, democracy, and governance by the rule of law, wherein the structure of governance is instituted according to these principles. There is no inherent contradiction between the two systems, Western and Chinese. The challenge is to find an innovative form of institution that can properly implement all these ideals. Woo's hope of building a nonconfrontational democracy or Tan's vision of a Confucian democracy, as described in the preceding subsection, have a better chance to succeed in China than anywhere else, based on the harmony-centered character of the Chinese heritage and the ready acceptance of the Western democratic ideal by the Chinese people and their government.

Although democracy is an ideal to which we may all aspire, China's large and diverse population, grand geographical scale, and complex social, economic, and political reality require that the implementation of democracy should be gradual, evolutional, and constructive in order to not create conflicts and chaos in the reconstruction process. To begin, the ruling elite must set a good example, and corruption must be curbed. True democracy should start with the internal practices of the party. Mechanisms of checks and balances and the rule of law must be established to enhance accountability, transparency, and openness. According to Mar and Richter (2003), there has been some progress made in governmental reforms in recent years. The restructuring of the administration has been under way since 1998. The anticorruption campaign has been enhanced. Village elections are now a nationwide practice. The People's Congress now plays a larger role in balancing the powers of the administration. Party membership is now open to owners of private and individual enterprises. Political experimentation continues at the local levels as well.

According to Hall and Ames's *Confucian Democracy* (Bell and Chaibong 2003), cultural politics is proceeding along two divergent paths. The first is the most recognizable in terms of processes of modernization associated with the extension of rationalized politics, economics, and technologies, all wrapped in the rational and moral consensus of the Western Enlightenment. The second form involves recognition of the mutual accessibility of cultural forms and processes leading to *ad hoc* and local sites of negotiation aimed at the resolution of particular problems. In the first of these two senses of globalization, the term "Confucian democracy" is oxymoronic. Hope for a combination of Confucian and democratic sensibilities depends on the success of the second form of globalization, a sense that recognizes the potential benefits of mutual engagement in which both Confucian and democratic beliefs and practices are seen as valuable resources for the improvement of modes of togetherness. China would be a good place for such experimentation and new forms of democratic institution.

New Economic Institutions

In many forms, entrepreneurship is the source of a new dynamism that has revitalized the domestic Chinese business environment and made it a new global destination for business and investment. Entrepreneurship and commercial networks are always identified as factors in the success of overseas Chinese business people in Hong Kong, Taiwan, and Southeast Asia. Pure entrepreneurship is now spawning thousands of new businesses in China. In the process, it is connecting China to the rest of the world. Entrepreneurship has found natural partners in technology because of the up-to-date knowledge needed, low start-up costs, and lack of geographic limits. Entrepreneurs in the Silicon Valley, Hong Kong, and China have revealed an openness to new ideas, tenacity in implementation, and the ability to look beyond their immediate situations to view opportunities on a wider horizon. Nowadays, almost all such entrepreneurs have a global outlook. In this age of globalization and rapid technological advancement, the global competitiveness of China would be greatly enhanced with governmental policies to encourage this group to remain creative and innovative. The past experiences of the Silicon Valley, Taiwan, and Singapore all support this strategy.

Technological development is one area in which China can learn much from past Western experience, but it is simultaneously an area in which China does not need to relive all the experiences of the West. By knowing what we know today, some of the development stages could be leapfrogged, effectively creating a newcomer's advantage. The development of communications infrastructure provides the best examples. China has been able to leapfrog specific Western technology, for instance, marketing cellular phones instead of laying copper telephone cables, laying down new fiber-optic cables in many areas, developing third-generation technologies, going directly into DVD and digital technologies without first investing in the analog counterparts of these technologies, and capitalizing on other nations' development of the Internet. China today is also a large consuming nation. The sheer size of the Chinese economy and its internal demand alone has provided China with many advantages through economies of scale. In addition, China is able to set new global standards and define new formats for future technological development, such as third-generation technologies.

One of the more immediate challenges facing China is its state-owned enterprises that, with some exceptions, are lacking in efficiency, competitiveness, market sensitivity, and consumer orientation. These deficits are all the product of recent socialist history. If left alone, these enterprises will go bankrupt, producing unemployment sizable enough to threaten social stability in China. Capital injections by the government can delay their demise, but it will not change the end result. There is an imminent need for the restructuring of these enterprises to adopt better corporate governance, improved accountability, and more transparency. Western experience is invaluable in this effort, and innovative solutions are urgently needed. In any case, the government should back out of its role as the biggest investor. Diversification of shareholding should be realized. Management authority should be returned to those with the expertise and interest in running the company, preferably with an incentive system to encourage performance. Additionally, a healthy legal system, impartial prosecution of criminals, and civil accountability should be established to prevent abuses of power. Protection of the shareholder's interests is a critical part in the development of corporate governance in China as well as a renewed emphasis on traditional values such as trust and loyalty.

The growing middle class, a hallmark of China since the policy of reform was adopted, has organized itself into independent associations pressing their independent interests. According to "Don't Break the Engagement", a recent report in *Foreign Affairs* (May/June 2004) by Dr. Elizabeth Economy, a senior fellow at the Council of Foreign Relations, there are more than 2,000 daily newspapers and 900 television stations in the country. Some have undertaken aggressive investigative reports of current political and social issues, such as government corruption and consumers' rights. Legal reforms, partially instituted because of China's entry into the World Trade Organization, have produced moves "toward an accountable regulatory environment with well-defined laws and well-trained lawyers and judges."

According to the same report by Economy, there were 120,000 lawyers in China in 2004, up from just 2,000 in 1978. More than 230 law schools were training an additional 80,000 lawyers in 2004. The number of lawsuits has increased dramatically as well with a staggering 70 percent lodged by ordinary citizens against the government ending successfully in 2003, compared to only 40 percent in 1990. A healthy legal system of civic laws, which the government is gradually legislating, is important to the Chinese people because social ethics dominates traditional Confucianism. Checks on state power is very much lacking.

China is still in the process of developing its own market economy, commercial laws, as well as economic management practices and rules for corporate governance. The opportunity to learn from Western experience is indispensable. However, China can improve upon this Western template by incorporating an additional ethical dimension in its institutions, a dimension that is lacking in the present Western system. Adam Smith's analysis of the market mechanism, *The Wealth of Nations,* tried to lay down the fundamental laws governing economic development and assumed the free market, guided by the invisible hand, was the best arrangement for organizing economic life. But very few people, even in the Western world, know of Smith's other great work, *The Theory of Moral Sentiments*, published in 1759 and revised by Smith in 1761. Both volumes share the same fundamental passion about the moral foundations of social life. At the heart of each of these books is an explicit recognition of fundamental contradictions within the market economy. Smith demonstrated that the free market is an immensely powerful force for impelling economic progress, but it is one with deep internal contradictions from an ethical standpoint, that is, the division of labor and pursuit of profit. Smith believed that class stratification was a necessary condition of economic progress because it facilitated the accumulation of capital and division of labor. However, he acknowledged that this rift amplified the possibility of class conflict as well as corruption of moral sentiments through the construction of social values that justified neglect of the poor and mean. He offered no solution to this contradiction.

Adam Smith's penetrating analysis is of the deepest significance in China's search for a moral touchstone to help the country find its way forward in the years ahead. Regional and wealth disparities are of incalculable concern to the Chinese government. Yet, it is misleading to suggest that Smith provided unqualified support to the free market. He did not, and his reservations were clearly of relevance to China's situation today. The central preoccupation of Chinese political practice for thousands of years has been the attempt to find a function for the state and nurture a social ethic that enables the economy and society to operate in a way that serves the wider social interest. Chinese philosophy has always centered on human needs and the improvement of government, morals, and value of human life. Thus, it becomes a complex challenge for the Chinese government to address the problem of income disparity and wealth distribution, adhering to the principle of social justice and equality without intervening in the free market economy.

The common theme of both Confucius and Adam Smith, according to Peter Nolan (2004), is that the market is not an intrinsically moral entity that should be allowed to dominate society. Restraint of selfishness, or benevolence, is a human moral foundation, unlike the pursuit of individual self-interest endorsed in the free market fundamentalism of the United States. Both thinkers emphasize reciprocal social obligations and duties as the foundation of a good society. Both regard the pursuit of wealth and position as damaging to individual fulfillment. Both regard education as the foundation of self-fulfillment and the morality that forms the cement for social cohesion. Both understand individual happiness to be the prime goal of a successful society. But they both believe that this is not to be achieved through the pursuit of ever-greater material consumption. Rather, Confucius and Adam Smith felt similarly that happiness is achieved through the contentment that derives from living according to the ethical norms evolved for the sustenance of a high level of social coherence. Each, similarly again, is scathing in their indictment of the possibility for happiness resulting from high levels of material consumption. So one of the challenges that the Chinese people face is establishing a market economy and social institution amenable to all these ideals and ethical considerations.

Energy and Environmental Challenges

Many Chinese harbor a misconception that modernization means chimneys and high-rises built to the sky. Everybody owns a car, a picture of a modern industrial Western city. In reality, this is not a good model to aspire to. As we have seen previously, despite their technological prowess, developed countries in Europe and North America are severely constrained in their choices about fossil fuel consumption because their economies, lifestyles, habits, and mentalities are still committed to the use of family automobiles. Even though active research is being conducted into finding alternative energy to fuel cars, it will be some time, if it is indeed possible at all, before any alternative fuels of significant value might become available at a reasonable price. If the price of oil continues to rise, even the developed countries will have no choice but to abandon fossil fuel reliance. Such a change will be very painful indeed. This is one path that China must not blindly follow! Instead, China and the Chinese people should celebrate its fortune that they do not have the burden of the inheritance of many second wave industries relying on the use of fossil fuels. Having the benefit of hindsight and with foresight, China should transcend fossil fuel-dependent industrialization. With ingenuity, it should aspire to build a sustainable and ecological-friendly economy and society.

With its immense population of 1.3 billion people and its limited natural resources, China cannot afford to use the same economic development model previously employed by Europe, the United States, and Japan during their own respective periods of industrialization. For example, according to Heber and Mills (2005), the average citizen of the United States consumes 27 barrels of oil annually compared with 1.7 barrels for the Chinese in 2005. While per capita use is relatively low in China, the country's overall consumption of energy and the resulting carbon emissions are substantial due to the large population and heavy reliance on coal. Already, seven of the ten most polluted cities in the world are in China, according to a World Health Organization (WHO) report of 1998. The situation is sure to have worsened since that time because China's pace of economic development is very rapid. In addition, the availability of fresh water resources creates another ecological problem for Chinese industrialization. If every Chinese person were to consume at the present rate of the United States, the total consumption would be at least eleven times greater than it is now. This, of course, is not sustainable, economically or ecologically.

Therefore, the greatest challenge for China in the third millennium is to conceptualize and implement an industrial development strategy that is sustainable and ecologically friendly. To start, China must not repeat the same mistakes that the developed Western countries have made, mistakes that are structural in nature but remain a source of ongoing dire consequences. They are not necessarily resolvable. Instead, China should take full advantage of the advanced technologies currently available from the world at large and adopt them as an integral part of its development strategy. The initial cost might be higher, but its benefits are immeasurable.

The concept of ecological consequences is best described by Liebig's Law of carrying capacity, which states that whatever resource is least abundantly available (relative to per capita requirements) sets an environment's carrying capacity. While there is no way to repeal this principle, trade helps to make its application less restrictive. People living in an environment where a shortage of some necessity, such as technology, limits their carrying capacity can develop exchange relationships with residents of another area that happens to be blessed with a surplus of that resource but happens to lack some other resource that is plentiful where the first one was scarce. The composite carrying capacity of two or more areas with different resource configurations can be greater than the sum of their separate carrying capacities. This forms one justification for globalization, having a federation of states, and forming a large country such as China.

Over the past centuries, the Western industrial powers have used colonialism to circumvent and extend the application of Liebig's law through their control of cheap oil in the Middle East, providing economical fuel for their own industrialization. Such amenable conditions are definitely not available to China. Even with an understanding of this principle, resources, advanced management, and technology remain the limiting factors of industrial development in China. China critically requires a new strategy for its industrial development.

For resources, options available to China include:

- Switching to renewable resources

- Slowing or even halting some industrial development, or at least limiting its fuel consumption and carbon emission and giving incentives to encourage fuel and environmental conservation

- Developing a strategy that can effectively achieve the first two points

Each of these options has their own preconditions and consequences. The first option may be the best strategy, but it requires technologies that may be immature, only marginally available, or not yet economically feasible, such as the use of solar, wind and tidal power, gas hydrates, hydrogen fuel, biofuel, and nuclear fission and fusion. Nevertheless, research for new technologies and sources of energy should not be abandoned, and it could eventually make any of these alternatives practical. The second option is unacceptable to most people in developing countries because this option directly puts limits on industrial development. The argument of people in developing countries is compelling. Why should they sacrifice the opportunity for a better life while people in developed countries continue to enjoy their lifestyle despite the heavy ecological deficits incurred? Arguments appear unlikely to convince citizens of developing countries otherwise. Limiting fuel consumption and encouraging fuel conservation makes sense if these efforts are combined with a legislated demand for the development and implementation of new technology that could produce better fuel efficiency and less pollution, such as super-lightweight vehicles, carbon emission-free fossil fuels, fuel efficient ecologically friendly buildings, and the kind of conservation measures that have been instituted in California. Ultimately, the combined strategy of the third option makes the most sense.

China should benefit from the experience of how the developed countries are dealing with their energy challenges, described previously, especially the part on conservation and governmental regulation on the use of motor vehicles. Unfortunately, the automobile industry remains one of the fastest-growing industries in contemporary China. Although China justifiably requires a transportation infrastructure to support its industrial development, one of the key strategies of the government must nevertheless be to discourage private ownership of cars because China and the world cannot afford such waste. Adoption of a "no privately owned car" strategy or its equivalent, together with other energy conservation measures, such as alternative energies for cooling and heating and the use of new technology in design and conservation, will help lower energy consumption and provide for the sustainability of China's social and economic development.

As a model for this type of sustainable thinking, Hong Kong's public transportation system is well known for its efficiency, comfort, and safety. Commuters travel wherever they want within a short period of time and with relatively low fuel consumption because of economies of scale. As a result, car ownership in Hong Kong is primarily a status symbol rather than convenience. A similar, well-designed public transportation system is the preferred transportation choice for dense urban centers of developing countries, from both economic and ecological standpoints.

Now is the time for the Chinese government to incorporate new laws, regulations, and disincentive programs, so the "no privately owned car" and carbon emission-free strategies can be realized. These strategies will simultaneously provide incentives for the building or improvement of new and existing public transportation systems. Once people and industry understand that the "no privately owned car" and emission-free policies have been adopted as a governmental strategy, all planning for the future will be decisively impacted. For example, consider city planning. Many advanced cities of Europe and North America have already adopted policies taxing and discouraging citizens from owning cars and introduced emission control policies for some states and established city centers. Because urbanization will continue to be one of the trends of future Chinese development, China can do even better than these Western urban centers by basing all city planning upon the policy of no privately owned cars. As a design criterion, this policy would foster imagination and innovation for new urban living, especially in many new cities that will be spawned away from the well-developed coastal cities. For example, a well-planned community could include a fleet of community-owned cars, which resident members can use on an as-needed basis. This and many other forms of cooperative ownership of facilities could also enhance our sense of communality, as has already been demonstrated in some North American cities. Instead of continuing to build new ring roads in Beijing, generating ever more traffic congestion and carbon emission, more and better subways and other transportation systems could prevail with the additional benefit of enhancing local communities for work and family. Commuter transportation networks between cities also have to be enhanced. Without the competition of private cars, intracity, intercity, and interprovincial transportation will be improved with the net effect that Chinese industrialization will be accelerated.

In summary, the challenge facing China and its people in the new millennium is immense. At the same time, globalization and technological advancement have offered China and its people a golden opportunity for a reconstruction of its political, social, economic and cultural ideals, traditions, and institutions. If the Chinese people can rise again to meet these challenges in an imaginative and innovative way, the world will surely benefit. The key is not to follow blindly down the same path as the West. It is to face their challenges and transcend them with new ideas, new strategies, and the application of the best innovation and technology China can learn from anywhere in the world.

Concluding Remarks

Our journey has shown us how different, yet complementary, the Chinese and Western cultures really are. We have seen how differences in physical environment dating back to the Ice Age have resulted in very different thought patterns, philosophies and worldviews. Yet, despite the many differences, both provide a valuable record of our heritage, allowing us to evaluate the various dynamic forces behind the rise and fall of civilizations. China, in particular, has a long and well-documented legacy reaching back thousands of years. It reached its height during the Medieval Ages, when it was likely the most advanced civilization in the world. As a consequence of the country's long history, Chinese planners and policy makers are more strategic thinkers, looking farther into their past, as well as looking further into the future.

Yet in the last several hundreds of years, the young United States has easily surpassed both China and the rest of Europe, to become the biggest and most influential superpower on the planet. But with great power comes great responsibility. The United States has the advantage of youth—it is more creative, innovative, energetic, and idealistic than other countries in the world. It has set a great example for democracy and freedom. Yet it suffers from inexperience and impatience, which is exacerbated when it constantly changes leadership as often as every four years. That inexperience, combined with a persistent desire to impose its own ideologies on the rest of the world, has unfortunately caused some resentment. Even though America may have all the best intentions, there are many people in the world that despise what they see as American arrogance, self-righteous attitude, and unilateralism. The Bush doctrine of pre-emptive war has worsened this situation. As we watch events unfold in Iraq and the Middle East, and listen to American strategies on the war on terrorism, we are reminded of the lessons of the Vietnam War described earlier in this book. The Vietnam War was one of the only times that opposing sides sat down after the war to evaluate why things developed and happened as they did. The conclusions documented by the Americans clearly indicate that a severe lack of understanding about each other's cultures, histories, and motivations, caused a complete breakdown in diplomacy leading to millions of unnecessary deaths. The American leaders should take a serious look at history and make stronger efforts to seek better-balanced diplomacy.

The advent of North Korea's nuclear program offers an excellent lesson that diplomacy can achieve objectives that war cannot. In 2002, the United States labeled North Korea as one of the three countries on the "axis of evil," along with Iran and Saddam Hussein's Iraq. In 2003, six nations got together and started the now famous Six Party Talks with the goal of achieving a nuclear-free Korean peninsula. China not only hosted these meetings but also played a major and constructive role in the discussions. On July 16, 2007, after many setbacks and repeated negotiations, it was confirmed by United Nations inspectors that North Korea had shut down its nuclear facilities. The United States is now negotiating directly with North Korea to normalize their relationship. It is interesting to compare and contrast this with what happened in Iraq. We strongly believe that in order to win the war on terrorism and bring peace back to the Middle East, the United States will need to advocate skillful diplomacy, as well as increase cultural and religious tolerance and understanding. It will also need the assistance of other more neutral countries and the United Nations. Moderate Islamic majorities will have to play a key role. But it will not be achieved by military might.

China and the West face different challenges in the new millennium. Each of these cultures exists as it does today because of the products or by-products of distinct cultures, histories, and traditions. Each civilization is progressing through its own stages, pursuing diverging paths of cultural, economic, social, and political development. Globalization and technological advancement will improve dialogue and communication among different cultures. Cross-cultural understanding can provide many objective lenses and perspectives through which we can view and improve ourselves. Those varying perspectives can also help to guide us through predicaments. But our objective should not be uniformity. Instead, we should aspire for harmony in diversity—a global community where every culture can flourish in its own way.

It is clear that relations between China and the United States are at an important juncture. According to Chinese Ambassador Zhou Wenzhong (speech in New York, September 2005), in 1978, two-way trade between China and the United States totaled merely 990 million U.S. dollars—less than one billion—and mutual investment was virtually zero. In 2004, trade volume between the two countries reached over 169 billion U.S. dollars. China is now the most important market for U.S. industrial goods such as airplanes, as well as agricultural produce such as fruit and soybean. The number of projects in China with U.S. investment exceeds 40,000, with a total paid-in investment of 50 billion U.S. dollars. Several Chinese companies have also set up business in the United States.

The rapid growth of the Chinese economy, however, is quickly becoming a global issue. China has been growing at a rate of over nine percent a year over the past twenty-five years. In that same period it has moved 300 million people out of poverty and quadrupled the average Chinese personal income. And all this has happened, so far, without catastrophic social upheavals. The Chinese leadership should be commended for this historic achievement (Newsweek, May 9, 2005). Even so, on a per capita basis, China is still very much a Third World country, striving for better living standards, and facing many of the social and ethical problems typically encountered in the development of Third World countries. There is no doubt that China is in need of a cultural and spiritual renewal. But although it is taking only small steps right now, it is bestowed with one of the most unique opportunities of our time. It has a chance to build new social, legal, and political institutions as well as new ideals and traditions that will have profound and lasting consequences for the entire world, not just the Chinese people. However, limited resources, as well as environmental and ecological concerns, currently constrain the development of China. Sustainability is the key. These are all areas where the U.S. and the rest of the world can provide expert advice and guidance for our mutual benefit.

On a personal level, it is our hope that the ideas in this book, both Chinese and Western, will resound with our readers and find a place in their lives. We believe that the Chinese and Western cultures, philosophies, and ways of thinking, are all very complementary, like yin and yang. For example, in this book we have discussed the traditional Chinese values of harmony in diversity, benevolence, balance, cooperation, self-cultivation, tolerance, deference, and the Western sense of justice, liberty, individuality, equality, and fair play. These are all values that when combined, will make us better human beings.

It is our hope that with sincere dialogue and a willingness to understand each other's history and cultural biases, politicians and everyday people will be able to work together to improve each other's societies and the world as a whole. In particular, we feel that continuous dialogue and sharing between China and the West can have a beneficial impact on our global village in the 21st century. Learning from each other will help both civilizations to attain a new dynamic balance. Hopefully, it will result in a level of world peace, harmony, and prosperity unlike anything humankind has ever witnessed.

Bibliography

Adams, Bert N. and R. A. Sydie, *Classical Sociological Theory*. Thousand Oaks, CA: Sage Publication Inc., 2002

Allinson, Robert E., ed. *Understanding the Chinese Mind: The Philosophical Roots*. Oxford University Press, 1991.

Ames, Roger T. *The Art of Rulership*. University of Hawaii Press, 1983

Ames, Roger T. and David L. Hall. *Daodejing: Making This Life Significant, A philosophical translation*. Ballantine Books, 2003.

Ames, Roger T. *Wandering at Ease in the Zhuangzi*. Albany, NY: State University of New York Press, 1998.

Arrighi, Giovanni, et al., ed. *The Resurgence of East Asia: 500-, 150-, 50-Year Perspectives*. Routledge, 2003.

Arrighi, Giovanni. *The Long Twentieth Century: Money, Power and the Origins of Our Time*. Verso, 1994.

Bakken, Borge. *The Exemplary Society-Human Improvement, Social Control, and the Dangers of Modernity in China*. Oxford University Press, 1999.

Bairoch, P. "International Industralization Levels from 1750 to 1980." *Journal of European Economic History*. Fall 1982.

Barrow, John D. *The World Within the World*. Oxford University Press, 1990.

Behnegar, Nasser. *Leo Strauss, Max Weber, and the Scientific Study of Politics*. The University of Chicago Press, 2003.

Bell, Daniel A. and Hahm Chaibong, ed. *Confucianism for the Modern World*. Cambridge University Press, 2003.

Bodde, Derek. *Chinese Thought, Society, and Science: The Intellectual and Social Background of Science and Technology in Premodern China*. University of Hawaii Press, 1991.

Braudel, Fernard. *Civilization and Capitalism, 15th-18th Century*. Vol. 1 and 2. Harper and Row, 1984.

Brecher, Jeremy, et al. *Globalization from Below: The Power of Solidarity*. South End Press 2000.

Calvin, William C. and Derek Bickerton. *Lingua ex Machina*. MIT Press, 2000.

Carter, April and Geoffrey Stokes. *Democratic Theory Today*. Polity Press, 2002.

Cheu, Hock-Tong. *Confucianism in Chinese Culture*. Pelanduk Publication, 2000.

Ching, Julia, and R. W. L. Guisso. *Sages and Filial Sons: Mythology and Archaeology in Ancient China*. Chinese University Press, 1991.

Cohen, Paul, and Merle Goldman. *Ideas Across Culture*. Harvard University Press, 1990.

Cook, Scott. *Hiding the World in the World: Uneven Discourses on the Zhuangzi*. State University of New York Press, 2003.

Courchene, Thomas J. and Donald J. Savoie, ed. *The Art of the State Governance in a World Without Frontier*. The Institute for Research on Public Policy, 2003

Crane, Edward H. *Civil Society vs. Political Society: China at a Crossroads*. Cato Institute Conference, Shanghai, China, November 10, 2004.

Creel, H. G. *Confucius and the Chinese Way*. Harper & Row Publishers, 1949.

Curtis, Alan, ed. *Patriotism, Democracy, and Common Sense*. The M. S. Eisenhower Foundation & Rowland & Littlefield Pub., 2004.

Dawson, Raymond. *The Legacy of China*. Cheng & Tsu Co., 1990.

De Bary. *The Liberal Tradition in China*. Chinese University of Hong Kong Press, 1983.

Deikman, Arthur J. 1996. "'I' = Awareness." *Journal of Consciousness Studies* 3, no.4.

Dent, Harry S. *The Roaring 2000s*. Simon & Shuster, 1998.

Diamond, Larry and Marc F. Plattner, ed. *Democracy in East Asia*. The John Hopkins University Press, 1998.

Dittmer, Lowell and Samuel S. Kim. *China's Quest for National Identity*. Cornell University Press, 1993.

Donald, Merlin. *Origins of the Modern Mind: Three Stages in the Evolution of Culture and Cognition*. Harvard University Press, 1991.

Duesterberg, Thomas J. and Herbert I. London, ed. *Riding the Next Wave*. Hudson Institute Publication, 2001.

Economy, Elizabeth. Painting China Green. *Foreign Affairs*, May/June 2004.

Fingarette, Herbert. *Confucius: The Secular as Sacred*. Harper & Row, 1972.

Forman, Robert K. C. 1998. "What Does Mysticism Have to Teach Us About Consciousness?" *Journal of Consciousness Studies* 5, no.2.

Frankforter, A. Daniel. *Civilization and Survival*. Vol. 1. University Press of America, Inc., 1988.

Frankl, George. *Blueprint for a Sane Society*. Open Gate Press, 2004.

Fukuyama, Francis. *The End of History and the Last Man*. Avon Books, 1992.

Geaney, Jane. *On the Epistemology of the Senses in Early Chinese Thought.* University of Hawaii Press, 2002.

Geller, Ernest and Cesar Cansino, ed. *Liberalism in Modern Times.* Central European University Press, 1996.

Geller, Howard. *Energy Revolution: Policies for a Sustainable Future.* Island Press, 2002.

Gibbon, Edward. *History of the Decline and Fall of the Roman Empire.* Penguin Press, 1994.

Giddens, Anthony. *Runaway World.* Profile Books, 1999.

Giskiu, Howard and Bettye S. Walsh. *An Introduction to Chinese Culture through the Family.* State University of New York Press, 2001.

Gold, Thomas, Doug Guthrie, and David Wank. *Social Connections in China.* Cambridge University Press, 2002.

Graff, David A. and Robin Higham. *A Military History of China.* Westview Press, 2002.

Gregory, John S. *The West and China since 1500.* Palgrave MacMillan, 2002.

Graham, A. C. *Yin and Yang and the Nature of Correlative Thinking.* National University of Singapore, 1986.

Graham, A. C. *Disputers of the Tao.* Open Court, 1989.

Griffith, Samual B. *Sun Tzu: The Art of War.* Oxford University Press, 1963.

Hansen, Valerie. *The Open Empire: A History of China to 1600.* W. W. Norton & Co., 2000.

Hall, David L. and Roger T. Ames. *Thinking Through Confucius.* State University of New York Press, 1987.

—. *Anticipating China.* State University of New York Press, 1995.

—. *Thinking from the Han.* State University of New York Press, 1998.

Haw, Stephen G. *A Traveler's History of China.* Cassell Reference, 2002.

Heaton, Herbert. *Economic History of Europe.* Harper & Brothers, 1848.

Hinsch, Bret. *Women in Early Imperial China.* Rowman & Littlefield Publishers, Inc., 2002.

Ho, Eugene Y. C. 1994. "Passages from Gibbon's Decline and Fall of the Roman Empire." *Intellectus* 30.

Hsu, Cho-Yun and Katheryn M. Linduff. *Western Chou Civilization.* Yale University Press, 1988.

Huang, Ray. *China: A Macro History.* M. E. Sharpe, Inc., 1997.

—. *Broadening the Horizons of Chinese History: Discourses, Synthesis, and Comparisons.* An East Gate Book, 1999.

Huang, Chun-Chieh. *Mencius Hermeneutics.* Transaction Press, 2001.

Huber, Peter W. and Mark P. Mills. *The Bottomless Well.* Basic Books, 2006

Hucker, Charles O. *China's Imperial Past*. Stanford University Press, 1975.

—. *The Ming Dynasty: Its Origins and Evolving Institutions*. The University of Michigan, 1978.

Hurtgen, James R. *The Divided Mind of American Liberalism*. Lexington Books, 2002.

Ignatieff, Michael. *Blood and Belonging: Journeys into the New Nationalism*. Farrar, Straus, and Giroux, 1993.

Ivanhoe, Philip J. *Confucian Moral Self-Cultivation*. Hackett Publishing Company, Inc., 2000.

—. *Chinese, Language, Thought and Culture: Nivison and His Critics*. Open Court, Carus Publishing Co., 1996

Ivison, Duncan. *The Self at Liberty: Political Argument and the Arts of Government*. Cornell University Press, 1997.

Jia, Lanpo and Wenwen Huang. *The Story of Peking Man*. Foreign Language Press and Oxford Press, 1990.

Jia, Wenshan. *The Remaking of the Chinese Character and Identity in the Twenty-first Century*. Ablex Publishing, 2001.

Jones, Peter. *An Intelligent Person's Guide to Classics*. Gerald Duchworth and Co. Ltd., 1999.

Jullien, Francois. *The Propensity of Things: Toward a History of Efficacy in China*. Urzone, Inc., 1995.

Jullien, Francois, *Detour and Access: Strategies of Meaning in China and Greece*, Urzone Inc., 2000.

—. *A Treatise on Efficacy: Between Western and Chinese Thinking*. University of Hawaii Press, 2004.

Jun, Li. *Chinese Civilization in the Making, 1766–221 BC*. MacMillan Press Ltd., 1996.

Kasinec, Wendy F. and Michael A. Polushin. *Expanding Empires: Cultural Interaction and Exchange in World Societies from Ancient to Early Modern Times*. SR Books, 2002.

Keller, William W. and Richard J. Samuels, ed. *Crisis and Innovation in Asian Technology*. Cambridge University Press, 2003.

Kohlberg, Lawrence. *The Psychology of Moral Development*. New York: Harper & Rowe, 1983.

Kohlberg, L. and E. Turiel. *"Moral Development and Moral Education."* In Psychology and Educational Practice, edited by G. Lesser. Scott Foresman, 1971.

Kohn, Livia and Harold Roth. *Daoist Identity: History, Lineage and Ritual*. University of Hawaii Press, 2002.

Korten, David C. *When Corporations Rule the World.* Berrett-Koehler Publishers, 2001.

Kluver, Randy and John H. Powers, ed. *Civic Discourse, Civil Society, and Chinese Communities.* Ablex Publishing Co., 1999.

Kruger, Rayne. *All Under Heaven.* John Wiley & Son, 2003.

Kung, Hans. *A Global Ethic for Global Politics and Economics.* Oxford University Press, 1998.

Kupperman, Joel J. *Learning from Asian Philosophy.* Oxford University Press, 1999.

Lal, Vinay. *Empire of Knowledge: Culture and Plurality in the Global Economy.* Pluto Press, 2002.

Lanpo, Jia and Weiwen Huang. *The Story of Peking Men.* Foreign Language Press and Oxford Press, 1990.

Lei, Haizong. *The Warring States (475–221 BC): The Modern Period in Ancient China.* LEWI, Hong Kong Baptist University, 1943.

Li, Chenyang. *The Tao Encounters the West: Explorations in Comparative Philosophy.* State University of New York Press, 1999.

Li, Jun. *Chinese Civilization in the Making, 1766–221 BC.* Macmillan Press Ltd., 1996.

Li, Xueqin. *East Zhou and Qin Civilizations.* Translated by K. C. Chang. Yale University Press, 1985.

Liu, James T. C. *China Turning Inward.* Harvard University Press, 1988.

Liu, Li and Xingcan Chen. *State Formation in Early China.* Duckworth, 2003.

Liu, Xin. *The Otherness of Self: A Genealogy of the Self in Contemporary China.* University of Michigan Press, 2002.

Lloyd, G. E. R. *The Ambition of Curiosity.* Cambridge University Press, 2002.

Loew, Michael, and Edward L. Shaughnessy, eds. *The Cambridge History of Ancient China.* Cambridge University Press, 1999.

Loureiro, Rui Manuel. 2000. "News from China in Sixteenth-century Europe: The Portuguese Connection." *Oriental Art,* no.3, vol. VLVI.

Mackerras, Colin. *Western Images of China.* Revised ed. Oxford University Press, 1999.

MacNair, Rachel M. *The Psychology of Peace.* Praeger Publishers, 2003.

Mahbubain, Kishore. *Can Asians Think?* Key Porter Books, 2001.

Major, John S. *Heaven and Earth in Early Han Thought: Chapters Three, Four, and Five of the Huainanzi.* State University of New York Press, 1993.

Mar, Pamela C. M. and Frank-Jurgen Richter. *China: Enabling a New Era of Changes.* John Wiley & Sons (Asia), 2003.

Mazarr, Michael, J. *Global Trends 2005: An Owner's Manual for the Next Decade.* St. Martin's Press, 1999.

McBryde, Isabel, ed. *Who Owns the Past?* Oxford University Press, 1983.

McGilvray, James. *Chomsky: Language, Mind, Politics.* Polity Press, 1999.

McNamara, Robert S., et al. *Argument Without End: In Search of Answers to the Vietnam Tragedy.* Public Affairs, 1999.

McNamara, Robert S and James G. Blight. *Wilson's Ghost: Reducing the Risk of Conflict, Killing, and Catastrophe in the Twenty-first Century.* Public Affair, 2001.

Meyer, Milton W. *A Concise History of China.* Rowman & Littlefield Publishers, Inc., 1994.

Mithen, Steve. *The Prehistory of Mind: The Cognitive Origins of Art, Religion and Science.* Thames and Hudson, 1997.

Mitter, Rama. *A Bitter Revolution: China's Struggle with the Modern World.* Oxford University Press, 2004.

Moore, Charles A., ed. *The Chinese Mind: Essentials of Chinese Philosophy and Culture.* University of Hawaii Press, 1968.

Needham, Joseph. *Within the Four Seas: The Dialogue of East and West.* University of Toronto Press, 1979.

Needham, Joseph. *Science in Traditional China.* Chinese University Press Of Hong Kong, 1981.

Ng, Tai P. *Chinese Culture, Western Culture, Why must we learn from each other?* iUniverse, Inc. 2007.

Nolan, Peter. *China at the Crossroads.* Polity Press, 2004.

Northrop, F. S. C. *The Logic of Sciences and the Humanities.* World Publishing Co., 1947.

O'Brien, Robert and Marc Williams. *Global Political Economy: Evolution and Dynamics.* Palgrave MacMillan, 2004.

O'Hara-Devereaux, Mary. *Navigating the Badlands.* Jossey-Bass, 2004.

Overmyer, Daniel L., ed. *Religion in China Today.* Cambridge University Press, 2003.

Pohl, Karl-Heinz and Anselm W. Muller. *Chinese Ethics in a Global Context: Moral Bases of Contemporary Societies.* Koninklyke Brill, 2002.

Pohl, Karl-Heinz. June 2003. "Ethics for the Twenty-first Century: The Confucian Tradition." *Ex/Change*, no. 7.

Polanyi, Michael. *The Tacit Dimension.* Routledge and K. Paul, 1967.

Pomeranz, Kenneth. *The Great Divergence.* Princeton University Press, 2000.

Prazniak, Roxann. *Dialogues Across Civilizations.* Westview Press Inc., 1996.

Price, T. Douglas, and Gary M. Feinman. *Images of the Past.* 3rd ed. Mayfield Publishing Co., 2001.

Proctor, Robert N. *Racial Hygiene: Medicine under the Nazis.* Harvard University Press, 1988.

Puett, Michael. *The Ambivalence of Creation: Debates Concerning Innovation and Artifice in Early China.* Stanford University Press, 2001.

Raphals, Lisa Ann. *Wisdom and Cunning in the Classical Traditions of China and Greece.* Cornell University Press, 1992.

Rees, Martin. *Our Final Hour.* Basic Books, 2003.

Reding, Jean-Paul. *Comparative Essays in Early Greek and Chinese Rational Thinking.* Ashgate Publishing Co., 2004.

Roberts, J. A. G. *A History of China.* MacMillan Press Ltd., 1999.

Robertson, Robbie. *The Three Waves of Globalization.* Fernwood Publishing, 2003.

Robinson, William I. *A Theory of Global Capitalism: Production, Class, and State in a Transnational World.* John Hopkins University Press, 2004.

Rodrik, Dani. *Has Globalization Gone Too Far?* Institute For International Economics, 1997.

Ropp, Paul S. 1994. "Women in Late Imperial China: A Review of Recent English Language Scholarship." *Women's History Review* 3, vol. 3.

Rosenwein, Barbara H. *A Short History of the Middle Ages.* Broadview Press, 2002.

Samli, A. Coskun. *In Search of an Equitable, Sustainable Globalization: The Bittersweet Dilemma.* Quorum Books, 2002.

Sato, Masayuki. *The Confucian Quest for Order: The Origin and Formation of the Political Thought of Xun Zi.* Brill, 2003.

Schrecker, John E. *The Chinese Revolution in Historical Perspective.* Praeger Publishers, 2004.

Shand, John. *Philosophy and Philsophers: An Introduction to Western Philosophy.* McGill-Queen's University Press, 2002.

Shankman, Steven and Stephen W. Durrant. *The Siren and the Sage: Knowledge and Wisdom in Ancient Greece and China.* Cassell, 2000.

—. *Early China/Ancient Greece: Thinking Through Comparisons.* State University of New York Press, 2002.

Slingerland, Edward. *Effortless Action.* Oxford University Press, 2003.

Stavrianos, L. S. *The World Since 1500.* Prentice-Hall Inc., 1966.

—. *Global History: The Human Heritage.* 3rd ed. Prentice-Hall Inc., 1983.

—. *Lifelines from Our Past: A New World History.* M. E. Sharpe Inc., 1997.

Strayer, Joseph R. *Western Europe in the Middle Ages*. 3rd ed. Waveland Press, Inc., 1991.

Stiglitz, Joseph E. and Shahid Yusuf, ed. *Rethinking the East Asian Miracle*. World Bank and Oxford University Press, 2001.

Stuart-Fox, Martin. *A Short History of China and S. E. Asia*. Allen and Unwin, 2003.

Tainter, Joseph A. *Getting Down to Earth: Practical Applications of Ecological Economics*. Island Press, 1996.

Tan, Sor-Hoon. *Confucian Democracy: A Deweyan Reconstruction*. State University of New York Press, 2003.

Teggart, Frederick J. *Rome and China*. Berkeley: University of California Press, 1939.

Toffler, Alvin. *The Third Wave*. Morrow, 1980.

—. *The Future Shock*. Bantum Books, 1971.

—. *The Power Shift*. Bantum Books, 1990.

Tomasi, Luigi. *New Horizons in Sociological Theory and Research*. Ashgate Publishing Limited, 2001.

Toynbee, Arnold. *A Study of History*. Oxford University Press, 1972.

Tucker, Mary Evelyn and John Berthrone. *Confucianism and Ecology: The Interrelation of Heaven, Earth, and Humans*. Harvard University Press, 1998.

Turnbull, Percival. 2004. "*Roman Empire*." Microsoft Encarta Online Encyclopedia.

Wagner, Rudolf. *Language, Ontology, and Political Philosophy in China*. State University of New York Press, 2003.

Wang, Gungwu. *To Act is To Know: Chinese Dilemma*. Eastern Universities Press, 2003.

Wang, Robin R. *Images of Women in Chinese Thought and Culture*. Hackett Publishing Co., 2003.

Watson, Burton, trans. *Zhuangzi Basic Writing*. Translated. Columbia University Press, 2003.

—. *The Complete Works of Chuang Tze: World Philosopher At Play*. New York: Columbia University Press, 1968.

White, Ralph K. *Fearful Warriors: A Psychological Profile of U.S.-Soviet Relations*. New York: Free Press, 1984.

Woo, Edward P. H. *In Search of an Ideal Political Order and An Understanding of Different Political Cultures*. Novelty Publishers, Ltd., 2002.

Wood, George S. Jr. and Juan C. Judikis. *Conversations on Community Theory*. Purdue University Press, 2002.

Wortzel, Larry M. *Class in China: Stratification in a Classless Society.* Greenwood Press, 1987.

Zey, Michael G. *The Future Factor: The Five Forces Transforming Our Lives and Shaping Human Destiny.* McGraw-Hall.

Zhang, Dainian. *Key Concepts in Chinese Philosophy.* Yale University Press, 2002.

Zhang, Wei-Bin. *Singapore's Modernization: Westernization and Modernizing Confucian Manifestations.* Nova Science Publishers Inc., 2002

List of Chinese Classics Used

易 經	Yijing
道 德 經	Daodejing
書 經	The Book of Documents
詩 經	Shijing: The Book of Poems
孝 經	The Classic of Filial Piety
禮 記	The Book of Rites
荀 子	The Book of Zunzi
莊 子	The Book of Zhuangzi
論 語	The Analects
大 學	Daxue: The Great Learning
中 庸	The Doctrine of Mean
孟 子	Book of Mencius
淮 南 子	Huainanzi
國 語	Guo Yu: The Book of Nations
左 傳	The Book of Zuo
春 秋 繁 露	The Spring and Autumn Annals
史 記	The Book of History
孫 子 兵 法	The Art of War

Index

978-0-595-41846-6
0-595-41846-5

Printed in the United States
103867LV00004B/79-249/A

9 780595 418466